CHASING BLACK
UNICORNS

MAREK ZMYSŁOWSKI

CHASING BLACK
UNICORNS

HOW BUILDING THE AMAZON OF AFRICA
PUT ME ON INTERPOL'S MOST WANTED LIST

Translated by Paul McNamara

TABLE OF CONTENTS

Introduction	7
I'll Show You	11
A MacBook and a Soya Latte	47
Memento Mori	61
Ten, nine, ignition sequence, start	83
In Desert and Wilderness	103
The Lust for Money	115
Cops and Robbers	131
VIP Pass	151
Springboks vs. All Blacks	173
From 'I don't know I don't know' to 'I don't know that I know'	195
Jaguars and Leopards	221
Blood River	239
Kidnapped	255
Houston, we have a problem	277
David and Goliath	303
Miss World and the Terrorist	345
War and (the Lack of) Peace	381

To my Mom – the epitome of beauty,
wisdom and tenderness

UNICORN:

1. A mythical creature appearing in myths and legends, possessing a single horn in the center of its forehead, portrayed with the head and body of a white or red and black horse.

2. In business and the new technology sector, a private company financed by start-up capital reaching a value of a billion US dollars.

While all the events described in this book are true, the names of certain individuals have been changed due to fears for their safety. The names of others I modified out of mercy. I just wanted to spare them the embarrassment.

INTRODUCTION

It was 14 January 2018 and my holiday was coming to an end. I had spent the last five years mainly on planes and in places such as Lagos, Accra, Johannesburg and Nairobi. I was one of the founders of Jovago. com, the largest hotel booking website in Africa, which eventually merged with Jumia.com, currently known as "the Amazon.com of Africa", and went public on the New York Stock Exchange. My subsequent companies, HotelOga and HotelOnline, developed software for hotels and facilitated the expansion of such players as Expedia and Booking.com on the African continent.

In actual fact, we were one of the first companies in Africa with whom these tech giants decided to work. During all these years, I managed to avoid "African bad PR": terrorists, kidnappers, corrupt politicians, high-ranking officials and unscrupulous competitors. I was really lucky and, by my own example, improved the statistics related to doing business in Africa and dispelled stereotypes around this topic.

However, that was when the statistics decided to catch up with me. On January 14th, I was flying from Warsaw to London for a meeting with the directors of an investment fund. I was supposed to negotiate its involvement in my upcoming ventures. Put in simpler terms, I was supposed to ask a few bankers in expensive suits for their money. Actually, it wasn't their money at all, but that which had been invested in their fund. Guys in expensive suits had always made an impression on me, until I discovered that they really work for other guys in T-shirts. That is the beauty of the financial markets.

1.30pm – an Uber dropped me off at the airport exactly two hours before my departure. I was with my life partner, Yaritza. Her plane to Brussels was to take off a short while before mine and I intended to accompany her right to the departure gate. As we had already checked in online, all I had to do was to go with my hand luggage through security check and passport control. So, for the moment, I suppressed my romantic notions concerning the equality of all mankind and used my business cards, filled to the hilt with air miles, in order to save time by joining the priority queue, the one for those who thought they were a cut above the rest.

2.45pm – Yaritza was now safely on the plane, which had by then certainly reached an altitude of several thousand meters. Brussels, just as Warsaw, lay in the Schengen Zone, which makes traveling just so much easier, a fact we frequently take for granted. The journey to London, however, required the Polish Border Guard to check my documents more thoroughly. So I stood there, on my best behavior, in front of a politely smiling lady wearing her stiff, border guard uniform, and handed over my passport.

2.49pm – As my mind was otherwise occupied, I didn't notice that I had been standing at her window for quite a while. The queues on either side of me were moving along nicely, while the female border guard, still staring intently at the monitor, made a phone call. Then the smile disappeared from her face.

2.51pm – Suddenly, two border guard officers appeared out of nowhere and directed me to leave the queue. They did not respond to any questions while leading me to the rear of the terminal.

The secluded room I found myself in was less than four square meters in floor area and was bereft of windows and door handles. The gentlemen from the border guard patrol had not taken my bags, however. That's a good sign, I thought. Surely, it's all been a misunderstanding, probably something wrong with my passport. Those issued abroad are often considered a bit suspicious.

The guards told me as they were leaving that someone would be along shortly. I asked them to inform the airline that I could be delayed for my flight, a request which amused them visibly. In any case, I rang my lawyer and assistant to give them a report of what had happened to me.

3.05pm – Three new uniformed border guards arrived. Bigger and less friendly looking than the previous ones. As they took my watch and personal effects, this was the last time I was still able to precisely register the chronology of events. When they then informed me that I was being arrested and would be placed in custody in the notorious Mokotów Prison in Warsaw, I broke out in a cold sweat. I was then placed in handcuffs and led outside through the terminal, no doubt becoming the biggest attraction for any passengers traveling through Frederic Chopin Airport that day.

I managed to get one of the guards to tell me, as far as he knew, that I was being sought by the government of Nigeria, which was accusing me of "large-scale financial fraud". A crime for which, according to their laws, one can get anything between seven to 21 years' jail time. In a Nigerian prison. All I knew was that my arrest had been caused by a Red Notice, meaning the fugitive category with the highest level of threat on the Interpol list, one which is issued on behalf of a government seeking out a particular criminal. Although it is designed to be used for catching terrorists, murderers and drug barons, it is also used to target business rivals and political enemies, seeing as Interpol members also include such democratic and incorrupt countries as China, Iran, Russia and Turkey.

I had absolutely no idea what would happen to me, nor any knowledge of what the procedures looked like in such a situation. Up to then, my greatest crime had been breaking the speed limit in urban areas. I became enveloped by the greatest fear, concerning if or when I would ever see my family and my beloved again, and whether I would be able to survive doing time in a Nigerian prison. Built during the colonial period, they are crowded with 10 times the number of inmates they had been designed for. Instead of running water and electricity, they have rats, insects and an internal prison hierarchy. I was already imagining leaders of prison tribal groups fighting over whose plaything I would become, if some killer disease didn't get me first.

The January sun had already set when I was carted off to prison and directed into a cell. It was only the following day that I was to stand in front of a state prosecutor and find out anything whatsoever as to my future fate. The prison guard was as clueless as myself with regards to what would happen to me.

"As far as I know, you can even be put on the first plane to Nigeria tomorrow," he said and closed the cell door.

That first night in prison, after countless panic attacks, attempts to meditate, uncontrolled weeping, push-ups, praying to all the gods I could think of and walking around in circles, I was finally able to calm down and get my shit together. I had no clue as to how and when I would manage it, but I swore to myself that I would get out of this cluster-fuck alive and well. And that I would then share my story.

Chapter 1

I'LL SHOW YOU

By the age of 23, I had already planned my own funeral. This is, however, not the story of a spotty, desperate kid who decided to end it all, having been listening to depressing rock ballads and ostentatiously showing off his "valley of woe" to his friends. No, sir – I did it for the money.

But let me start at the beginning. Even before the funeral in 2006, at the age of 19, I had found my first job – as a door-to-door insurance broker, although brokers preferred the term 'financial advisor', as it sounded more trustworthy. After all, 19 is the perfect age for having such a job, right? As it turned out, I was pretty good at flogging insurance policies and sold so many of them that I was promoted to Head of Operations in one of the largest companies of this type in Poland. When, in time, all that easy money came to an end, it occurred to me that the funeral services sector would be a great business idea, for it certainly seemed in need of new blood, so to speak. A couple of people, however, including the Polish undertaker mafia, did not like the idea of someone new coming in and stirring things up. Poland's so-called 'skin hunter gangs' cash-for-corpses scandal had barely died down, and now they had to deal with new technology I intended to introduce into the sector.

Following my undertaking enterprise, I sought further adventures so intensively that I ended up in Africa. It was there I met people who first invested in my business, but once I became superfluous to their requirements, they planned to get rid of me using, of course, their friends in the police and government of Nigeria.

Before I get into this period of my life, however, I had paid my dues in Koszalin, a leafy town, beautiful in its own way, a stone's throw from the Baltic Sea. It really was a bit of a backwater. Don't get me wrong – I'm proud that I'm a Koszaliner (if that's the term) and that I come from this enchanting place. While still being a mid-sized city, it is a damn long way from anywhere. Although Koszalin is leafy, peaceful, safe and spread out, half of Poland thinks it's nothing more than a coastal resort. In fact, you need to travel a good half-hour by bus to reach the Baltic Sea, something you then have to spend half your life explaining to other fellow Poles – so it should be back to school for those dunces to brush up on Polish geography, please.

Koszalin is one of the towns in former German-occupied 'Recovered Territories', which became part of Poland after the Second World War, and from which German residents were expelled, while Poles from eastern and central regions settled in their place. However, there were exceptions, one of whom was my great grandfather, Jan Szubert, a Pole who had spent many years living as an émigré in Germany and who never forgot his roots.

Before the War, Jan had led a relatively peaceful life with his wife and a number of children, including my grandmother, in south-western Germany. He was an engineer responsible for building beautiful mountain roads. He conducted this as far away as possible from the political whirlwind enveloping interwar Europe at that time. As a Pole in Germany, during World War II he found himself in a complicated situation, to put it mildly. He miraculously avoided arrest or being forcibly conscripted into the Wehrmacht. Once his family had survived the War, they decided as soon as it was over to put into operation a plan they had drawn up several years previously, namely to return to Poland. My great-grandfather believed that since Poland had won the War, things there could only get better. He clearly did not appreciate, however, the capability of the Soviet Union to make a bad situation worse. Poland, seeking to revive itself after the fighting ended, welcomed with open arms engineers who possessed civic construction experience most of all. Jan Szubert was thus given the task of supervising the clearance of forests and the commencement of the building of a military airport near

Koszalin. And that's how he ended up in this region. Alongside him was my grandmother, then a teenager, who got to know a handsome young man who had been transferred from the heart of Poland and who did not yet know that one day he would be the best grandfather in the world.

I can clearly remember my childhood holidays spent at my grandparents' home in the country, drinking warm milk straight from the cow, the German sweets sent in packages from aunts and uncles who had, however, moved from 'wonderful' communist Poland to the 'dreadfully rich' capitalist West Germany. And I can still recall rummaging through 1000 page-long catalogues from Quelle, the German mail order company, containing all the toys, clothes, computers and other goods from 'the filthy rich West' kids like me, trapped behind the Iron Curtain, could only dream of.

It is no accident that I bring up the topic of where I come from at this point. Among other things, it's thanks to Koszalin that I am where I am today, or to put it more precisely, thanks to the overwhelming desire as a teenager to get the hell out of there as fast as I could. It was surely that which drove me to study in Poznan, then take on Poland and further parts of the world. Of course, you only begin to appreciate small town life once you have put being intoxicated with big cities and all the fast life attractions and dangers they have to offer behind you, and moved back to where you came from. It was only around the age of 30 that I began to appreciate the unique flavor of Koszalin, just as I had done that of halva and red wine.

Coming back to the above-mentioned spotty teenager, although it was never so bad that I had to walk around with a paper bag over my head, as some characters in American comic books, I did not feel comfortable with myself. I'm speaking here about my time in junior high school, which was a newly created entity due to educational reforms at that time. My year, comprising children born in 1986, was the vanguard of those who instead of going to seventh class in primary school, went straight on to junior high. This was the charm of being born in 1986 – first the Chernobyl disaster, then junior high. It was not going to end well.

As everyone in Poland knows, being in junior high was often more difficult than being in a military camp, especially if the only sporting activity in which you had no equal was wolfing down sweets against the clock. If, therefore, you happened to be quite a short fat-ass, a) boys did not take you seriously, which is lame, and b) girls did not take you seriously, which is even more lame. So self-confidence was not something I enjoyed too much. My weight problems made me the target of nasty jokes from classmates who were, after all, then fighting for a place in the peer-group pecking order. Because of this, lonely, sad and ashamed of my appearance, I isolated myself from the group more and more. And because I hadn't been able to lay my hands on any book or cassette brought out by a life coach up to then, I buried my sadness and stress in eating sweets. Thus I spent several long years trapped in this vicious circle. The worst times were during periods of hot weather, when you had to walk around in T-shirts which highlighted my belly and man boobs. One morning, I decided to wrap my torso in clingfilm to hide the fat. Unfortunately, someone in my class noticed my little trick and did not shy away from loudly informing everyone about it. Later that very day, I ate an awful lot of sweets.

In my first ever love letter, one which I wrote to a girl whom I had met at summer camp, I devoted a whole paragraph to telling her that although I was sure that she would be embarrassed to be seen going out with such a fat-ass in front of her friends, I promised to lose weight, as I had started to play soccer. She never wrote back. I must have given her the wrong address.

Two years had passed in junior high before I managed to summon up the courage to 'chat up' a girl from another class. We had known each other for a long time and I remember that she had never laughed when others had made fun of me. So I thought she was a safe bet, because even if she said 'no' to me, she would do it in such a way as not to hurt my feelings. How wrong was I – "Marek, you must be nuts, I would never go out with you! You walk around with these fatty lumps, because you yourself are like a walking lump of fat. How could you even think that someone like me could go out with someone like you? Yuk!"

That same day, I ate even more sweets than the time I had decided to cover myself in clingfilm.

I imagined how simple and pleasant life must be for those who were not fat like me, when you have the opportunity to talk with whoever you like, with no risk of being laughed at due to your appearance. But

I talked myself round in this way: "All of you who are laughing at me today might be popular in junior high, have the prettiest girls in school smiling at you, and should have a page on Wikipedia just for being 'awesome', but in 10 years' time it will be me who is world famous and it will be you trying to catch my attention." And that is how my dear Koszalin, or its teenage inhabitants to be more exact, formed a trait within me which was later on to have an impact on my future, namely this 'I'll show you' impulse, meaning the necessity to prove I was worth something.

Many years passed, however, before I realized that if you have to prove your worth to anyone at all, it should be to yourself first and foremost.

Meanwhile, however, I still had to study, which I did neither with great zeal nor with particular distaste. Studying and getting good grades came easily to me, a trait for which I was frequently labeled 'nerd'. Sure, if you're fat and get straight As, you must be a nerd, right? Sometimes, I even deliberately did badly on tests so as to be able to hang out with the popular kids, busy complaining about some stupid teacher and, for a moment, to feel part of a group. When it came to senior high school, I was happy to go there because it was the only chance I would get to meet "Her".

"Her" name was Marysia and she was, so to speak, totally my type. A tall, enchanting blonde with long, lightly curled hair, she viewed the world through gorgeous blue eyes. Unfortunately, among the myriad of positive qualities she possessed there hid one fundamental flaw: she didn't give a damn about me. Although I was besotted like a lovesick fool, there was no chance of anything happening, other than that which I could do for myself. If you know what I mean.

But she was quite nice, especially from the second year of high school on, when I rapidly and unexpectedly grew in height and lost weight thanks to the hormones which rage through puberty. Actually, it was down to the cult computer game *Tony Hawk's Pro Skater* which got me fascinated with real skateboards – doing ollies and kickflips in real life burns a lot more calories than showing off with combinations of keys on a keyboard. While I wasn't doing it to raise my hopes, at least she eventually replied to my "Hiiiiiiiiiiiii!".

One time, I heard that she was going to some kind of party with her friend, and had arranged to meet them in town. I put on my glad rags and headed off for the rendezvous point, just so I could say "Oh, hi, what a coincidence? I just happened to be walking around in the best clothes I have". Unfortunately, it turned out to be a house party at the home of her then boyfriend. As you may have guessed, that evening did not go particularly well. As with every other evening during that time, I spent it at home with my parents.

I also have a family, and it is rather special to me. We were a very typical family unit for the time, the so-called two-plus-one model. My parents kept to this model for the first 14 years of life, until my brother was born. Up until my father had completed his life's ambition of "becoming a real man" (which in Poland requires you to do the following three things – build a house, then father a son and plant a tree), we lived in a block of flats made of pre-fabricated concrete in one of Koszalin's many communist-era suburbs. Although my dad was an army officer, let's just say that the Commander in Chief at home was my mother. A teacher, you know the type – whether you were a genius or nothing of the sort, everyone had to finish school in her opinion. So, whatever I happen to believe today, it's thanks to her that I went out into the world with my head held high – she presented quite a specific attitude on certain questions, such as motivation and encouragement to find my own way in life, providing support whether you needed it or not. To cut a long story short, when I came up with my plan to conquer the world, or at least to attract the attention of girls at school, she laid out my life on a sheet of A4 paper.

"Let's be honest with each other, son", she said one day. "With you we need to... I mean, you need to plan out your life and concentrate on a particular task. You're good at math and physics and we have such a great university here in Koszalin. You'll graduate, then I'll talk with my school principal and he'll get you a job teaching at our school. It'll be quite funny, us being colleagues, now won't it?"

"Uhhh", I replied, feeling rather terrified, not looking up from my computer. "And Dad will help you build a house, right beside ours. And later you'll get married, we'll all bring up your children together."

"Uhhh", my dad replied, also feeling terrified, not looking up from the television screen.

"I mean Zosia, our neighbor's daughter," Mum went on. "She's so nice and I think she likes you."

And that's how I came to the absolute certainty that, despite losing several kilos in the so-called meantime, Koszalin was a bit too suffocating for me, while Zosia, the neighbors' daughter, undoubtedly too plain. I mean that already I wasn't just thinking about girls and skateboards, but had other more serious ideas, such as Mark Twain's saying that "Twenty years from now you will be more disappointed by the things you didn't do than by the ones you did do. So throw off the bowlines. Sail away from the safe harbor. Catch the trade winds in your sails. Explore. Dream. Discover."

I therefore decided to move to Poznan, a crazy distance of 200km South from Koszalin.

It was a thoroughly considered decision – I must have spent at least half an hour thinking about it. Although, at the time, I had no idea what it was I wanted to do with my life, the Technical University of Poznan sounded fairly impressive. Actually, I was really influenced by their promotional film, which showed some guy in a white lab coat playing around with a remote controlled robot, being winked at by a girl from his study group, while the whole thing had music from Pitbull playing in the background. Now, how could I turn down something like that?

It so happened that at that moment Marysia was in pain, because her boyfriend had dumped her "for that slut Marzena from biology and chemistry class", and I happened to be, as usual, in the vicinity. So, bit by bit, we became closer and in a serious way. To be more precise, I gave her my homework to copy before lessons. And I even called her on the phone once or twice. She said many nice things, such as "I really like talking to you" or "You're a real friend, thanks for helping me with math". What a disaster.

But I decided the following: as Marysia wasn't sure whether to study in Poznan or Warsaw, I came up with a diabolical plan. I had a friend in Poznan and made a deal with him that he would move out of his flat for a couple of days and leave me the keys. You don't want to know what I promised to give him in exchange for this favor, but from time to time I still miss the white Nike Air Force trainers I had got from the United States and which were the first such pair in our small town.

Anyway, I told my Marysia that I have a place to stay in Poznan and that we could go there for the weekend, wander around, see the city and stuff.

She agreed!

I spent almost the entire night before our departure on the internet, reading articles like "How to read her signals", "Five sure ways to initiate foreplay" and "How not to let her know you're a virgin".

Everything in Poznan went to plan. After a long, really long walk and seeing the sights, at last we went my friend's apartment to relax a bit. The time then came for Stage 2, which I called "Whatever is on Cable TV and Chill". We collapsed onto the sofa and watched a movie while sipping wine. At that was it. I sat there paralyzed. I didn't have the courage to try anything. We had one bottle of wine and drank it. But when push came to shove, I just froze.

But there was another night and I got the impression that Marysia was sending out clear signals. Surely she had decided that she must take matters into her own hands, as she certainly couldn't count on this neurotic ex-fat-ass skateboarding show-off to do anything. At least, that's how it seemed to me. We spent the day walking around various departments at the University of Poznan, the Academy of Economics and the Technical University. As Marysia was suffering from a lack of sleep (probably due to waiting for me to make a move), while we were on the bus her head suddenly found itself on my shoulder. The problem here was that at one of the colleges we were visiting we bumped into Karol, our school's "man about campus". He was the kind of guy who was always chosen to be first on any team, while I was chosen last – the kind of guy who girls called up when they wanted to be kissed, while I was the guy they called when they needed help with math.

As the Academy of Economics just happened to be having an open day, almost our entire year from Koszalin was there. Marysia didn't like Karol – she thought he was an asshole. Clever girl. We wanted to slip away, but Karol noticed and called us over, and so there was nothing we could do. We had something to eat together, wandered around the city and then he very generously proposed that we put him up for the night, as what was the point in him spending money on a hostel seeing as I had a place to stay. I desperately tried to find a reason to turn him down, but couldn't come up with anything. In the end, I agreed to take him in, thereby screwing up my second and only chance of any possible action with Marysia. I was sure that she wouldn't have the nerve to engage in any sort of sexual activity if there was another boy in the house.

How wrong was I.

That night Karol scored with Marysia three times.

I was lying in the other room, listening to their moans coming through the wall, and thought of Poland, or more precisely famous Poles. First, a fairly long time about the murderer Karol Kot, dubbed the Vampire of Krakow, then about the serial killer Zdzisław Marchwicki, the Vampire of the Coalfields, who never admitted to the crimes of which he had been accused until his dying day. I wondered whether there had ever been anyone like this in Poznan.

Come the morning, when Marysia's moans had finally subsided, I floated somewhere between sleep and daydreaming, my fading consciousness producing an image in which I had inflicted upon Karol a cruel and painful death.

Marysia went back to Koszalin and I never spoke to her again. Let her do her own math from now on, is what I said to myself.

Revenge against Karol was one thing, but money was another. So it actually worked out that both Karol and I ended up doing the same degree. I never gave in to the feelings I had against Karol following that first night – in fact, he suggested that we rent a flat near the university together, seeing as it would be cheaper than renting separately. And that's how we became flatmates.

I started my university studies, where once again passing exams seemed much easier for me than for everyone else. So, once again studying was the easy part, while relations with the opposite sex were the very opposite – terrible, in fact. I passed everything I needed to with flying colors (apart from gaining the recognition of girls) and generally it seemed that I would get straight As. But like every self-respecting Polish student, I was permanently short of cash. Although there was hope of a scholarship on the horizon, I would have to figure out something until then.

I was still getting some pocket money from home, but parties in Poznan were not the same as parties in Koszalin. And every guy needs a drink from time to time, seeing as I had to try and find a way to fit in. So, usually about a week after Mommy's monthly bank transfer, I was just left with memories of money. I thought about tutoring children in math and physics. I was pretty good at that sort of thing, and even if I wasn't great, it would be good enough for those Poznan thickheads.

Then one day, I turned up at tutoring classes hungry, so after an hour's work I took myself off to a supermarket with 20 zlotys to buy some bread and a piece of sausage. Those were some high times. I also quickly realized that my monthly bank transfer from home was the last form of control my dear parents had over me. I would have to do something to change it. Then one evening, when I was desperately counting my pennies, which were to cover the price of my bus ticket and something to eat, Karol dropped in, grinned and said that he had just become a "financial advisor". I had no idea what it meant, but "financial advisor" sounded more or less like "a ton of money", so I immediately asked my greatest friend/foe to get me in there. After all, if he could, then I could too!

And this was the beginning of the end of my academic career.

It was 2006 and the financial intermediary machine was up and running in Poland. Banks had begun to push 30-year loans on people in Swiss francs with interest rates below inflation, while billboards promoting investment funds with 30% rates of return offered further temptation. Pension funds were going crazy, while insurance companies were selling "real beauties", meaning long-term regular savings programs exempt from taxation (so-called 'saving insurance policies').

Everyone wanted to get under the mattress of the average Pole and convince them that anywhere else would be better to keep your money, on the condition that it was in the account of some financial institution. And every Pole who didn't have savings, but had some kind of secure employment, was pushed into getting mortgages, meaning you got real money for buying or building a house with the house itself as collateral.

And financial advisors were the guys who were responsible for moving the money from being hidden beneath Mr. Average's mattress to the accounts of financial institutions, or fixing Mr. Average up with bags of money from these institutions, which he could use to buy a house, money he would later have to repay with interest. If, after several years, the loan turned out to be too much of a burden, then Mr. Average could take out a new loan to pay off the old one, and so on. For being involved in this whole process of moving cash from one pile to another, financial intermediaries, sorry, 'advisors' received a generous commission on the value of each and every transaction.

A number of such firms on the market grew using standard methods, meaning most of the commission was put into media marketing and the opening of snazzy offices on busy city streets. Others invested most of their profits into sales structures, where the advisors earned several times more than the competition, but had to find both clients and employees on their own through personal recommendations. And it was at such a company that I ended up.

I had no idea then either of the sector or of the company, or whether the movement of savings into investment funds and the taking of mortgages was good for Mr. Average. 'Financial advisor' sounded impressive and was associated with money and fancy suits. They didn't need anything else to convince me.

I will never forget the first and last job interview of my life. I presented myself, in the classic way, in my high school graduation suit and was as stressed as it was possible to be in this situation. The Office for Financial Advice was to be found in a prestigious building in the center of the city. In the waiting room, I noticed several fellows just like myself, dressed in high school graduation suits they had long since outgrown. Attached to the wall was a flat screen TV, showing a 24-hour business channel, an endless stock markets ticker moving along the bottom of the screen. On the coffee tables there lay catalogues taken from Porsche and Mercedes showrooms and Rolex and TAG Heuer outlets.

Some finished their interviews within five minutes, while others emerged only after an hour.

I know, because I had arrived two hours before my appointed time, due to the fact that I couldn't sit at home in such an excited state.

Eventually, my turn came.

"Taking my monthly earnings and the amount of time I spend at work into account, an hour of my time is worth 1,000 zlotys. Why then, as your future boss and mentor, should I invest my time in training and managing you?"

I hung on every word my future manager had to say.

"We recruit talent already in their first year of studies, we aren't looking for experts in finance or lending, we make them. Why? Well, which do you think is easier? Find a guy with an encyclopedia of economics in his head and teach him to develop qualities such as openness, class, eloquence, style and charm? Or find smiling, ambitious, communicative, intelligent, creative people and teach them the fundamentals of finance? Do you believe that you have something within you that will allow you to achieve success, as well as sufficient amounts of confidence to work with the richest people in this country and to speak with them as equals?"

I was so stressed that I don't even remember my answer.

"Thanks for dropping by. We have several candidates for each position; if you get to the next stage, you will receive a phone call from us in two days' time," the young exec informed me in a relaxed tone of voice, seeing as he was dressed in a suit much better cut and significantly more expensive than my own.

If I had been fascinated by the concept of financial advice before the interview, now I was ready to sacrifice a kidney in exchange for such a career. I don't need to add how long those two days seemed and how many times a minute I checked to see if my phone had rung by any chance, and if the battery was still fully charged. Every few minutes, I called friends to make sure that the connection was working. Of course, I now know that what counts in the financial advice sector is how much you sell, not the job interview. So basically they hired everyone, as it would take a just few weeks of work before their value became apparent. The questions were constructed in such a way as to get rid of those who were potentially incompetent salespeople, as even a rubbish salesman would be able to persuade his parents to invest in something which would also be helping their son in his career. The questions were meant to reveal those who were prone to using manipulation, as for them all that would count was sales and only sales. They were supposed to have a mercantile attitude to life, meaning that they had to be ready to do anything for money, to be part of the gang. They were also expected to look the part.

In a word, I was the perfect candidate. They would have taken me on immediately, if they themselves hadn't had to wait two days before calling, merely to create an atmosphere of exclusiveness – "Marek, congratulations. You made it right to the top of the list of candidates invited to attend our training course..."

That day I went crazy – I bought some expensive beer and opened the last jar of my mother's stuffed cabbage rolls. "From next month on, I'm only eating in restaurants," I thought to myself.

I then arrived for the introductory training. Time: Friday evening, seeing as if you're a student and you come to this, instead of drinking vodka with your buddies and then pulling girls, that means you're serious about this job. In the room there were around 40 guys just like me. Young, good-looking men in outgrown suits, ready for anything, but having no idea what 'anything' meant. There were just a few girls. Just as the hands on the clock showed that it was seven o'clock in the evening, a guy entered the room who was well over six feet tall, wearing a beard and glasses and with a such a piercing stare that when he looked in my direction I immediately felt as if I had done something wrong, although I had no idea what. There was still a bit of a buzz of conversation in the room. This towering man stood in the middle of the room not saying a word and with a delicate smile glanced around at those present. When the room eventually quietened down, he slowly and majestically said:

"When Big Daddy talks, the kids listen". He said this in such a quiet but forceful way that no-one laughed. Everyone froze. "Currently, in this country there are several hundred financial advisors. If, in the next ten years, Poland achieves such a economic boom as Spain has done in the last decade, this means that a further twenty thousand people will find employment in the financial advice sector. While the annual commission paid to advisors will reach six and half billion zlotys. Annually ... Today you have the opportunity to begin fighting for a piece of that pie for yourselves. Today you will get the opportunity to gain a view into the way our business works, the secrets of its success and discover why we are the best in Poland. But if you are expecting a box of tricks, you'll be sorely disappointed. We stand for only one thing: HERE WE WORK OUR FUCKING ASSES OFF!"

The towering man then delivered such a sermon that we almost fell off our chairs. He painted a vision of big bucks, expensive cars, a chick for every day of the week and one other thing: "This is a job for those who go the whole way!" he continued.

If you recall Ben Affleck in *The Boiler Room* or Leonardo DiCaprio in *The Wolf of Wall Street*, here I experienced just the same, only a hundred times better. This guy was a master at public speaking and brainwashing. His height, his German accent, the timbre of his voice and the tempo of his speech all caused the biggest badasses in the room to keep their mouths shut. He looked and sounded like a Polish version of Tony Robbins merged with the aggressive business manner of Bobby Axelrod from the TV series *Billions*.

"This is work on commission because, if you work your asses off, this commission will give you unlimited earnings. We don't work on a 40-hour per-week permanent contract here, because you know what that is? A situation when a young guy works his ass off and gets a handshake from the boss if he produces results for the company. But if that company makes a loss, he gets told to 'fuck off'. Most young people in Poland working full-time contracts are carrying around their dickhead boss on their backs and if he, as an entrepreneur, takes a hit, it's they who get fired, not him! A full-time contract isn't participating in the profits, but participating in the losses! Now is the moment you are standing at a crossroads. It is you who will decide if you choose a safe full-time contract or will you choose the work of a financial advisor, which is connected with responsibility and independence. As long as you're young and single, you can make such a decision. Once you have a wife and kids, you won't take such a risk. If not now, then when?" he continued in his broken Polish syntax.

And we lapped it all up like cats drinking milk. The towering man chattered on for 45 minutes, but when he finished I was already a different person. At the time, the company was called Efect, and the towering man named Felix. Today, he's a legend. Business-wise, he's had an enormous influence on me. Felix created one of the least known but also the largest, and certainly most controversial, financial empires in Poland, while at the same time taking thousands of young salespeople, managers and businessmen hungry for success in a brand-new post-communist Polish economy and changing their lives.

He was eventually killed in a tragic accident, flying his own private plane. Although I saw him for the last time 10 years ago, even today my adrenaline level rises when I hear the classic Nokia ringtone which I had set for when he rang me. Actually, for many years while doing business, I wanted to be just like Felix. You may laugh at all that neuro-linguistic programming, life coaches, gurus and the whole gamut of pseudo-psychologists, but the truth is that something got into my head then and stayed there. I really believed that if I worked sufficiently hard, I would achieve success.

And goddammit, it worked.

I found my place in this new reality very quickly. Felix had noticed and begun to like me, which for me was something. I needed attention and for someone to tell me that I was cool and would become somebody. Above all, Felix believed in me. Well, not so much in me, but basically in the income which I could generate for the company.

I soon got my first real opportunity. I was sent to a female client in order to sew up my first contract. It was necessary to drum it into her head that it was high time to set aside 10% of her salary for her pension. I was as nervous as hell, and my boss furnished me with such standard phrases as "Don't come back without a contract" and "If she says she needs to sleep on it, tell her you'll wait in the living room", and other such things. So I went. The meeting took place in a café, which is always worse than at a client's home, as the client may always leave a café, but they have to ask you to leave their home. That's how were trained.

I remember that first sale as if it were yesterday. We were sitting in Kociak café on St. Martin's street, the same one in which my parents had gone on dates during their studies. In some way, I got to like having meetings with clients there. The decor and the menu had not changed much since the time my parents were young. The old, wooden, but still elegant, chairs had hosted many buttocks of the communist proletariat. Although the jellied desserts served in long, narrow dishes were garnished just as my aunts used to do, the prices were right up to date. As the restaurant decor did not attract a millennial crowd, despite its fantastic location, one could always find a free table there, even during rush hour. Probably, it was already only being visited by long-time customers out of feelings of nostalgia.

My client was called Ewa, a 30 year-old computer graphic designer, single and earning far more than the average national salary, aware that she had no chance of a pension from the state budget. She was already afraid of it, because I was the one who had placed that fear within her. There was the fear, there was the need to secure her future. There was a need, so there was a solution. The regular, long-term setting aside of 10% of her salary, not counting what the state social insurance fund took. I pulled out all the stops, played my A game and eventually closed the deal. I was ready for any question, any excuse, and if she just did not want to decide, to tear up the contract there and then.

"I have to sleep on this decision, can we meet in a week?" said Ewa, asking the standard question of a client losing their nerve.

"What kind of decision do you want to sleep on? On facing hunger during your retirement, if you don't do something about it right now?"

"Yeah, I m-m-mean no. I know that, b-b-but..." she began to stammer. "Well, it's about this investing... So will I have to set aside 500 zlotys every month for thirty years? And what happens if I don't have the money?"

"If you don't have the money, you also won't have it for your food and accommodation! Have you taken that eventuality into account? After all, as long as you have two hands and a head on your shoulders, you will always have money. If you happen to suffer an accident, you'll have money from your additional insurance after all," I explained in a quick, assured voice, as if it was the most obvious thing in the world, implying that I was amazed she was asking such things, as none of my hundreds of imaginary clients had never had such strange doubts.

"Yeaaaaahhh, I knoooow. But this contract which I have to sign now, after all it has so many pages of small print, and perhaps I should read through it in peace and quiet? Give me a few days, perhaps?"

"Ewa, there is certainly no problem, it's just absolutely unproductive. If you only start reading it, further questions will come into your head with every paragraph until you get yourself into a total muddle. After all, that's what I'm here for, in order to explain it. If you don't trust me or that the product which I have proposed for you is the best, we'll start reading through the contract together. I have the time. Please read and ask any questions."

"No, ok then, after all I trust you... but..."

And that's how this ping-pong argument went on.

At the back of my mind was Felix's training in closing a deal. The largest room in which the evening training sessions had taken place was just an enormous corridor with several doors leading to smaller rooms.

"Imagine," he taught us, "that you are here in this corridor with a client. And he wants to get the fuck out of there. Each one of these doors represents an excuse which they could use. 'I don't have a stable job', 'I've got to ask my mother', 'I don't know how much I can save' and other such bullshit. During a sale, you've got to close all of these doors. The only one that stays open, because you can't close it, is the door which is called..." and here Felix took a red marker and wrote on one of the door frames: 'I'm stupid'. "With a client you are to conclude your arguments in order that the only way they can turn down a product from you is the excuse: 'No, because I'm an idiot...'"

And how did my meeting end? With pen touching paper. I secured her signature on the form and earned my first 1000 zlotys. In an hour. Being 20 years old and having a few days experience in finance, I met a total stranger who had presented me with all of the information concerning her financial situation during our first meeting (including the state of her savings). She had signed a document obliging her to invest money over the next 30 years and then gave me the contact details of 14 (standard in our company) of her friends (names, addresses, telephone numbers, professions, in order for me to ascertain to what degree of income they had and whether it was worth me visiting them). I could now call them, say I was Ewa's financial advisor and arrange a meeting. She also promised that she would inform them in advance and set up the meetings. If there was ever a turning point in my life at which I had began to believe in myself, believe that I was able to make money and that my life would be really good, then that was it.

Do you remember that famous Hollywood scene when after some big success a hero policeman, reporter or stockbroker returns to the office and everyone stands up, applauds and slaps him on the back?

The next day in our office, everyone wanted to bask in the reflected glory of my awesomeness when the boss praised me from a height and said:

"You see? You see? This Zmysłowski got a contract signed from nothing and what about you?"

Either I was so good at it, or the business was so easy, or the clients so naive, or the sales system introduced by Felix so brilliant. Time was to show that it was a bit of everything.

My first salary in Efect, which was actually the first real salary

I had ever received, amounted to 15,000 zlotys. It was 2006 and this was astronomical money to me, five times the salary of my parents. I didn't have to look at the price of anything that was just an everyday item. I bought myself proper shoes, a Hugo Boss suit and a briefcase. I began to look like a financial advisor. As my subsequent salaries were even better, I got myself my first real watch – an Omega Seamaster – the same kind James Bond wore. Suddenly, it turned out that I was really good at something. Suddenly, it turned out that others were trying to keep up with me, not me with them.

Then the high-life began. The best restaurants, the best drinks. The doormen at the clubs began to recognize our faces and let us in ahead of those waiting in line. A box seat near the dance floor was always found for us. Bottles landed on the coffee table. Girls are somehow more willing to talk to you when you are in the best box seat with champagne, having earlier seen you get in before everyone else. I don't know why, but that's just the way it is. Or I do know...

Anyway, it's not important. It began to seem to me that I was better than everyone else, because here I was in my teens, earning more dough than university graduates with years of experience, although I was still shy around girls. Even though it was all going to my head more and more and I looked decent enough, inside I was still the small, neurotic fat-ass who didn't want to go anywhere. My friends then decided to help me out.

"A virgin at university? That's just absurd. Don't worry, we'll sort it out."

We drove to a cat house, or as they say in intellectual and artistic circles – a bordello. It was a huge villa on the way out of Poznan. At the beginning, I was taken aback that there were no markings outside the ordinary looking house, but later I figured out that the pink fence was a sign, and a pretty unambiguous one at that. We drove up to a huge gate and waited. After a moment, the biggest muscleman I had ever seen in my life came out. In a suit he looked like a black and white lump of timber. He peered into the car and, with a bored look, shone a torch on all of us, then mumbled:

"Welcome, gentlemen".

The automatic gate began to open. We drove into a courtyard, where there were already several Mercedes and Audis parked.

"It must be ok, wealthy clientele come here," I thought. The guys clearly had already had experience, because as soon as we crossed the threshold they dispersed around the rooms. I, however, had to plough my way through all the formalities with the brothel keeper, I mean the lady in reception, then ordered the most expensive vodka and Red Bull in my life from the bar and was led to a large room with an enormous sofa on which the girls sat.

The poor little things were sitting there just in their underwear. Weren't they cold? However, I was getting very warm and started to feel my throat going dry. So I asked for another vodka and Red Bull. The girls promptly figured out that they were dealing with a novice and one of them quickly decided to take advantage of the situation.

"Hiiiiii there, I'm Jessica. May I join you?"

I was so stressed that I didn't know what to do with myself. At last, a woman was interested in me! And Jessica was experienced and engaged me in conversation. And while she was at it, she asked me to buy her a drink, and another, and another. Of course, I kept up with her, although I was impressed at her ability to metabolize alcohol, and was pretty drunk myself. At last, Jessica invited me to a room.

So how did the little trip upstairs go? Nothing happened. I spent an hour massaging her back, because she was so tired and sore. In the end, she still managed to get a tip out of me. Later, the time came to pay for the drinks and then I realized that my wages were not as astronomical as I had thought... I then figured out that you can get the most money out of a customer through them buying drinks, while Jessica's vodka rather had no alcohol in it. Ladies and gentlemen, I stand before you – Marek Zmysłowski – business whiz kid.

The guys, of course, had a ball while I became a laughing stock, although I was slightly surprised that no one had the courage to laugh in my face. However, this entire situation aroused a competitive envy within me – 'I'll show you!' at expert level. I decided that it was high time to lose my virginity, but it would have to be an operation that would bring me everlasting respect. A conquest which none of those assholes could ever deride.

And then I thought it over.

Since the beginning of my studies, I had been active in an inter-varsity student association. For, *Nomen est Omen,* future financial advisors, but not pitching bullshit at Mr. Average trying to make a living, rather pitching bullshit at the CEOs of enormous listed companies. We used to meet fairly regularly, while every so often consultants from McKinsey and PricewaterhouseCoopers came to see us, looking to recruit new talent and quite willing to share their knowledge. For us young guns, barely 20 years old, they were almost gods and I decided that I would do something for the first time with a consultant goddess, something I should have done a long time ago.

One beautiful day, the exquisite and diabolically intelligent Ania appeared at our university. I was enchanted and desired that she be my first. She was a tall, elegant blonde with unbelievably big, extraordinarily bright eyes. At the same time, she had a lot of class and charm, as well as having recently completed a PhD.

Ania had spent all day at a conference organized by our university and I, of course, followed her around and took every chance to chat her up. When she laughed at my jokes three times, I threw caution to the wind and quickly asked her to go for coffee. She agreed!

Later, we had a few more dates and started going out together. During the first few weeks, I didn't invite her round to my place, because I was still living with Karol and I somehow feared a repeat of the situation with Marysia. But then again, Ania had her own flat.

And that's how the final barrier came down.

My sexual initiation allowed me to make a break from the mental fat-ass of the past. Although he would always return at moments of weakness, he would no longer be constantly whispering in my ear that I was not good enough.

And that 'first time' itself? It wasn't so bad. I'm sure today Ania recalls those 10 seconds with the greatest affection.

From that moment on, nothing could fence-in or stop me. I went hard into battle and after a while was pulling in a minimum of 30 to 40 grand a month as a financial advisor. In 2007, aged 20.

Nothing devalues money as effectively as working in finance and earning money on "forms", meaning contracts signed with clients. Now, a coat from Hugo Boss did not cost 2,000 zlotys, but one 'big form'. An hour's work, if you had access to good clients. It was then I understood that if you earn just to spend, you will never earn as much so as not to want more, because there is always something newer, more wonderful, more expensive that you don't yet have. You bought a boat? Someone has already ordered a bigger one. You bought a new Ferrari? Great, the newer models are already coming out.

Working by myself, it was difficult to break through the ceiling of tens of thousands of zlotys a month. It's also different when a financial advisor changes into a manager, who is building his own team of advisors, who in turn become managers recruiting advisors, who in turn... and for maintaining this structure, you will receive a commission for every form signed.

It was in this way we discovered multi-level marketing (MLM).

So MLM + financial advice = money, lots of money. And becoming even more rotten.

From that moment on, we began a massive recruitment drive. As I had almost no friends in Poznan outside the company, I was left with recruiting people on the street. We did not recruit through job advertisements, as we were looking for badasses. And badasses don't look for jobs. Jobs look for badasses. So I went down to Półwiejska, a street in Poznan's shopping district where the young and beautiful people like to be seen and where I went to watch them. I suppose I don't have to say that you need a lot of confidence to approach complete strangers? I was like a hawker of perfume, or a Jehovah's Witness. Once I had identified someone, it more or less went something like this:

"Excuse me," I said cheerfully, pretending to be late. "Do you by any chance know where the recruitment office is?"

I simultaneously scratched my right cheek with my left hand, so that my new gold Rolex would catch their eye.

"It's somewhere at the university," they would answer looking at my watch. "But there's a temping agency here. A bit further on."

"Oh, thanks. I have no idea about it. I'd say such things are only known by those looking for work."

"Ha, ha, ha!"

"Are you looking for anything by any chance? You see, I'm asking, because I'm going to the recruitment office to place an ad. I need real pros. What do you do?"

"I'm studying. Sometimes I hand out leaflets."

"Leaflets?"

"Yeah, I'd be happy to change to something else, if they paid better."

"Excellent, wait, let me give you my business card... Hold on, where do I, I... Oh, damn it, I left it in the car. Will you come with me? It's just here, twenty meters away."

And I led them around the corner to where I had parked an Audi RS4 or a Mercedes CL65 AMG I had borrowed from the boss for such 'hunting expeditions'. I opened the door, took out my business cards, handed one over to a guy amazed by what he had seen and set my stopwatch. He usually rang back within the hour.

I don't know why I took a fancy to the BMW Z4. Maybe because Bond had driven the previous version... I decided I needed a badass car. Badass in the teenage sense.

Between making a decision and actually buying something, ordinary people spend time on the internet searching for information. In the end, we are talking about a car worth over 250,000 zlotys. But not Marek Gone to his Head Zmysłowski. Having got the idea that morning, by the evening I had sauntered into a BMW showroom saying:

"Good evening, I'd like a Z4 please."

The salesman was dumbstruck.

"But..."

"A black one."

Initially, he didn't believe me. He mumbled something that if I wanted to lease it, I would have to have my own down payment to the amount of blah, blah, blah. I put a gold card on the table and said:

"Take what you need as my down payment and give me the Z4. I'm in a hurry."

And that's how I bought a car in which I had never even sat. The highlight of the most immature era of my life.

Ordinary people do it in a way that the more they earn, the more they spend. In Efect, the more we spent, the more we earned. You could say we were passionate about our work and wanted to change the world. But let's not kid ourselves – the best motivator is having no way out. If you have a gun to your head in the form of high monthly expenses, you have to work your ass off. The boss was happy that we were renting bigger and bigger apartments and leasing yet another, even more expensive car. If an additional guarantee was necessary, he rang the bank and the bank gave us what we needed, because the whole company was too big a client to turn down. At that time, we were one of the biggest firm of financial intermediaries in Poland. But the boss was happiest when the boys gave in. Meaning when they became fathers. That was the Holy Grail of guns to the head.

Although I had passed the first year of university no problem, I only got through the second – when Efect turned up – by sheer force of momentum. Once I started making money, I somehow lost the desire to study... oh, well.

In order to pass on an individual basis, you had to go to a young PhD student who was earning less than the cost of your suit. You apologized for being late and used one of the hundreds of sales techniques in order to gain the PhD guy's sympathy. Getting Cs was no problem, Bs a pleasure, but sometimes I fought for an A, just to check whether I was the best salesman in my own universe.

In the third semester, I didn't turn up for lectures even once. I thought to myself: "Give me a break, I'm making big bucks here, my life is sorted, the Z4 is streaking through the streets like lighting and then I come to college and see those troubled students who are shitting their pants with fear, because now there's a test in the theory of the design of mechanisms. Design of what?"

This was a stage where I went from one extreme to another – from a shy, helpless boy to a smug asshole who believed he was better than everyone else. I would have to get a real kick in the ass in order to change my attitude to people.

But let's not get ahead of ourselves.

I didn't take the exams. If once I had seen studying only as a springboard to a career and a better life, now I didn't see a whole lot of sense in it. Why bother, since I was already earning multiple the salary of someone who had recently graduated from university with a Master's degree?

I focused on my work. From today's perspective, I have an ambivalent attitude to that period of my life. On the one hand, I recall Felix's words: "There are two kinds of company directors. Those who have MBAs and those who have assistants with MBAs". And it was hard to argue with that. Today's system of education was established when access to information was very limited. For a long time now, universities have not been the best places to gain knowledge, experience and contacts. In Poland, there has never been an academy teaching real entrepreneurship. Now, everyone can learn what they want and what they need. Universities resemble factories for the unemployed, because the government, while of course ensuring one's education, has divorced it from the realities of the market place. In any case, that is how it seemed to me. It was a time when I had every complex global issue immediately solved in my head and was amazed that no-one else had come up with these solutions before.

I tried university studies four more times in the years which followed. Each time, my enthusiasm lasted just one semester. Although studying was easy, there was an internal rebellion as to what a waste of time it seemed to be. Never in my life has the situation occurred where the lack of a degree has had a negative impact on me directly. On the other hand, I saw how friends who had completed MBAs at renowned universities such as Harvard or Cambridge were using a wide circle of contacts which they had made there. I had to make such contacts by myself on the golf course. Or in strip clubs.

However, by 2007 my thoughts were elsewhere. In the office there was a crazy race going on to have the best sales results, to secure the largest number of forms from Mr. Average who, thanks to us, would be assured of a fairly good retirement or a wonderful house, due to having taken out a mortgage in Swiss francs. The boss promised that the best would be able to choose their own region of Poland in which the company was not yet operating and build up the structure from nothing. I slaved away like an idiot to get even better results. The sales system, which was unbelievably effective for the time, became second nature to me.

In our office, the working week began on Friday, as every Friday every team had what was called a working club. The training session started with a summary of the sales figures for the previous week. It was important to laud the guy with the best result, while giving a good bollocking to those consummate deadbeats who had not performed:

"Where the fuck is your turnover, Zmysłowski?!" the boss would ask rhetorically, sometimes referring to the number of signed forms. The next part was a summarized version of the motivational talk I described earlier, reminding us why we were there (for the dough). It didn't matter how many times we had heard it, by the end we were pumped up with just the same energy. This energy was necessary, because at the end we came to the declarations: "Zmysłowski, grab yourself by the balls. Does it hurt? Good, because that means you still have them! And now tell me, since you have balls, how many forms will you fill out this week?!"

Each one of us outdid each other so as to impress the boss. When it came to implementing the plan so as not to have egg on our faces, we worried about that later. We used a particular unit in order to assess the value of each form signed by a client. A form which undertook to save 200 zloty per month for five years produced 127 units; a thousand zloty per month, 635 units and so on. For each unit, you would get from four to 10 zlotys, depending on how long you had been at the company, your position and the number of people in the sales structure. I don't know why, but the 'working club' is one of the most pleasant things I remember.

On Saturdays, everyone gathered at the office around 11am. Some had come straight from a party, which happened to me a couple of times. My internal alarm clock goes off at 9am, even though at 7am I was still with the gang for a morning fit kebab! Another time, a girl I had met at a DJ's console a few hours earlier made me breakfast. I couldn't remember her name and I felt a bit awkward asking it. I was also very angry with the manufacturers of make-up which can make an angel out of a monster. People who pull the wool over the eyes of guys who are drunk or can't see very well should be put in prison. Fortunately, the scrambled eggs tasted pretty good.

How much would I give now for the ability to regenerate myself as I had then.

Saturday was the day when financial advisors arranged their appointments with their prospects (potential clients) for the whole week. Why Saturday? Because statistically people answer their phones more often at the weekends. We analyzed the quality of the recommendations, meaning the contacts to the friends of our clients, on a scale of one (the best) to three (the worst) regarding two factors, namely money and their relationship with those recommending them. Money-wise, the No. 1s were lawyers, doctors and architects, while No.3s were the proverbial check-out girls at the corner shop. The richer your prospect, the more potential they had of affording greater monthly savings or a higher interest rate on a mortgage. And the more you earned from the "forms".

If you wanted to earn the most, you had to have the most appointments with No. 1s. Good financial advisors only met with No. 1s. Rich people have rich friends and it was important to stay within this circle. The less able or beginner salespeople had to make do with meeting No. 2s, or, God help us, No. 3s and hope that the check-out girl from the corner shop had a richer sister, and that this richer sibling would agree to meet the financial advisor of her check-out girl sister. And here's where we come to the relationship between those recommending and those being recommended.

Our telephone patter was, at the time, masterful. It may seem a bit stupid, but I was wonderful at manipulating the person on the other end of the line.

"Good morning! Is that Franek?" speaking loudly and cheerfully, because old friends greet each other loudly and cheerfully.

"Oh, yeah, it's me..." Franek would say, unwittingly confirming his identity while wondering if he should not have recognized us by now.

"We don't know each other yet personally..." Franek breathes a sigh of relief that his memory hadn't failed him. "But we have a mutual friend, Heniek. You work together in the same office."

Of course, Franek knows Heniek, but we must be good friends with Heniek since we know with whom and where he works. So we are in.

"Oh, yeah, I know Heniek," says Franek already feeling calm.

"Wonderful!" I say cheerfully, "Because you know, I've been Heniek's financial advisor for a while now (which means three days) and Heniek told me that you're a man who doesn't like throwing money down the drain. Is that true?" This stupid question answers itself, because everyone says 'Yes', so we are in agreement once again.

"Yeah, ... sure," says Franek.

"Wonderful, so I could also give you an hour of my time to conduct a professional financial analysis, which will help you make the best financial decisions. I'll do it completely for free, because you know Heniek. I have two times I could meet you, Monday at 5pm or Wednesday at 8pm. Which would suit you better?" – a question giving Franek the illusion of choice.

"Uhh, Wednesday at 8pm, probably," replies Franek.

"Wonderful! So I'll put that in my diary. I'll definitely be there, so could I ask that you also write down the time of our appointment, ok?"

In the end, the salesperson takes the address before hanging up. Although Franek has no idea what has actually happened, he remembers that he has to be home on Wednesday evening, so as not to embarrass Heniek.

Good salesmen only call the best friends of their clients who have already been to told wait for his call. Out of 10 phone calls, they get 10 appointments, and that's the way it works.

But if you call prospects with 'weak relationships', you have spent all day Saturday until the evening working like an agent in a call-center in which nine out of 10 people turn you down, while the one you have made an appointment with will say that 'something has come up' at the last minute. The minimum number of appointments a week amounted to 12, while those with 'weak relationships' were double-booked, meaning you would have two meetings arranged for the same time. If none of them were called off, you could always send a colleague from the office who was going through a dry patch.

Those going through dry patches moped around the office, ruining everyone's mood. Everybody realized that their days in the company were numbered – with no recommendations you weren't able to make appointments, with no appointments you were unable to sell anything without selling anything, you didn't earn money. And so you dropped out, because you weren't able to work for long for free. Dry patches were, therefore, natural selection at work in the jungle of finance.

Mondays were for weekly discussions with our immediate superiors, during which we wondered how you could be so fucked up as to declare such high sales targets during the 'working club' and then, looking at the number of appointments, wonder if there was any chance whatsoever of securing that 'promised fucking turnover'.

Every Wednesday evening there was a meeting, or a proper sales training session, for all financial advisors. Meaning basically the only time devoted to building up your knowledge of finance which, on the one hand, helped you understand what was going on the financial markets (to cut a long story short 'All institutions want to make the most money out of you'), and on the other hand, allowed you to find ways of impressing clients with your knowledge: "Remember, Zmysłowski you have to know at least 1% more than the client for them to consider you an expert. But 1% is more than enough."

The remaining time was filled with meetings with prospects and parties. I was in my element. For fish in an aquarium, that aquarium is their whole world. And I was at the top of mine, mainly because I didn't become discouraged. I constantly recruited and visited clients who nobody from my company wanted to go to. As I recall, one client recommended me to another. Not just to one but to 14. A financial advisor does not leave an appointment with a client without getting 14 names, addresses, telephone numbers and information about what they do. And this was before Facebook and other social media. We checked out these recommendations and decided whether the client could have available funds and whether to call and arrange an appointment. Every advisor wanted to meet lawyers and doctors. However, I was less discriminating, especially when I was threatened by a dry patch. So, for example, one of my potential clients was clearly a farmer near Szamotuł. I thought to myself, "Farmer or not, I'll give him a call."

I called, arranged an appointment and went.

I raced off in my 2.0 liter Z4 (which looked like a 3.0 liter M Power, I swear) down some awful little forest trail. When I arrived at my destination, my car was so spattered with mud it was hard to see its color. Eventually, I came to some farmhouse, whose door was opened by an old man of the forest, at least that's the impression I had. An old, decrepit man exhausted from working in the fields. Absolutely no financial potential. I could have wheedled my way out it by saying that I had got lost and so on, but something struck me, or someone to be more exact, namely the old man's wife. A peroxide blonde of about 30 with enormous silicone breasts, showing an equally enormous amount of cleavage. Together they looked comical. "Hhhmm," some things you don't do for money, I sighed. I immediately understood that this guy must have money. A lot of money.

They sat me down at a table, both of them sitting opposite me.

"Have you got anything interesting for me there, sonny?" the old man asked, while I wasn't able to concentrate on anything else other than his wife's cleavage. It was good that I was truly an experienced professional. Thanks to this, I was able to constantly build up a need and then automatically satisfy it. I told him about what I had to offer and gave him a bunch of talk about how he wouldn't always have the strength to shovel manure, that the time would come when he would have to live off his savings. And the cost of living won't necessarily go down, and here I looked knowingly at him, then at his wife. And I already knew that he had got the message:

"How much would you like to invest per month?" I eventually asked him.

"Oh, I don't know", he replied, "Not too much, because I don't understand all of it exactly, you understand. Maybe at the beginning around 10,000 zlotys. Per month."

In the blink of an eye, I had calculated my commission and realized I that if I wanted to lease a new Porsche 911, I had just earned my own down payment. Filling in the form was so much more difficult in that very moment, as I was struggling not to look at his wife's cleavage, as well as not to grin like a Cheshire cat.

Another time, I went to see the owner of a scrap yard. I drove onto the premises and, looking for the office, found a hut completely covered in mould. I got out of the car and was almost run over by a tractor carrying scrap. The driver shouted some very abusive language and I gave as good as I got. The scrap dealer, my potential client, walked up to me. He constituted such a hideous apparition that I felt nauseated. Filthy clothes, a dirty face and soiled hands, one of which, of course, he extended in order to greet me. It took a lot for me to literally get a grip and shake his hand.

"Nice toy," he said lisping slightly and smiling, thereby exposing his crooked teeth.

"Yeah," I replied, even though I have always been more eloquent.

"The sports version," he said trailing his hand along the body, causing me to wonder in despair where the nearest car wash was. He didn't pay any attention to me, however, only saying, "I also like sports cars."

He pressed a button on a remote control fob. The gate of a garage hidden among the piles of scrap opened and standing inside was a red Ferrari F430. In a fucking scrap yard.

I signed a contract with him and made a huge pile of money. Decidedly too much, too easily and too quickly.

"Zmysłowski, now is your time," the boss started another motivational speech with his German accent, and my dopamine levels immediately shot up. "We'll conquer another town, we'll open new branches and you'll get the chance to open one of them. You're going to Chorzów in the South of Poland. And from there you'll conquer the whole region! Soon you'll be a very rich man."

Although previously I had counted on Wrocław or Krakow (much nicer and bigger polish cities), Felix sold it to me that now Chorzów seemed a hundred times better.

And in this way, I said goodbye to Poznan once and for all. On the way, we still had a weekend party with all of the newly-minted regional managers. Meaning two days of drinking and partying. For this purpose, the company had rented a whole castle in south-western Poland. Although there were easily 200 of us there, this number was supposed to have doubled that evening, but more about that in a moment. The car park was full of the managers' cars, motivating the young guns with the revving of their engines, including models such as the Porsche 911 turbo, Audi R8, RS4, S6, Mercedes C63AMG, as well as a load of S3s, Golf GTIs, Lancer Evos and M3s. Salespeople from the Mercedes and Audi showrooms came in their own cars to the party. You could take a test drive and sign a leasing agreement for a car straight away. If you did that, the boss was, of course, well pleased.

The company was totally dominated by the male sex, not because men are better salespeople than women, but simply because the manner of indoctrination, motivation and management, and perhaps the recruitment preferences of the managers, resulted in only two out of every hundred financial advisors being female. Of course, this complicated things when it came to office parties. But a way around this was found.

Before the party had started, two coaches with hostesses pulled up to the castle. That night, the nightclubs of Wrocław must have been particularly empty. After motivational speeches from Felix and other managers, the promotions and bonuses being doled out, the company's successes and plans being outlined, the Polish blonde bombshell pop star Doda appeared on the stage. Oh, the things people do for money. Apparently, the bar had been drunk dry by 2am and the hotel staff had to drive round to surrounding 24-hour liquor stores for supplies. The bar staff stopped serving alcohol around 5am, when we came upon the idea of taking down the knight's armor on display and dressing up in it to create a Slavic version of Gladiator. It was a miracle that nothing happened to anybody. Although the swords and replicas had not been sharpened, they could have done a lot of damage to any jackasses who ended up with just black eyes and bruises. The body of a man who's drunk is extraordinarily flexible and can take almost anything without the trace of a blow, which otherwise would have him end up in hospital. Although some of the hostesses got scared and wanted to go home, they had no way out, as we had got the coach drivers drunk. Others drank the same as us, or disappeared into rooms with some of the advisors. Some couldn't wait to get to their rooms, they were in such a hurry. I remember that I wasn't able to use any of the toilets in the restaurant, as somebody was either puking their guts up or screwing someone else.

On Sunday, suffering the greatest hangover in the world, we were supposed to sign additional documentation connected with the opening of franchises and a contract forbidding competition, guaranteed by a bill of exchange to the value of 5,000,000 zlotys. Everything altogether came to around 20 pages. Although they were documents I had seen for the first time in my life, none of us then considered the details. We were a band of brothers and we were conquering the world!

After signing the documents, I got into my Z4 and drove to Chorzow with a hangover. And already waiting there for me was an apartment of 100 m² rented by the company. True, it had a view of the coalmine, but it was still something.

I got down to work. First, it was necessary to assemble a team, then train them up and send to them out into the world. They start by selling contracts to their friends, parents, aunts and uncles, then their friends, and then the friends of friends. To tell the truth, I was scared. It's a different thing to go out into the street, bullshit a few students and send them to the main office in Poznan which deals with the rest. Here it all depended on me whether we would make money or not. Equipped with a great wealth of know-how, I decided that, just as in Poznan, I didn't have the time to browse through CVs. I went from restaurant to restaurant and sought out handsome, eloquent bar men. Some of them thought I was gay and I don't blame them. In any case, a good barman is, above all, a good salesman, and I needed this kind of person. This time the gimmick with the business card took place in the Z4, not the Audi RS4, but this was Chorzów, not Poznan.

As promises of quick and plentiful cash had always worked, soon

I had assembled a team of handsome and hungry young guns. It was necessary to move to the next stage, namely training. As I wasn't as good as my boss, the beginning was painful. All the motivational clap-trap which had to instill a desire to work in my team, well… it didn't go great for me.

The biggest problem for me was that for some time I myself had not been convinced whether this work was making me happy or was completely ethical. I didn't want to get out of bed in the morning, in the office I quickly lost patience and got irritated when someone wanted something from me. I simply stopped liking people and started to avoid them. And this was perhaps the worst thing which can happen in a sales and management job. I counted the hours from Monday to Friday, until I could just get into the Z4 and head off down the motorway to Krakow, driving 200km an hour and partying the weekend away. I didn't know it at the time, but these were the classic symptoms of burnout. No-one had either warned me or prepared me for it.

I was having more and more problems with the cheating of my clients by my own financial advisors, who were ever more creative. Sometimes a break or a pause in a sentence can cost tens of thousands of zlotys: "Everything which you pay in, you can take out after five years." I was starting to receive difficult telephone calls at the office, that we were a gang of fraudsters, that they would hunt me down and strangle me.

All of this resulted in me devoting much more time to training staff than I should have. I wanted them to know what they were doing, so that they would suit the investment product and the associated risk to the client. So that they wouldn't sell an investment contract for a 1000 zlotys per month for 10 years to someone who was earning 2,500 zlotys per month. So that the client would know what they were buying.

There's an irony to the fact that when, many years after I had left the company, my father suddenly died and the time came to cash in on the insurance policy which a work colleague had sold my parents, it turned out that the amount paid out was missing a zero from the end compared with the figure that my 'co-advisor' had presented them with. And the fact that my folks had trusted him was down to me.

Coming back to Chorzów, not all of my team turned out to be sufficiently tough. In the sales business, the most difficult thing is dealing with being turned down by a client, which people frequently take too personally. In the place of those who left we had to take in new people. And the staff training had to start all over again. Although Felix had always said "You need to build quicker than it all gets fucked up", the worst thing here was that I didn't have time to deal with my own clients. Before, it was all simple. I went to someone, signed a contract with them and earned three, five, 10 thousand zlotys. One contract a week was enough. Now, I could only dream about such money. Even worse, I had to pay for the cost of running the office, the assistants, office materials and so on. My people were not bringing in too much money, while my commission from their work amounted to pennies. I had put a lot into all of it and at a certain moment started running out of money. I was not prepared for this. I had become very unused to not having money.

This caused a drop in motivation. This lack of motivation lowered earnings even more as, after all, this was dependent on the quantity and quality invested in sales. So, I began to earn even less.

More and more often, I asked myself the question: "Do I really want to do this? Do I want to be pushing saving insurance policies on people for the rest of my life?" As long as there was money, I was living an illusion, in a bubble of happiness. If I felt bad, I went somewhere, bought something and it was lovely. But the bubble then burst. One October evening in 2008, in my 100 m² apartment, I ran a bath, hopped in, closed my eyes and took a deep breath. I tried to feel as light as possible, just to float carefree on the water for a moment longer.

The phone rang. I looked at the display. It was my boss.

I let the air out of my lungs and I slid under the water. The phone rang a little longer and then went silent.

Chapter 2

A MACBOOK
AND A SOYA LATTE

Several days later, I rang the company and told them I was leaving. It was not an easy decision, as it meant an admission of failure, but floundering in stagnation was even more difficult.

The first few days were strange. I was used to hard work, morning phone calls, unbelievable pressure to achieve targets issued from above, which I then passed down the line. And now it was waking up at 10am, breakfast, coffee and… that was it.

I hung around the city a bit, although 'city' isn't the right word for the Upper Silesian Industrial District. When a bus pulls up to a stop, the back doors are still in Chorzów, while the front doors are already in Katowice. So I drove and walked around and went people-watching. Especially those who were older. You could see the enormity of the hard work they had experienced in life and, at a certain moment, I realized that I knew nothing about such work. That I had only driven my white ass around in a sports car and encouraged people to transfer money from one bank account to another. That was the moment when, just for a second, the problems with my feelings of my own self-worth returned. I wondered whether I had achieved anything at all, or whether my work had served any purpose other than making money. Every other man on the streets of Silesia had spent half of his life in the mines digging coal, which had given all of us electricity and heating. While I had been selling dreams.

I thought about all of this and felt the idea growing within me that real work was this kind of work. A physical cleansing. Hardship, toil and dirt. Coming home with the feeling that you had done something worthwhile. Only then could you appreciate life.

And I would have qualified to be a miner, damn it, if I hadn't seen a certain guy at a coffee shop first. This guy was undoubtedly the first hipster in Poland, as silk scarves and slicked-down mustaches were not even fashionable in Warsaw at the time. He was drinking a soya latte from a paper cup and tapping away at the keyboard of a computer with a shiny apple on the back. Apart from the two of us in the café, there wasn't a living soul around.

"Do many IT guys work in this city?" I joked.

Glancing up from his monitor, he looked me up and down. He perceived a well-dressed man with an expensive watch and recognized that he could suffer responding to this idiotic taunt. But he didn't push the boat out, in this regard.

"I do," he said.

"Aha, and you make a living from something like that? Tapping at a keyboard, I mean."

He heaved a sigh.

"You can," he retorted. "I build start-ups, man. You can make millions out of it."

Well, fuck me. He used the magic word.

I immediately forgot about what I had just planned regarding becoming a miner and quickly returned home.

On the way, I started reading and opened up so many pages in the web browser that my phone crashed. By the time I had arrived home, I had a terrible headache. So I turned on the television and sat on the sofa to relax for a moment.

It just so happened that there was a report about Nasza Klasa [Our Class], a Polish clone of Facebook. Although what happened to it later and why is another story, but when they said how much the portal was worth I nearly fell over. Then they smoothly moved on to the subject of start-ups as a global trend, showing a café in California in which some geeks were sitting at tables, tapping away on MacBooks. Each one of them armed with a soya latte, and each of them earning millions. At that time there was still something in the phenomenon of Silicon Valley.

I thought to myself, "If these dweebs can do that, I'll show them that so can I."

In one minute, I decided that I would be just like them. At the beginning. Because later I would overtake them, lap them and then buy them out. I got up and ran to get a soya latte. And a MacBook.

In the following two weeks, I had become an expert on start-ups. At least in theory. I downloaded everything I could find on the internet regarding this subject. First in Polish, then in English and later using Google Translate. With such knowledge in my possession, I started thinking about plans to conquer the world, maybe even all of Poland.

I succumbed to start-up fever. Just like the gold fever which had broken out in the Canadian Klondike region at the end of the 19th century. Gold-diggers from all over North America travelled to the small town of Dawson City. At its height, the town had over 40,000 inhabitants, which was 40 times more than before. It's the same with start-ups. Marc Andreessen, the legendary Silicon Valley entrepreneur, investor and founder of the internet browser Netscape (again for kids today, this went out with the dinosaurs), once wrote that "Software is eating the world". Our parents' concept of a bank with no people is crazy, while we think it's crazy to have to go to a window at a bank just to make a transfer.

Technology is literally entering our refrigerators, which can now order our groceries for us. The world has suddenly understood that there's money in the internet and that it was enough just to click it into your own wallet. And everyone started clicking.

What's obvious has its own consequences. Whenever I got a great idea, it turned out that someone had beaten me to it. I had clearly discovered this subject several years too late. On the other hand, however, as it happened to be the moment when the world was appreciating start-ups, it was relatively easy to find investors. It wasn't necessary to explain why it was necessary to pump money into it. Only an idea was required. That's the way it seemed to me.

During my period of greatness at Efect, my buddies and I started to get involved in a particular game, namely speed dating. 20 guys and 20 girls participating in the game. Once the order is given to start, you have three minutes to speak with each girl. For those three minutes you tell them whatever trips off your tongue. I always said the same thing: that I used to work as a financial advisor, but that working in a corporation wasn't for me, that I had packed it all in, had given up a great car and, because I now wanted to change the world, was dealing with start-ups, yadda, yadda, yadda. In the end, the girls chose with whom they wished to continue the conversation. If they made the same choices, we had a match. So in the end, my buddies and I had marked them all off. That way we knew how many of them were interested in us.

Just so that we understand each other, I wasn't looking for a woman. Not in that way. With a little effort, I could have had 80% of the chicks I wanted. Ok, maybe 50%. Alright, 40%... ANYWAY! We just went there for fun. The guy who had the worst result had to buy a round of beer in the pub. Although it happened to me several times, usually it went well. A few times, I walked away with a full house.

And it was at one such meeting that I got to know Kasia. She wasn't taking part in the activities, but had organized the whole thing. She was a fairly well-recognized person in this field and had successfully run the Halves of the Orange [Two Halves of an Orange] project. If you haven't heard of it, it was the first company in Poland which focused on ensuring that singletons had fun. When I heard about it, I then understood that I had found my big business idea, as the company was operating strictly offline as an exclusive club beyond the world of the internet. Its members paid a monthly fee, for which the club organized their time, but there was almost no trace of them on the net. I decided to put on my superhero costume and rush to the aid of these wretched singletons deprived of internet games!

Of course, it all began with a big gimmick. I introduced myself to Kasia as an experienced professional, who had already had some success. She believed it, because I can be very convincing when I want to be. We went for a coffee. Then another.

"Listen, Kasia", I pontificated, "There are five million singletons in Poland. Five million people who may want to use our portal. Do you know how much money that is?"

"But ..."

"I know, I know what you want to say, that dating websites are already out there. I know they are. And that's the thing. We won't be a dating website. We'll be a portal for singletons. You know, those who are single by choice. Or for those who don't have a choice, but have become used to it. We'll employ the best journalists and fill the service with loads of content for singletons. You know, it'll be a kind of Nasza Klasa for unmarried men and women, meaning those who are unattached. For Christ's sake, it's a great idea. We'll make millions from advertising. Every investor possessing at least the IQ of a grass snake will throw everything into it and be running to the ATM to get dough for us."

Dear readers, if you bought this book in order to find out how to establish a start-up, you can give up reading the rest of this chapter. But if you are interested in how not to establish a start-up, print out what I am about to say, make a picture of it, put it on the desktop of your MacBook and write it with a marker on your cup of Starbuck's soya latte.

In working at Halves of the Orange, I made absolutely every possible mistake that a big-headed start-up amateur could make.

You start by accepting a certain 'flying by the seat of your pants' thesis on the basis of your own, subjective experiences. Put simply, as something seems logical or in line with everything you've ever learned, you believe it to be true. Meaning you're making an educated guess. What's more, you try to prove this thesis or, to be more precise, confirm it. Meaning you'll choose and pay attention to those facts which confirm it, while ignoring and dismissing those which don't. And this is the recipe for a stupid business idea.

If I had to outline a hierarchy of errors, I would admit that one big fuck-up appeared (let's call it the Great Fuck-up) which brought down the edifice of the project, one which was no longer capable of bearing the weight of the smaller fuck-ups (Common Fuck-ups).

This is the way, more or less, it seemed to me:

The Major Fuck-up: I prepared a very detailed plan simply based on educated guesses which were, in turn, confirmed through confirmation bias. I only concentrated on those facts which confirmed my ideas and ignored those which could have said differently. As it seemed to me to be the perfect plan, I put all the money I had left into it. The fundamental assumption was that, as there were loads of singletons in Poland suffering from a lack of entertainment tailored to their needs, we would rapidly gain huge momentum. That was clear. A divine wish.

The First Common or Garden Fuck-up: This was when TV stations started to discuss problems with Nasza Klasa's efficiency, as there was a moment when the service worked very slowly and was continually crashing. The founders of this project had not expected the success which came to them. As I was convinced that soon there would be a second Nasza Klasa, I immediately invested a load of money into servers. If Nasza Klasa had been based on what I had bought, I would have shot down the road like the Road Runner running from Wile E. Coyote.

The Second Common or Garden Fuck-up: Because I was entirely convinced that we would achieve success, I constructed the portal to facilitate the easy addition of content from the countless journalists invited to join the project. You know, they were meant to be able to increase the volume of content with articles, films, photographs and other such crap. And this of course caused the portal to be very complicated, take a long time to be developed and, above all, was simply expensive.

Meanwhile, none of this functionality had ever been used, as we had not got to the stage of being able to employ anybody.

The Third Common or Garden Fuck-up: The most embarrassing of all, as it underlined the absurdity of the entire project, namely that we assumed, as I have said, that there were loads of singletons, that we would create content especially for them and that they would be on our portal night and day – but what does this actually mean for singletons? Or as people say on 'the internets', what content? There is no such thing. If we write a great movie or book review on the net, it can be read by someone who's single or not. There was nothing which could cause a singleton to feel especially catered for by our portal. Maybe something as idiotic as 'Ten ways to pick up girls/boys'. But we were meant to be, first of all, a portal for those who were single by choice and who, according to my stupid 'educated guess', were not looking for love at all (they're always on the lookout, only they won't always admit it). Secondly, how much of this shit can you produce? We would have run out of subjects after five articles.

The Fourth Common or Garden Fuck-up: Hold on! My name is Marek Zmysłowski and recently I persuaded a farmer to pay 10,000 zlotys per month for 10 years as part of investing in our product. How long could it take to find an investor ready to invest only two million zlotys in a portal which would soon be the second Facebook? With this idea in the back of my mind, I wasn't really bothered by how money was evaporating at a terrifying rate and having nothing to show for it.

Meanwhile, reality turned out to be a bit more complicated. I would go to an investor, sit facing an old marketing ace and tell him: "Hey, man, soon there will be hundreds of thousands of singletons here, advertisers will be killing each other for the opportunity to be on our website, on the leads alone you'll earn millions" (Note for marketing-speak novices or those who haven't seen *Glengarry Glen Ross*: put very simply, a lead is the data of a potential client and the more leads you have, the greater the amount of tentatively interested clients to whom you can direct what you have to offer).

And he would reply, "Yeah, you know I advertise on Onet and WP [two major Polish news websites] which right now have traffic which you won't have for about 500 years. I get leads from equally big partners. Why should I put two large ones into something which I've had for ages? And, what's more, with no certainty that I would ever get it back?"

I was crushed. Me, the best salesman in the world, with the whole gamut of convincing, almost sincere smiles, was not capable of selling such a product for such a pittance as two million zlotys? Jesus, surely it was because I no longer had the Z4. I'd had to get rid of it. Dreams, however, do not feed your stomach or fill a petrol tank.

The Fifth Common or Garden Fuck-up: The last nail in the coffin, namely the parent syndrome. I was so in love with my project, that I didn't perceive its faults. The idea is perfect, only the circumstances, the clients, my partners, the market, those stupid immature Poles, namely everything else is fucked up. Not me. And if the facts contradict this, that's too bad for the facts. I didn't draw any conclusions. All the indications that I had made a mistake I interpreted as being false, while all those which confirmed my vision even to the slightest degree I raised to the rank of key arguments. The more it fell apart, the more money I put in to fix the situation.

When the money ran out, so did Kasia's patience. And then I learned a very important lesson. The relationship between partners is a bit like that of an old married couple. You have your ups and downs. In marriage, it's not only about the sex being good, or regular anyway. A married couple should also be friends. And if something goes wrong, then that friendship is a kind of airbag. Myself and Kasia were not friends. We had nothing in common. When the business collapsed, we fell into an abyss from which there was no return. We tore into each other like animals and our paths went separate ways.

I left the project without so much as a red cent. Literally. I didn't even have enough to cover the rent on my 100 m² apartment, which, to be honest, I should have given up a long time before. So although I had to get ready to move, I was still convinced that start-ups were where the thing for me. The 100,000 zlotys I had put into Halves of the Orange eventually came back to me. Not in the form of a financial profit, but constituted the price of one of the most important lessons of my life. I only learned that much later.

I was still a Great Pretender. I wasn't poor, because only poor people were poor. I was still a rich man with temporary financial issues: "I don't really like the flat anyway", I persuaded myself. "I'll find something smaller. Money will turn up..."

Then something happened which woke me up. In the Katowice branch of Efect there worked a great young guy. His name was Szymek and I immediately got on well with him. Some people just suit each other. At the time, I suited a lot of people, but not many people suited me. There was money, fancy cars and girls. I couldn't complain I didn't have friends. But of all the people in that group, Szymek was the one who never wanted anything from me, even though he didn't have very much himself. In Efect, he had particularly bad luck. He was a nice kid, but without the sense of doing something for the hell of it that was necessary to achieve success in this fucked-up business. Honestly speaking, in fact, I had always considered him a bit clumsy. He was just too good and too nice a person. Besides, he just trusted people too much. When someone proposed going into business together, he agreed, putting up his flat as collateral. And guess what? The business never took off and Szymek got into difficulties. He had received the flat from his parents and was now wondering how to tell them about his troubles.

And that was the only time when he asked me whether I could help him out.

And that was the only time when I wasn't able to help him out.

I had made loads of money. My life had been one big party. The dream of every hedonist. When the money was there, I could afford anything. But when it ran out, I didn't have enough for the most important thing. Just one year earlier, I would have been able to help Szymek out and would have done it without batting an eyelid, even though it would have cost me half a million zlotys. And now I had to tell him that I couldn't do a thing for him. I was his only lifeline. Unfortunately, that lifeline was ready to snap.

And it seems to me that was the moment when everything changed. In the space of one moment, I had gained humility. I recognized that this was the end of all this swaggering around and that it was high time to take a step backwards. Maybe even two steps. Because living on as I was would not only have achieved nothing, but would in fact hurt those close to me.

A few days later, I became a barman.

I packed everything in and, together with my friend Szymek, went off to conquer Warsaw. The plan was to find basic casual work, which would provide some money, while allowing me to slowly devote some time to start-ups. Szymek intended to find work in car sales and first got a job at a BMW showroom. Without going into details, I will just say that Szymek also took his previous experience to be a lesson, a diabolically effective one. He had turned out to be a great salesperson and I, a terrible judge of character. From BMW, he was poached by Audi and later went to work for just better and better brands, including Ferrari. Now, he manages premium showrooms and makes a ton of money doing it. He's got a beautiful wife and great kids. And later he ended up saving my ass on many occasions. And he's a real friend.

Coming back, however, to those days, I had to drum up some work and there was only one option. I had previously worked as a waiter while still at high school in Koszalin during the summer holidays. Now I looked the part and had sales experience to offer as part of the deal. I went to photocopying outlet, had 200 CVs printed off and distributed them where I could. A few days later, I already had two jobs. Every week day from 5pm to 1am, I worked in the bar of the Mercure Grand hotel, which belonged to the Accor group. At the weekends, I worked from 8pm to the early hours at Utopia. Do you know what Utopia was? Only an exclusive gay nightclub that is famous all over Poland.

However, before I started working there, Maciej Prostak, an old friend from Efect, got in touch. He's one of the best financial aces I've ever had the pleasure of meeting, not only in my professional but personal life, although we had had rough start. To put it simply, both of us were really good at what we did and there had always been rivalry between us, sometimes healthy, sometimes not. But ours went the healthy route. In addition, Prostak impressed me with his unbelievable self-confidence and charisma. He must have made an impression on everybody with a name like Prostak [Simpleton], as well as coming from a place with the weird name of Wąchock, a town whose name is the butt of many Polish jokes (true story), I had expected some loser worn out by years of bullying in school and the neighborhood yard.

Although Maciej had heard something about my unfortunate venture into start-ups, it had clearly not discouraged him. He had also got into the subject, but far earlier than I had. He not only had an idea, but also an investor. So he helped me out by proposing we work together, warning me, however, that at this stage the money wouldn't be very good, especially knowing the way we worked at Efect. But instead, there would be share options and I could stay in an office with a bed and a bathroom right in the city center, on the condition that I would manage to be up and ready before 9am and not leave a trace of myself behind.

Well, what could I say to such a proposal? Of course: "Hey, buddy, I'm in." It was through this that, within a week of arriving in the capital, I had achieved my initial plan. I had work, which gave me some money, and could work on start-ups. Sleeping in the office became more and more comfortable, although once the head of a certain large bank found an old black sock under his seat.

But all of this took a lot out of me. Mainly health wise. I was working on start-ups from morning until the afternoon, before running off to Accor. And then at the weekend, as I said before, at Utopia. I wasn't sleeping much at the time. It was then I learned respect for my own work. After all, I saw how much I would have to pay to chase my dreams. It's impossible to describe in just a few words the different world into which I had arrived. But I felt great there. At least in Utopia. Working there brought many unexpected benefits, as although it was a gay club, that did not mean that everyone there was gay. For example, when I was there, all the barmen were straight, while the customers were, well, you know, gay. Here I mean the male customers, but there were also lots of gorgeous girls coming to the club. Really, the most beautiful and sexiest women in the city went to there on the assumption that they would be left in peace. With gay men all around them, no-one would be chatting them up or staring rudely at their almost completely naked bosoms and other outstanding attributes. They could let their hair down and be free. And that's the way it was. Insofar as around three in the morning, after a few drinks, girls would suddenly say that all of this asexual bullshit is totally overrated. That they really could use a handsome, well-spoken heterosexual man.

And the only handsome, well-spoken, and above all, heterosexual men at Utopia at three in the morning were the barmen. And I had never had so many women as I had working those six months in a gay club. And what kind of women they were.

There were some comically hair-raising situations. Once, I was standing at the bar and suddenly saw a suspiciously familiar face. I racked my brains and remembered that it was a client from my time at Efect. He spotted me, came up to me, smiling. Then the small talk started. And this was a problem, because the guy just wouldn't shut up and was wagging his tongue worse than a market trader. And I then knew that tomorrow all of my old friends at Efect would find out about my failure of becoming a bartender after a "career" in finance.

It turned out that the last thing this guy had a desire to do was to come out. So no-one knew anything about my new bartending gig. Later, several times I saw my old clients, including those from among the 100 richest Poles list. Some of them quickly disappeared on seeing me. Some pretended that they were just there on a social visit, and kept pointedly repeating it. Others couldn't give a fuck.

I also had a great time working with Maciej on his start-up. We built the first price comparison website for financial products in Poland. Maciej was a more experienced manager than me and did not make the mistakes which I had made, one after another, at *Halves of the Orange*. We also had great investors. One of them, Andrzej, had introduced a certain well-known dark-colored carbonated drink to Poland. So let's say he never lacked money. He also didn't lack a laid-back nature, which I discovered during one board meeting when he pulled out my previous day's underpants from the chair he was sitting on.

Things went much worse for me in Accor. Generally, I was bored with the job. At Utopia there was fun, there were girls, there was drinking alcohol with the customers. Celebrities dropped in, someone hit someone, someone was kicked out by the doorman for arguing, someone complained to the doorman and the doorman ended up shouting at someone else. In Accor nothing went on. Absolutely nothing. There weren't even very many guests. Have I mentioned tips? At Utopia, this amounted to a second, even a third salary, on top of my basic 1,500 zlotys. And remember I was only working weekends. At the hotel, I was getting 1,500 zlotys per month and it was a pretty good day if you got 30 zlotys in tips.

I remember once in the hotel a financial advisor was signing up a client. I observed him. He was as useless as tits on a bull. If he had worked in my team, he would have soon been out of a job. By some miracle, however, he brought matters to a conclusion. And I know he made 500 zlotys on the deal. Meaning that in half an hour he had made about the same as me standing there for over two weeks. Forgive me if this sounds cocky, but I could have called that loser's boss at any moment and immediately I would have had a job. There were no companies selling such products in Poland then which would not have welcomed me with open arms. But I had pangs of conscience about selling anything at all. When the client left, this loser came to the bar for a drink. His hands were shaking from nerves. Without asking, I poured him a scotch.

"On the house", I said. "Congratulations."

I had lost all passion for such work. I had a vomit reaction to insurance or mortgages. I had already moved on, both in heart and mind.

But my new dream life was constantly throwing up challenges. Soon, it turned out that the start-up was developing very slowly and I found myself in a situation which I couldn't allow myself to be in, namely waiting for a paycheck.

I was fired from Accor.

Was it because I was too good? Not exactly. Due to disobedience. I hate it when someone tells me what to do. Especially when they are talking nonsense. When I get onto a website and want to set up an account, but can't because I get a message saying "Your password is too short", "Your password requires at least one digit" or "Your password requires at least one capital letter", I usually put on the voice of Bruce Willis and say "You won't fucking tell me what password I should have". Then I go to the competition.

In Accor there was a female manager who thought she knew it all. Anyway, that's what it looked like. A woman who had all the answers and who loved to demonstrate it. "That's wrong", "That's bad", "Change that", "Put this here and that there" and so on. Every time I tried to get her to understand that she didn't have a fucking clue what she was talking about, I heard "I've been managing this bar for three years and know better". And how can you argue with a person like that.

Once, she came to me and said:

"We have guests at Table 3."

"We'll sit them at Table 7. It's free and I have just cleaned it", I replied.

"Table 3 hasn't be cleaned yet."

"Clean Table 3 now. They are already sitting there."

"Now, I'll be unnecessarily waving a dishcloth in front of them. Next time, could you please look and see if there's anything already ready."

"Don't argue, just do what I say."

And then I heard those famous words: "I've been managing this bar for three years and know what should be done and what shouldn't."

I just couldn't hold myself back: "Yeah, and I suppose it's no accident that you haven't been promoted in three years."

I felt ecstatic, letting it all come out. I only forgot that she was my boss and not the other way round. And how much longer do you think I was working there?

Once I had been fired from Accor, I was left with only Utopia. But I had more free time, and I did need it because it was then for the first time that the idea came to my head to get into the funeral services business.

Chapter 3

MEMENTO MORI

In the beginning there was the word Well actually, PowerPoint slides. In analyzing various issues (read: "browsing the internet"), I reached the extraordinary general conclusion that everywhere a technological revolution occurred, great fortunes had been made. Or to put it another way, if you did not choose to have wealthy parents and had not gone down the route of organized crime (I don't mean politics), the greatest chance of making a fortune was to base it on change. Meaning to establish a business in an area undergoing a sudden transformation, or cause that transformation itself. If you hadn't managed to latch onto a political transformation, there was always a technological transformation. That's what happened when the amazing properties of crude oil were discovered (as a side note, the first commercial oil field was established in 1854 – in Poland, in fact – which led to a revolution in the industry. Go and Google "Bóbrka oil field"). That's what happened when computers were invented. A hardware revolution caused the world to speed up and its founders are the world's richest people today. Computers would never have become mass-market products without a software revolution, when it turned out that, with the aid of a computer, we can do everything and solve all our problems, even those which we didn't have before computers came along. Later came the internet, which caused thousands of small markets to be merged into one enormous market. Then social media and lastly, smartphones. Awaiting us is Big

Data, Artificial Intelligence and the Internet of Things. In every such revolution, some part of the market died and something entirely new and much bigger took its place. Nokia, MySpace, Kodak, Blackberry and Yahoo either took their eye off the ball regarding market revolutions, did not keep up with change, do not exist anymore, or are a just shadow of their former selves.

The conclusion reached from such thoughts was the following: it's worth seeking out an area in which it seems nothing could ever happen. One in which the roles of the moguls and minions were doled out years previously, but then, thanks to new technology, fuck it all up from within.

Another of my assumptions was to be the one and only for a long time to come. Although I knew that I would have to compete aggressively with those who had created the status quo, I didn't desire to compete with my own imitators. Because you know yourselves what it's like. You come up with a great idea and in six months you won't even be the market leader among the companies which have exploited your idea. This is why the business must be so 'out-there' in order to have certainty that no young gun will want to take it on.

Although start-ups go beyond being a financial fashion, the fashion for start-ups is a double-edged sword. Conferences, fame and fancy offices with free food attract a lot of 'wannabepreneurs', namely mediocrities living in a dream world and constantly building something which will change the world, but not yet knowing how to either monetize or get it going. Such people ruin the market and piss off those involved in it, but fashion also attracts extraordinarily talented people, who otherwise would have chosen another career route, when the recruitment of geniuses sees millions being spent on it (by corporations) or promising fame (the scientific route). Start-ups have provided options for both. In fact, this is how NASA recruited the best talent to work for the space programs of the 1960s, as working there provided both money and fame. And so success with members of the opposite sex.

But running funeral services was not really going to attract members of the opposite sex.

And this how the concept of Mementis was born. I just happened to be at home for dinner, when my mom recalled that a neighbor's family member had died and what a nightmare it had been to sort the formalities for the funeral.

"What? You don't like it?" asked my mother concerned, when I spat out my soup in amazement.

That was it. A funeral services brand that would confirm all my assumptions! The sector was almost entirely offline. Undertakers were hyperlocal companies without the knowledge, budget or, above all, desire to invest in new technology. A bit like the hotel sector in the 1990s, which overlooked the technological transformation and allowed such giants as Expedia and Booking.com to become established, and who today are the biggest players on the market despite not owning any hotels.

The heads of funeral services companies were the proverbial mustachioed gentlemen sitting in their comfy chairs, convinced that, over their dead bodies, nothing was going to happen to their line of business.

Mistake. Ladies and gentlemen, I give you Marek Zmysłowski, code name: Tombstone, the personification of the last nail in the coffin of Polish undertakers.

I got down to work.

Right from the beginning of my adventures with start-ups, I made the assumption that you could achieve success only when a burning consumer need was met with the aid of technology. It was necessary to identify and find this need as quickly as possible. Or create it.

Considering it further, I came up with a charming, I mean working, hypothesis.

The undertaker's customer is not the deceased, only the family member organizing the funeral. Statistically, Mr. Average organizes two and half funerals during his lifetime. On the one hand, it is very difficult to foresee when this will occur, while, on the other hand, there are only a few or several hours available to choose an undertaker. Usually, it works out that a doctor or priest turns out to be extraordinarily helpful in this situation, recommending a 'very reliable' funeral services company, whose number they just happen to have and, in order to relieve Mr. Average of this onerous task, makes the call and places the order himself. All taken care of – the competition hasn't a chance.

Or perhaps we could take into account that this Mr. Average, the customer of the funeral services company, is more or less 30 to 45 years old. Families often award this task to someone younger, who is in a condition to bear up emotionally and deal with the formalities. Slowly, this age group in Poland is becoming the first generation of heavy internet users, namely those who use the internet on a daily basis at work and in their private lives. They have consumed and created content.

As time marches on, chances will increase that Mr. Average will not necessarily listen to the priest or the doctor, and instead of making a final decision, will take out his phone and see what the internet has to offer in this regard. And find Mementis.

Mementis was supposed to dominate the organic and paid search results, have absolutely the best website, a proper 24-hour call center etc. Western-level quality at Polish prices.

The second advantage which Mementis was meant to have was a marketing strategy.

Mementis was supposed to have the greatest number of services covered under one brand, every one of those loosely connected, but connected with… departing this world, such as grave-cleaning, legal aid in making and executing a will, insurance, help with acquiring the Polish state funeral allowance, funeral loans, help with securing compensation, writing eulogies, and even planning your funeral while still alive. I hoped that thanks to all of this, the Mementis brand would become recognizable. Simply recognizable. And that this would allow us to build up a huge advantage over the competition. Although I wasn't going to send a newsletter offering funeral services to all users of Poland's most popular email service, I had already sent one offering a wreath-sending service on behalf of the customer for All Saints' Day.

I put everything I had thought through onto 15 PowerPoint slides. 15 slides which were supposed to help me make some money.

Following my adventure with Halves of the Orange, I knew one thing, namely that if I was going to lose money in a spectacular fashion, it was going to be someone else's money. If I was going to make costly mistakes, someone else was going to pay for them. Secondly, I had no other option. I was broke. I had no chance of getting a loan nor the nerve to ask my parents, who had already helped me so much. I thought to myself that I would get the money for my business from a venture capital (VC) fund.

Put very simply, a VC fund differs from individual investors in that, while they do invest, it is not their own money, but that of their limited partners.

Funds make money most often by charging a management fee, which is usually interest on assets (not only profits, but also all of the capital being managed). Of course, they also get lots of bonuses, if their investments end up with larger so-called 'exits', meaning exiting their investment by selling their shares to someone else at a profit.

To a large degree, investment funds, venture capital in particular, are responsible for the global start-up boom. On the one hand, they are inclined to be much more daring about investing in projects at a very early stage. On the other hand, each one is looking for billion dollar projects with the potential for a rate of return hundreds of times that invested and which is meant to cover the losses incurred in the tens of start-ups which have never passed the point of breaking even, where income finally exceeds costs. If one also focuses on the disproportionate rates of return, the VC market is highly polarized: a very narrow band of leading funds and a whole bunch of mediocrities, which basically earn money to pay their managers through management fees. Funds with successes under their belt will attract the best start-ups with the highest probability of a large exit. Less well-known funds have to try much harder to seek out interesting projects when the chances of something coming out of it are so low anyway. The struggle between funds for the possibility of investing in the hottest start-ups is no less intense than the struggle which start-ups face in becoming noticed by the strongest investors.

Whether an investor is strong or not, money is money. In order to increase the likelihood of success, I built a database of all the VC funds I could find, of which there were around 40. I wrote a nice email and sent it. Five replied.

The one that was most interested was a VC fund in Wrocław, which, following a preliminary conversation over Skype, invited me for a chat at their headquarters.

At that stage, I was completely broke. My lavish lifestyle had resulted in me being in huge debt, despite the big money I had possessed during my days at Efect and Halves of the Orange. But there was nothing that I couldn't manage. I got to Wrocław by hiding in the toilet on the train. I only had enough money for a one-way ticket. If I had paid my fare, later I would have spent the entire meeting wondering whether I would have to return without a ticket and play hide-and-seek with the conductor. Really? I decided to get the stress out of the way immediately, so that later my thoughts would be there where I wanted them.

"Alright, tell us about this business then," the Wrocław investor asked. Apart from him, several other guys were sitting in the boardroom. Everyone examined me carefully.

"So you see, it's like an Online Travel Agency, only this is a one-way journey, ha, ha," I added. No-one laughed. So I continued: "We're an internet service, thanks to which you can arrange a funeral over the internet. And if not arrange, at least ask for help in organizing it and in finding the nearest undertakers. We don't have to build our own funeral service facilities, as our clients will be using those already existing, which will pay us for each customer. We'll organize the nationwide promotion of our service, mainly through the Internet. The cost-per-click rate is ridiculously cheap, as our competition has not yet seen the need for advertising on the net. The conversion rate is high, as it's the type of service only people who are genuinely interested search for. In addition, according to Google Ads Keyword Planner, the term 'funeral' has tens of thousands of searches per month. People are looking for this information and the competition is asleep as usual. They have not noticed that the market is changing."

"Because it isn't changing," observed an investor.

"Alright, but I want to change it."

"Mr. Zmysłowski, do you know what you are aiming at, at all? Do you know what the funeral services sector in Poland actually is?"

"Of course. I know everything and have planned for everything."

Bullshit. If only I had known, I would have never got involved in it. But more about that in a moment.

I returned to Koszalin, paying for my ticket like any good citizen.

Two days later, I received information that my 15 slides had been valued at 1.5 million zlotys, while I was to receive a little over 700,000 zlotys and 49% of the shares. That's how much funding was ready, once the formal requirements had been fulfilled, of which more later, and to be paid into my account.

"You are investing in a presentation of a bunch of slides. A very risky idea which will be run by a young entrepreneur with a lot of failures behind him," I wrote to them, throwing caution to the wind, "And that doesn't bother you?"

"Correction," began their reply. "We're investing in the lessons we hope you have learned from these failures."

It was then I learned, almost incidentally, that in the West no-one is treated seriously in business if they don't have at least one failure behind them. There they approach things with the right assumption – that you only learn through your mistakes.

Whether my new investors, the investment directors of this VC fund, were visionaries looking far into the future, or just simply found it easy to spend money belonging to someone else, remains a mystery.

"Don't piss it away on a new sports car," I heard at the beginning. I burst out laughing.

"I'm serious," said the guy from the VC fund. The board of the previous fund they had invested in had started its venture into new technology by leasing two Porsche 911s. I moved to Wrocław, set up a company and the bank account into which the money was transferred. I travelled around Poland by train. I resisted the temptation to buy a Porsche and literally stayed on rails, traveling the length and breadth of Poland. Been to Sieradz? I have. And Konin? Or Tarnobrzeg? I spent so much money on train tickets, that if the Polish State Railways had conducted a rail miles scheme, that one freeloading train ride I took wouldn't constitute 1% of what I would be due.

And it was during these journeys, that I comprehended the weakness in my concept. Convincing investors that the Internet would revolutionize the funeral services sector was easy. Convincing the sector itself was a completely different story. I now understood what the head of the fund had in mind when he asked me if I knew what the Polish funeral services sector actually was.

It is one enormous mafia. As I could write a separate book about the adventures I had trying to find partners, I'll just cite a few interesting incidents.

Setting the scene: one of the small towns in southern Poland. I visited an undertakers' run by a hideously ugly woman with massive hooters. She received me in her office, I gave her a presentation and outlined the form of cooperation, the KPIs or key performance indicators, profits and forecasts, at which she interrupted me at a certain moment, looked deep into my eyes and asked: "Hold on a second, are you even over 18?"

I was dumbstruck.

"Well now sonny, show me here your ID. Ya want get money out of me, do ya? Going on about these yenternets," the old lady squawked. "Folks only watch pornos and drink beer in those yenternets."

I had intended to say that, on the contrary, the Internet was the future, that it would carry the torch of enlightenment and enormous profits, but fuck it, I just lost my drive to do so. They ordered me to leave. They said it several times, so there was no room for misunderstanding.

Then in Słupsk, a town in northern Poland, I went for a meeting with a certain owner of a funeral services company who seemed very nice over the phone. And that was true. A friendly older gentleman, very elegant with a pleasant personality. He told me a story of how this mafia worked with the first crematoria in Poland and sent in additional bodies as 'padding', to be burned alongside those meant to be there. What a wonderful story to start a relationship. I had just started to tell him about Mementis, when he raised his hand and said: "Just a moment. We have to wait for the owner. I've already phoned him."

I was a little surprised, as I was sure that it was him I had arranged to meet. And then things got weirder when the owner arrived. Two huge motherfuckers stepped out of a black Mercedes S Class. Dressed in black leather of course. One of them had some kind of tattoo of his bald head and it was him who sat down opposite me.

"Talk, sonny."

What's all this 'sonny' about? Everywhere I went, this word always came up.

So once again, I spoke about profits, KPIs and so on. When I finished, he looked at me and asked: "So this all fucking means that I'm supposed to pay you per funeral. How much?"

I didn't know too much then about the undertaking business, but I did know that the margins were not the worst. On average, customers spent 6,000 zlotys on funeral services, as that's what the state funeral allowance amounted to at the time. The funeral services companies had always manipulated the options on offer, as well as taking advantage of the customer's lack of knowledge regarding materials, to somehow always come up with a figure of 6,000 zlotys. Moreover, the customer did not have to pay a penny from their own pocket, as the undertaker sorted out all the formalities with ZUS, the Polish National Insurance Office, until it transferred the money directly to the undertaker on behalf of the customer. Maybe the government was slow to pay up, but it always paid up. This, when mixed together with the customer's vulnerable emotional state, resulted in the perfect set up to crank up margins on everything on offer.

So, with the certainty of a former financial advisor, I thought: "Okay, I'll throw out some figure and we can negotiate if necessary. I'll have to get a sense of the threshold price in order to secure a customer. Meaning one which a partner will complain about, but will be inclined to pay."

"A thousand zlotys," I said.

The owner's face turned bright red. He took my business card from the table and threw it back in my face so hard that it cut my forehead.

"Get the fuck out of heeerrreeee!" he informed me at a rather high volume.

And so I got the fuck out of there. Maybe I had not been forceful enough in suggesting that I was willing to negotiate?

It was only later I discovered that, several weeks before our meeting, the nice older gentleman had lost his undertaking business in a game of poker. For the bull-necked goon with the tattoo on his noggin, I was probably the first client he had ever had in his life. A legal client, I mean.

But my most interesting escapades lay ahead of me. Not put off by these teething problems, in the end I had managed to secure some partners and launched a nationwide campaign. We landed on television thanks to an advertisement for funeral insurance in cooperation with 4Life Direct, an insurance company which had made a grand entrance into the Polish market. We were on billboards on the streets and on the metro, promoting funeral planning which proved to be controversial. And then it all kicked off, when suddenly I came to the attention of such friendly institutions as the Polish Undertakers' Association and the Society of Polish Undertakers. Meaning those who were shaking the market up at that time.

This was because I had assumed that I would come in with new technology and would put these helpless mustachioed old men out of business. Only it turned out that they were not so helpless and had far-reaching influence. They all stood together in opposition to me and things got very unpleasant.

Remember the 'skin hunters' scandal? If you don't, you should because I didn't. Obviously, I need to work harder on my research methodology. Next time I will check, just in case, whether the sector in which I plan to do business is not involved in killing people. To cut a long story short, the 'skin hunters' were Polish paramedics and doctors in Łódź who aided in the killing of their patients, for which they were paid a commission by local undertakers. As to how many of the parties involved have blood on their hands, I will leave that for you to decide, dear reader. Meanwhile, however, I received a phone call from a Mr. Skrzydłaty, a so-called whistleblower who had exposed the corruption of the Łódź funeral services market and its links with those in the health service. He had tried very hard to come out the hero of the scandal, giving money to impoverished children, becoming a patron of sport and so on. And so he called me up and said that we should have a drink together, as he respected me greatly.

And I stupidly went. He showed me his office. The guy is undoubtedly a megalomaniac. To get to his office, you have to climb a flight of about 200 steps all in one line, just like a Mayan Temple of Inscriptions. And the office is just on the second floor. Then, we are sitting there talking over a glass of whiskey when he says:

"You see, Marek my boy, something bad has happened. We took our eye off the ball regarding you coming into the market. And now you're too big and too well known for us to shut you up without arousing suspicion."

Afterwards, he burst out laughing. So did I. Because what else was I supposed to do?

I left this place with my life flashing before my eyes. Although he never said anything directly incriminating, that didn't matter, since I had the strange conviction that the whole meeting had been one enormous threat: "If you jump, no-one will be there to catch you when you fall."

A few days later, my phone rang. A low, drunken male voice asked whether I had watched the documentary entitled *Necrobusiness*. I replied that of course I had. Why should I have to admit that the last occasion I had time to watch a film they were still making silent movies? He said he was one of those featured in the documentary, that he knew I had been to see Skrzydłaty and that I had to be careful because...

And he told me things that made me go hot and cold at the same time. I was probably the youngest person in the business and was afraid that if I stepped on someone's toes, they would never leave me alone. Although Skrzyładty has managed to block the broadcast of *Necrobusiness* on Polish television through legal means, it's available on the internet. Just sayin'.

Coming back to business, a 'concerned citizen' then informed the Polish Office for the Protection of Competition and Consumers of the activities of Mementis. Meaning a sector which had given rise to the 'skin hunters' and a load of other scandals (it's enough to Google 'undertaker scandal' and the town of your choice), was now concerned about the operations of a certain website. I couldn't have come up with it myself. They accused me of pretending to be an undertaker, when I wasn't one at all. It would be like accusing Booking.com of offering hotel reservations, when they don't even own a single hotel. I thought I was going to go crazy.

Of course, I had to explain everything in great detail. The inspectors from the Office of Competition and Consumer Protection did not have a grasp of the technology any better than the undertakers. I explained that I was a middleman, that I offered additional services and so on. The inspectors requested that I initial every single contract of the last six months and send them on for their perusal. This ran to around 2000 pages. I spent the entire night signing that shit and today have a larger right than left forearm, which could only have been caused by this. In the end, they didn't do anything to me, as they couldn't find anything to catch me out on. Actually, this didn't concern catching me out, but my noble competitors simply doing everything possible in order to make my life as difficult as possible. It was clear that they had come away with the assumption that I would give up all by myself.

However, they did not know whom they had crossed. They also didn't know that nothing motivates me more than the possibility to show someone that I can manage. In other words, 'I'll show you' suits me.

And, incidentally, they had crossed someone who had no way out because, firstly, the investor was starting to become impatient, as the business was growing at a slow rate, and, secondly, if this company was laid to rest then I was going to spend the rest of my life working at a supermarket checkout.

Every so often, I even struck back. Once, a customer called to say that his grandmother had died and that the body needed to be collected. At the time, I had got it into my head that I would get to know the customers better if I answered the phone myself. Even at three in the morning. So I said that I would send a team over. After the people working at my partner funeral services company had travelled to the location, they called to say that the body had vanished. What do you mean, vanished? As it turned out, the doctor at the hospital had shoved "some papers to be signed" in front of the customer, which he did as he thought they were from the hospital. However, they were no such thing, but a contract with a funeral service company, whose employees arrived to collect the body five minutes later. Five minutes. Once my customer had finished talking to me, he noticed that Granny had vanished. By the time he had figured out what had happened, my people were already there.

I was furious. I had circumstantial evidence that the doctor was a classic 'skin hunter', who must have rung the undertaker before old woman had died. So I decided to get the guy. A few days later, I sent a couple of undercover detectives to the hospital. We had them rigged up Hollywood style. Each had three cameras, a load of microphones, transmitters and other gadgets. They told the doctors that their "beloved granddad is not long for this world" and begged "Please doctor, save him!". Following this, they recorded fantastic material in which the doctor came out of his office in order to convince them to sign a contract with "a friendly funeral services company".

Although the doctor was soon fired and the undertakers in question fell into difficulties, I had no intention of giving up. In fact, I offered this as part of my services and wrote to every undertaker in the country that if they had any problem with a dishonest priest or doctor who was drawing customers away to their competitors, I had people who could record this and publicize it. Put simply, I led them all to understand that they were no longer above the law. Each undertaker would have to carefully consider whether it was worth using such a method to gain customers. Whether something would get back to their direct rival in town and not whether they wanted to use my services. To be blunt, I set them against each other. They were not afraid of me, but of each other. And it worked. Perhaps they understood in the end that I was cleverer than them and left me alone. In any case, their actions against me were not as crude as before.

Competition is one thing, but dealing with customers wasn't easy either. It slowly dawned on me that the technological revolution in funeral services would not occur as quickly as I had outlined in my 15 slides.

The one thing I certainly wasn't missing was adventure.

Once, I answered the phone at night and experienced the most absurd conversation in my life:

"Hello," a haughty female voice said down the line, "My name is Żaneta Więcławska (the name ha been changed – you'll soon understand why). My mother passed away during the night. She died in her sleep, having lived five and eighty years. I would now like to fulfill my daughterly duties."

"Fulfill what?" I thought to myself.

"Could you tell me," the lady continued, "how much would cremation cost?"

Well, she should have come to the point straight away. I calculated the cost of the service and then heard: "My mother was fitted with a pacemaker. Would that be a problem?"

"A procedure to remove the pacemaker would be necessary, which is conducted before the cremation."

"And how much would that cost?"

"An additional thousand zlotys."

"Thank you for the information, I will have to think it over."

At which point she hung up. Two hours had passed, when the phone rang again.

"Hello, it's me again, Żaneta Więcławska. Regarding that pacemaker, the problem has been solved. You may come for the body…"

And that's the kind of thing that happened day after day.

The greatest problem Mementis faced turned out to be – wait for it – a lack of growth. This did not concern even the typically high cost of acquiring customers online (CAC – customer acquisition cost) or the customer lifetime value (CLV). The problem was that I had misjudged the speed of market change. Or rather its slowness. Even though Polish customers knew that priests and doctors were often corrupt to the core, in order to have peace and quiet they allowed themselves to be drawn into the routine of the old system. The last thing they thought about at such a moment was to go online and shop around.

But instead I thought of a plan, one which would make me a lot of money. If it took off. Because the only thing which was going to take off was my beloved investor, the VC fund.

The investors became really unbearable to deal with. They rang me daily to enquire about progress. In the end, I got annoyed and told them to leave me the fuck alone, because I was intending to buy them out. The 'I'll show you' alarm went off once again and a damn good thing it did. They immediately agreed to sell their shares and at a very fair price, with the addition of my delayed payment. This was because, firstly, they had already ceased to believe in the project and the possibility of breaking even seemed attractive. Secondly, that which was probably the decisive factor, namely that they could now report to PARP (the government agency which had awarded them several million zlotys in EU funding, of which there will be more later) that the Mementis project had been concluded successfully, as they had managed to sell it on. From then on, they needed nothing more from me. Although they hadn't earned anything, it had allowed them to build up a positive reputation with PARP, from which more funding would certainly come.

Now, a few words on where my investors had got their money. During that time, the EU launched the Operational Program 'Innovation Economy', Measure 3.1 Initiation of Innovation Activities, or just called '3.1'. The rule for awarding financing was as follows – one had to put 2 million zlotys into the pot and the EU would throw in 18 million zlotys more. Next, all of this money had to be invested in companies involved in 'the initiation of innovation activities'. In Poland, around 5o investment funds applied. And you know what? Up to 30 of them are under legal investigation today. Because these sons of bitches, instead of investing in the market, immediately siphoned off all the money. The members of the fund, their families and friends, all established fly-by-night companies, then transferred the money to themselves. Then the newly established companies collapsed, because "you know, it was a start-up and most start-ups have a way of failing". In fact, one of these '3.1s' was my VC fund. It is only now, with the benefit of hindsight, that it was a little strange that I could only spend the money they had invested in Mementis on the digital agencies, advertising agencies and legal firms which they had stipulated.

Although I was left with an almost dead company and in debt, I no longer had an annoying investor. Thanks to this, I could now do what I wanted with Mementis. And I already had a plan regarding what I wanted to do.

Having the rest of the money in my account, I decided to move offline. Whatever you say about the funeral services sector, it is characterized by a fairly stable demand for its services. Indeed, annually it 'serves' about 1% of the population. If such a company is run in a transparent manner, it potentially becomes an attractive element of the stable parts in an investment fund portfolio.

In more developed countries, such as the United States, the UK or Germany, large funeral services companies are listed on the stock exchange. But in order to end up on the stock exchange, previously someone had to conduct consolidation in those countries. Someone bought up small family businesses, rebranded them, standardized processes and, by issuing public shares, floated them on the stock exchange (or as the boys in the business say, they conducted an IPO, an initial public offering). And by the way, this someone ends up with enough pin money. Several million dollars' worth. It goes without saying that I had hatched a similar plan.

In the meantime, I started talks with a certain Dutch investment fund, which had consolidated the sector in the Benelux countries several years previously and floated its company on the stock exchange. And now it was showing preliminary interest in repeating this trick in Poland, as long as I found a minimum of 20 undertakers which could be assessed as having a minimum price of one million zlotys each.

To cut a long story short, the strategy to achieve flotation on the stock exchange comprised of three stages:

The selection of 10 well-functioning undertakers in 10 cities and the commencement of a soft consolidation, based on the unifying of brands and the purchase of shares (with deferred payment) from the owners. As part of their duties, the owner was obliged to maintain income at the same level for a minimum of three years following the sale of shares.

The purchase of an additional 10 undertakers facilities. The further unifying of standards and processes in the companies taken over in order for them to look like one properly managed body. Flotation on the stock exchange, the accumulation of several million zlotys for further expansion.

As the plan was risky, I needed the help of a very experienced partner to organize the mergers and takeovers, but I also had a project on the side that was starting to take off and which was beginning to demand more and more time.

Some time before, when I had dreams of a not very concrete vision of floating the undertaking business on the stock exchange and was fighting to achieve profitability, I met a friend, Gregory, who told me about a very interesting company in the United States, one which had not yet entered Poland. In short: the long-distance checking out of cars before purchase. So you want to buy a car, but don't have the time or the money to travel the length and breadth of the United States in order to find a car in a decent condition? You call us and we have our man there and in a jiffy you have the information needed to decide whether it is worth traveling to Miami or Atlanta.

It seemed like an interesting business and I had some experience in seeking out partners in local markets, as well as workers who dealt with this kind of thing. So I decided to use my resources to diversify the risk exposure connected with the development of Mementis itself. And that's how MotoRaporter was born.

Well, to be precise, OK-AUTO was born first. The project was supposed to be financed in the long term jointly by Mementis and Gregory. The first money was put up however only by Mementis. The project showed potential, but required way more money to be poured in. I offered Gregory co-investment proportional to the shares percentage he wanted to have. If a company is raising money and you have, for example, 10% of shares, and you want to stay at 10%, you need to chip in 10% of the amount being raised. Otherwise your shares will be diluted. It's simple mathematics, but Gregory didn't quite get it. He didn't want to put any money in, but didn't agree for his shares to be diluted either. In his mind, the fact of giving us his 'one of a kind idea' he stole from the USA was enough to get all the benefits with none of the risks or costs. Well, that's not how things work. We parted ways, killed OK-AUTO. I started building Motoraporter on my own, while Gregory launched a competing company, also alone. I guess the chemistry never worked between us. Sometimes it's better to break up a relationship early. I always wished him well.

I started to look for a business angel for both projects who, like a real angel, was supposed to fall down from heaven to help develop the business, consolidate the sector and float it on the stock exchange. Without a cash injection, I could consider my plans, if you'll excuse the pun, dead and buried.

As it happened, there was a meeting of the Pomeranian Group of Business Angels being organized in Szczecin, for which I managed to qualify in order to present my idea. So I got on the train and went. This time, I paid for my ticket, which I treated as symbolic social advancement, in comparison with the previous occasion.

My presentation was due to take place between talks on investment opportunities in retirement homes and a chain of 24-hour self-service cafés. I don't know if this is an occupational fetish, but I immediately got the idea to merge both businesses

There were about 50 businessmen over 40 years old in the room, of whom half looked as if they had just turned up for a free lunch. Which was actually a good sign, because the best looking ones are those who have a reason for pretense. Those who have the real money often don't give a fuck about their appearance and whether their shirt has been ironed or not.

In order to loosen up the atmosphere, I started with the classic joke that as I could see several people that didn't look their best, they were the ones I wanted to give my business cards to. The room burst into laughter. It was plain sailing from then on. I made it into a show. I described how Mementis was this amazing company, the prospects it had, how it was changing the market for the better, how rosy its future was. I also showed them the prospects of the fledgling MotoRaporter being developed by Mementis at the same time.

As they say, all power corrupts, but PowerPoint corrupts absolutely.

What a wonder that that during the networking sessions only one person came up to me. Marcin. He had my immediate respect, as he was the same height as me. He gave me a broad smile and gave off the impression of someone who was friendly and laid back. He asked me a couple of extra questions, we exchanged business cards and that's all I saw of him.

The fact that I had travelled across half of Poland to talk to one person was a very good reason to spend the rest of the evening at a bar in which the female bartenders danced on the counter every half hour.

The next morning, I was woken by a headache, which was no surprise taking into account the unbelievably warm and cheap vodka which I had had occasion to tank myself up on. What was a surprise, however, was an email waiting for me in my inbox once I had fired up my smartphone, whose battery had run out during the night.

It was an email from Marcin: "I'm in. We'll start with 300,000 zlotys, with an option of a further transfer of funds once the set goals have been carried out. One condition, I join the board and we work together. I like this business and it seems to me that I could gain greater value from it beyond money. Give me a bell within 3 days max, as I'm off on holiday, but I can send you the money before my flight anyway."

As I had been blessed with good fortune with people, I followed it through.

Hopping into bed with someone who you've just met most often ends wonderfully or terribly. It's the same in business. I decided to risk it.

"It's a deal, here's the account number. We'll go through the details on your return" – I decided to rub him up the wrong way a little, as if he wanted some trust from me, let him show the same.

The money landed in the account the next day. They're the kind of deals I like.

A month later, when Marcin had returned to Poland as brown as a berry, I invited him to go for a steak. We chatted a bit about trivial things, a bit about the past, a bit about Mementis, when suddenly I became very honest.

"You know," I said, "It somehow slipped my mind earlier, but there's still one important issue."

"What?" asked Marcin.

"Actually, it's this... I must have forgotten to tell you when you joined the company that we are 200,000 zlotys in debt. I mean not as much as I forgot to tell you, but you forgot to ask..."

Marcin was just about to put a piece of steak into his mouth. He held the fork still in mid-air. Then, very, very, slowly he laid the meat back onto the plate and, through gritted teeth, muttered: "Tell me that once again. But slowly so that I definitely understand it."

What can I write? He got fucking mad of course, and he was right to be. He didn't call me for two days, but later we laughed about it. He told me that I really was a good salesman. That I had talked up the business so much, that he had forgotten to check the financial issues. Well, if truth be told, I know several people in Poland with whom he would have ended up much worse off.

Marcin turned out to be an old pro. He knew exactly what was going on in this game. There are moments when I wonder whether I took him in, or he took me in. Jesus, I still don't know. One thing is certain: he didn't come out of it too badly, as he's always telling me that he likes me. And after all, when someone tells you that they like you, they're always telling the truth, right?

Unfortunately, following months of traveling the length and breadth of Poland looking for companies with plans to buy up undertakers, there was nothing to show for it. We were several decades ahead of the market. Everyone wanted to sell their undertaking business, as who wants to deal with stiffs when you can take a quick and easy, and above all, large sum of money. Insofar as it turned out, some of these companies were operating entirely illegally, others had horrendous debts, while yet others had complex ownership problems with, for example, the owner having died 10 years previously. In addition, the companies usually didn't possess any physical assets. The buildings were rented from aunts and uncles, the vehicles leased and the money held in private bank accounts. So absolutely nothing. There was actually nothing to buy. You would have to spend more on a consulting company to turn this mess into an auditable company than the company was itself worth. The guy from a Dutch fund, who had come to check out the situation, could only bang his head against a brick wall before leaving quickly.

On the other hand, however, MotoRaporter had begun to grow and properly so. Marcin's coming in had brought more investment. The Polish Enterprise Foundation got in contact, as it also wanted to chip in. As you can easily guess, we made halves, even thirds of ourselves in order for the company to make the best impression. This time, thanks to Marcin, we made money.

And here we are talking and, meanwhile, Africa was getting closer in leaps and bounds.

Chapter 4

TEN, NINE, IGNITION SEQUENCE, START

And just as everything was coming together, as one more time I began to believe in success, once again I had to experience a sense of 'I'll show you'. I know today that this trait is both my greatest asset and greatest curse.

It was 2011. We had already set up our company headquarters in Warsaw. Closer to the investors, closer to the money (the version for investors), closer to the best nightclubs and the most beautiful women (the version for our friends) and closer to home (Hi, mum!).

Anyway, I was sitting, drinking coffee in a restaurant on the Old Town Square. Not some shitty soya latte, but normal, regular strong coffee for real men. I had grown up. I was looking at some news on the net, when I suddenly heard: "What's up, Marek!"

I knew that voice from high school. A shiver went up my spine. It was Karol, the guy who had screwed Marysia – my Marysia. The human body has an extraordinary capacity to subconsciously recall emotions and the smells and sounds connected with them. Just as the sound of the ringtone of the phone of my ex-boss Felix had burrowed its way into my consciousness forever, so that within a millisecond Marek, the mature and self-confident businessman, was transformed into the neurotic Marek craving acceptance. So I didn't even deserve to be drinking such strong coffee after all.

"What's up, What's up, it's been long time," Karol said, unceremoniously sitting down at my table.

"Karol! It's been a long time! Sit down and tell me everything," pretending to be excited as best I could.

Both of us gave the abridged version of what had happened to us since the last time we saw each other in the apartment we had been renting together. Both of us tried to slip in information about our greatest number of successes, while trying to appear extremely modest on the surface. Both of us pretended to be attentively listening with all our strength, while analyzing the statements of the other and trying to figure out whose life had turned out better. It was one of the strangest and most awkward conversations of my life. And one of those which was to influence my fate.

At that time, Karol was working for McKinsey, one of the best and largest consulting firms in the world, regarded as a breeding ground not only for business talent, but for business sharks, total automatons working 14 hours a day and calculating mathematical formulae in Excel quicker than Excel. The company was renowned for attracting the best talent from the best universities already at an early stage of their studies. In the States, this practice was conducted on such a scale that McKinsey had earned the nickname 'McHarvard'.

During my first year at university, I had even applied for an internship at McKinsey, but failed the math tests, which dented my pride and my faith in my mathematical ability. But I had quickly forgotten it, once Efect and my adventure as a financial advisor had turned up. Now, I was clearly behaving like a true Christian, as I had turned the other cheek and got slapped once again. Then Karol won over 'my' Marysia and now he was working at 'my' McKinsey.

As well as that, Karol started talking about a company called Rocket Internet, a kind of McKinsey for internet companies. It had been founded in 2007 by the investment fund of the three Samwer brothers, which only invested in its own projects, built from scratch by partners employed for the task. The dozens of companies it controlled on five continents altogether employed over 30,000 people. The Samwers were the absolute gods of the internet business, as everything they touched turned to gold. They sold their first internet service for $35m 100 days following its coming into operation, and later it only got better.

Once Rocket employed you, it sent you to the other side of the world where, just as in consulting, you were thrown in at the deep end, while the demands placed on you, if we're talking about results, were literally and metaphorically out of this world. As every soldier wants to serve in the US Navy Seals and every driver wants to race for Team Ferrari, so every entrepreneur or manager in the internet sector wanted to gain experience at Rocket.

And just as McKinsey only took the best, most hard-working, most intelligent and most ambitious students 'in the class', for its high positions Rocket would only take those who had worked at McKinsey or had been former investment bankers...

So Karol was trying to get a job at Rocket.

Third time's the charm. Karol, old buddy – challenge accepted.

"May I have the bill, please," I called to the waiter. I already had a plan of grave urgency in my head and wanted to find myself behind a desk with a laptop as soon as possible. Dealing with a business having a little less to do with graves.

Of course, both myself and Karol acknowledged how wonderful it had been to see each other again after so many years and that, of course, we must keep in more regular contact. Of course, we haven't seen each other since. It was just difficult to find a table in a restaurant with space for both of us (Karol is also almost 6½ feet tall) – and our egos.

The meeting with Karol and our conversation about Rocket awoke a strong need in me to see the world. Poland was beginning to suffocate me.

Having been brought up on Hollywood movies and MTV music videos, I continued sucking up Western influences, knowledge and motivation from TechCrunch, Mashable and Wired. It was in the States, in Silicon Valley, that fortunes had grown in business online. It was in San Francisco that a real revenge of the nerds was taking place, who were now changing the world by tapping away at their keyboards. After high school, I had 'escaped' from Koszalin in order to do, experience and gain more.

Within a few years though, Poland had become my Koszalin.

My problem rested on the fact that, surprise, surprise, I didn't know anyone working at Rocket. According to what I could find on LinkedIn, 99% of Rocket's senior management staff came from Germany, France and Israel. So all I was left with was their website and 'Careers' tab, something which had I had regarded my whole life up to then as a wailing wall for life's victims.

It was time to park my ego at the door – I took a deep breath and clicked to see what they had. Among the typical corporate categories of business intelligence, legal, marketing, sales HR and finance, I found exactly what I was looking for: co-founders. Of course, Rocket wasn't looking for partners for itself, but for the companies it had established.

The Samwer brothers had turned the classic investment model used in the capital market around. The standard way is that an entrepreneur with an idea starts a company, develops it and then puts capital together for development by securing an investor.

The start-up sector had moved the stage of securing an outside investor forward as far as to the idea, something I myself had experienced.

The Samwers had gone even further. They knew perfectly well which businesses they wished to build (most often this was a tried and tested business model from the States which was to be implemented in less-developed markets) and already had investment funds ready for this purpose, but lacked... partners who would fall in love with a certain business idea and, like a parent, adopt it and bring it up as their own. And it was for this purpose that Rocket needed an army of pros bored with giving PowerPoint presentations on consulting and Excel presentations on investment banking, those who wanted to feel what it means to create a business from scratch and bite the bullet. What Rocket didn't know was that it also needed Marek Zmysłowski, who was bored with Poland and its online undertaker trade.

The only location available as part of the 'co-founders' tab was Egypt.

"The Pyramids and kitesurfing is fine for me," I thought.

The requirements were all too clear: "completion of an MBA at a reputable university, a minimum of two years' experience in a top consulting firm, investment bank, venture capital fund, private equity fund or a start-up."

It was this "or a start-up" which gave me my only hope.

I dug out the CV from when I was looking for work as a barman in Warsaw, emphasizing some things, exaggerating or lying a bit about other things (especially regarding my knowledge of English), and finally made a PDF. I then included a covering letter which went like this: "Although I know that I do not fulfill 90% of the requirements, I know that I am way better than those neurotic straight A-student-terminators from McKinsey, therefore I am begging you to call me! In exchange, I will get you a discount on a funeral. Offer valid while stocks last."

Then I clicked 'send' and went to bed.

So that's how my application to Rocket looked in general terms. No contacts, just a CV sent through their website. Of course later, when some journalist asked me about this, I said that "I was recruited by a reputable headhunter agency, which had been trying to get me to work for Rocket for over a year". Fame doesn't make itself, you know.

The next day, I had naturally forgotten all about it. My responsibilities connected with MotoRaporter and Mementis reappeared and I threw myself into the whirlwind of work, which is how my failed venture with Rocket Internet had come to an end.

Anyway, that's what it looked like.

Because it was about two or three weeks later that an email arrived beginning with the words: "Dear Mr. Zmysłowski, Thank you for your interest in Rocket Internet. Would it suit you if a preliminary interview took place tomorrow?". I didn't read any further, as it's difficult to read anything and perform a victory dance at the same time.

The preliminary interview took place through Skype the very next day, as Rocket doesn't beat about the bush. Everything there is done in a quick and concrete manner. I didn't prepare too much, as how demanding could an interview be with an assistant of the assistant of yet another assistant?

Very demanding, as it turned out. Because the role of this assistant was to connect me with a certain Frenchman, who was then responsible for Rocket's operations in Africa.

The conversation went something like this:

"Good morning, Marek, it was very nice to hear from you, your application was very interesting, blah, blah, blah," the Frenchman began politely.

"Blah, blah, blah," I replied, as I'm also able to waffle.

"At the outset, I should stress that we are urgently looking for partners in Africa."

"Yes, I know, you mean Egypt… Yes, I read about it on the website," I interrupted him.

"Aaah, well, the information hasn't been changed in six months. Everything is changing so dynamically, that we haven't had a chance to update our announcements. There's no point. We're constantly recruiting people. I am currently looking for a founder in Africa who will start by building up a business in Lagos."

"That Lagos in… Portugal?" I asked hopefully.

"Lagos. In Nigeria..." and here the Frenchman paused for me to take this in. He was clearly used to such reactions. Lagos, a city of 20 million without public transport. In a country of 200 million people. I only knew two things about Nigeria – Boko Haram and the scam involving a Nigerian "prince". "So, you no doubt associate Nigeria mainly with terrorism and fraud?"

"You're able to read my mind."

"There is no lack of problems in this country. However, it doesn't change the fact that its economy is growing at an extraordinary pace, due to new technologies to a large degree. Over the next 20 years, Nigeria will undergo a transformation as that which Poland has experienced during the last two decades. The only difference is that it is four times bigger than Poland. Nigeria is the most populous country in Africa and the most difficult in which to build up a business. But if you manage to pull this off, expansion into the remaining 53 countries of Africa, comprising of a population of one billion people, is just a question of time."

"You've convinced me," I replied, as that was all that was necessary to get me really interested in Nigeria. The Frenchman had found my motivational button. Even if little of what he said was true, I had found my own revolution during which I would make my fortune. I had found the size and scale, along with the international aspect, which I had found lacking in Poland.

"Could you now summarize the last five years of your life in one minute?" the Frenchman gave me my first task.

The next part of the interview went on in a standard fashion.

Meaning as you would expect in talking to a top corporation or a consulting firm. A load of questions checking your abilities regarding thinking quickly and analytically.

Apparently, answering questions whether you are up to the challenge is the easy part. The real question is whether you will want to meet the challenge in the long term.

"I have achieved relatively a lot of success in terms of my own niche brand and Poland itself. I have been hungry for achieving success, but by an order of magnitude. Several orders of magnitude. You look like the kind of people who could teach me this," I said in a direct, completely honest manner. A couple of years later, I found out that hunger was the Frenchman's key word.

"Tell me more about building up the online funeral services business. But please, focus on the problems involved. Go ahead and complain."

The son-of-a-gun surprised me. On the other hand, there's no better nation at complaining than the Poles.

"Let's start with the fact that those in the undertaking business who provide the services thanks to a platform which we have built… to put it diplomatically… have absolutely no understanding of the internet. The sector does not attract… how should one say this… the most intelligent and most ambitious people. Corruption is a natural part of it, in that it's not called corruption, but a marketing channel. Gangsters in BMWs (apart from those in Z4s, as the ones who drive Z4s are cool), local crime barons and money laundering paint a typical picture. In order to persuade a sufficient number of companies to join us, I had to travel personally to the forty largest cities in Poland, where I had over 10,000 sales meetings, in which I above all explained how the internet would influence changes in the sector within the next few years. Attempting this either by email or telephone would have been pointless."

"But I read that you are one of the biggest players on the market."

"I understand how PR and marketing works and take advantage of it."

"How do you make money?"

"We receive a commission on income made by the funeral services company. This is the weakest link in the whole process, in that even the greatest Neanderthals have become geniuses at creative accounting."

The conversation lasted for several more minutes, until it ended along with my hopes.

For a long time afterwards, I went over by what miracle I could have made such a fool of myself. It wasn't enough that my sector was completely unattractive in itself, but I entered the conversation as a total sucker who couldn't even deal with such a banal subject. How could I have said that we were continually verging on bankruptcy? That Poles don't get my business? That I had moved in mafia circles? Of course, I had told him a bit about all the great things, about the additional funeral services, about the transportation of the deceased and the cleaning of graves. Then I had mentioned MotoRaporter, but even screwed that up as, I don't know why, I had to say that it had been established in order to diversify Mementis's income. What a disaster.

There's a pretty common scene in movies in which the main character is seen wandering city streets following some spectacular catastrophe. It's dark, because this always takes place at night. The streets are lit by the harsh light of not particularly effective streetlamps. Our hero is wearing a scruffy raincoat and looks worse for wear. Of course, as if on cue, it starts to rain. He enters a harbor, looks at the sea, the waves roaring while he continues to suffer...

Okay, so nothing like that happened to me. Three days later, however, an email arrived saying: "Dear Marek, we would like to invite you to our office in Paris for two days for the next stage of the interview process."

In my mind, I patted myself on my back. Zmysłowski, you've still got it. I held myself back from showing too much joy. There remained a list of things in my head which could still go wrong. I decided not to say anything to anyone yet. Especially Marcin. If he was going to kill me, at least let him have a good reason for doing so.

I wrote him an email that I was taking a break from the company for a few days just to relax, news which he took well, in fact, as he knew just how much blood, sweat and tears I had been putting in recently.

It was high time to deal with the gaps in my education concerning Africa. All I had learned in school was that Europe had colonized Africa, but something hadn't gone right. Then Europe had liberated

Africa, but something hadn't gone right. At the same time, thanks to the lady who had taught me geography, I knew all the capital cities of Africa, but couldn't locate them on the map. I was an ignoramus regarding the 'this Continent', just as 99.99% of the populations of Poland and Europe are too. We knew nothing about it, for us it is a 'dark spot' on our map.

I started my research with the most reliable source of information for every millennial – YouTube. I watched all the right documentary films concerning Nigeria, South Africa, Kenya and several smaller countries. I got to know the stories of foreign journalists who had passed themselves off as diamond traders in order to gain access to corrupt politicians in Congo. I watched a report about a boy who rode a motorcycle taxi around Lagos in order to make money for his family and finish his studies. I discovered what Nollywood was, namely the Nigerian film industry, which produces more movies than Hollywood. But it was the large number of film reports from CNN on newly established businesses which worked their way into my imagination. In the end, I watched a street survey in Nigeria in which the journalist asked girls the best number of boyfriends to have at any one time. The average answer worked out at 2.5. The reality being described there was so far from everyday Poland, so exotic and simultaneously intriguing, that I couldn't stop thinking about it.

Two days later, I flew to Paris in order to get to know the people who would make my African dream possible. I landed at Charles de Gaulle and headed for the city center. They say that the French only speak French. I can assure you that it's total bullshit, as half the French people there spoke Arabic very fluently.

"As-Salaam-Alaykum, uvulevu alley?" asked the driver.

"Do you speak English?"

No, he didn't. So I showed him the address of the office, written on my smartphone, located in the 9th arrondissement. We drove for half an hour, passing the Stade de France. It made an amazing impression on me.

However, Rocket's French headquarters did not make such an impression. Here I was going to the offices of one of the most powerful internet companies in the world. I expected glass and metal. The assistants' roles were to be played by models and coffee was to be served in Ming-dynasty cups at a Louis XIV-style table.

On the contrary, the office was located in a small, sand-colored tenement which, although nice, did not meet my expectations. On entering, I saw a gigantic open-space office and instead of the above-described assistants, at least 100 snotty-nosed kids tapping away at MacBooks.

Each one, of course, sipping a soya latte.

I was welcomed by an assistant who, while certainly not having any experience in the modeling industry, had the broadest smile I had ever seen. During the whole day, I had four meetings with managers from several departments at Rocket, namely marketing, global venture development, customer service and financial operations.

They grilled me really intensely. Each one of them gave me several cases to work on (each of which would have required an entire day in normal circumstances), returned after an hour to talk over my work and grill me with questions for another hour. The tasks mainly concerned problems which Rocket had encountered in Brazil and Indonesia, countries which had the most similar demographic structure to Nigeria. Or at least among those in which Rocket was already operating. What surprised me was that absolutely everyone who I either saw or spoke to in the office was white. By the end of the day, I was so dog-tired that I nearly fell asleep on the running machine at the hotel gym. I hit the hay early in the hotel, so as to report for a meeting the following morning, summing up my rubbish efforts.

Soon the meeting began, attended by myself, the 'president for Africa' (the Frenchman with whom I had spoken earlier) and another 'president for Africa'. Also French and white. Because, as it later turned out, a project at Rocket usually had two, even three managers. They complemented each other, while being rivals at the same time, which allowed for an extraordinary increase in the effectiveness of their operations. At least in theory.

"Please tell me," I first asked. "Were there so few people interested in Africa that you invited me here after that dreadful job interview?"

They laughed, with one of them then adding:

"It's not what you think. We get dozens of applications daily. The problem is that few of them have the combination of skills, character and experience that we demand. We need someone who will be able to build a project in an unfavorable environment, dealing with clients, competition, organized crime and corruption. Whoever can get their foot in the door where business is failing and find creative ways to save it. Someone who understands that building a business online takes place offline. Frankly speaking, your application would have gone in the bin, if we hadn't noticed that you had worked in the undertaking sector. We knew what this kind of operation was connected with in Poland. Up to now, everyone we had employed had snapped. They couldn't handle Africa. But looking at what you have achieved, we have no doubt that you'll manage. Africa is not as Third World as Poland."

"Very funny," I thought to myself when he started laughing at his own joke.

"Okay then," the other interrupted. "We have two options for you. The first is as follows: our company, Jumia, is the African Amazon.com. Its small team numbers barely one hundred people."

During the best time at Mementis, I had about 30 permanent employees in the office. I couldn't let them know that.

"We need someone who will take over the management of our online marketing team responsible for all of our African markets. You will have a twenty-person team under you and complete freedom of operation. Currently, the development of this department is our most urgent need, as the company has been operating for a year and is beginning to achieve its first successes. So it's high time for the next move."

"Or the second option," the other guy added. "We'll drop you into Africa and you'll build a project completely from scratch. We have several ideas which we intend to implement."

It was a difficult choice, and I felt under my skin that a lot may be riding on it. Even though I had no idea what lay behind it, I thought of choosing door no. 1. The company had been in operation for over a year. A ready-made project. Clients already there. Success, a perfect addition to the portfolio. Yes, certainly. As only No. 1 made any sense, I said:

"Only No. 2 makes any sense for me."

As they both smiled, I knew that I had chosen the right answer. Well, keeping in mind what they had told me about their needs, I was convinced that they required a troublemaker who would bulldoze his way into any jungle. It was also an advantageous entry point for me, as although I had described myself on LinkedIn as a 'director of online marketing', the risk was too great. The kind which I really knew was a typical, standard, text-book start-up. Meaning starting something from nothing. Building structures, organizing a base, implementing technology and securing clients – 'with bare hands'. Only this time I had an investor behind me with an unlimited budget and operational support which, at the same time, gave me a large degree of autonomy and allowed you to feel like an entrepreneur. Meaning the best of both the corporate and start-up worlds. That's at least how it seemed to me then.

"Alright then," said one of the presidents eventually. "We are really convinced that we will sign a contract with you even today. You have impressed us, in that that you're not afraid to take up the challenge. Therefore, you may choose the sector in which you would like to operate."

They presented me with four options to choose from and I discovered then that the African start-up market mainly dealt with copying tried and tested ideas from around the world. So I could have started an African Uber, an African GrubHub, an African OLX, Booking.com or Expedia – that is some of the biggest internet companies in the world.

"Regardless of your choice, you will be entirely responsible for all aspects of the company's operations, starting with the budget and ending by chasing down every customer in order to get a positive review," they said, sending me away to some restaurant on the ground floor of the building. I was to sit there with my thoughts in peace and quiet.

"As-Salaam-Alaykum, keseke jevuser?" the waiter asked.

"Do you speak English?"

No, he didn't. I put €10 on the table and pointed to the first good dish I saw. I wasn't even able to read its name.

The meal, as it turned out, was beer. Tasting it, I appreciated its alcoholic strength and fizz. But I wasn't concentrating on the taste. I wasn't concentrating on anything. Except the screen of my smartphone.

Deep down inside, I felt that getting into online travel would suit me best – travel for business or pleasure always has positive associations. The possibility of cooperating on a daily basis with airlines and hotel managers seemed a nice perk for the difficulties of working in Africa.

"At least I'll get lots of free coffee and discounts on flights, not only on funerals," I thought.

I returned to the office and told them that I would create a clone of Expedia. They were little surprised that I hadn't even asked about the conditions, but I had simply forgotten about them. They brought in the contract. I looked through the documents: a budget of $10M dollars for the first two years, 2% or the stock, plus another 2% if the firm achieved its KPIs, as well as a car, an apartment and a cleaner. And, of course, a salary. A five-figure sum every month, plus bonuses awarded at the end of the year. In dollars.

Although I had already earned more money, that was through decidedly more stress and less fun. And here there was the prospect of life without major problems, above all, without that which had always bothered me the most. That if I failed, I would lose my own money. This was different, in that I really hadn't gone there for the money, but for the adventure and experience. The money was just a bonus (in brackets, it was only much, much later that I discovered that, in signing this contract, I had become one of the company's worst paid employees).

We finished up late in the evening. The metro had stopped running. They wanted to call me a taxi, but I said I would prefer to walk. The next morning, I had a flight back to Poland. I wanted to see as much of the city as possible. I mean, coming all the way to Paris not to see the Champs Elysées, the Louvre or the Eiffel Tower? No way!

The quickest route on Google Maps showed me that in order to see everything I wanted I would have to walk a good 10 kilometers. But what's 10 kilometers to a strong, young man? As I had to be at the airport at 6am, there was no point going to sleep. And as Rocket was paying for the hotel, I didn't have a great sense of losing anything in using the time I was due in a hotel bed. I set off.

Never, ever do this. You may head off on a night time stroll around Brooklyn, the forbidden neighborhoods of Lagos or the favelas of Rio de Janeiro. But not Paris. Three times I had to run away from people who instead of saying "How are you?" shouted "How much have you got?!"

I don't think I have ever been so afraid in my life. I was actually happy that I would be working in Nigeria and not this fucking Parisian urban jungle.

Of course, I neither saw the Eiffel Tower, the Champs Elysées nor the Louvre, as the desire for a stroll immediately disappeared and I caught the first taxi that came along. Instead, I took advantage of my time in the hotel.

When I returned to Poland, I first told my parents. For half the way there, I put together a plan to prevent my mother getting a heart attack. The only thing which came to my head was to talk for hours about the money and the challenges. I was counting on Mom not thinking to ask: "But where exactly will you be working?"

"But where exactly will you be working?" Mom asked after 30 seconds.

I turned pale. So it hadn't turned out the way I planned, but what could I do? Lying to my mother usually just wasn't worth it.

"Well… in Nigeria," I said quietly.

"Ambitious, son, as usual. Several of my students work there now and I'll put you in contact with them. Just look out for yourself!" Mom replied.

"Wife, I have a feeling that we're going to have gorgeous, coffee-colored grandchildren," my dad commented in his own peculiar way.

Talking to my parents was the easy part. Now, a much tougher task awaited me.

I went with Marcin for a steak…

We talked about this and that, until finally I cut to the chase.

"Have you ever heard of Rocket Internet?" I asked.

"Sure," he replied, chewing his steak, rare as he usually chose. "A global giant. They're cleaning up."

"Weellllll… what would you say about you buying me out of Mementis and MotoRaporter, finding someone to take my place, sorting things out with the investors and directing expansion, so that I could go to Nigeria and start up a new project for Rocket Internet? Great idea, don't you think?"

Marcin was just about to put a piece of steak into his mouth. He held the fork still in mid-air. Then, very, very, slowly he laid the meat back onto the plate and, through gritted teeth, muttered:

"Tell me that once again. But slowly, so that I certainly understand it."

And that's just what my relationship with Marcin was like. For the second time, I had hung him out to dry. For the second time, he was fucking mad. And for the second time, he forgave me. I even think he respects me. Well, I mean I suspect he respects me, because up to then no-one had ever left him hanging before. Anyway, we quickly came to an agreement. He told me that he would have done the same. Because once he had done the same when he took the decision to move to Japan.

He told me to get ready for a lot of new experiences. He said that it would open up my horizons and that I would never look at the world in the same way again. Now, with the benefit of hindsight, I can say he was 100% right. Fortunately, he was really fired up about MotoRaporter and going it alone didn't bother him. Additionally, he took on the responsibility for sorting out things connected with the Enterprise Foundation. Normal investors would collapse into a panic if, just before a contract was to be signed, one of their partners suddenly ran off to Africa. I didn't have much time. Just two weeks. That's all I had to sort out all my affairs in Poland. Work became a whirlwind.

The first port of call on the list was the hospital of the Polish Ministry of the Interior. In order to secure permission to travel to Nigeria, I had to get vaccinated against yellow fever. But as I was aware that I was going there for at least a year, and who knows maybe longer, I got everything which was recommended. Typhoid fever, tetanus, measles, hepatitis B, hepatitis C, polio, meningitis…

"But sir, you can't take them all of them once." the doctor told me.

"Why can't I?"

"Because it will overload your body!"

"I'm big and strong, I'm leaving in two weeks and don't have time to waste."

"But the vaccination for hepatitis is only effective after three doses."

"Don't talk, just give it to me. I'll get the rest once I get to Nigeria."

The doctor sighed and added without much conviction: "At least don't drink any alcohol today."

I promised I wouldn't. Also without much conviction.

Once my yellow International Certificate of Vaccination had been stamped, I could apply for a visa. I paid my money and sent in the form. I was lucky. My appointment was arranged for the following day. Wondering what I could do for the rest of the day, I came up with a great idea.

To my great surprise, I found an African restaurant in Warsaw. It was called *La MaMa* and was on Anders Street. I just had to go there.

What was even a better surprise was that they served cuisine mainly from western Africa, including Nigeria. Unfortunately, the waiter was a Pole who had never been to Africa. I asked him for several typically Nigerian dishes. I got pepper soup, boiled goat's head, goulash with every sort of reared animal meat in it, including the skin. Together with the goulash, there were fried slices of something which reminded one of the harder and less sweet variety of banana known in Europe as the 'imported, chemically treated, pumped with gas for quicker ripening' type. To drink, I got Nigerian *Star* beer, produced by Heineken. Everything tasted… basically, I don't know what it tasted like. Each dish was so spicy, that I didn't feel anything other than my tongue being burnt.

Now already worried, I thought I would never become a fan of the cuisine of my new homeland, when the waiter brought some palm wine.

Such wines are produced from the fermented juice of the flowers of various kinds of palm. The longer these wines stand in the sun, the longer they ferment and become stronger. This wine had been standing a long time, a very long time. And it saved my relationship with west African cuisine.

The next urgent matter to be sorted out was the visa, the embassy and so on.

Rocket had sent on all the necessary documentation and I had arranged my meeting with the consul by phone. He was a tall, broad-shouldered nice guy who looked around 30 years of age. I was surprised such a young man was in such a post. I was prepared to guess that he had got this job through family connections. Which could have been true. The truth could also have been that I was not able to assess his age correctly. Due to the higher concentrations of melatonin in their skin, black people simply age more slowly. As I heard a few months later in Nigeria: "Black don't crack."

Then I realized that this was the first time I had ever sat face to face with a black person. This the curse of our Polish everyday reality. The word 'Pole' could be replaced with 'white Catholic'. This sets our default position at barely corked xenophobia, regardless of how many Will Smith movies we have seen. If we are brought up in a homogenous environment, we are not able to practice tolerance towards those who are different from us.

I had considered myself to be an open-minded person. However, I just wasn't able to take my eyes off my interlocutor. I was captivated by his behavior, his manner of speaking and, out of pure curiosity, couldn't look away while he was filling in the documents. At a certain moment, I got scared: "Jesus, what if I'm a racist and don't even know it?"

I had left dealing with the most difficult thing until the end. Telling a certain woman about my plans… Klaudia was a tall blond beauty who looked like Charlize Theron's younger sister. We had gotten to know each other six months earlier, when she packed in her career as a dancer and had started studying journalism. From then on, we were inseparable. Insofar as when we weren't arguing and didn't want to kill each other. We had broken up and then got back together after a break of a few weeks.

The funeral business is merciless on your nerves and emotions and my partner was effective in helping me forget about this. As this was my first serious relationship, I didn't know whether it was normal to try to blot this stress out by creating even more stress in my private life. My father never raised his hand to my mother. Dad never even spanked me, in fact. When it comes to myself, however, I don't hide the fact that I'm able to aim my words in way that can hurt more than physical blows. As a boy, I was brought up by a woman of extraordinary strength and grew up with enormous respect for the opposite sex. But Klaudia was proof of the theory that madness is a form of beauty. A theory which I was to confirm several times thereafter.

Once, when I came back too late from a party with some friends, she expressed her dissatisfaction by welcoming me with the pepper spray I had given her several weeks earlier. Another time, during an argument, she pulled a knife from a drawer in an attempt to strengthen her line of reasoning. I wasn't in a position to listen to it in the end, as I was in a hurry to get to the shop for bread and milk. During one of our break-ups, when I was already completely convinced that it was time to put an end to this circus and had stopped answering her calls, I got a text from her saying that if I didn't show up at the apartment within 30 minutes, she was going to jump out of the window.

"But we only live one floor up," I calmly observed, which wound her up even more.

"Don't argue with me! You've got to come back straight away or I'll jump."

Even though I had had enough of these silly games, I still had a conscience and called the police to report that someone might be in danger. A police patrol just happened to be in the area. Then there was a phone call from the local cops, which wasn't what I had expected.

"Klaudia is with us, but with regard to the procedures related to this kind of call, we have a duty to bring her in for observation to the psychiatric clinic on Nowowiejska Street."

I needed a moment to digest this. In my mind, I was wondering just how many doses of pepper spray I was now going to get as gratitude for such an experience. This time, I went there straight away. In a normal hospital, each patient, even if they are coughing blood and barely able to walk, can have themselves discharged whenever they like. Being discharged from a psychiatric hospital isn't that simple. It was Saturday and the doctor would not see her until Monday. So Klaudia had an involuntary weekend in a renovated 19th century building in the city center. I felt sad, stupid and responsible for the entire mess. When Klaudia saw me, however, she threw her arms around me and, wonders never cease, also apologized. We were back together that Monday.

Until Friday. It really was a typical rollercoaster relationship. However, she took the news of my departure exceptionally calmly. We both acknowledged that there was no point in arguing, since we wouldn't see each other for at least several months. And I had bought a one-way ticket to Nigeria.

"If we see each other again and still want to be with each other, we'll have to get engaged. Are you happy?" she asked seductively.

"Sure, I'm happy," I responded nervously, having absolutely no idea what she meant.

Later, I found out that Klaudia had been screwing around behind my back, left, right and center. Sometimes even at parties which we had attended together. So just as with Marysia, I hurt like hell, but in the end I somehow ceased to care anymore.

Chapter 5

IN DESERT
AND WILDERNESS

That day was the first time I had sat in a wide-body aircraft. Meaning one in which economy has 10 seats in a row, not six or four like in some crappy little plane. An Emirates Airlines Boeing 777 is nothing to be sneezed at. I remember the first moment I felt the ecstasy. Which passed after just three minutes. Or more precisely, when it turned out that I was sitting in the middle seat of the middle row with a sweating fat-ass on either side of me. I've always had a weakness for curves, but not those of the male variety. In booking me a ticket in economy class, Rocket Internet was sending me a signal that they spend a lot, but only on things which produce growth for the company.

The plane left the runway with all the noise and grace of a rhinoceros pregnant with twins. The journey was uneventful, however. After 30 minutes, I got bored looking at the clouds out the window, an image which was being streamed on the headrest monitor from the external camera.

I wasn't able to sleep. I only managed to get some shut-eye straight after takeoff during my subsequent years in Africa, when flying an average of four times a week. I got a whole multimedia package going and decided to catch up on the entire Harry Potter movie series. And that's how I passed the time on the way to Dubai, from where I had a direct flight to Lagos.

It was already late in the evening, just before 11 pm, when we landed there. But the airport, which is rightly considered one of the most magnificent in the world, seemed not to notice that it was time to hop into bed and get some sleep. Actually, all of Dubai has no idea of what sleep is. Night-time traffic is the same as during the day. On the other hand, the temperature is far more bearable.

My departure to Lagos was not to take place until the next day at 11 am. Although I supposedly had a hotel reservation, I don't know anyone who would spend their first night in Dubai in bed. And I had no intention of doing so either. This city had summoned me.

I got into a taxi, gave the driver $300 in cash and told him that he was to show me as many places of interest as possible, but above all take me from one end of the city to the other. I wanted to "feel Dubai". Normally, I would have done this while jogging, which is the way I most often discover a city while traveling. However, in the case of Dubai, I wasn't sure if the weather or the traffic would allow it. The driver was extraordinarily keen to take on the task. Since he hadn't protested or wanted to haggle, I surely must have given him three times too much. Well, no-one has ever become poor by giving. In any case, the taxi driver came from India and told me his own moving story in detail along the way, how he had spent 10 years working in Dubai, until he was able to bring over his wife and children. They hadn't seen each other for a decade. And we complain about conducting a 'long-distance relationship' between Koszalin and Warsaw. During this beautiful story, I also understood that whoever hasn't heard English spoken with an Indian accent, doesn't know much about life.

One of the stops on our trip was the Burj Khalifa, 829m tall, including the antenna. I ordered the driver to stop, got out, looked up and said in awe:

"What the fu…"

"Yes, yes," the taxi driver agreed in his Indian accent, nodding his head as if he had understood exactly what I was thinking.

Although it was night, it is never dark in Dubai. I'm sure that there are more streetlights on there than in the whole of Africa. In driving around, I looked at the people, the cars and the buildings. I quickly understood that I would never get to like Dubai. I was like Truman

Burbank in *The Truman Show* and everything was so plastic, pretty and artificial. Anything that was ugly and cheap was hidden away. Pakistani laborers are brought to building sites from special districts outside Dubai in buses with tinted windows, so that the sun doesn't bother them. And so that the sight of them doesn't bother those born in the Emirates, standing alongside at the traffic lights. Sitting in their Lamborghinis, receiving monthly salaries from the government just for being... Emirati citizens.

After two hours of driving around, I arrived at the Conrad Hilton Hotel. Quick check-in, a short dip in the pool and then I collapsed into a huge, comfortable bed. In the hotel, I noticed an interesting rule. The receptionists were beautiful white girls who spoke with the same harsh east European accent as mine. The staff in the restaurant and spa had Asian features. The cleaning staff were black.

"It's surely a coincidence," I told myself. "There is absolutely no reason to think that in this region we could be dealing with the slightest element of racism and class division."

As the hotel was really good, I didn't shy away from unpretentiously bragging once I had 'checked in' on social media. Hey, who wouldn't? Oh, how much artistry can one dish out from a selfie, with the addition of Instagram filters. Your ego won't massage itself, you know. As a cover, I put up some generalized, amazingly deep motivational quote from Google about personal development. These days it just doesn't do to be vain.

After a couple of minutes, I received a private message. It was Gosia, an old friend.

"Hi Marek, are you in Dubai?"

"Yes, but I'm flying further on in the morning."

"The morning is still a long way away. Drop in."

After which she gave me the address. As it turned out, Gosia was flying with Emirates Airlines as member of the cabin crew – one doesn't say 'stewardess' these days. A few days earlier, she had been promoted to cabin crew chief and that night it just happened to be her birthday. Well, of course, it would have been very impolite to turn down such an invitation. Even more so, since I remembered Gosia as being a gorgeous gal, while the party she was inviting me to was a pool party, which would surely be followed by an after party.

I didn't need to be asked twice. I left and went by one of the hotel taxis.

On arriving at the villa where the party was taking place, the Mercedes S class in which I had arrived turned out to be the least impressive car there. In the pool next to the house, in which you could have organized the Olympics, there were lots of girls splashing around. All of them were beautiful. Gosia explained that she had mainly invited her colleagues from work. Meaning 'cabin crew', meaning 99% women. I will only add that Emirates deliberately employs staff from around the world so that on board the greatest number of beauty types, I mean languages, will be represented.

"Are you sure I should be here?" I asked, feigning modesty.

"Stop it! You're special. A buddy from Poland has a special pass. I still remember how you saved me from that drunken gorilla in a night-club a couple of years ago."

Although I had only saved Gosia by pretending that she was my girl-friend, I didn't protest the point. Then, I had almost got the proverbial punch in the face from this thug. This was an the appropriate moment to accept such gratitude.

"I love such rules, Gosia!" I laughed and was, a moment later, already in the pool.

My African adventure had begun in a truly interesting way.

In the morning, I turned up at the airport late, tired but happy.

Dubai International doesn't just have a lounge for business and first class passengers – they have an entire terminal section for this. Well, I had to just suck it up and show my passport at the entrance to the terminal for regular folks. I went through check-in, security and immigration control like a hot knife through butter. Boarding for my flight had already begun.

I ran to the gate.

And froze. The queues were longer than those for toilet paper in communist Poland. In front of me, there were dozens of passengers armed with enormous suitcases, backpacks and colored bags. All of them were waiting to enter the plane. Didn't they know that you can leave your larger bags at the check-in desk?

Thus, for the first time, I came across the famous Nigerian trait of trying to carry colossal amounts of hand luggage on board. The check-in time of every flight to and from Nigeria always takes terribly long. And always following the same format. The ground crew first ask, then try to convince people to follow common sense, then attempt to negotiate until finishing by threatening either not to let them on board or to cancel the flight.

In the end, they manage to gain control. Later, having flown this route many times, I started to suppose that this was a kind of game between the passengers and ground staff. A game following which the opponents shake hands and go their separate ways.

When, in the end, I found my way around the now-familiar Boeing 777, I didn't feel right. I knew there was something different than usual, but didn't know what. Eventually, I figured it out. There was only one white man on the whole plane. Me.

"Hello adventure, I'm coming," I chuckled to myself. I reached for the book I had picked up at the airport, Paul Collier's *The Bottom Billion,* which was meant to help me understand the reasons why some nations are wallowing in poverty. I also had a printout of the annual report of Priceline, a NASDAQ-listed company and the owner of Booking.com, which was meant to help me better understand the online reservation business. I read them alternately for a time, but wasn't able to concentrate. I found it very difficult to concentrate in fact. Although I was sitting by the window, in the seat next to mine a beautiful girl was sleeping. Her eyes were hiding beneath lids bristling with the most wonderful lashes. Her breasts, covered with a figure-hugging black top, rose and fell as she breathed. Her long, curly, ebony-black hair danced to its own rhythm in the light turbulence. This girl was phenomenal. I remember exactly what I was thinking at the time.

That if she didn't stop snoring so much, I swear to God I would shout "There's a bomb under my seat!" and get the plane turned around.

As she didn't allow me to read at all, I pulled out my phone, switched on a 'Calm down' playlist on Spotify and fell fast asleep. It was high time to sleep through the Arabian Peninsula and the Persian Gulf. After partying all night, I would have fallen asleep on a bicycle. But it was not given to me to drift off to the Land of Nod, as the chainsaw – pardon me – my enchanting neighbor woke from her nap, sensed the call of Instagram and decided to take some photos. And it had to be through my window. Wishing to or not, I looked out through it. There were no clouds at all. We were flying 12 km above the Earth and the only thing you could make out was vastness. For a while, I wondered whether Mark Twain had ever had a chance to see such sights, until I remembered that he died in 1910, a fact which clearly answered my quandary.

When, after several hours, we were approaching Lagos, the plane became enveloped by clouds and the machine started to shake a bit. The pilot switched on the 'Fasten Seat Belts' sign and informed us that we were soon about to land.

However, that 'soon' lasted pretty long and still all I could see was cloud. I had wanted to see Lagos from a bird's eye view and knew that the airport lay almost in the city center. I had expected to view a great African metropolis, millions of people scurrying around like ants on the streets and skyscrapers in the financial district. Meanwhile, all I could see was a great white nothing.

Eventually, at a height of a few hundred meters, the plane broke through the clouds. I saw for the first time what Nigeria looks like from the air.

I saw a sea, no – sorry – a red ocean of sheet metal roofs covering ruined hovels leaning almost to the ground. The fact that some were covered with wavy corrugated sheet metal makes my comparison with the ocean entirely appropriate, even if this was an ocean of only dirt and dust.

Fortunately, this depressing sight finished as quickly as it had started. The place of the filthy roofs was taken by unevenly laid asphalt and within a moment we had landed. The pilot thanked us for the flight, while my travel companions started to get ready to disembark.

I however moved off to be first at the exit. Despite all the negotiations on the ground, most passengers had taken loads of stuff on board anyway. I preferred to be first, because otherwise I would have had to stay in my seat for another 100 years.

The stewardess opened the door.

"Welcome, Africa!" I shouted.

"Fuck off!" Africa shouted back, directing a blow of terrifying heat straight into my face. Which made me take a step back.

"Oh no, you won't get me that easily," I thought, then jumped down the the steps and raced to the air-conditioned terminal.

Which wasn't air-conditioned, but that wasn't what dismayed me the most. I saw thousands of people, but heard a million. The first thing I discovered on coming to Nigeria was that you don't speak here. The one and only thing you do is shout. If you meet two men from the the Yoruba tribe on your way who are jumping up and down, gesticulating and screaming to high heaven, there is a strong possibility that they are in the middle of a calm discussion about the weekend weather forecast.

Soaked with sweat, even today I don't know whether I did this from fear or the heat, but I headed in the direction of customs. Now, where was it? The corridor in the terminal was long and dark – there was no air-conditioning, because there was no electricity and so no light. Anyone landing at any airport in the world automatically looks for the signs directing one to baggage reclaim, passport and customs control or the exit. I couldn't find any signs. So I waited with a heavy heart for that whole crowd of passengers with their elephant-sized hand luggage, before whom I had managed to get ahead, and started walking behind them. We arrived at customs, which was comprised of three check-points. They didn't serve all the travelers at once. Although you had to go to each as they individually sorted out 'different stages of customs inspection', you didn't visit one after another at all. The information delivery system at Lagos airport takes the appearance of three guys standing at checkpoints and roaring incessantly. If you can hear any-thing, or above all, see anything, maybe you will manage to understand where they are directing you. If you don't, you only end up annoying them.

I came to the checkpoint and stood in front of an official dressed in a T-shirt and jeans.

"Oyinbo! Welcome! Do you have anything for me?" he asked with a smile.

It was in this manner that I encountered corruption in Nigeria for the first time. And I only mention it, because he was the first person I had spoken to in the land of the Sahara. 'Oyinbo' is a word which means 'white person' in Nigeria. If someone in the street doesn't know your name, they shout 'Oyinbo' at you. Meaning the equivalent of 'Nigger' or 'Boy', insofar as whites don't have the right to be offended by 'Oyinbo', as it was the whites who exploited the blacks, not the other way round. 'Oyinbo' is often also said out of admiration for your skin color. Light skinned Nigerians also can be called that in public.

For a moment, I wondered what stupid thing I could to say to feign idiocy.

"Maybe I could… pray for your good fortune?"

I think I didn't notice his blushing, just because of the dark color of his skin. A smile appeared on his face, he glanced at my passport and ordered me to move along. When I later told people who had already known Nigeria for some time about this, they always told me that this was a brilliant move. Nigerians are very religious. All of them. Muslims and Christians. So it is worth keeping this in mind sometimes. Especially when they are trying to extract a bribe out of you. They get all awkward and usually withdraw.

I went further on. According to the information which I had received in an email the previous day, a driver was meant to be waiting for me, wearing an orange t-shirt. As I hadn't seen anyone of the kind in the arrivals hall, I headed for the exit, hoping that maybe he was waiting for me in the car.

Although he wasn't waiting, several others were. All of them, as it happened, were wearing orange T-shirts. At one moment, they started shouting at me. All at the same time. One of them used sign language to show me that he would take me into town. Sign language in that he pretended to be turning an invisible steering wheel in the air. Another guy wanted to change money. As still another waved an identity badge under my nose, showing that he was a certified airport taxi driver, I wagered he wouldn't kidnap and eat me.

I had no idea how to act in such a situation. All I did was say "No, thank you." They shouted even more. Some of them started to beckon me with kissing sounds. Although in Europe we consider this rude, the most eminent Nigerian scientists have discovered that even quiet kissing sounds are audible in the worst noise. A different sound frequency or something like that. In any case, as I felt hounded, I quickly returned to the arrivals hall. Today, in hindsight I can laugh about it. Now, whenever I'm at the airport in Lagos, Abuja or anywhere else, I can perfectly tell who is in Nigeria for the first time just by looking at them.

I decided to wait for the driver at the airport restaurant, but then remembered that I had no local currency. While I was Warsaw, I had gone to a large and really very good bureau de change.

"Hello, I'd like to change 500 zlotys into naira."

"I'm sorry, into what?"

It was then I found out that only one country in the whole world recognizes the Nigerian naira. Circumstances had therefore forced me to take dollars and change them locally. Not far from the airport restaurant was a bureau de change. I gave the cashier $100. And he gave me five kilos of waste paper. At the end of the 1970s, there were 2 naira to the pound sterling. But later inflation kicked in. Now, one dollar was almost 350 naira. However, if you are reading this book later than 24 hours since it was published, it is highly likely that this figure has changed by as much as several hundred percent. Oh, such are the charms of emerging economies. So I received around 35,000 naira. In fives, tens and twenties. Meaning in wads of banknotes at least three inches thick.

Two hours. That's how late my driver was, and it was only after several weeks in Nigeria that I understood that this was the norm concerning punctuality. Poland is certainly not a country where the state railway company apologies for the train being 30 seconds late, as in Japan. Students turning up at a quarter past the hour is a common occurrence. In Africa, however, time is treated in a metaphysical manner. If you ask someone how long a journey will take, he will not tell you in minutes or hours, only 'short' or 'long'. We have watches, they have time. And if someone complains, they will apologize and promise to be better. And later they'll do exactly the same.

The airport for the commercial capital of the largest economy in Africa seemed nightmarish. Not only were there frequent power cuts and the reign of general chaos, but it had a mere eight gates, while access to the terminal was along a single route. From the car park, we had to drag our suitcases along an uneven, sandy road for about 15 minutes. A similar level of disorganization was caused by the building of a new terminal alongside by the Chinese, which was to change everything within a few years. I hope they finish it before I die, I thought to myself, looking at the gigantic arrangement of scaffolding which we had passed. I could hear screaming everywhere, but began to get used to it after a while.

Getting out of the airport car park took us an hour. If you haven't been to Lagos, you have no idea what a traffic jam is. It's a paradox, but the stress goes down with every passing moment. The closer we were to the center, the more modern the buildings outside the window seemed. It was only later, I discovered that the airport doesn't lie in the best part of Lagos, so inevitably, the closer to the center, the better. Along the way, we entered by driving over the Third Mainland Bridge. It is 12 km long, and is the longest in Africa with a motorway running across it with three lanes on either side. Along the bridge expensive cars passed, almost all of them SUVs, a phenomenon which has its own story, of which there'll be more in another chapter. In the distance, I saw billboards advertising banks, cell phone networks and internet deals, thinking "Zmysłowski, it's ok. Money can be made here."

In an emerging economy, the most important pillars of development are the banking and telecommunications sectors, as it is only based on such infrastructure that you can build other businesses and develop the economy further.

We left Ikeja, passed the already mentioned Third Mainland bridge and drove to other parts of the metropolis: Ikoyi, Victoria Island and Lekki. There were very many people everywhere and almost every one of them was holding a cell phone. Believe it or not, there are more active SIM cards in Nigeria than people. And the population numbers around 200 million or more, as it is difficult to provide a precise estimate. However, such a large number of phones is caused by the very poor quality voice and internet connection offered by telecoms companies. Years will pass before the infrastructure will be at a satisfactory level. People often have two or three phones, each with a card for a different operator, in order to increase their chances that at least one will work. Thanks to this, they somehow manage to maintain contact with the world. And then they can continue to roar at each other.

God only knows when it got more modern and a little bit greener. In the past, Lagos was located on islands. Later, during a demographic boom, it grew in an uncontrolled manner, taking up space on the mainland. This was where the poorest lived, while the islands turned into enclaves for the rich. There are very few places in the world where you can see such enormous social stratification as here. Some drive the newest Mercedes and BMWs, while others run barefoot.

The home which had been prepared for me was located in a residential part of Lagos called Lekki. The neighborhood still displayed the remains of former days. Among the office blocks of glass and steel, you could sometimes encounter old colonial villas. Such juxtapositions of history and modernity make a stunning impression.

When I was left at my 'new home', hidden behind a three-meter-high fence, I felt a bit like being in a dormitory. A large house with many bedrooms and a bathroom. A communal kitchen shared with other residents who, probably as I, had been sent by Rocket from various corners of the world in order to start up numerous enterprises. A house in which the cook/cleaner/housekeeper assigned to us ruled. It was clean, fairly quiet, although a little too warm. I was to live there for the first few months, until I had acclimatized and found a place of my own to rent.

I was used to sleeping and generally functioning in lower temperatures. The evening had just fallen, the journey from the airport had taken three and a half hours, despite it being just a drive of 20km. I was dog-tired as the entire journey, including the stopover in Dubai, had taken 39 hours. I opened the window as wide as I possibly could, naively hoping for a cool night breeze, hopped into bed and fell asleep as soon as my head hit the pillow.

Chapter 6

THE LUST FOR MONEY

My relationship with Africa is neither easy nor pleasant. Although it has been full of passion and wonderful, sublime moments, it has also had more unpleasant times. On this basis, both Africa and I should have gone for relationship counseling.

For every newcomer, their first few weeks in the 'Cradle of Civilization' is an idyll. Everything around you – the people, the buildings, the streets and the natural world – is fascinating.

After a few months, however, every expat goes through a crisis in which their enthusiasm decreases, while their irritation with cultural differences grows and grows. Ninety-nine percent leave Africa after a year.

Those who stay, have made the transition from 'infatuation' to true love, a love found in those with greater understanding. There are very many things in Africa which I don't like and often drive me around the bend. Many of them I describe in this book. However, it doesn't change the fact that my love affair with her has become one which is for better and worse. Sometimes we argue and slam the door, but I love and respect her and can't imagine life with her not there. Now however, it's time to return to the first night we spent together.

About five in the morning, I was awoken by boiling drops of sweat streaming into my eyes. The air conditioning had stopped working as the generator had been turned off for the night. But even if it had been on, it wouldn't have been of any use anyway as, after all, I had left the window open. Well done, me. I looked at my forearms and got scared. Four large red spots on the right and three on the left – mosquito bites. On just seeing them, they started to itch like crazy. Oh, wonderful, I thought. I haven't even been here a day and have already caught malaria. In the 21st century, malaria spread by mosquitoes still kills over a thousand people a day in Africa, which is no joke.

If you don't get medicine in time, malaria will kill the healthiest person and certainly wouldn't have any problem in dealing with a young whippersnapper from Poland, totally unused to local bacteria and viruses.

There are no vaccinations for malaria. Once caught, the parasite can immediately attack its host or remain lurking in the body for many years and attack unannounced. You think you have flu, having forgotten about that exotic holiday from years before, take medicine for something you shouldn't have and wham! Your life may just come to an end, even while lying in the most luxurious European capital, as it will enter no-one's head to give you anti-malarial drugs.

I googled the symptoms I was to expect in the next few days and rationalized things to myself by saying that I didn't deserve such beautiful karma and that everything would be OK. And, above all, I closed that fucking window. I went to take a cold shower to reduce the temperature of my body and spirit. The water flowed out more slowly than the piss of a 60 year-old man with prostate problems, because, without a generator, the pump wasn't working, of course. In hindsight, everything seems so obvious now. I cooled down after about 15 minutes of raging at the stream of water and went back to sleep.

Up to now, I've had malaria three times and, fortunately, it's been fairly mild. Something like flu.

The driver had mentioned that he would call for me at 7am so as to have me at the office by 8am. So I expected him to turn up before 9am. He arrived at 8.45am. The journey to the office took only 10 minutes, a distance you could have walked if it hadn't been for the scorching sun, the lack of sidewalks and the threat of being run over by mini-buses traveling at insane speeds.

Rocket has taken one of the elegant colonial villas as its base. The residential part of Lagos, the most toffee-nosed place in town in a very pleasant and leafy neighborhood. Close enough to the sea to hear its sound, but far enough not to have fish swimming around in the office. In the garden outside the house there were plastic chairs on which young people sat working at their computers, shaded from the sun by large parasols. The garage had been transformed into a mini-warehouse and package collection point. In the corner there stood and huge satellite dish with a diameter of about 10 meters pointed directly up into the sky.

I went inside and my eyes met one large open space office – the headquarters of Jumia, namely the African Amazon.com, which Rocket Internet had started up just a few months earlier. Every square meter of the formerly splendid sitting room and bedroom was now designated as office space. In one of the enormous bathrooms, a conference table had been placed. In the other, the cleaning ladies ran a laundry for the employees. In the kitchen, someone cooked them all dinner. Each one of them sat on colorful plastic chairs. Population density: about one person per square meter of floor space. Everyone was busy with emails, telephone calls or energetic conversations. There was a lot of strong positive energy. I soaked it all up. This was the moment. 8000 kilometers from home, in another hemisphere and on a different continent, I felt that same shiver of emotion. We were building something from scratch, changing the world or, as it seemed to us at least, maybe we could make some money out of it. Yes, siree, I think I'll find my place here.

"Do you like it?" someone asked me from behind, startling me from my reverie. It was Tunde, one of the cofounders at Jumia, a Harvard graduate, who had founded his own online store in Nigeria, when Rocket Internet pulled into the port of Lagos and made him an offer he couldn't refuse. The German internet behemoth then took over his mini-company and started to build Jumia on its foundations.

"They boys from Paris called and said to give you the attic. It's all yours – there are the stairs," he pointed to a super-narrow metal spiral staircase in the corner. "Congratulations and good luck," he said and left.

I pulled myself upstairs, hitting the ceiling on the way. The attic wasn't so bad. There was a mini-kitchen, a large bedroom divided by a partition into two mini-offices in which two people could fit, meaning six in a Nigerian start-up. And, of course, a large bathroom, meaning my future board room. There was also a small closet, which was basically a large wardrobe which you could walk into with a small window, allowing you to peep out and see what was going on in the street. I took a chair and table from one of the micro-desks and threw them into the closet. In this way I created the CEO's office.

Although there was no air-conditioning, I found a fan, plugged it in and aimed it at my sweaty face. I sat down, switched on the laptop and started my historic first day at work in Africa.

The meeting in Paris had allowed me to better understand the philosophy of the company. Although Rocket has been accused of copying, it prides itself on precision and effectiveness in conducting business, while remaining unappreciated for its vision and courage. Because without vision and courage you won't invest in a business in the Developing World, which has no chance of making a profit during the first 10 years and eats up more money than a coal mine. This vision largely rests on the idea that capitalism wins. And that capitalism does more good than bad. And that governments won't bother them too much in this regard. And that Rocket wants to be there and perform for you.

Internet companies, especially those in which Rocket is involved – online trading, auction platforms, as well as social media – are characterized by frequently conquering everything or nothing. The network effect is crucial: the larger you are, the quicker you grow, as people come to you because you are big. You have to lure everyone in and give them something they will want to relate with on a daily basis. For example, in Poland the online auction site Allegro managed to gather and build up scale in time. It concentrated such a critical mass in sales and purchases, that there was nothing left for the global giant eBay to take. And it's not the first time eBay entered a new market too late.

The story of Rocket Internet and the Samwer brothers actually started much earlier than 2007, which is the official date of the company's foundation. Nine years earlier, a certain little-known German management school student, Oliver Samwer, wrote a Master's thesis entitled *American Start-Ups Achieving The Greatest Success – A lesson for other entrepreneurs*. In 1999, when eBay was already a powerful force in the USA, but did not exist in Europe, three brothers from Germany, Oliver, Alexander and Marc Samwer, contacted eBay with a proposal that they would develop its business on the continent of Europe. Maybe the Samwers were young, but they hadn't dropped out of the sky. Their father ran one of the largest legal firms in the German city of Cologne, while their great-grandfather had been the founder of an insurance company. However, eBay sent them packing, not having any idea of how, by doing so, they had created a dangerous three-headed hydra. Because what did the Samwers only go and do? Copy eBay and launch it in Germany under the name of Alando (just don't confuse it with Zalando, although that's their site too). They pumped several million euro into it with the effect that three months later humble eBay raised the white flag in order to negotiate a buyout with the Samwers. In the end, this came to a figure of $50m. Genius in its simplicity. Copy some big American idea in Europe, then sell it back to those you've copied it from. Or its direct competitor.

In 2000, they copied several American start-ups, merged them together into one large body and launched them under the name Jamba. They released a paid subscription service for ringtones and wallpapers for telephones. Remember Crazy Frog? That was Jamba, in fact. Four years later, the business was bought by the American giant Verisign for a lot more than a quarter of a billion dollars. Not enough? In 2010, they sold CityDeal to Groupon for 'a nine-digit sum in dollars'. CityDeal – a clone of Groupon.

The Samwers have been successively putting the premises of Oliver's 1998 Master's thesis into practice.

At that point, many would have cashed in their chips and left the casino. But not the Samwers. They had just started. These quick deals had given Rocket the label of being a clone factory. That's not exactly true. It's stupid to say that just copying an idea is enough to ensure success. The difference between markets mean that innovation is not necessary at the top next to strategy. But at the bottom. In this regard, Rocket should get a badge for being a leader in innovation.

The successes mentioned here must have changed its way of looking at business, because Rocket announced that it would be building long-term ventures. Since it was attacking markets which did not yet have Amazon, Alibaba or Booking.com, it could just as well create local leaders which would not be sold to the internet giants, but would compete with them. Its mission became the creation of the largest ecosystem of trading platforms outside of China and the United States. Meaning a market sufficiently big enough to achieve at least the same income as Alibaba or Amazon.

The tactic was pretty simple: choose a market to attack, starting with the largest, and do absolutely everything, regardless of the scale of the costs, in order to become the No. 1 player. Which would then grow due to a growing market.

The tactic works if there's money from investors, but getting this money from investors, apart from a thousand and one other aspects, comes down to one simple thing. Growth. If you generate growth, investors will shower you with money. And you can shovel it into the firebox of a locomotive or put it in a rocket, it'll move things on. What did all of this mean to me? A huge fucking load of work.

It was April 2013. The launch of the service was set for 5 August. On this very day, there was an article planned about the start of Jovago, which was to appear on TechCrunch, the best known internet business site in the world. We were supposed have a working site with reservations available at thousands of hotels in Nigeria at least, as well as hundreds of reservations conducted by our first real customers. If something didn't go right, the article could have surely been postponed, but certainly not at the whim of Oliver Samwer. In a particular email which was leaked to the press, Samwer wrote that he demanded that founders sign plans with their names in blood and that the launch of a company was to be like blitzkrieg. I can neither confirm nor deny this. In any case the date was not for moving, unless I wanted to return home as fast I had arrived. And I had a lot to prove, both to myself and everyone around me.

Following the launch of the site, the expected growth in key performance indicators, such as the number of reservations or active hotels on the platform, was to be maintained at a level of 20%. Monthly. As the deeper you enter the forest you can't see it for the trees, the most important indicators became those concerning the satisfaction of returning customers, the cost of securing new users, the speed of page upload, brand recognition etc.

But everything in turn. The building of the platform itself, meaning the website, was carried out by a five-person team assigned to this task and based in Porto, Portugal, where Rocket's technology center was located, meaning a farm of developers building technology for internet companies founded by Rocket all over the world.

Defining their task did not take me very long.

"Build me a Booking.com MVP" was the order. MVP is an acronym for Minimum Viable Product. This meant building a version of the site in the simplest way, but still advanced enough to fulfill the most important demands of its first users. At this stage, losing time on technological nuances was idiotic, because we had no idea what the market wanted as yet. By far the most important thing was to secure a sufficient number of hotels which would agree to their rooms being booked through our website. Sufficient in the sense that the user coming onto the site would have the subjective feeling of having an appropriate level of choice, allowing them to make the best decision.

In the preliminary report which had been prepared for us by a biiii-igggg consulting firm from one of the so-called 'Big Four', whose name I really shouldn't reveal (it was PricewaterhouseCoopers), it was written that there were 1,500 hotels in Nigeria. I already knew that this was bullshit. And I was right. There are 1,500 hotels in Lagos alone. Such discrepancies arise from pure ignorance.

Consulting firms. Big companies, big marketing, big words and at the end of the day a guy is left with a few PowerPoint slides put together by an intern. The problem here is that neither the people working in these fabulous firms nor their interns had a clue about the hotel market in Nigeria. Even if they had stumbled across a hotel, it would have merely seemed a bump in the road to them because the difference between the European and African definitions of an hotel is vast. Here there are no signboards or neon signs. No-one needs any of this and it could only end up causing problems. Before you know it, tax collectors will turn up, along with people extorting tribute, all sorts of snake-oil salesmen and, of course, Zmysłowski with his entourage telling them about the magic of the internet.

A typical hotel in Africa is a very large villa divided into bedrooms. There are from 20 to 30 rooms, plus a canteen. Such accommodation is considered to be a three-star hotel. But a consultant only sees some kind of mean hovel, adjusts their expensive glasses and pronounces it to be some kind of shit-hole, not a hotel. The trouble is that what a hotel is or is not isn't decided by a consultant from New York, but a customer from Nigeria.

The consultant Rocket had sent 'to help' me for a few days didn't know this either. I remember how he told me: "I've made a list of companies with whom you should work. They'll secure customers and partners for you, as well as help with recruitment."

"What do you mean?" I said annoyed. "I haven't worked my ass off to now pass the work on to someone else. This is my job and I intend to be bound to it."

"You won't manage on your own. You're totally new in Nigeria, not to mention all of Africa," the consultant pronounced, thereby arousing the monster which had been sleeping within for some time: 'I'll show you'.

I got down to work.

The fact that hotels had no internet access did not pose any obstacle. We simply acknowledged that we would employ people who work offline. The customer would book a room using our website and my guy would go there and make the reservation in person. Half the rooms are always empty, so there would never be such a problem as overbooking.

This temporary solution would be completely sufficient for the first few months of operations, I thought. In the second stage, we would put a call-center into operation, which would remind hotels of upcoming reservations and ensure that the rooms are available (just because the room is free on the day of booking doesn't necessarily mean that it will be free on the day of the customer's arrival). When hotels begin to receive a sufficient number of additional bookings from Jovago, comprising a significant proportion of their income, then they would start treating us seriously. Then we would be able to train them up gradually, and then force them to regularly use the panel (third stage), which we will create for them. On this they will be able to update prices and room availability. Stage three may occur after one year, maybe five. The market was to have been verified by then.

During my first week I visited 50 hotels, meaning all I could find on Google Maps and those which my driver from the airport knew and who now stayed working for me. I quickly hired an assistant, who was meant to deal with organizing the office when we had people working there. She was a Nigerian called Bertha and had worked before in Jumia, although she very much wanted to join a new project in the hotel sector. Since she was good enough for Jumia, she should turn out to be fine for me. It was only later that I was to learn a lesson from her about poor recruitment strategies.

I would just walk into a hotel from the street, as there was no opportunity to arrange meetings beforehand. Fortunately, the Nigerian hotel sector has a thing about the manager spending most of his time on site. And the receptionist usually did not cause me any problems.

My conversation started with: "Good morning, I've flown in to see you from Europe. I'd like to speak to your manager, please. It concerns sending large groups of customers to your hotel."

My opening line contained sufficient information to arouse interest, without any unnecessary details about some internet thing.

"Aha, one moment, please sit down," the receptionist would say. I didn't sit as I don't like someone telling me what to do. Apart from that, I wanted to be always within her sight, so that she wouldn't forget that someone was waiting.

"There's some white man to see you," I heard behind my back. That's how my meticulously prepared presentation was boiled down. Not important why I came, just important that I was white.

The most crucial element were the negotiations concerning the commission, which the hotel had to pay. Once a contract had been signed, it would be difficult to negotiate (especially upwards) and news travels fast in this sector. One poor decision could decide the company's income for the next 10 years. I had to understand just how much hotels were in a position to pay for customers. It was a difficult decision, insofar as the hotels themselves didn't know it themselves, because the cost of securing a customer was one great unknown to them. Someone builds a hotel and people come sometimes. How and from where? Nobody knows.

Intuitively, I knew that the less developed the market, the greater the opportunity for a higher commission ceiling, before the hotels learn the technology and the arrival of online travel agents.

Easier said than done. Nigerians like to haggle, make no mistake. In turn, negotiating terms that are too expensive may end with the hotel giving us increased hotel prices. When our customer comes to a hotel and sees that he'll get a lower price at the reception, then of course he'll ask for that lower price. My plan was based on commencing negotiations with a proposal of 50% as long as I wouldn't be kicked out or, as had happened with the undertaker mafia in Poland, the negotiations would last up to the point where my interlocutor doesn't just complain, but loses it. Although we managed to sign contracts with the first few dozen hotels with a commission of 30%, within a few years the contracts had come down to about 20%.

Another important challenge was how quickly the contracts were signed. We couldn't invite customers to use a service with just a few hotels in the database. First, we had to secure the hotels and only later start up the platform on the net. This wasn't so easy, however.

Following the signing of a contract with one hotel, I went to another, and this guy says to me: "Just wait a minute, my friend. Yesterday, you signed a contract with my good friend. You were to give him lots of new customers and nothing has changed in the meantime."

And there was no way of explaining that everything would take off when we had more partners: "What do you mean more? There will be more of us? There will be more of us for you to divide out your customers? But then it's not worth it for me."

The typical problem of the chicken and the egg. Everything should have been done simultaneously. Put all your effort into securing hotels and, at the same time, launch an advertising campaign to secure customers. We needed to secure hotels much quicker. In passing the deadline imposed by Rocket, I realized that although the contracts signed with the hotels may not have expiry dates on paper, the patience and interest of those who had signed may run out.

During the first month, I had secured 40 hotels on my own, traveling the length and breadth of Lagos, having numerous encounters with the police, the local inhabitants and others, of which more later.

Securing hotels did not depend only on signing contracts. You had to photograph every part of the joint, namely rooms, restaurants, pools etc., then write down the information regarding the facilities and prices. Then you had to put it all into the system. With an internet speed allowing you to upload one photo in five minutes at best. This worked out at almost a whole day for one hotel. But we had to secure an average of nine new hotels daily in order to be ready to launch the system.

In order to do this, I needed people. A lot of people. It seemed to me that I had sufficient knowledge concerning the process of securing partners in order to start the process of replicating it. So I told Bertha to place an announcement on local online employment websites. Bertha asked me if I was sure this was a good idea because... but I didn't want to listen as, at the end of the day, who is the start-up guru here? Me or Bertha?

Well, since it was me, Bertha placed the announcement and, as it was late, we went home. I was interested how quickly I would manage to gather a team. I needed at least 20 people and hoped that I would manage to gather as many CVs during the following week. It would be even better if I had 30. Just so I would have something to choose from.

10,000 came in. That's how many emails were waiting for me the next morning.

"Quiet. I don't want to hear one word," I said to Bertha.

"But I didn't say a thing," she replied smugly.

"You said 'I told you so.'"

"I didn't!"

"But you wanted to."

"Maybe a little."

Well, this time I didn't try to defend myself from seeming like one of those arrogant foreigners who come to Africa like a lord, only quickly to lose face.

It was obvious that 10,000 emails was only the beginning of my problems, as a cursory look at several of the résumés showed that the applicants were lying through their teeth. One guy was 18 years old, but had two college degrees. Someone else had five years' professional experience, four of which was as "Bill Gates' assistant". Someone else wrote that he had worked for four years as a "project manager in the Internet". Well, well, Nigeria is not only big, but young. One third of the population is aged 20 or less. And most of them are unemployed. At least officially. They look for work using every conceivable way.

Another question was the quality of the education received. Of course, not all of them were lying. Most of them stated the truth. Unfortunately, just because someone had finished school didn't mean that they could write or even count well. And I'm not joking. So in the end, I got what Bertha was trying to tell me. In Nigeria, you recruit through advertising but above all through personal recommendation and multi-stage theoretical testing. The most basic positions require 15 people to turn up at an appointed time, when they are placed in one room. They sit at computers and take tests on intelligence, knowledge, analytical skills and so on. It is only then that the time comes for conducting proper interviews.

Although my team had a painful birth, eventually it was brought into the world. On the first day, half of the new workers were late. The most decent of them only half an hour, the record holder three hours. In Poland, I would have given them their marching orders, but when I thought to myself that I would once again have to go through the recruitment process... I just gritted my teeth and started to teach them that their reason for being late was not traffic, but the fact that they left home later than they should have.

In time, I learned just what amazing entrepreneurs my employees were. Even too amazing sometimes, which isn't always good for an employer. A low level of trust towards employers in the jobs market, being used to poor salaries, late salary payment and poor treatment by management persists. Everyone protects themselves as best they can. One guy, who I had employed as a researcher, earned money in the laundry at the weekends. In the evenings, my driver 'ran his own business', meaning he changed foreign currency at the airport by cheating new arrivals. Some had two, or even three jobs on the side. They gave each employer what they were required to do with the least effort, which is obvious in such a situation. The best employee at Jovago had two full-time jobs. One with me and another somewhere else. And he maneuvered between both so smoothly, that I didn't notice for three months. Others never even turned up for work, sending a 'subcontractor' instead. The salary which I paid was divided in half. He took one half and paid the other to his own guy. Then he himself had enough time to work in two other places.

In the restaurants and nightclubs of Poland, it was no problem for me to find people who worked as barmen or waiters with passion. They always said that they loved their jobs, trained themselves up and went to competitions, wanting to be the best. In Nigeria, I frequently got the impression that everyone only had one ambition: to become the boss. To be exploited in order eventually to be able to exploit. Nobody wants to be a waiter. Everyone wants to own a restaurant. I don't know how much the perception of being the boss and low wages are to blame in this case, or to what degree a simple Freudian need to be an important person dominates the hopes of others.

Jovago's sales dream team was personally trained by me and ready to go. It was high time to secure hotels. It was obvious that they couldn't be found on the internet as, after all, it was us who had created the first real hotel website. We needed a creative approach. First of all, my people and I ordered taxis and ordered the drivers to go to every hotel they could find. This method turned out to be pretty effective, but had its pluses and minuses, as they say. While it was effective, firstly it cost a lot and secondly took up more and more of our time. Initially, we created just a small circle of hotels, but as out database grew, we needed to move out further. Often this was into places which the drivers did not want to bring us. And these guys are not easily scared. So we had to think up new ways. And that's what we did.

The Okadas came to the rescue. These are guys who ride motorcycle taxis, some of the most fearless people I've ever met. Or the craziest, which actually amounts to the the same thing. I'm sure you've often seen pictures from African cities showing four guys and goat riding on a motorbike. That's an Okada. They often turn into school buses by carrying six or seven young kids at the same time several kilometers to remote schools. In Lagos alone there are several hundred thousand Okadas. They see everything and go everywhere.

I stopped one on the street and said:

"Hey, do you know any hotels around here?"

"Yes, yes, a hotel. I'll take you."

"But only one."

"No, no. Lots of different ones."

"Wonderful. So do this: go to all the hotels you know and tell the manager..."

"They won't talk to an Okada. A poor guy like me, I can't afford a hotel. They know that."

"Tell them that your uncle is getting married and he's looking for a hotel for 120 people. Then they'll want to talk to you, because they know that the whole family will be at the wedding and the whole neighborhood will come to it."

"But my uncle is married."

"Tell them that you're looking for a hotel for a wedding and that's that. And that you need their telephone number to call and make a reservation. And then bring that number to me."

"But my uncle isn't getting married."

"For every number and address you bring and which I don't have in my database, I'll pay you 100 naira."

"Ahhh. That uncle of mine. Oh, yes, my uncle is getting married!"

By the end of the day, I had six new hotels in the database which cost me 600 naira, which back then was just under $5. The next day our entire team spent ordering every possible Okada to work for us in this way. Later, it wasn't necessary to order them. The news spread like wildfire. Within several weeks we had secured the data of 1,500 hotels in Lagos. Meaning as many as PricewaterhouseCoopers had said were in all of Nigeria. And we had paid $2,000 for this. By the way, rumors spread all over Lagos that there were going to be an awful lot of weddings in town.

We also worked in a similar way in other towns. But as they say, the faster you drive the fewer potholes you avoid. Actually, I don't know if that's what they say. That's what I say. Anyway, we were tricked both by the Okadas, who were meant to provide hotel contact details, and Jovago sales representatives who were able to create fictitious hotels complete with documentation and photographs in order to get the sales commission.

The first time I noticed something amiss was when I received a list of twenty hotels from a certain small town near Abuja. What caused me to wonder even more was that they were all located on the same street. What's more, their telephone numbers differed only by their last digit.

I called one up and said:

"Good morning. Is that the hotel?"

"Yes, yes, the hotel."

"Which hotel?"

"Which one are you asking about?" he asked back.

That's all I needed to know.

Checking out everything we had received took us a great deal of time. The biggest problem with securing these big and small hotels en masse turned out to be the catastrophic quality of the work of hotel managers and receptionists. Firstly, they weren't able to do very much, and secondly they practically couldn't do anything at all. Very often, the owner didn't even give them a computer, so that they wouldn't break it. In fact, their role turned out to be mainly picking up the phone and calling the boss.

Another delaying element was the ubiquitous waiting around for everyone. The less important must wait for the more important. This was especially annoying in the case of larger hotels. There the owner was frequently someone who had gained their property through hard work, or just corruption. Thus, the lord of the manor very much needed to show his superiority on occasion. It often happened to me that I arrived for a meeting and had to wait for an hour or two. And this was despite the owner having absolutely nothing to do. It was even worse in the case of owners linked with successive regimes. These were high-ranking military officers, ministers and other political figures. They could keep you waiting until you were a rotting corpse. Then when they graciously deigned to receive you, it was not a pleasant meeting, as such people were very negatively disposed to white people. This stemmed from the history of contact between those occupying the highest political and military spheres with Europeans.

I never got used to this, mainly because it greatly obstructed me in doing business. I couldn't arrange more than three meetings a day, as how could I be punctual when the time I was received and the time needed to get through the formalities did not depend on me at all. This of course changed once Jovago had become well known on the market.

The lust for money always wins out in the end.

Chapter 7

COPS AND ROBBERS

Imagine an enormous city of 20 million inhabitants. Throw into this an almost complete lack of public transport and the traffic jams that come with it. Colossal traffic jams.

Sometimes we sit in a traffic jam in central London or New York in air-conditioned cars or buses with our favorite music playing and moan as if an hour here or there would make any difference whatsoever. In Lagos, there are people who spend five hours commuting to work and another five coming home. And they work 10, sometimes 12 hours. Most of the sleep they have in their lives is found while traveling.

Public transport only exists to a very limited degree. Even though supposedly there is some kind of city transport company which organizes bus routes, the very few buses it has are overcrowded and in very poor condition. Even according to the very liberal Nigerian regulations concerning vehicle roadworthiness.

I've already mentioned the Okadas. Although there are lots of them, they can only move around within one district, maybe two. They are also prohibited from traveling on main roads. That's what the city authorities have decided. Allegedly, this is due to safety reasons, because the Okadas are crazy fuckers. They carry passengers without helmets and operate on the principle that the rules of the road are for suckers. You have to admit that they get you from A to B very quickly, which does involve a significant risk of the customer losing their life along the way. But the Okadas are fearless and really hard-working guys.

Of course, they display no understanding concerning the decision of the city authorities and break the ban on moving between districts as often as they can. Then, when the brave police spring into action, real problems may begin. In any case, if one morning the city turns out to be completely impassable, it usually means that the Okadas are holding another of their many protests. If they don't move, all of Lagos comes to a standstill.

Apart from the fearless motorcyclists, there are also the 'danfo'. I'm sure you know what a Volkswagen Transporter looks like. I'm not talking about the oldest model from the 1950s or the later hippy love bus version. I mean the third generation boxy one, which you used to see on the streets in the 1990s and the early 2000s. Maybe you or someone in your family had one. If so, I can guarantee you that today your VW Transporter is traveling the streets of Lagos. I suspect that such vehicles comprise at least half the freight brought here by container ship. Having being driven around Europe, they would never be in such a bad state as not to be able to go on for another 20 years in Lagos. There are tens of thousands of these cars here.

One day, I had a meeting arranged at a nearby hotel. It was about 10km away, which is a stone's throw in Lagos terms. And so I thought that I might go by danfo so as to get to know the local people better, understand those customers with whom I crossed paths daily, and put myself in their shoes.

And so I went to the bus stop.

"Excuse me, which number goes to Ikoyi?" I asked a waiting passenger. The poor guy probably had a speech impediment, because he just muttered something to himself, which sounded more or less like "dumb white guy". Or he surely had a headache, because he tapped his head several times.

Alright then, so imagine a long street on which 20 of the same yellow VW Transporters are parked. Of course, there is no such thing as a route number or even a sign with a destination on it. No, sir. Simply the driver stands in front of the bus and shouts where he intends to go, that he's cheap, that 'danfo good', that there's only a few seats left, and so on. Although hearing anything in this cacophony was borderline miraculous, eventually I managed to find one intending to go towards

Ikoyi. He had just pulled in, which I considered a stroke of luck. I was first and would be able to choose my seat.

The vehicle had about 5,000,000km on the clock. It wasn't especially old. Maybe 30 years of age. Although you could see rust here, there and everywhere, the driver managed it in a typically Nigerian way: he had just got used to it. The headlights were covered with metal grills. Perhaps that's why they were still in one piece when the rest of the car displayed the traces of a billion minor collisions. Vertically protruding spikes had been mounted on the rear bumper 'so that they don't travel without a ticket' explained the driver, who was clearly a witchdoctor in his spare time, as he was able to read my thoughts.

I peered inside and understood that Nigerians love to tune down their vehicle's interior. Everything had been gutted. Instead of the original seats, five transverse wooden benches had been crammed inside. But the front row right behind the driver constituted something like first class, with luxury guaranteed by two chairs screwed to the floor. You know, two normal kitchen chairs. Unusual perhaps, but at least they had back support. When I sat myself down on one of them, the driver chuckled, no doubt thinking of the fortune I would have to pay for the privilege. This came to around 50 cents. Every danfo driver has to have a license and pay taxes in the normal way. So one could consider him to be honest. Insofar as one stems from the other.

Then the rest of my traveling companions started to enter the vehicle. Each one in turn was more and more surprised at the presence of a sweaty European on the bus. That day, I discovered that a normal VW Transporter can even carry 30 people. Because when we pulled away, there was 29 of us, including the driver. And even though I was initially perturbed by what was going on during loading – because sometimes you have to call a spade a spade: we were more like goods than passengers in this vehicle – I later acknowledged that another person could have easily travelled in the driver's lap.

I somehow survived the entire journey. Fortunately, I was sitting by the window and, even more fortunately, the window could be opened. Otherwise, I would have been boiled, steamed or fried to death. I returned to the office with my own driver. I considered my experiment with mass public transport as having been completed at this stage. Not so that I would discover anything about people, but that I recognized that I had started with too extreme a method. Being driven around everywhere has its advantages. You can try to work in the back seat, as long as the road has more smooth sections than potholes. During the first few months, however, I was overcome by an infinite longing to get behind the wheel, every now and again.

"It's not a good idea," Bertha said as usual.

And I, of course, put up resistance. As no one recognizes a Polish driving license, I therefore found out how to get a Nigerian one.

One of the boys on the team had a cousin who was the brother of the sister of someone who was a sub-contractor for someone working in the Department of Transport. He proposed a very simple and efficient solution. Officially, I didn't have to get a new license, just extend the old one as it had expired. Well, here a certain problem appeared. In order to apply for a new one, you had to have a scan of the old one.

"No problem, I'll sort it out," said my new assistant.

When she returned, I nearly fell off the chair. I held in my hand the scan of the driving license of a total stranger on which my photo had been stuck on over his, I assume using a program like Paint. And in the place where before the guy's name had been written in pen, there was now a white box in which my data had been entered in Times New Roman.

"For God's sake, even the greatest cretin would notice that!" I shouted.

"He won't notice," this guy retorted, "In fact, for this purpose you also have 4,000 naira. There are four civil service administrators. They are people who are poor and ill. One is blind, another has short term memory loss and forgets to check the paperwork, yet another is obsessively nervous and writes certain things into the computer faster than you think. Their assistant has asked me for 20,000 naira for 'operational costs'".

And although that is how I got my own license the following day, I still had to wait. 10 hours in a Nigerian transport office is a bit like 10 years in a Polish one.

Armed with an brand new and totally legal document, I set off into battle in Lagos.

On YouTube you can watch a film from a junction at Meskel Square in Addis Ababa. In Lagos, it was more or less the same, but twice as congested. Although my first journey as a driver lasted an hour, I aged a year during it. I got honked by absolutely every car passing me.

"I'm in my own lane, for Christ's sake!" I screamed at one of them, not being able to take it anymore. "You're the one barging in, while overtaking four cars overtaking each other!"

In Lagos, driving lanes are only, well… a sort of suggestion. The drivers see them and may use them. But usually they don't. After many months in Nigeria, I can even say that that it isn't actually that stupid. The greater the congestion, the closer the cars drive to each other and five lanes are created from three. Thanks to this, more cars move forward per minute… until they completely block the next junction. But this style of driving is by no means the result of being an asshole. Rather it's due to a desire to live. If drivers in Lagos didn't drive like this, they would starve to death, as the commute home would take at least three weeks.

Another one of these drivers who was pushing in from the right, drew right up beside me and bared his teeth in my direction. Following this, he folded back his wing mirror, then mine, waved goodbye and I was left with the folded-back wing mirror. I wanted to stop to adjust it, but immediately the horns of dozens of cars sounded. Everyone honks their horn here. Constantly. When sometimes I go for a drink with my buddies, we joke that car producers in Africa should fit several kinds of horns. If you wish to overtake, you press horn No. 1. If you'd like to barge into a lane, horn No. 2. If you want you to tell someone that you're tailgating, so they should graciously slip out of the middle lane, No. 3. And if you simply desire to tell someone politely to get the fuck out of the way, No. 4. As they say everything with the aid of the one and the same horn, you haven't a chance in hell of understanding what the fuck is going on.

It's the same with full headlights. At night, you just drive around with them on all the time. So you can see all the better all the time. Simple. So the guy coming from the opposite direction can't see anything? Let them go and see an ophthalmologist.

They also use their full headlights during the day, alternately with the horn. Often Poles flash on motorways when they believe that an Opel traveling at 180kph is going too slow and should move out of the way. In Lagos, this is normal practice. In fact, it's very funny. Nigerians can be very slow. You have to wait ages for everything. Nobody's ever in a hurry. "I'm coming, I'm coming" only means "I intend to come to you soon. And I'll probably do so". And he'll arrive in three hours. Time itself has several varieties, namely: although 'the present time' refers to something which should be happening now, don't confuse it what should be happening 'right now'.

'Right now' means very urgent with a greater probability of it happening. But with no guarantee.

'Now' means 'soon, perhaps'. It's the opposite of what we consider to be now. If someone tells you that they'll do something 'now', it means that maybe they'll do it later, but definitely not now. Basically, this is almost not now at all, perhaps…

'Now, now', meaning a kind of 'soon'. If someone uses 'now, now' in a conversation they are certainly thinking of something that will happen shortly, in a moment, very likely before long, and maybe even soon. Certainly 'now, now' should happen quicker than 'now', but it's still unclear whether it will happen at all.

Then we come to 'just now', or 'later'. If someone says they are doing something 'just now', it means that they'll do it in the not-too-distant, very near future. Which will happen shortly, soon, before long, presently, when it happens…

But when Nigerians get into a car, each one of them turns into Michael Schumacher. The logic behind drivers' behavior is fairly complex. Once, I was returning home, drove into a closed residential district and had about 800 meters to go. And here from the opposite direction a guy was flying along about to cut me off. He was driving against the traffic and flashing his lights. We had stopped almost bumper to bumper, when I see the guy jump out of his car, shouting: "Didn't you see that I was flashing you?!!"

So the guy had given himself right of way. He considered that since he had flashed, this meant that he could drive on, while I should have reversed 500 meters. Oh no, my friend. It's not going to be like that. And I had to frighten him a bit, because I already knew that in Nigeria such conflicts are won by he who scares his opponent the most. And the arguments were on my side. Because apart from a fine for driving against the traffic, he would also get a compulsory psychiatric assessment. I also had to get his attention and hint that I had a lot of money and could pay a doctor to establish a diagnosis, have the poor unfortunate put into a straitjacket, have him placed into a cell and throw away the key.

It worked. I won.

In wishing to be in accordance with my duties as a reporter, I must mention here that once I did manage to take a wrong turn. It happened as I was in a hurry and just missed my turn. I had the choice of driving 200 meters against the traffic or making a two-kilometer detour. You know the choice you would have made in such a situation. I drove against the traffic. It was night time, not a living soul to be seen. What could go wrong?

Only that just as I entered the street, two policemen jumped out from behind a proverbial bush. And 'Stop!'. I pulled up. They came over. When they saw a white man behind the wheel, their faces broke into smiles so wide that night turned to day. It was then for the first time that I saw with my own eyes what drivers' experience of the police was. And it looked as if I would have to hand over 1,000 naira. Meaning it always starts from 20,000. But later, depending on one's negotiating skills and self-confidence, it would end up at a thousand. The whole 'transaction' could last five seconds or go on for an hour. And just to be clear, I'm not talking about a fine at all.

"Of course, of course. You could have made a mistake. Of course. We don't want to punish you with a fine. But you have torn us away from our duties. We could have been earn… supervising traffic somewhere else. Yadda, yadda, yadda."

As I didn't have any cash, we drove to an ATM. I handed over the money, making out at the same time that I was very sorry. But really my blood was boiling.

"Are they always like this with you?" I asked as I was leaving.

"What's like this?"

"These bribes?"

"What? You gave a bribe? That's against the law. I have to arrest you."

"But maybe you didn't take it."

"Of course I didn't take it. It was just a normal transaction."

"Oh yeah? And what did I supposedly get for a thousand naira?"

"This," he retorted unhesitatingly, taking the Nigerian highway code from his breast pocket. He smiled, saluted and left.

But at that time I hadn't yet figured out just how widespread the procedure of milking saps for cash was. Had I known, I would have certainly not decided to do what I'm about to tell you.

One Saturday, I was driving home about 4 am. You must realize that is the most dangerous time to be out, as everyone is returning from parties at which they got drunk or high. And I only had a few streets to go. In front of me there was an old Toyota. Swaying from side to side. The driver had absolutely no control over the direction he was traveling in. I wanted to overtake him, but it just couldn't be done. The guy was unpredictable. I drove behind him for about a kilometer, until eventually I saw a police car in a roadside car park. Which didn't deign to show any interest in the drunk driver. So I pulled off the road, parked near the police car and got out. I walked towards it and saw that the police officer was laughing his ass off. Although this should have alarmed me, my self-preservation instinct was obviously on vacation. The cop rolled down the window. I pointed my finger at the departing drunk.

"Did you see that?" I asked.

"I saw it, I saw it. Saw that you didn't have your seatbelt fastened."

A thousand naira.

The real rollercoaster ride occurs when you come to a roundabout. There are three types of these junctions. The first is the type where right of way is held by those on the roundabout, the second by those entering, while the third is typically Nigerian namely: first come, first served. Sometimes an exception to the rule appears: if you are traveling in a huge SUV and others aren't, you always have right of way.

One of the most characteristic phenomena on the streets of Lagos are street sellers. You're standing in traffic when several youngsters run up to you with stuff to sell. They've got anything you want. Snacks and drinks are par for the course. But once I personally saw one little shyster trying to palm off a kitchen sink onto a danfo driver. As normal, through the window. Once the transaction was complete, the sink was taken into the van, with one passenger surely having had to hold on their lap for the entire journey.

I availed of their services once. I was dying of thirst. The air-conditioning had broken down and Lagos in summer can boil you alive. I pay about 50 naira. I open the bottle and drink all of it at once. Oh, that hit the spot! I move towards the junction and see a policeman who orders me to stop.

"Why were you stopped at a green light?" he asked.

"Maybe for two seconds. I was drinking water."

"Maybe for two seconds. But it's not allowed."

A thousand naira.

Equally fascinating is the question of parking in the city. There are very few car parks. People leave their cars on the street, often completely unperturbed that they're blocking all of the traffic. The following situation is standard: you're traveling on a three-lane road and suddenly, out of the blue, a gigantic traffic jam appears in front of you. You spend a hour in it until the mystery is solved. In front of a shopping center, parked cars are standing on two of the three lanes. Simply that. I mean they have to do their shopping, right?

When you drive around the city, you can see that the infrastructure of Lagos was once magnificent. The basic structure of the city was built during the 1960s and 1970s, when there was oil and prosperity, and 10 times fewer people.

Once, I was driving along, for want of a better word, a dual carriageway. It was already dark. I was tired, having spent all day behind the wheel. I was close to home. There would be nothing to do, but hop into bed and go to sleep.

Suddenly, I see an enormous hole in front of me. Later my colleagues told me that there had been local flooding, which had simply washed away part of the road. I turned the wheel rapidly, the car swerved and by some miracle I avoided the trap. As I had lost control of the car for a moment, I had to pull over. And then the darkness was lit up by the roof lights of police car standing nearby. Two police officers slowly got out of the car.

"Why did you change lanes without using your indicator?"

"For God's sake, maybe you can see there's a hole in the road."

"Is that a reason not to turn on your indicator?"

"And shouldn't you do something about the hole instead of standing here and waiting for suckers to pass?"

"And do what?" they said, put out. "Do we look like road workers?"

I know what you're thinking – a thousand naira. Oh, no. Not this time, not after such a rush of adrenaline which went to my head. I jumped out of the car and yelled into their faces. I had almost been killed for Christ's sake, because those sons-of-bitches, instead of making the hole in the road safe, preferred to lay in wait for someone they could tap for a bribe. I spun such bullshit at them that, even today, I don't know how I thought it up. Including that I was the fiancé of the daughter of the current president's brother-in-law (the color of my skin was somehow not enough to consider me a liar), that I knew the chief of police, that they wouldn't get a red cent out of me, but I would pay their boss 10 times what they wanted to have them fired and thrown in jail.

I don't know what worked. Maybe my bullshit talk, or maybe they just understood that they weren't going to get a penny out of me that evening. I had had enough. Although I had heard a lot about crime in Africa, here in Lagos the only thieves I came across up to then were the police. A thousand naira isn't really very much money. Something around $3. I often preferred to pay it rather than wrangle with the cops. They know full well that the naira is Mickey Mouse money. And that the really valuable currency for a white expat is his time. That's why when they secure a victim, they torment him for two, three or four hours. And they are most happy to bring him down to the police station, as they know that the longer they keep him, the greater the chances of having their palms greased.

My experience with road traffic cops shows that they have neither any real power nor are held in any regard by the Nigerian people. Especially the local police and traffic cops. They actually can't do anything to you. They don't carry firearms, at the most they have a truncheon, but are afraid to use them on white men (as they are certainly the managers of large corporations) or the drivers of luxury SUVs (as they are certainly members of the president's family). Serious consequences would be threatened. A police officer orders a driver to pull over who then simply lays into him. And what does the police officer do? In Poland, he would call headquarters for support, then a car chase, a helicopter, stingers and live broadcasts on YouTube and 24-hour news stations. And then a good beating in a dark corner of the police station and a few years in the slammer. And here? Nothing. Policemen on foot often don't even have a radio to call for support. Even if they had, they wouldn't do it. After all they would never admit to their colleagues that they had received a total dressing down.

Now knowing everything, I noticed ever more desperate attempts by the police in order to effectively carry out their duties, while simultaneously thinking up new ways to play around with them. Usually, when I saw a policeman on foot waving me down, I slowed down as if to stop. I switched on the interior light in the car, because that's what you do in Nigeria before an inspection. Then the cop can see how many people are in the car. When the police officer noticed my white face, he usually smiled from ear to ear as he could smell his thousand naira in the air. Once he had moved slightly to one side to be standing by the door, I floored it. I had managed to catch them out several times in this way until I slipped up. Because once, there were two of them standing 100 meters apart. I had just made a jackass of the first when second jumped right in front of the hood. I had to pretend that I was stupid, saying that I didn't know their intentions: "Well, gentlemen, I didn't know you would stop me, I thought you only wanted to check that I wasn't a terrorist. Sure I switched on the light, so I'll cooperate, yadda, yadda, yadda, I'm very sorry, yadda, yadda, yadda."

A thousand naira. For each of them.

But the cops quickly adapted to the governing circumstances in the city. It twice happened to me that, having pulled me over, they started letting the air out of my tires. Just to prevent me from racing off. Besides that, they repeatedly tried to get into the car. The first five minutes of the conversation concerned me opening the passenger door for them. I would never agree to it. If they got in, they could do what they wanted. As long as they're standing outside, I'm in control of the situation. However, in regard to everything which I have cited, one has to add two 'buts'.

Firstly, you have to smell the cop as very often – and almost permanently at night – they work trashed. If they have been drinking, that's half the trouble. But sometimes they are so high on drugs that they could black out during the inspection. You need to be very careful with such cops. If he's on foot, it's best to escape right away. But if you have a suspicion that he's carrying a firearm, you should never do this under any pretext, as they will start shooting immediately.

Secondly, in Nigeria there exists a unit called MOPOL, meaning the Nigerian Mobile Police. And it's better that you don't cross paths with these sons-of-bitches. They wear black uniforms and are armed. And not with regular handguns either. A regular automatic pistol can kill one person a second. A toy for geeks. MOPOL officers carry machine guns and by no means just to look tough. Actually there is no fear of them stopping you on the street. But if they do, stop and do everything they demand of you. There is no fooling around with such people. They are gods, and gods are characterized by vanity and arrogance. If even for a moment a police officer in a black uniform (meaning a person who will alone decide whether you live or die) feels that you are not showing him appropriate respect, you're going to have problems. The best you can expect is a severe beating and many hours in a cell. It's no accident that Nigerians refer to them as 'Kill-and-Go'. Once I saw with my own eyes what these motherfuckers are capable of. I was driving through the city, this time fortunately with a driver, when three Igirigi armored personnel carriers were driving behind us. We were stopped in a traffic jam, when suddenly out of nowhere masked people appeared who started stoning the APCs. There was pandemonium. The private cars around us started to escape, driving through market stalls and forcing their way through the sidewalks. My driver was alert and had started to do the same. But MOPOL meant business. It's officers jumped down from the APCs and sprayed the whole neighborhood with Kalashnikov rounds. In saying 'Kalashnikov', I mean exactly that and not some imitation weapon. The Mobile Police have tens of thousands of them in stock. They probably still come from 'the old days'. So I felt as if I was in war zone. I only later discovered that the squadron had gone to a local market to capture the leader of a criminal gang, and as this gang did not very much want to hand him over, they organized an ambush.

In Lagos, there exists a certain practice of attaching yourself to police convoys. Such convoys usually escort various government bigwigs or businessmen. In Poland, it sometimes happens that drivers take advantage of the situation. I recall when a Polish Member of Parliament drove so closely to police car racing along with its sirens on, that the cops inside thought that someone wanted to help the suspect they had in custody escape. However, in Nigeria this is commonplace. A limousine and three MOPOL police cars force their way through the city and 10 minutes later the convoy comprises 20 cars. And sometimes it happens that the police shoot one of the drivers in pursuit, considering him to be a terrorist, or pretending they considered him to be one.

There is also the question of roof lights. In Poland, although you may purchase police roof lights in shops, if you use them there will be serious problems. But not in Nigeria. You can buy them anywhere and anyone who has enough money can use them. This is such a far gone social ill, that many drivers simply ignore roof lights. This is why when a really important person is driving through the city, police officers jump out of their cars and shout at drivers that they have to pull off the road or get shot. The problem here is that there isn't always anywhere to go, as in many parts of the city high curbs have been installed so that drivers don't drive into restricted areas, which usually means that it is simply impossible to move. Something which the police cannot understand. And later in the newspaper one can read that the police shot a driver believing him to be a threat to a VIP.

There are really a lot of such articles in newspapers and on portals here. Fortunately, this will surely change soon. Every such incident arouses enormous commotion. And now everyone has smartphone with still and video cameras. Lots of material is appearing on the internet. If MOPOL doesn't clean up its act soon, it will face enormous riots. So big that they won't cope without help from the army. And the army supports it unwillingly.

To cut a long story short, I lost my desire to drive in Lagos fairly quickly, a decision which was finally confirmed by events the following day, when I attempted to go to one of the hotels in the port district of Apapa with the aid of Google Maps. My sat-nav brought me to the middle of nowhere, where, at a certain moment while making a u-turn in a cul-de-sac which I had entered, I was surrounded by several men with sticks who started to beat the car, hoping that I wouldn't move and would give them what they wanted. Instinctively, I pressed the accelerator and would have driven over a guy, but luckily he moved. It was not until I was at a safe distance that I was hit by a stream of hot adrenalin rushing through me and my heart started to beat like crazy. Suddenly, I missed my old buddies the cops, who were at least fairly cheap and predictable.

Once I had arrived home, I rang my driver and told him that he was back in the game. And I put information up on Twitter not to use Google Maps if you're going to Apapa. 5000 Nigerians retweeted it and burst their asses laughing.

Subsequently, I drove very rarely. Only at the weekends when my driver was off.

Having your own driver is a comfort, as long as he knows the city and is able to use maps. Which was never certain. Anyway, my adventures with my driving assistant began when brought me to work along some weird road. Once, twice, three times. Finally, I couldn't contain myself and asked him why he was driving around in circles. He replied that it was the only route he knew. The ability among drivers to read maps is, you could say... poor. As a result, this two kilometer journey took us 45 minutes. Just to make it clear: my driver wasn't trying to pull the wool over my eyes. He had no reason to, as I was paying him a daily rate. The quicker he brought me from A to B, the longer he could nap while waiting for me.

I must admit that my life calmed down a lot once I had decided to travel in the back seat. Even though several unpleasant situations later occurred.

One of these happened literally a few weeks after I had set things right with my driver. We had an old Honda Accord. We were going to a meeting in a hotel, were pressed for time and had a really long distance to cover. My driver drove onto a dual carriageway. I should explain that in Lagos if a Nigerian suddenly needs to take a piss, they believe – rightly or wrongly – that it's better to stop on the slip road leading on to the dual carriageway rather on the road itself. And that's exactly what we stumbled across. We had to stop. My driver used a few choice words as even he understood that his fellow countryman had behaved badly. And then we heard some weird sounds followed by a mighty collision. They laptop which I was holding on my lap flew forwards between the seats and broke the windshield. Glass flew everywhere. The shock lasted several seconds, after which I turned around and saw that our car no longer had a trunk and lying within arm's reach was the radiator torn from a huge truck.

People ran towards us. But mainly to gawk. Here, very few help the victims of accidents. Mainly due to the fear of being blamed for the whole thing. And a culprit must be found, after all.

We jump out. An old Mack truck, certainly at least 30 years old, had cut through our car like a hot knife through butter.

"Call for another car," my driver shouted to me.

"What? We've had an accident, for God's sake."

"Exactly. Soon the police will be here. There are going to be problems. Then it will turn out that it's all your fault, because you're white and can afford to pay for it."

I listened to him. I called my assistant at Jovago and he sent me another car in which I went on to the hotel located barely a kilometer from the accident. I had no time to think. I just went straight to meeting. I signed a contract on very beneficial terms, chatted about nothing and had early supper with the owner. It was only when I returned home that the memory of the event returned and I began to shake. An enormous truck inches from my back. Fortunately, it had very high suspension. It was only thanks to this that it our trunk wasn't shunted forward and I wasn't squashed to a pulp. Of course, we never got the money back for our written-off car. The driver of the truck was drunk while his vehicle had faulty brakes. He was thrown in the slammer and will stay there until he pays us compensation. And if he doesn't pay, he'll spend a long time there yet.

The next day, I made a decision to buy an SUV. And not just any kind. In Nigeria, you see loads of SUVs driving around. New and old. Swanky ones and ruins-on-wheels. Here, the Toyota RAV4 is a laughing stock. Something like the Kia Picanto in Europe. On the other hand, G-class vehicles are only driven by those who have enough money to do so. So I decided to take the largest one I could get my hands on. My choice fell on the Toyota Sequoia. Why? Because it is the largest in the Toyota series and a reliable vehicle which can be repaired by any street mechanic should it break down. And in Africa this could save your life. Additionally, we fitted bull bars both front and rear, which would basically transfer the crumple zone to anything that had the audacity to square up to us.

Another time, my driver took his eye off the ball while coming out of a car park and dented someone's Mercedes. It wasn't really anything, just a small scratch. Out of the car jumped a woman who was apparently a well-known lawyer in Lagos, and who suddenly started shouting at me. That I was a piece of shit because she earns more in an hour than I earn in a month, that she would never pay for the repairs, that she would get me and so on. It was not until she noticed that I was recording her that she relented somewhat. And I put the recording up on the net, because I found it hilarious that she was bawling her head off as if we had devoured her mother at the very least.

But that was nothing. I got out and politely told her to relax, that our car was insured, that here were all the documents, that we would sign them and then she could inform our insurer about the matter and they would refund the cost of the repairs. To which she replied no, that we would have to pay right now. To which I replied, no way as I'm not paying a lot of money for insurance so as to have to lose more money in such situations. To which she replied by calling the police. Her own police, who were no doubt in receipt of generous and regular payment, as they arrived with a ready-cooked version of events.

I didn't have time for this bullshit. As I was not the culprit, but my driver, the police had no right to detain me. So I left him there and went off to do my own work. He was a clever guy, knew the reality of the situation and I believed that he would manage.

Which was a mistake. The police confiscated my car, hauled it off to their impoundment lot and then let the air out of the tires, as they later stated 'to ensure that all damage was covered.' I later had to go to the police station at night, pay the lawyer whatever she wanted and then ask them to pump air back into my tires. And of course 'parking fees', which by no means came to a thousand naira.

Only once did a really dangerous situation occur with a loaded Kalashnikov being pointed at my head, one which involved the Nigerian State Security Service (SSS), meaning their kind of local FBI. I was traveling with a driver from Lagos to a conference in Ibadan, a city located several hours drive away. The entire journey was one of incredible misfortune. It began with a 'routine inspection' by customs officers, who were standing on the motorway looking for vehicles illegally imported into Nigeria. And it somehow happened that when the officers saw me on the back seat, they very quickly made contact with headquarters and established that my Toyota Sequoia had, for customs purposes, been brought into Nigeria as a … boat. My car would now of course be confiscated and I would be brought to the police station to provide an explanation.

I knew perfectly well that if the car was going to be taken, I would never get it back. And getting myself out of the police station wasn't going to be cheap or quick either. However, I strongly maintained that this was a misunderstanding. One of the guards got into our car and so we made our way to their miserable headquarters located 45 minutes drive away. The rest of the merry band of customs officers and policemen (10 in total) hopped into the back of their pickup and drove behind us. As I expected, my unwanted passenger suggested that if I scratched his back (and those of his friends), he would scratch mine. 20 minutes later, we had finished up at 200,000 naira. Now it was only necessary to find a working ATM. After half an hour, I waved my new buddies goodbye.

Everything was just wonderful, but I was already an hour late for my talk. I ordered my driver to fly through the city as fast as he could. However, Yemi (my trusted driver and sometimes bodyguard) didn't know Ibadan too well and, because of the rush, went through a gate he shouldn't have. The conference was taking place in a conference hall in the city museum in Ibadan but, as luck would have it, this was right next to the headquarters of... the Nigerian FBI, whose car park we had driven into with our tires squealing. This scared the guards out of their slumber who jumped up as if on fire. And these gentlemen weren't as lenient towards white men as others in Lagos as, firstly, this wasn't Lagos and, secondly, these were just normal officers, but undercover agents. And I was about to painfully find this out.

I ordered Yemi to ignore these screaming motherfuckers and quickly reverse. Yemi hadn't yet managed to put the car into reverse gear when shots rang out and we were forcibly dragged out of the car, thrown onto the ground and placed in handcuffs. I could forget about the conference. It took us two hours to explain that it was all one big misunderstanding, that we had mixed up the gates, and that I wasn't a spy who wanted to take over their headquarters. Here we were helped out by the conference organizer, who had found out about the commotion in the neighboring building and came to get us out. He threw out the names of some people involved in the conference and we were released. It also pays to have connections in Nigeria.

And that's how my life in Nigeria rolled along.

I had travelled thousands of kilometers there, either on my own or with a driver. And I thought I had seen it all when it came to the cops' shenanigans, but they managed to surprise me every time with their creativity in screwing people out of money.

A few weeks later, after returning to Lagos, I heard shots ring out while I was working. Uncomfortably close shots. I peered carefully through the window and saw between 10 and 20 policemen armed with Kalashnikovs. They were running around the streets and shouting at a group of men who hadn't even attempted to escape.

I was scared, but, what do you know, I was the only one who paid any attention to the entire situation. The guys in the office just went on working, as if nothing had happened.

"Hey!" I shouted, "They're shooting."

"It's the last Friday of the month," replied one of the boys, not looking up from his laptop.

"Those guys down there are drug dealers. The junction below our office is their haunt. On every last Friday of the month, the police come and put on a little show. They shoot a bit, shout a bit and then the dealers give them their share and it's all over."

"How's that?"

"A police officer is just a man, Marek. And he also likes partying at the weekend. But he doesn't get paid until next week.'"

Chapter 8

VIP PASS

Within several months of launching the site, the booking results in Nigeria were good enough that we could think about opening offices in other countries. At same time, we had to regularly visit the hotels which were bringing in the biggest earnings, namely those in Abuja, Port Harcourt, Jos, Ilorin and Kano, the biggest cities in Nigeria apart from Lagos. The only option was air travel, because of the lack of rail connections and the dangerous and, above all, long journeys by car.

Then the moment came when I was forced to put my life at risk. Meaning using African airlines. Although it was true that Arik Air, by which I was supposed to fly to Accra in Ghana, wasn't on the European Union's blacklist, I was still afraid. Especially in Nigeria, which had just suffered a commercial airline disaster, when Dana Air Flight 992 crashed into a Lagos neighborhood while attempting an emergency landing shortly after take-off. My imagination pictured a patched-up, 40 year-old Boeing or Airbus with stained seats and doors that wouldn't close.

Eventually, I packed my bag and told my driver to take me to Murtala Muhammed International Airport, as Lagos airport is called. Since it wasn't my first time in Lagos, the journey there was slightly shorter than usual, a mere two and a half hours. In fact, there was a joke doing the rounds in Lagos that if someone dropped you off at the airport, you would be checking in at a hotel in Accra before they got home.

We got there in the end. My driver was so happy that he was getting three days off… while I was standing in a 30 meter line.

Even though I wasn't sure what the cause of the line was, I supposed it was surely due to safety reasons, because, as everyone knows, safety is all important. At a certain moment, I was approached by chap with an absolutely illegible badge who asked "VIP pass? Fast track?"

"No," I replied, because I didn't have any such pass. Of course, the guy wanted to 'help' me, a fact which, unfortunately, I didn't get at the time.

From what I could see, Lagos has one of the worst organized airports in the world. I dare to say that it's like this, because you simply have to cough up money for everything. The more problems you have at an airport, the greater the chance that you'll just lose patience and want to slip someone a few bucks to save yourself the trouble. And there are hundreds such people at this airport, just waiting have their palms greased.

Anyway, I was still standing in line, at the only entrance to the airport through which a river of new passengers was ceaselessly flowing to all the international departures from Nigeria. And all of them have truckloads of bags, there being just two baggage conveyor belts, only one of which is working, as its operator went to the john two weeks ago and hasn't come back yet.

I waited 40 minutes. Mainly because every minute I was being overtaken by sly bastards being led by other sly bastards with illegible white badges.

"Out of the way. VIP pass. Fast track!", a sly bastard with a badge grinned at me, leading his flock to the entrance. And there I was, standing with my mouth open, soaking with sweat and mad as hell.

When eventually I got inside, I immediately recalled that the airport didn't have air-conditioning. Meaning that it wasn't working right at that moment. Which, by the way, is the standard answer to the question as to why there is no Wi-Fi in Lagos hotels. I mean it's there, but just not working. Meanwhile, the next line awaited me. This time it was check-in, which you can't do online in Lagos. This isn't due to it being technically impossible. It simply pays more to piss passengers off.

I was there so long, that I thought I was about to set down roots into the ground, while more people were constantly passing down a special 'corridor' beside me, marked with two posts and a rope. Despite me being certain that they had appeared at the airport long after I had – VIP pass. Fast track.

Before I had even got to the check-in desk, two uniformed officers appeared in front of me.

"Please open your bag," one of them said.

"What?," I replied amazed, "Here? In the middle of the departures hall? I have a million things in there for God's sake."

"We'll check to see that you are not taking any contraband out of Nigeria."

I gritted my teeth and opened it up. The guard put his hand in, but didn't make the slightest move.

"Maybe you have something for me?" he asked quietly with a cheeky grin.

"I've said a prayer for you," I said, giving the standard answer, letting him understand that I had spent some time living in Nigeria and wasn't a complete sucker.

The guard grimaced. He put his hands into the clothes, felt around and closed the case.

"You're a bit of a joker," he said in the end, smilingly sarcastically. "I suggest the next time you buy a VIP pass," and went off to harass the next traveller without one.

When my turn eventually came, a nice lady printed out my boarding card, took my case, attached a professional-looking sticker to it with a bar code, put it on a huge, super-modern conveyor belt after which… she made that kissing sound as loud as only they can do in Nigeria. At which a young guy came running up, grabbed my case and carried it off to the baggage room. The conveyor belt was just like the hotel Wi-Fi. It's there, but not working right now.

Finally, I checked-in. Now there was only the security inspection and…

Yeah, right.

Yet another charming man whom I met that morning was 'a gentleman from the immigration department'. I say 'a gentleman from the department', because he wasn't the real immigration officer. That guy was awaiting me. Meanwhile, however, I had to fill in a departure card. You had to put down your full name, date of arrival, date of departure, passport number and a few other things. Once it was filled in, 'the gentleman from the immigration department' took the document and gave me a receipt in exchange. And that's it. So no-one reads the form you have spent several minutes filling in sweating like a pig (because of no air conditioning). I didn't know about it then and now have run all out of ideas what to write. I've been James Bond, Antonio Banderas, Conchita Wurst, once even I granted myself the liberty of being former Nigerian president, Goodluck Jonathan.

People's love of bureaucracy is an amazing thing. Because you have total power over some area, regardless how small it is, and feel special. Plus you have an opportunity to make a few bucks on the side. One of my friends once went on a trip to Cross River National Park. As he was dying for a piss, he hopped out of his jeep. Suddenly, a battered old 4x4 pulls up and a guy with a badge jumps out, claiming to be a guard. Pissing is forbidden... And you have to pay a fine.

"Sir," my friend says, "but leopards, chimps and elephants all piss here."

"An elephant may. But not you."

And that's how it is. It's not about the fine itself. Sometimes, it's not even about a bribe. It's only about being someone important in that particular place, even if just for a moment.

But let's get back to the airport, where I had been stuck for two hours. After the document stage, there was a normal, totally un-exotic security check, which mainly differed from a European security check in that it didn't work. Only three of the eight conveyor belt luggage security scanners were staffed. Which, of course, meant that I had to wait my turn once again. At the same time, there were five lines of people. So it was necessary to have another airport employee who, through waving his arms around and shouting, decided just which line could approach the security scanner. Of course, priority was given to passengers accompanied by the gentlemen with illegible white badges. It wasn't until you actually got to the conveyor belt that you could throw your things onto it, as only one person at a time could approach the scanner. In this way, everything was drawn out even more by the time it took to put things on the conveyor belt and then take off them off. Because, of course, there was no way anyone could have got themselves ready for this beforehand.

I met more assholes with a VIP pass just a few meters further on. Where the real immigration officer was waiting. He checked everything. Your passport, visa and vaccination certificate. As if I was entering Nigeria, not leaving it.

"Are you taking any carvings out of the country?" the customs officer asked. I didn't really know what to say.

"What kind of carvings do you mean?"

"Wooden carvings."

So I'm standing in front of him with a small item of hand luggage after three baggage checks and he's asking me if I'm talking any carvings out of the country.

25 minutes later, I'm standing in front of him once again. I didn't know that I couldn't take more than $10,000 when crossing the border. But I was going to Accra on business for God's sake. And as I expected certain costs, I had twice that amount on me. I was stupid to admit to the whole amount, but was afraid of being caught out by a thorough search. Which now gave rise to a clear problem. What the fuck was I supposed to do with the 10 'big ones' I wasn't supposed to have? Although I knew that the immigration officer would gladly 'keep' it for me, that wasn't the issue. There was no bank at the airport, I was running out of time for my flight and doubted whether anyone would manage to come and collect the money beforehand.

My attempts to negotiate didn't work on this occasion. I had way too little time until my flight and even less patience for such a conversation. So I did the only thing I had left up my sleeve. I rang a certain friend. She is the consul of a certain small, very wealthy European country, which both sends many important people to Nigeria and receives many important guests from this country. And she would know what the fuck was going on with this fucking VIP pass. And I was right. She knew. A lot. So much that I quickly decided to buy one, once she had put me in contact with the right person.

This was the best investment I had made since moving to Nigeria. The 'right person' in question was a guy called Freddie, a guy who stood out from the crowd. He wore a slightly extravagant, but good quality and tastefully tailored outfit. A blue blazer, red trousers, a pretty good imitation Rolex on his wrist, as well as manicured nails, all accompanied by a perfect British accent. And if you have studied in the UK, you evidently have wealthy parents. So you yourself must be rich. And if you are rich, no-one will give you any trouble. You can always frighten a white expat with the threat of revoking his visa. But no-one can take your passport.

In addition, Freddie had the best price in the whole airport. The best, meaning the highest. 10 times more than what the those jackasses with the badges were charging. My intuition told me that here Freddie was in a league of his own.

"What's the problem, Marek?" he asked, without the formalities.

"I have too much cash on me."

"Who told you that?"

"The customs officer."

"I'm sure he was joking. He's known as a real joker."

Together we went to the customs officer. It was a bit like running to complain to your older brother and coming back to face the neighborhood bully with him.

"Hi Josh," Freddie said, "How're you doing?"

"Hi Freddie," the officer replied, "'I'm doing great."

"My friend Marek here told me a really great joke. Supposedly you didn't want to let him through because he had too much money on him," that's to say, he burst out laughing and did it in such a natural way that Nicolas Cage should take acting classes from him. The customs officer also laughed along.

"Okay, okay," Freddie went on, "but we need to be serious now, because Marek is in a hurry."

"Of course. You said you have how much money?"

"Twent...," I didn't manage to finish, as suddenly I ran out of breath. That's how I usually react when someone elbows me in the ribs.

"A thousand dollars," Freddie said helpfully.

"Oh, that's fine."

And that's how I passed through customs. I got the impression then that, with Freddie's help, I could have taken out of Nigeria not only a carving, but a live elephant, tusks and all. I would have led it through on a leash. Freddie would have said it's just an overgrown bulldog and everything would have been alright.

Just as a side note, I later found out that if you're a white expat, the customs officers check to see that you're not taking out too much money. But if you're an average black traveller, they check to see if you're taking out too little. Because they're afraid you're fleeing the country. Once, I sent one of my employees for a training session which was taking place in Gdansk. I didn't give her any money as her flight, accommodation and meals were all paid for, plus she had a minder in Gdansk who had Polish zlotys for her. I was sitting in some meeting and she rings crying to say that they didn't want to let her through, as she didn't have enough money. It was good I knew Freddie by then. He sought her out in the terminal and gave her $500. No receipt. I settled up with him later with a good bit extra.

Meanwhile, we plowed further on.

"VIP pass," shouted Freddie. The suckers who didn't have Fast Track looked at me with utter contempt. Well, what can you say? As Julian, the king of the lemurs in the movie *Madagascar* put it: "It's nothing personal, it's just that we're better than you."

So I finally reached the gates. The last thing which awaited me was boarding. But I wasn't really concerned with that. Now I was a VIP, while the girls from the airline were smiling very warmly at Freddie.

I said that the last thing I had to face was boarding. Actually, no. Because it turned out that those smart airport administrators had thought up yet another way to screw money out of travelers.

At a European airport, you sit down on a seat, you wait until the ground staff open the gate and you walk through. But not in Nigeria. Because here you must first go through pre-boarding. Of course, pre-boarding takes place in many airports, not only in Nigeria. But here it takes on such a bizarre form. Which is connected with… yet another round of checking bags and documents. So another bag check, another document check, another attempt to screw you out of money. I just wanted this to be over quickly. I pulled Freddie by the arm, but he didn't even react.

"What's going on?" I asked. "Has my VIP pass run out?"

"What do you mean? It's just that here VIPs board at the end."

Nigerian pre-boarding is based on shoving passengers into a special waiting room the size of the public toilets at Warsaw Central Station, and with a similar smell. Because there is not only no air-conditioning, but not even a window. Which is extremely irritating, as when everyone eventually boards the plane you'll be gleaming with sweat, with your clothes stuck to your skin and stinking to high heaven. It's worse flying tourist class. Even worse if you have to go straight from the airplane to a meeting.

And what surprised me the most that day? That the Boeing 737-800 looked better than anything that I had ever flown in Poland. As well as the fact that the crew were only late for the take-off of their own plane by half-an-hour. Obviously, they didn't have a VIP pass.

Later, I worked with Freddie many times, and the influence and possibilities of this man have never ceased to amaze me. Since I've gotten to know him, my airport life has become much more straightforward and pleasant. Mainly because Freddie sits at the top of the hierarchy of the guys with the badges. These gentlemen call themselves 'Protocol Officers'. I've often seen one of these badge men using Fast Track to lead their suck… I mean their customer along, until an airport official appears on the horizon, which is when they suddenly disappear, leaving their customer high and dry. Of course, this must have been a real big cheese, as all of the other services were clearly drawing on the material benefits, which were by no mean small, from working with the badge men. At the same time, Freddie is on first name terms with the airport director who, by the way, is also an immigration officer.

And the most important thing is that Freddie never lets you down.

The whole procedure works on the badge men paying off every possible airport official who has the power to make life difficult for passengers. Usually, they settle up at the end of the day. But sometimes, a badge man has a bad day and has very little to share out. Then the official may express their dissatisfaction, usually doing this in the most ostentatious manner. Once I was flying to Addis Ababa and saw with my own eyes (or even heard more with my own ears) how this works in practice. A large crowd had gathered at the security check and since there was a crowd, the badge man responsible for that sector soon appeared. He quickly found an impatient, but tight-fisted traveler. When I say tight-fisted, I'm thinking about everyone who hadn't pulled in Freddie. So this customer bought himself a VIP pass and a moment later was, along with his guide, moving through the crowd to get to be first in line for the baggage security scanner.

"Back in line, like everyone else!" the customs officer screamed.

"But I have a VIP pass," the customer muttered and pointed to the badge man.

"I'm sorry, but he is not an airport employee. You must take the matter to the police."

"Olufunke, what are you saying?" the badge man said in amazement, "For God's sake…"

"I don't know you," the officer interrupted, screaming at him so loudly that you could hear him at the other end of the arrivals hall.

"Quiet, quiet. After all we have a deal."

"Are you accusing me of taking bribes?"

"No, no. I'm sorry. I'll come this evening and we'll talk ok?"

"I don't talk to strangers," the officer replied haughtily, after which he turned to the unfortunate customer and said: "You may go on. It's not your fault that this man cheated you."

So this time the badge man was lucky. Maybe this had happened for the first time and the officer was just giving him a warning. But a few times I even saw the culprit being led away by the police. Of course, he wasn't put in jail, but yet another name was added to the list of those to be paid off.

No such things ever happened to Freddie. I had the impression that if anyone ever tried pull rank with him, the next day they would be out of a job. Usually, the other badge men stay out of his way. I've often seen and heard them at the airport entrance, arguing over customers and threatening each other with prison, death and all sorts of curses. Sometimes fistfights break out and, with each badge man having his supporters, it sometimes turns into a real shit storm. But when Freddie speaks, nobody dares to protest.

This guy became something like a friend to me. I know that he'll always welcome me to the airport and really be happy to see me, just like a long-lost member of the family. Whenever I have to fly anywhere from Lagos, Freddie is always waiting there for me at the entrance. And then he works his magic.

Once I was a step away from being late for a flight to Dubai. By the way, if you think that due to this arrangement planes will wait for their passengers, then you're wrong. As long as the crew aren't late, the fact that a passenger is missing doesn't bother anyone too much. Of course, as long as they've already paid for the flight.

I had arrived at the airport at 8.30am and the flight was to depart at 10.00am. It's impossible to manage this in Lagos, when in the restaurants here I wait 45 minutes for French fries. Or rather it would be impossible to manage, had I not gotten to know Freddie. Once I had jumped out my taxi, all sweaty and mad, I saw my guide waiting. Do you think he was nervous? That he was rushing me? That he was nervously looking at his watch? Not at all. Instead, he just smiled broadly and held out his hand as if greeting a cop.

"Freddie, this is a very important meeting. If I fuck this up, I'll have to fire myself."

"Relax. We have time."

"How do we have…"

"Sit down," Freddie grinned, baring his immaculately white teeth.

Beside him stood a well-worn but still working wheelchair. I immediately understood what he had in mind.

"But what? Right here? Everyone will see it for God's sake."

"So…?"

So I sat down. Some flunky of Freddie's grabbed my bags and we headed off on crazy race around the airport. As the security check had already been sorted out (read: paid for) at the entrance, they let us through with no loss of time. And there were about a billion people in the terminal.

"Out of the way, sick person coming through," Freddie shouted and the crowd parted like Moses at the Red Sea. And I really was close to death. From my sides splitting with laughter. We passed the first checkpoint right after check-in when Freddie changed his spiel.

"Out of the way. This man has lost his wife in an accident. He's got to accompany the coffin. Let us through."

"I would like to offer you my sincere condolences on your loss," the airline official said earnestly, handing me my boarding card, at which I put on a pained expression and nodded my head slightly in appreciation. We went on. Freddie was racing so fast, that I thought I was going to fall out of the wheelchair.

"Jesus, can I have your autograph? I love Real Madrid!" shouted 'the gentleman from immigration', once Freddie had told him that my name was Sergio Ramos, a fact which I had confirmed while filling in the departure card. "I hope your injury doesn't turn out to be too serious."

The real immigration officer turned out to be Freddie's cousin, who just stamped the passport, not even looking at the first page.

Then there was a cursory check at pre-boarding and I was ready to fly. I got out of the wheelchair and Freddie laughed and went on his way. And the look on the faces of the other passengers? – priceless. For everything else, there's MasterCard.

The funniest thing in all of this was that day I was flying by Emirates Airline. New planes fly into Lagos and, as they don't have their own personnel on site, they use outsourcing. This is why one person often fulfills several roles. So the girl who had earnestly expressed her sympathy at the loss of my wife was now smiling at me flirtatiously, saying "Have a nice flight, Marek." I knew well she had recognized me, although she tried hard not to show it. And it was only then that I understood everything. That it had all been an illusion. A spectacle. That none of the airport staff had believed that I was accompanying a coffin, that I was paralyzed or that I was playing for Real Madrid. Freddie had simply paid them all off to pretend to be idiots. That the only person who had been completely taken in was me.

I was finally convinced just how unlimited Freddie's powers were, only very recently. I was sitting in the airport café, half an hour before my flight to Nairobi, when I realized that I didn't have my vaccination certificate on me. Once, a long time before, I was in Scotland. I had driven by car to a place called Portree on the Isle of Skye. A policeman approached and asked me where I was from. When I told him I was from Poland, he explained the basic rules to me:

"You see that single yellow line there alongside the curb?" he asked. "That means you can't park here. And here, on the other side where you have a double yellow line, that means you REALLY can't park here."

So in traveling from Nigeria to Kenya I had to have money, a passport and a visa. And I REALLY had to have my yellow vaccination certificate. But didn't. And I was totally convinced that not even Freddie could help me in this situation. Because even if he had bought off all the officials at the airport, I wouldn't be able to take them with me to Nairobi. And what would I say then? After all, he didn't know anyone there.

Actually, I'm not too sure about that last statement, but more of that in a moment. Meanwhile, however, the time to board was fast approaching and Freddie had come to check whether everything was okay.

"No, it's not okay, Freddie," I said with resignation in my voice. "I forgot my vaccination certificate."

20 minutes later, my plane took off from the runway. And where was I then? On it, of course. The son-of-a-gun had arranged a new vaccination certificate within seven minutes. It had my full name, my details and stamps confirming all possible vaccinations. Seven minutes. It was of no importance that this was a 'temporary' certificate and that I had to get a new one on my return.

But one day Freddie was ill. And I, as luck would have it, had to fly to South Africa that day for a conference (read: an hour talking business and the whole evening getting hammered, meaning closing business deals). So I had to manage on my own. Just in case, I had turned up at the airport three hours before my flight. It was even a little too early. Half an hour before check-in opened, I was already in line for it. And with me was my Nigerian girlfriend at that time, who had decided to accompany me to the airport.

We had been standing there a good 20 minutes, whispering sweet nothings to each other, while the whole time we were being observed (meaning, joking and gossiping) by the ground staff preparing to open the check-in gate.

Mixed-race relationships arouse great interest. And often extreme emotions, especially in Nigeria. If a white man is going out with a local girl, it most often concerns fat, disgusting engineers or sailors getting committed to an aging 'permanent club socialite'. A relationship between two young independent people based on love rather than an exchange of benefits is just too much for some people.

Frequently, I was the object of scorn and dislike from young rich Nigerians, because I was going out with a member of their tribe or fellow national. Because I had taken one of their best women. My partner also often became the object of envy from other women, who linked all of her professional success to her relationship with me, which was total bullshit.

Unfortunately, her extraordinary beauty did not lessen the envy she experienced.

The ground staff were talking away in their own tribal language,

Igbo, not realizing that my girlfriend, Keyshia, also came from the same tribe and understood everything they said.

She didn't want to say what exactly they were commenting on. They must have been nasty, especially one airport employee with a close-cropped hair, as Keyshia was becoming more and more annoyed. Knowing her personality, I knew that this could end up in a screaming match and even serious disruption to the operations of the entire airport. Keyshia never lets such things go, until the other person realizes who's going to come out on top. But a blazing row was the last thing I needed right now, especially without Freddie by my side.

Fortunately, check-in had just then been opened, and I was the third in line. Kissing Keyshia on the forehead, I asked her to wait for me a short distance away and not get into a discussion about it. Once I had got my boarding card, we could move to another area and say goodbye in a normal way there. Although she agreed to such a deal unusually meekly, this didn't arouse my suspicions. I stood in the line. A moment later my turn came and I threw my case on the conveyor belt, which, as usual, didn't work.

Suddenly, just as my boarding card was being printed, I heard a huge ruckus behind me. An enraged Keyshia and the short-haired airport employee, who was even more enraged, were screaming at each other and energetically waving their arms in the air.

As such things often end in a fistfight, without giving it much thought, I ran over to protect my woman. I jumped between them, holding back the airport employee with one hand and gently pushing my girlfriend away with the other. I just didn't foresee that the airport employee would start bawling as if someone had torn her skin off. People ran towards us, including her colleagues and airport security.

And here I was for Christ's sake, with no Freddie in sight.

They led us out of the crowd and brought us to an airline office 'to explain everything.' Although I had my boarding card, I was just concerned about my baggage. Right after we had entered, I noticed that the room had bars on the windows. And I did not like this at all. They ordered us to sit down, while they, completely ignoring our presence, blatantly started to set out what they were to say to their boss, so that it would look as if we had started the row. There were 10 people in the room and, although none of them had seen the incident, they all made out that we were to blame. This set off my partner once again and now I had to go between calming her down and negotiating with the airport officials in order to clear up the situation. I told her to record everything. I also turned on the recorder on my iPhone and discretely slipped it into my pocket.

After a few minutes, the boss of this doghouse, I mean airport, arrived. An old Nigerian. Fat and wrinkled, and wearing the Ankara, the traditional Nigerian dress for outdoors. He completely ignored my girlfriend, as well as the short-haired provocateur. I was the only one he asked for an explanation. When I finished, he laughed in a particularly unpleasant manner and asked: "Why did you stick your nose in? Now you will have problems. When two broads argue, men don't stick their noses in. They'll sort things out themselves."

And so this fucking Neanderthal sexist now got me going.

"I'm not surprised what this airport works like, this since there are people like you running it. I'm not interested in your tribal traditions, this is an international airport. Which means that its staff, including you, are bound by international behavioral conventions regarding its passengers, and especially regarding women. Don't you know how your employees are supposed to behave towards passengers, which is what they are paid to do?"

And this got him going.

Usually, I'm a good judge of character. However, this time I fucked up. Because I was really upset, I had failed to realize that I was dealing with the holder of an enormous ego who was extremely sensitive about his personal dignity. Which he now considered I had assaulted.

He let out a roar like a cross between that of an elephant and a hippopotamus. He screamed and waved his arms around like a man possessed. In his tribal language of course, so I had no fucking clue what he was on about. But it sure wasn't anything nice. It was the first time in Nigeria that anyone had laid into me with such force. Actually, the first time in my entire life. I was dumbstruck. I wasn't concerned about my flight anymore, but just simply wanted to avoid ending up behind bars.

Several new people now appeared (altogether almost 20 people, not including me or my girlfriend). They began to calm him down. Someone showed us the door.

"Let us go into another room," he said.

As there were no bars on the windows, we gladly accepted his offer. The guy commenced a 15 minute lecture on respect for older people occupying high office, etc. This time, I had no intention of interrupting anyone. He also suggested that my great-great-great-great grandfather may have done something unpleasant to his great-great-great-great grandfather, which may have had an impact on the current atmosphere of prejudice between us. I nodded, unconvinced.

"There's no point in dragging this out," he said after dragging things out for 15 minutes. "I knew you were recording the whole thing. If you erase the recording right now and sign a declaration that you were the ones who were aggressive, you'll both be released and you'll manage to catch your flight."

I looked at my girlfriend and she looked at me. We had to concede defeat in this battle. We did what was required of us. Half an hour later, I was already on the plane and my girlfriend was on her way home.

"Did he ask you to clean out the folder with the erased recordings?" I asked her on WhatsApp.

"Of course not :)" she replied.

I still have the recording. In case the current head of the airport ever becomes the president of Nigeria, it may come in useful.

When I landed in South Africa, I immediately filed a complaint with at the airline desk. They listened to me very carefully, before saying: "You said you've been living in Lagos for a fairly long time now. So you know yourself what things are like there."

Then they said something along the lines of "We're very sorry" and "It won't happen again", but I had already stopped listening. Because can they indeed be blamed for the fact that "that's the way it is" in Nigeria?

Insofar as I believed myself to be the victim that day, six months later in Ghana I only had myself to blame.

I had also come to Accra for a conference. I think I have already outlined what this actually means. At the afterpa… I mean the deal-closing meeting, I got to know a team of several very nice Italians, who invited me to their place for a drink. As this drink had turned into several drinks, they proposed that, instead of returning to my hotel, I crash out on the couch at their company apartment.

So that was great. Until I woke up and found I had only half an hour to get to the airport. And as I mentioned earlier, my girlfriend in Lagos was as beautiful as a mountain sunset, clever as bunch of encyclopedias, and – which is highly relevant to this story – as explosive as a dump truck driving through nitro-glycerin plant.

As luck would have it, that was the day that she had planned for us to attend a mind-numbingly boring reception. And if I missed my flight and failed to avail of this dubious pleasure, I could be sure that it would have been better had I never been born.

So I just brushed my teeth and, a moment later, was in a taxi.

"I'll pay you $100 if you get me to the airport in 15 minutes," I shouted. The driver must have felt as if he were in a movie, as he shoved the car into first gear at lightning speed and tore off to the sound of squealing tires.

Even the fundamentally undeniable bravado of my driver, a man who had got into the spirit of *The Fast and the Furious*, wasn't enough to help me in my hour of need. Because we were in an old Toyota Camry, which could have easily had a million kilometers on the clock. And wasn't able to go faster than 60 km an hour. At least it was a very eco-friendly journey, in that it didn't pump any fumes into the environment, but directed them into the car interior. In such a situation, it seemed funny to me to see a little 'no smoking' sign placed inside.

In any case, I had to say goodbye to my hundred bucks. It later turned out that my Italian friends were based only five minutes by road from the airport. So I only had myself to blame. I could have asked them.

Although check-in had finished, the airline lady was still at the desk. Initially, she didn't want to give me the time of day, but of course my personal charm won her over. Plus 20 dollars. To cut a long story short, she issued me with a boarding card. Luckily, as I had come to Accra for only one day, I had only one small piece of hand luggage and no cases to fool around with. I thanked the airline lady and put myself into airport inspection mode. Meanwhile, however, as I found out later, the lady had called those working at the airline desk at the gate to inform them there was another klutz racing to get to them. But they replied that the boarding process had finished, that they did not intend to open it again, that she was dumb and should get the boarding card back because if she didn't, they would tell the boss on her. And the poor girl had only $20 to share out for God's sake. Well, I mean how the fuck would you be able to share out such chump change with five people? If I had given her a hundred bucks, everything would have gone smoothly and my lady wouldn't haven't had to be so terribly scared.

I had just taken off my belt before the security check when someone suddenly grabbed the boarding card from my hands.

"What are you doing?" I asked in amazement, when I saw the lady in question.

"Check-in is closed. You secured this boarding card illegally."

"What are you talking about? You gave it to me yourself."

"Not at all. You took it from me."

"How could I have taken it since you would have had to print it out?"

She didn't reply, just simply ran off.

"Are you going or not?" asked the security officer. So I went. And everything went fairly smoothly. Right up to the gate.

Because there the check-in lady's colleagues had cast a strong veto. And I had no dollars left.

"If you don't have a boarding card, you can't pass."

"My boarding card was printed, so it's valid. Unfortunately, your colleague stole it from me for which she'll go to jail. And all of you too for aiding and abetting in a crime."

They weren't taken in. The two girls who were running the show remained inflexible. Perhaps they had received news from the check-in desk that if they negotiated they would get a 'premium' out of me.

The girls stood at a glass door with steps leading downwards behind them. And little further below. A group of passengers for my flight. They were waiting for the bus which to would ferry them to the plane. The absurdity of the situation drove me round the bend.

"For Christ's sake, all you have to do is get out of my way," I barked, "It's enough for us to open that door and in three seconds I'll be with the other passengers."

"It's not allowed."

And we went round in circles. In the meantime, the bus pulled up. The passengers got on. The engine was running, but the vehicle had not yet moved off. It was as if it was waiting for me. Of course, the driver couldn't have had any idea of my situation, but by now everything looked so fucking crazy that I was starting to lose my mind.

And then I did something stupid. Really stupid. Don't ever attempt this at any airport you're at.

"Too bad. I'll take the next flight," I said in a sad tone and walked away a bit. The girls and the two guys with them finally understood that nothing had come of their 'premium'. They started to gather up their things. Their work was clearly done. Well, while they were moving their things, they moved a little to one side. And what did Marek Zmysłowski do? He raced forward, swung round them, pushed through the glass door and ran down the steps towards the bus.

Which had already departed. I was 10 seconds too late.

"Fuck! Fuck! Fuck!" were the words I used to express my disappointment. I didn't know what to do now. I also didn't realize what was actually going on around me. And a lot was going on, as the girls had called security.

"YOLO," I thought to myself.

And I ran. The passengers were already climbing up the stairs fairly quickly and unfortunately there weren't very many of them. So as I ran up to the plane, the steward had already started to close the door.

"Wait! Wait! There's still me!" I shouted. I saw everything in slow motion. The doors were closing slowly, suddenly they stopped closing and then, in a short instance, they started opening again. I saw the head of the steward emerging from behind the door.

"Are you also flying with us?" he asked in amazement.

"Yes!" I replied and felt a wave of happiness rush over me.

"No, stop!" a voice behind me interrupted.

And the fun was all over.

Right behind me, two guards were gasping from exhaustion, who were very determined that I not board that flight. With that, they took me off to the air traffic control tower which, in fact, I enjoyed as I had never been in one before.

The supervisor was there to greet me. I don't know why, but he was certainly the person there who made all the decisions. The guy seemed fairly nice, called me 'brother' all the time and seemed genuinely worried about my fate. I explained what had happened. I told him that the stupid chick at the check-in desk had stolen my legally-issued boarding card and he ordered his people to bring her here. Then everything that I had said came out. That they had ordered her to take the card back from me.

"I understand you brother, I really do," the supervisor said, "But you ran onto the runway and that I can never forgive. You must be punished. The police will deal with you and what they will do is no longer my concern. At the same time, I must place your name on this airport's blacklist. You will never be able to use this airport again."

Yeah, right. The following week I had another four return flights to Accra planned.

Luckily, I had an ace up my sleeve. Sometime previously, I had got to know a great guy at a party. He was totally crazy, in the positive sense of the word. It later turned out that he was the sales director of a large African airline, who should know some people. I called him up and outlined the situation for him and he promised he would call back and organize some help.

And that's what happened. After several minutes, the supervisor's phone rang.

"Hello? Yes. Yes, he is here."

Then he was silent for a moment, listening to the torrent of words streaming out of the receiver.

"Well, since you… that's clear… undoubtedly, we are dealing with a misunderstanding here."

He replaced the receiver and looked at me with almost fatherly concern.

"It seems as if the security camera has malfunctioned and not recorded your alleged run around the airport. And our security guards are not sure whether you got on the bus with the other passengers."

"What do I have to do to make this happen?"

"Nothing. I declare you not guilty. You only have to sign a declaration that you have nothing against us. In the end, our job is to ensure the safety of our passengers. How could we have known that you are such a respectable man? Apart from that you must write that you are bound to obey the rules governing the airport in Accra and will follow the directions of the staff of the airport and airlines."

"That's no problem. Anything else?"

"No. You only have to pay a fee for transportation to the terminal."

"How much?"

"A thousand dollars."

"Riiight ... and how much does a trip to the ATM cost?"

After that, everything was okay. They booked me a ticket on the evening flight. I spent the entire day in the airport's special VIP lounge. I was extraordinarily taken up with sampling the local drinks served there. I knew that it was better to anesthetize myself now, as later on it may prove too late. I texted my girlfriend that I had been robbed at the airport, that I was injured and that I couldn't get out of Ghana.

However, she only wrote back: "If you don't manage it, then you will be injured."

In the end, I owe you one more explanation. It may seem to you that the head of this African airlines called the supervisor and got me out of trouble. Nothing could be further from the truth. He had called his own friend, a man well known for being able to sort out anything in Nigeria. But someone who also had influence in Ghana.

Yes. That was Freddie. A man who had his own friend and counterpart in Ghana.

Chapter 9

SPRINGBOKS VS. ALL BLACKS

Nigerians adore football. They're crazy about it here, especially the English Premier League. The inhabitants of Lagos can bring the city to a standstill while celebrating a victory by Hull City or some other less well-known English club, when the English people themselves say "Hull what?".

But we're not talking about football today, at least not the kind played with a round ball, but about a certain rugby match.

It was the year 2015, so I had gotten to know Africa pretty well by then. I had also gotten to know lots of great people. And if you know great people, sometimes stories, such as that which I'd like to tell you, come out of it.

"Hi, what are you doing on Saturday?" my friend Jimi asked when I picked up the phone.

"I don't know. I haven't even thought about it."

"Great. So fly to Johannesburg. We're having a birthday party there. Only not too late, because before the party we're going to a match."

"What kind of match?"

"You'll see."

He hang up and I booked the tickets straight away.

In any crime statistics you read, it always turns out that South Africa has the highest rates of murder and rape. On the other hand, the same statistics show that the crime rates concerning tourists are lower than anywhere in the world. People who go there can't believe that the level of safety in South Africa is no different from that in Italy or Spain. Okay, it's obvious they don't wander around slums, but stay in tourist areas and see the attractions aimed at attracting them. Of course, they'd have something different to say if they were living there every day.

I had been to South Africa pretty often and somehow survived. Up to then, I had mainly visited Cape Town, but now I was to fly to Johannesburg for the first time. And Cape Town, my friends, is the African equivalent of Monte Carlo. Only incomparably better. In this region, the seasons of the year are the other way round from ours, so all the most beautiful people in the world go there in order to flee winter. Because there is no city like Cape Town in the entire Southern Hemisphere. Not Buenos Aires, nor Rio de Janeiro, not even the more modern cities of Australia offer as much entertainment and sunshine as this town, one which is small in terms of Southern Africa. Only half a million people live in Cape Town itself, with another three million in the surrounding area. 1000 people per square kilometer is almost a desert in African terms. Only fewer people live in, well, the desert. It's no surprise that celebrities tired of life in the limelight swarm around there like ants. But not only for that reason, as half of Hollywood and European showbiz winter in South Africa. So maybe it doesn't snow as much in Los Angeles as in Warsaw, but when you want to film a few scenes where the sun is shining and the characters need to run around the streets in open shirts, where better than South Africa?

In fact, I had gotten to know Jimi in Cape Town and he's a dream contact for every young white new arrival from Europe, wishing to break into these 'golden circles'. Jimi is an international model of Nigerian origin, who later transformed himself into the owner of a modeling agency and a nightclub. Even though he no longer graces the covers of the most popular magazines in the world, he still knows everything and everyone.

"Drop in today, I've booked you a table next to Selita Ebanks."

Selita Ebanks was a Victoria's Secret model, who had appeared in Kanye West's famous short film *Runaway*. I had a weakness for this song, actually more for Selita, and Jimi damn well knew it. When Jimi organized a party, the most beautiful people were always there. There, where Brad Pitt or the Beckhams come for business or pleasure, hundreds of the hottest people on Earth swan around, hoping to be plucked from a world of anonymity. And thanks to Jimi, I sometimes had the chance to swan around too.

When I was coming in to land at Johannesburg for the first time, I looked out the window and wasn't sure whether I had overslept and missed my stop. Because it looked more like Chicago or somewhere like that, than anywhere in Africa. Glass skyscrapers, hundreds of thousands of vehicles and millions of ant-like people scurrying here and there, seemingly without any purpose. The airport was like something from a different continent. I wasn't completely surprised by it all though. Whenever I was feeling tired of Africa and either couldn't or didn't want to fly to Europe or the States, I booked a flight to Cape Town. A few days spent on its beautiful beaches, eating at amazingly cheap restaurants where they make the best coffee in the world and the seafood and steaks are so good it's difficult to watch your waistline, as well as going to the best nightclubs in the Southern Hemisphere, recharged my batteries for the next few months of the daily grind in Nigeria.

Jimi was such a great buddy that he would pick me up from the airport in person, even though no 'protocol officer' was necessary and the drivers waiting on passengers to arrive had their names printed on cards and didn't have to shout 'Malik Zmayslowsky' throughout the entire arrivals hall.

The road to the stadium reminded me a bit of the Africa I knew. Here in these areas, the poorest inhabitants of the city live and whose poverty was nothing like that in Nigeria.

And the stadium itself – well, what can I say? Of course, now in Poland we have magnificent modern stadiums. Although Ellis Park isn't any more beautiful or modern than those in Gdansk or Wroclaw, it is a mighty structure. It holds 62,000 people and, when sold out, makes an awesome impression. And that day it was. Because the Springboks, South Africa's national rugby team, were playing, causing the entire nation to hold its breath.

The Springboks' opponents that evening were New Zealand's national team, commonly known as the All Blacks. And renowned for, among other things, the *Haka* ritual warrior dance, their black rugby shirts, the late lamented Jonah Lomu who died in 2015 from a heart attack, and, above all, for steamrolling through everyone with fucking unbelievable force.

The match was part of the 2015 Rugby Championship, an annual tournament in which, apart from South Africa and New Zealand, the Wallabies, Australia's national team and Los Pumas from Argentina, also participate.

Once, by some miracle, we had located our sector and then our seats, Jimi asked me:

"Have you noticed anything strange?"

"Yes," I replied, "We're the only blacks here. Oops, I mean you are."

"Ha! That's exactly right," said Jimi, praising my powers of observation. "But look straight ahead over there. Do you see the flags of the All Blacks?"

"Sure I do. That must be the Kiwis' sector."

"Well, not necessarily. Most of South Africa's black fans are sitting there."

"Umm… I don't get it."

"Well, I see have a lot to tell you about this country."

So it was here I discovered what racism is really like in Africa. It was all explained to me, a white European, by a black African, which would have been impossible but for our friendship and a great deal of distance. Both from me and him. Mainly from him.

The Apartheid system is an inseparable element of the history of the Republic of South Africa and I wouldn't even dare to figure it out here. I'll just limit myself to outlining it in layman's terms. Before the 17th century, this was what you may call real Africa. Then the Dutch arrived, then the Germans and still later the French. And in the end, as is their custom, the Brits, who kicked everyone else's ass. Meanwhile, enormous diamond reserves were discovered in the region, which resulted in the necessity of 'defending civilized values', in which the defenders of such values were the British, as the USA was getting ready for their own civil war and had no intention of sailing to the ends of the Earth. So the British defended their civilized values fiercely, until they had conquered and plundered the entire country. Thank God no-one discovered oil, as the Americans would have eventually decided to defend democracy.

The new order was based on the absolute dominance of the white man, which didn't even change after 1910, when South Africa secured its independence. It was only then that the whites went full on with racism. The blacks weren't allowed to go to school, earn money, vote or use medical services. In fact, they were not allowed to do anything. This state of affairs lasted until the 1990s. South Africa, after the USA, was the only country after the Second World War to propagate racism through institutional means.

The first attempts at reform were forced through by Nelson Mandela, who mainly forced them through from prison where he spent 27 years for terrorism. Whether this was justified is still a bone of contention, even among Africans themselves, whereas obviously judgment concerning the actions of Madiba, to give Mandela his tribal name, is often decided by the color of skin of those passing it. So for some whites he's still a thug, while for blacks, a hero. But for everyone, a legend.

The end of Apartheid only occurred during the 1990s. There were more and more protests, despite being brutally silenced by the governing regime. Sanctions by the international community became more and more severe. So the gentlemen in power allowed Mandela out and he used the opportunity to run in elections which his party, the African National Congress, won, allowing him to become president.

Anyone who thinks that racism ended with apartheid is wrong. According to my observations, there are at least three kinds of racism in South Africa, even though I'm not a sociologist and there's a high probability that my experience does not describe the complexity of the issue.

The first kind is the one we know very well. Whites hating blacks. Or at least treating them with contempt. People say that South Africa has weakened under black-led governments and maybe that is so. Reforms have been introduced too slowly, the country is getting poorer and many whites are simply leaving.

"And let them fuck off," said Jimi during the break. "Nobody needs them here anyway, They are usually old, completely backward people. For them a nigger is a nigger and that's that. They are not able to get used to the fact that they are no longer the masters here."

"But they are right about the fact that under the governments of the African National Congress a lot changed that was to their disadvantage. You can't deny that," I said, because I really think that myself and Jimi and I always speak to each other honestly.

"Of course not. But it's hard to see how it could have been otherwise. They had it way too good for decades. It's not possible to raise the entire black population so that they have the same as the whites. Part of the white population had to be brought down. Apart from that, since it was they who didn't allow us to be educated, they are to blame for us having uneducated and inexperienced people in power. Mandela was so old that he grew up during the period when blacks still had their own universities, so he managed to get educated. As for those who came later, well the less said the better. It's only now that the first generation not forbidden to study is coming through. You'll see how they change the country," he replied.

But they haven't changed it yet. The blacks are getting more and more impatient. And the whites are getting more and more worried about their future.

Once, we were with Jimi at a Cape Town restaurant. It was such a strange place, in that 30 years earlier they wouldn't let a black man in, and now it was only they that packed out the place. Apart from that, the serving staff were white and probably found it difficult to come to terms with blacks summoning them by clicking their fingers.

In fact, I had just finished a grilled springbok, when a terrible ruckus broke out. Some blacks had jumped up from their tables and started throwing plates and glasses on the floor, after which they attacked the white waiter. It took a security guard to break things up.

In the end, I was amazed that out of all this swarm of people, the guard only threw out one guy. The waiter who had been attacked by all the black customers.

"Kaffir," Jimi whispered.

"What? What do you mean Kaffir?"

"'Kaffir' is the most racist word in South Africa," Jimi began to clarify, "Stronger than good old 'nigger'. In calling a black man that, you usually leave him with no choice. If he doesn't hit you, he'll never forgive himself as long as he lives that he turned out be such a pussy," Jimi explained.

Although using such a word is illegal in South Africa, admittedly the punishment up to now had been slight and only in the form of fines. At the beginning of 2018, however, a new precedent was set.

A white woman, an estate agent, was sentenced to three years in jail for using 'the k-word' towards black police officers whom she had called to a crime scene. Someone had broken into her car and she just lost it. In a recording which was circulated on the net, she said the magic word 48 times.

Let's move on to the next form of racism, namely black racism towards whites, which is not based so much on feelings of superiority, as much as on reactive hatred. Undoubtedly, its classic form existed during the apartheid era. It's hard not to hate your tormentor.

Following the transfer of power, it was somewhat calmer, which was a miracle for which we can thank Mandela and his allies. Of course, ideas immediately appeared how to take revenge on the Afrikaners using administrative tools. The victims of such machinations were to be the Springboks themselves, the country's national rugby team. It was quickly established that the team's popular name and emblem (an inoffensive antelope), as well as their green and gold colors, were symbols of apartheid and, as such, should be immediately removed from the public space. Mandela himself was supposed to have vetoed the idea and forced through the thesis that following the transformation of power, South Africa would not suddenly become a black nation, but stop being a country for the whites. That a time of national unity was at hand and it wasn't allowed to take away the things the white people love. Because, firstly, "that wasn't the South Africa I fought for", and secondly that similar actions would be the best way to escalate a continuously ongoing conflict.

As we all know, Clint Eastwood is an amazing director. He made the movie *Invictus*, which dealt with this situation and depicted Mandela as forbidding the breaking up of the Springboks and the black supporters in the stands for anyone who had the Springboks in their sights. But the film also shows Mandela's Trojan work in building national unity in the face of the upcoming Rugby World Cup, which South Africa was hosting. The story of how Mandela worked together with the team captain Francois Pienaar is very true to life, insofar as it's portrayed in a typically idealized American style. The president breathed life into creating unity with the captain of the team, which in turn did the same for the whole team and then the whole nation. The Springboks got off their knees, won the World Cup (which actually happened) with wildly enthusiastic support of both blacks and whites, and they all lived happily ever after.

Unfortunately, today's team is threatened with suspension in all international tournaments. And this is due to South Africa's own minister of sport, who believes that there are too many white players on the team, which does not reflect the demographic structure of the country. Some politicians are threatening to confiscate the passports of the white rugby players, so as to prevent them from traveling to tournaments. To be frank, they believe that whites are to blame for the fact that not enough blacks play rugby.

No other country in the world has such an extensive quota system based on the color of one's skin as South Africa. It's changed so much, that it's gone from one extreme to another. Whites lose their jobs, because companies have to employ blacks in their places, who regrettably as yet do not have comparable skills or qualifications. The process of equalizing opportunities has lasted decades unfortunately. Quotas based on equalizing results at the 'exit point' (meaning how many blacks are employed in relation to whites) and not at the 'entry point' (meaning how many blacks have the same qualifications as whites) has quickly produced visible results. That's why they are liked by politicians facing approaching elections. At the same time, this approach has led to well-educated Afrikaners having to seek work abroad or working in restaurants and sometimes allowing frustration to lead them to call the clientele 'Kaffirs'.

The third type of racism is xenophobia or simply hatred. Black on black.

Once, I was traveling around Cape Town by bus. Whenever I come to a new place, I usually start my sightseeing with a morning jog around new neighborhoods or just catch a bus and travel the entire route. I love observing a city from the wings. In those parts where the normal inhabitants live and not weekend tourists. In many places you may read that using this means of transport is a form of Russian roulette, because sooner or later you will certainly be robbed, beaten up or even murdered. But I decided to use Cape Town's public transport system with the really cool name of MyCiTi and am somehow still alive, as you can see. That said, I only came across one unpleasant situation.

So there I was, traveling on this bus and it was a long journey, from the Sunset Beach villa district all the way to Green Point, as I really wanted to see the newly built stadium. Somewhere around the stop for Lagoon Beach, about half way along the route, the passengers getting on were all black, although MyCiTi isn't something that whites avoid.

Then, they started shouting at each other louder than usual. Of course in their local languages, so I had no way of knowing what they were talking about.

The driver, an Afrikaner, stopped and came out of his cabin. He was fat and ginger, with a puffy face. He simply started to separate the troublemakers, shouting at one, then the other. I was sure that in a second those fighting would take a break for a chat and then turn on their 'common enemy', but nothing like that happened. What's more, I got the impression that both sides attempted to explain to their side of the argument to the driver, as if he was one of the neighborhood defenders of justice.

Of course, the driver ignored it, as the only thing he did give a fuck about was the bus timetable, which had been screwed up by the ruckus. When he found his efforts were turning out to be fruitless, he gave me a look of resignation, which I interpreted as a racist act. Totally as if to say: "Christ, we are the only whites here. No-one but us will clean this shit up."

"Everyone out!"

"Wait a minute. Why should we get out since they picked on us?!!" asked one of the troublemakers accusingly.

"No, it was them!" someone from the other gang shouted.

"Yes, yes, I know," the driver replied, "but the truth is, I don't care. If you still want to punch each other, go ahead, I'll even bet on the winners. But take this fucking contest outside! Because if you don't, I call the police."

"I'll never understand those blacks," the driver said to me in an openly racist manner when we were alone.

"What actually happened?"

"I don't know and don't want to know."

When the apartheid system was dismantled, something new appeared. A jobs market based on supply and demand. And then something happened which the blacks never expected. Other blacks arrived and spoiled their party. Let's call a spade a spade (no racist pun intended). Because suddenly, just as the inhabitants of South Africa were going through the shock of the transformation, reading job advertisements and sending off CVs, the Botswanans, Zambians, Zimbabweans and Malawians came on the scene. During the apartheid era, South Africa was one of the richest countries in the world. Of course, if we're talking about the standard of living enjoyed by the whites, a class which was able to protest when the governing regime wanted to introduce a legal limit on the number of servants you could have in your home. But after the lifting of apartheid, South Africa offered black immigrants much better working conditions than in their home countries. So why work for Zimbabwean dollars worth shit due to rampant inflation, when you could earn a perfectly decent salary in South African rand? This sure sounds familiar to any rich country being a neighbour of a poorer one. However, the problem of locals rebelling against economic immigrants is a global phenomenon.

The result of this was that although the government had forced through better rates of pay for blacks, immigrants were coming in to these jobs at the old starvation rates. And therefore, despite South Africa having had blacks running governments for over 20 years, they still earn significantly less than whites. And they are losing patience more and more often, the evidence of which are spectacular anti-immigrant pogroms. Since 2009, thousands of immigrants have been killed in South Africa. Most frequently due to someone running into a machete or jumping into a burning tire.

You don't need to be a genius to figure out that one of the passengers was an immigrant – from Zimbabwe, if I remember correctly. I got the impression that the driver was disappointed that reality had taken him away from a game called 'oppress the nigger'. From having been a main player, now all he could do was sit on the sidelines.

"It's idiotic that the blacks don't even need us for that anymore. Racism, I mean," he told me in parting.

The things I've described here are only a small part of the issue. Perhaps a telling one, but still a small part. In Africa, and not only in the south, the issue is a bit more complicated, as xenophobia is perhaps a more appropriate word regarding these relations. There are 47 large African tribes, with 250 of the smaller ones in Nigeria alone. So when we talk about conflict, even between countries, this more concerns tribal conflict than national conflict. For example, in Nigeria, although the tribes live together and seem to form a country, this was a country created by an invader (Great Britain, of course) all of a sudden, just over a century ago, with the aim of financing the First World War. And we're also talking about tribes with a history longer than many of today's European nations. Tribal divisions have the ability to turn into truly nightmarish wars. You only have to recall the Hutus and Tutsis in Rwanda and Burundi. And just as a side note, it's extraordinary how Rwanda has transformed itself during the last decade and is now known as "the African Switzerland". I've been to Kigali and can confirm that there is no cleaner city in Africa. There is also no other African country which is developing as dynamically. In fact, Africans from all over the continent go there on their holidays, as it offers peace and quiet, the roads are smooth and well built, the city has functioning universities and financial institutions, while there are fantastic restaurants everywhere, offering delicious food at ridiculously cheap prices.

Xenophobia used to be a problem in Nigeria, mainly towards the Ghanaian diaspora. The feeling was mutual, as the Ghanaians also resented Nigerians, and maybe even felt xenophobic towards them also. This was because in 1957 Ghana became the first country to gain independence in the region, and many Nigerians emigrated there straight away. In turn, when Nigeria gained its own independence three years later, many Ghanaians recognized that there was oil and money there (this was before oil had been discovered in Ghana) and that there was no point in wallowing in poverty in Accra. So these guys went there and the other guys came here. And in Africa, we're talking about millions of people.

The effect of all this is that both countries are hosts to enormous minorities, and where you find enormous minorities there are also disagreements, and we all know that this doesn't just concern Africa. Eventually, it was believed in Ghana that Nigerians comprised too high a proportion of the population of the country and all of them were deported. As you may guess, the Nigerian government under the leadership of President Shehu Shagari retaliated fairly quickly by deporting over a million Ghanaians, right at the moment when Ghana was going through enormous economic problems. And these tit-for-tat actions gave rise to many, sometimes absurd, conflicts. One of the most important has not been resolved up to today, namely who makes better Jollof rice, a popular west African dish made of rice with vegetables and spices.

Once, I flew to Zanzibar. It's such a boring version of Africa: no terrorist attacks, no armed robberies, no coups d'état. Even in Tanzania, the country to which this island belongs, or to put it another way is a self-governing part of it, they don't know what's going on there. And the reason they don't is because nothing goes on there. Expats such as myself go there to go kite-surfing as firstly, the winds are great there, and secondly the views are really magnificent.

One of the gang I was with, who was intending to get engaged, had heard that Zanzibar City had the best jewelry store in this part of Africa. Which resulted in me losing at least three hours of good wind, because no guy on earth is capable of buying an engagement ring on his own, for Christ's sake. Especially if he has a lot of money to spend.

In fact, the jeweler, more than the jewelry store itself, made an extraordinary impression on me. He was an old Indian, who knew literally everything about precious stones. And, what was worse, he loved talking about it.

In the end, we managed, or I should rather say that my buddy managed, to choose a ring. He paid a mere $20,000 for one of the cheaper ones. If I were his girlfriend, I'd think twice about marrying such a skinflint.

When we were just about to leave, I noticed some stains of green paint on the entrance door window.

"What's this?" I asked.

"Oh, that? It's paint. Green paint."

"Oh, of course. Who'd have thought it."

"Well, sometimes they come here and they throw this and that at my store. Once eggs, another time tomatoes, and lately paint. I have the impression that someone in the neighborhood has bought a paintball gun."

"That's a bit weird," my friend observed, "If I wanted to rob a jeweler, I would have chosen rocks."

"I hope no-one takes your advice," the old Indian gentleman replied. "Thank God, no-one has attempted to rob me as yet. They simply don't like me because I have money."

"But you're an expat," I said in surprise. "Expats always have lots of money and boast left, right and center about it, and the locals prefer to be friends with them, rather than run them out of town."

The old Indian gentleman let out a deep sigh.

"Have you been long in Africa?" he asked.

"Well, almost two years."

"You should look a little further than the end of your nose. Because in Africa, if you're not white, you're black. You understand?"

"No."

"You're white, you're an expat. But if your face was of any other color, the most you would be is an economic immigrant. Meaning someone who comes and takes their jobs."

"But who defended them so as to…" my friend began, until the reproachful stare of the jeweler shut him up.

"Your friend has already been in Africa for two years," he shot back, "but I'd say you've only been here a week."

"Two weeks," he stammered. "I'm here on vacation."

At that, the jeweler spared us any further explanations.

There is, however, one other extremely pleasant aspect of racial difference. A different skin color adds several points of attractiveness, and the exotic is sexy. This can be seen in the black (or dark-skinned) members of the Polish showbiz scene. In Poland, they are considered to be extremely attractive, even though in their home countries they would be seen as average. If, of course, we're talking about beauty. However, if you're a white man, at least just a tad more attractive than Gollum, you'd better take a crate of Jimi hats, because HIV isn't the best holiday souvenir to end up with. And if you're a white girl… exactly the same applies. And African men go especially wild for chicks who, in Europe, are considered on the large side.

And if we're talking about pulling members of the opposite sex, the funniest were those attempts which didn't work out. Once upon a time, I was in Ethiopia, or Addis Ababa, to be more exact. Despite its history of more than a 1000 years, it was never completely colonized. So in this regard, Ethiopia is actually perhaps the most African country in all of Africa.

Addis Ababa is very clean, pleasant and extraordinarily atmospheric. The blood-sucking government there (although the current one just wants sweat and tears, not blood) has slapped a 100% tariff on new cars. Because of this, old, but beautifully restored VW Golfs and Passats, and loads of Soviet-era cars, travel around Ethiopian cities. There are fantastic shiny Ladas and Zaporozhets, the likes of which you would not even see today in Ukraine. Apart from this, there is a host of wonderful traditional dishes. Although Ethiopia suffers from enormous problems with hunger, this is not visible in the capital. I'm not going to give my two cents here. Other people much more clever than I will write books on social inequalities. Anyway, the cuisine is magnificent and to be found in pleasant restaurants with insanely low prices. And, of course, the most important thing – the most beautiful girls in Africa.

And there was one that I really got into. We had gotten to know each other at a party at a friend's house. It was intimate, with just a few people present. In going there and knowing whom I may meet, I decided to employ the 'intellectual' strategy of picking up women. With that in mind, I devoted several days to combing through the net in search of information on Ethiopia. And got quite absorbed, I must admit. Suffice to say that Ryszard Kapuściński's *The Emperor: Downfall of an Autocrat* ended up on my e-reader. I read the book from cover to cover and finished the last chapter while on the runway in Addis Ababa.

She was called Almaz, which means 'diamond' in Ethiopian, and I can certainly assure you that this shows that either her father was a witch-doctor or her mother was clairvoyant. She really was as beautiful as a diamond.

We quickly made contact and I started my spiel. I spoke with the tone of a know-all, at least regarding what I had read in *The Emperor*. Sometimes she nodded in agreement, sometimes she corrected me, but she generally looked at me wide-eyed, which I knew was a good sign. We talked the whole evening and she turned out to be a pleasant conversationalist. Almaz had studied in London and was extremely clever.

Did I tell you that my friend who had organized the party had a huge house? So some of the guests were traveling home afterwards, while others were staying over. Including myself and Almaz. But at the end of the party, when everyone was starting to leave and the time came to say goodbye to them, Almaz had disappeared from sight. She had simply left and gone to bed in her room. I was a bit disappointed. And even though there were a few beautiful 'Plan B' options remaining, I had somewhat lost my desire for them. I must admit that I had been enchanted by this Ethiopian diamond. So I said "See you, guys" and headed to my room.

A shower and into bed. I was lying there just in my underpants, when suddenly I heard light knocking on the door. I went over, opened it and saw Almaz. She had already managed to wash herself and change into something less formal. A tight T-shirt, which emphasized everything there was to emphasize. And that fragrance. She had put on the most exquisite perfume.

"Hi, come in," I stammered and quickly raced to the chest of drawers where my trousers were lying.

I sat on the bed and patted the duvet as a gesture of invitation. The girl came over and timidly took her place beside me.

Oh, Christ, that fragrance again…

"You know, I had a wonderful time talking to you this evening…" she said, fluttering her eyelids, with me now convinced that her eyelashes were a mile long and were the cause of the mighty tsunamis of southern Asia.

"Me too…" I replied in that cretinous, artificially lowered voice which I thought was meant to be sexy, but actually made me sound like an idiot.

"And I was thinking..."

"Yeeaahh…"

"I was thinking that it's wonderful that you are interested in our culture."

"Oh, yeeaahh?"

"And I wanted to give you a present. Something which will help you to find out even more about us."

"Oh, yeeaahh?"

"And that will have good memories of your time here."

"I'm sure I'm going to have good memories."

"Could you turn on the light please?"

Riiiiight, still waters run deep. I hopped from the bed and raced to the light switch.

I switched it on and quickly jumped back onto the bed and she gave me something thanks to which I would discover even more about Ethiopia.

A book. Fucking *Sweetness in the Belly* by fucking Camilla Gibb. After which she kissed me on the cheek and left. I must admit all the same that, once I recovered, I recognized it had been basically a sweet gesture.

Another more interesting story concerns something which occurred in my beloved Cape Town. I know a great restaurant there. I go there sometimes because Solveig, a really lovely Norwegian lady, is usually standing behind the bar. Once upon a time, she had been an 'expert' in marketing, but she packed it all in and headed for the hills. Or more precisely, South Africa. There she met a guy, they opened a restaurant and made a life together.

I said hello, we exchanged a few words, then I ordered a drink and sat at a table scrolling through my smartphone.

"Hey there, handsome," I heard from behind. I raised my head to look into the eyes of the person saying these obviously true, even nice words. Unfortunately, my eyes only got as far as the chest of my future partner in conversation.

"I haven't even sat down and you're already staring at my tits?" she laughed. "May I?"

"Only if won't bother you that I'll still be staring at them."

She waved her hand. As she sat down, I got a slightly better look at her. She was about 40, but looked about 20. Smooth black skin. Delicate, or at least delicate looking make-up, long black hair tied back into a pony tail. It was wavy and looked amazing.

Since our relationship had started off on a slight *faux pas*, I now felt authorized to keep looking at her cleavage. In the end, she couldn't think any worse of me now, could she? And she liked it. Every time she caught me doing it, she giggled sweetly. She didn't hide the fact that she knew. And she didn't pretend that she had put on that tight black dress by accident either.

We chatted away for 20 minutes. She kept playing with her hair and striking poses that were seemingly normal, but unbelievably sexy.

Everything went very naturally without any vulgar intrusiveness. At the same time, she was open and natural in an unstudied manner. Eventually, I recognized that it was a waste of time to continue the conversation.

"Tell me why," I asked, "you sat next to me."

"Did I have to have a reason?"

"I think so. You didn't sit here by accident."

"That's true," she winked.

"So you had some aim behind it."

"That's also true."

"And that aim was sexual," I smiled innocently, at which she burst into suppressed laughter.

"You are right once again," she agreed.

"So let's stop playing games. Tell me what you want from me."

"Are you sure? I wouldn't want you to think I was trying to use you."

"But I have absolutely nothing against you using me."

"Alright then, so…"

"And so?"

"I saw how you were talking to the lady behind the bar. Could you get her number for me?"

I just froze and then got sad. I had lost half an hour. But still, she had impressed me. In many countries in Africa you can still go to prison for being homosexual.

However, South Africa is completely different from the rest of Africa in this regard. Which actually isn't surprising, considering the differences between this country and the rest of the continent. And you could think Cape Town a Mecca for gays and lesbians in Africa, at least those who can afford a visa and an airline ticket. In any case, South Africa is the most liberal country in Africa, and Cape Town the most liberal city in South Africa. And I really had no idea of this and had yet to find out.

And if we're already on the subject, once I was on one of my many trips to Cape Town. As was my custom, when the toil and trouble of Lagos was getting on top of me. As we all know, it's hard to live an easy life. It happened to be the middle of the week and Jimi's club was closed, so we agreed to meet up at the Aces 'n' Spades, a nightclub with cult status in Cape Town. As I was fed up with being at the hotel and Jimi still had something to do, I decided that I wouldn't be waiting in my room until midnight like some loser, but just head out on the town earlier just to get myself 'merry', as they say. So I turned up at the Ace 'n' Spades about three hours ahead of the appointed time, with a strong desire to gain the respect of the men and the hearts of the weaker and fairer sex.

Alcohol works on people in different ways. After drinking, Poles have a way of either beating each other up or getting to know strangers who then become friends for life. Or at least drinking buddies, either at the bar or on the steps of the corner shop. This time, everything pointed towards the first possibility. At some point between my second and seventh whiskey, I got to know Hannes and Jomo and we got on like a house on fire. Haven't you ever sometimes come across someone who was a total stranger, but who you immediately felt was your best friend? That's the way it was with Hannes and Jomo.

It wasn't enough that they laughed at all my jokes, but they even surprised me with their knowledge of Poland. They not only knew about the Holy Trinity of 'Wałęsa-Wotyła-Lewandowski', but were also well-informed on Marie Curie, Krzysztof Kieślowski and, above all, the heart surgeon, Zbigniew Religa. It's worth recalling that Cape Town was the first hospital in the world to carry out a heart transplant, and this was in 1967.

"I'd like to get involved in transplantology at some point in the future," Hannes said.

"And what do you do now?"

"I operate on trauma injuries. You know, mainly traffic accidents, assaults and injuries, that kind of thing."

That was some achievement. The guy couldn't have been more than 35 years old, but looking at the wisdom in his eyes, I hadn't a shadow of a doubt that he wasn't exaggerating. Sometimes you don't need evidence to know that something is true.

We had another few drinks. Jimi had got delayed with something and wouldn't be there for another 45 minutes. It didn't really bother me somehow, as I was having a ball with my new friends and really was the worse for wear at this stage. Jomo suggested that it was time for a change of scene.

"Are you coming with us? My friends called to say that they're organizing a great house party."

"You don't have to ask me such questions twice," I chimed in. I was in a great mood and decided that I wanted to get to know as many wonderful people in my beloved Cape Town as I could.

As my head had started swimming at this stage, I ordered a bottle of vodka to go. Hannes ordered an Uber. I planned to revive myself a bit in the car, so that once again I could be like a young god at the house party.

"Either I'm losing form, or those whiskies must have been doubles."

I texted Jimi about a change of rendezvous point and to pick me up there.

"But Marek, do you know these people? Better wait for me at the bar!"

"Don't worry about it. They're okay, I know people."

I still managed to send my location to Jimi on WhatsApp so he could get there.

While in the Uber, the effect of the alcohol gathered even more strength. I felt weak and started getting hot and so asked for the air-con to turned up to the max.

"Nothing will happen to you," laughed Hannes from behind.

I can only recall selected scenes from what happened next.

I remember that the party took place in some large white villa. On the speakers, I recognized a set by Goldfish, a fantastic South African duo who create club music. Literally, every flat surface was occupied with bottles of alcohol. People were talking, laughing and dancing with each other, just exactly as it should be at any house party.

Actually, no. Not exactly.

Eventually, with what remained of my consciousness, I understood the catch. Namely, that there wasn't even one girl among the guests. Had I been sober, I would have noticed. But I wasn't. Apart from that, couples were getting together, dancing with each other and kissing. I also remember Jimi, who suddenly appeared with a girl who worked for him in the VIP lounge at the club.

I woke up in a large comfortable bed. Not my own, but in my own clothes. I rarely sleep like that if I don't have company.

Oh fuck. Company…

Where the hell was I? What time is it? What happened?

I got up and went straight to the kitchen. In which Jimi was making some scrambled eggs. He smiled at the sight of me. Well, no, not so much as smile as just burst out laughing.

"Relax," he said, before I had managed to say anything. "That hole in your ass is still its original size."

I found out what had actually happened the following day. As with every city full of tourist attractions, Cape Town is also full of tourist traps. And in this particular case, con-artists who take advantage of the naivety of newcomers. Such a con-artist gains your trust, by which you let down your guard. You don't notice them slipping something into your drink. Similar to those former customers of the Cocomo clubs in Poland who ended up drugged. The scene which may play out later depends on the type of tormentor who has managed to gain power over you. It may end up with you buying a round of drinks for everyone, a trip to the ATM, so someone can take care of your wallet, telephone or shoes... or you may end up raped or kidnapped.

Fortunately, I didn't come across real gangster, just more eloquent gays hoping to have a bit of fun at my expense, perhaps using some money from my wallet or the sale of my phone, as well as having a quick one with a completely unsuspecting Pole.

And my ass was saved, literally in this case, by WhatsApp. The service had just put 'live location' into operation, showing Jimi in real time where I was at a given moment. Jimi immediately knew what was up, as he knows a few tourists who had fallen victim to such scams. He dropped everything, or in fact did everything he could and managed to get there literally at the last minute.

And getting back to our rugby match. When, in the 46th minute of the game at Ellis Park, Jesse Kriel broke away to the left and then passed the ball to Willi le Roux who scored a spectacular try, thereby putting the Springboks into the lead, the blacks sitting opposite exploded with the same pure joy as the rest of the stadium. And even though the All Blacks eventually won the match, I understood that this country, despite everything, still had its future ahead of it. That these people want to live with each other. Maybe they are not yet able to do so, but it just so happens, after all, that time is on their side. Racism in South Africa will eventually die. And then Africa will breathe true freedom.

Chapter 10

FROM I DON'T KNOW I DON'T KNOW TO I DON'T KNOW THAT I KNOW

As I write these words, five years since I first landed in Lagos, I feel at home. I have fallen in love with this place, even though it's a toxic relationship. An addiction to Nigeria, despite its many drawbacks, its often strange inhabitants and even stranger customs. Here I have friends, and have somewhat gotten to know the culture, or rather cultures of this vibrant and vivid country. And above all, I have begun to understand the social mechanisms which govern here, as well as in other countries on this continent.

My frequently painful, but never boring discovery of this world, is perfectly described in the learning model created by Martin Broadwell in 1969. This model is based on four stages. As I think of it all now, the actions of every European or American in Africa can be divided into these four stages. Well, let's say four, because the vast majority, after reaching the second stage, usually say something like: "Fuck this! Nothing works here the way it should. I'm outta here."

Such a crisis most often appears after six months of being in Africa. At this stage, most expats at Rocket have crumbled and gone home. The record holder booked his return ticket the next day (by the way: bravo to the recruiter). If you stay a year, you'll stay for many years more.

Those who leave so quickly are making a mistake. Everything works here. Only in a different way. Sometimes in a very different way. And gaining an awareness of this is the first, usually the most painful stage of developing a business in Africa. It's the wrong intuition stage. That's the stage where you don't know what you don't know, because you think you know everything. But you actually know nothing. Simple, right?

And what don't you know? Anything. After about two or three months, a guy like me who thinks he knows everything about business, at least in his own field, realizes that he can throw at least half of his experience in the bin. Literally. One day, I turned on my computer and moved tens of documents with notes, analyses and other bullshit straight into the bin. It was simply taking up too much disk space.

Each one of us, including me, thinks that Africa is safaris, deserts and dried-mud huts. But according to the United Nations Organization, within a decade, half of Africans will be living in cities. 30 years ago, 1,000,000 people lived in Lagos. Today, it's 20 million. And things will get more interesting. The same research shows that by 2100, 80% of the world's population will be living in Africa and Asia. And that Nigeria will be the third most populous country in the world, following India and China.

What's more is that, within the next 15 years, the size of the middle class will double. Even now, it makes up a third of the population. Soon, it will be 60%. Of course, compared with the European or American middle classes, it's a bit poorer, but the facts are inescapable: there's going to be big money here. Although Rocket senses this, so do other tech giants. I spoke with people from Google, who wanted to expand their services into the Nigerian market. Of course, they had arrived loaded with all sorts of analyses for which they had paid hundreds of thousands of dollars. I was laughing at this a little as, after all, in Poland we say "Google knows everything".

This time, during these talks it turned out that Google didn't know shit. They wanted to develop their maps and introduce new functionality, when three-quarters of Nigerian drivers are unable to use its basic functions. But I've already described that.

Phones are yet another matter. There's a movie called *Crocodile Dundee* which, although set in Australia, matches the situation perfectly. So somewhere in the middle of the bush, the main character is with a lady, when they come across a guy who's jet black and covered in native war paint. Initially, she's nervous, but when it becomes apparent that the native has no intention of hurting them, she takes out a camera to take a picture.

"Oh no, you can't take my photograph," says the native firmly, in pretty good English too.

"Oh, I'm sorry. You believe it'll take your spirit away," she replies.

"No, you've got the lens cap on."

This kind of story could happen in any Nigerian village, although you would have to replace the camera with a smartphone. Today, there are 850,000,000 SIM cards in Nigeria. 40% of all phones here are smartphones. Although almost everyone has a phone, you wouldn't have heard of most of the brands, such as Tecno, Innjoo or Infinix. Most of them arrive in containers from various corners of the world and cost about $50, which is quite a lot of money for a Nigerian, but not so much as not to able to have two.

One example of a painful lesson for giants such as Google, Microsoft or Facebook is data transfer. It isn't enough that it's very poor quality and frequently crashes, but is also insanely expensive. Ignoring the rich for a moment, people here use the internet on their phones completely differently from 'civilization'. They're called smartphone zombies. So they have the same apps as you and I and apparently use them, but only every so often. They turn on data transfer, go on to FB, add a post, comment on something and then turn off data transfer. Notifications? Forget it. It's as if they don't exist. And then Google wonders why people don't use its maps as a sat-nav.

I remember a situation when an Evernote delegation came to see us at the office. Three white nerds straight from California, completely disoriented as to what was going on in Nigeria. They arrived with a consultant, who had been hired with the aim of conquering Africa. A guy born in Africa, but educated in the West. Dressed in an immaculate suit and speaking perfect English. Meaning a guy who was comfortable working in a corporation as if he was one of our us. And in exchange for such comfort, he just added the digit 1 in front of the fee on his invoices.

Anyway, Evernote had the brilliant plan to persuade all the couriers working at Jumia to use Evernote on a daily basis for making notes and using the basic functions of what was frankly amazing software. They looked a bit crestfallen when we explained that we were still at the stage of promoting Google Maps and Gmail.

On the other hand, it really is amazing how Nigerians know to the exact kilobyte how much data a particular application uses. And this is a very valuable indicator for anyone who wants to make a career in the start-up sector. Do you want to push a mobile app on them? It better use the minimum amount of data, otherwise you can forget about anyone downloading it at all. There's a rumor going around that once Mark Zuckerberg had visited Nigeria and realized what the problems were here, and how much money he was losing due to them, he introduced 'slow Fridays' on his return. Meaning he turned off 4G and LTE with all the data being transferred with the aid of GPRS and EDGE (that is older and slower data transfer technology). So as to make his people aware just how Facebook was being used in one of the biggest markets in the world.

Another fun fact. People in Europe often talk about the 'four screen theory'. Although this is actually gradually becoming obsolete, we still accept that we use a computer for activities taking longer than 30 minutes, tablets for activities lasting three to 30 minutes, smartphones from 30 seconds to three minutes (despite smartphones replacing tablets more and more often) and, finally, smartwatches for activities up to 30 seconds. Maybe it's a bit of an exaggeration, but we can generally accept it as true. In Africa, however, only one screen counts. The smartphone. Everything is done with the aid of one. Shopping, banking operations and making contact with people. You have a computer at work. As long as you work in an office. At home and everywhere else, the internet is accessed through a smartphone. The audiobook business is a great example of these differences. Audiobooks in the West are gaining popularity among those ambitious individuals who want to make their every minute more productive and listen to a book while driving, cleaning the house or working out. In many African countries, the consumption of audiobooks is driven by... school pupils. When an exam is getting closer and you have to study in the evening, but there is no light because the generator stopped working, your phone battery might be your only solution.

On the other hand, however, you have to remember that access to the internet means that you immediately have yourself a potential customer. I'm not talking about purchasing power here. One time, a certain consulting group whose name I shouldn't really mention (okay, it was Boston Consulting Group) recommended market research regarding the adoption of technology in developing countries, including Nigeria. And so BCG came up with the fact that more people in Nigeria use Facebook than the internet. Immediately, their research methodology was called into question, suggesting someone had made a boo-boo. It eventually came out that many people use Facebook, not knowing what else the internet may be used for. For some, the internet is on a computer, while Facebook is on a phone.

You seek out customers mainly through education. Nigeria is one of the few countries in the world where Google uses TV and billboards to advertise an internet browser, a product so basic to us.

In Europe, we have grown up with the internet. It has evolved before our eyes. It has hopped from device to device. Africa joined the game at a completely different moment and perceives everything completely differently. When cell phones first appeared in our world, for a long time there was a clear division: a telephone had a landline, while a cell phone you kept in your pocket. Then, when cell phones gradually pushed out telephones, perceptions evolved. Now, when someone asks if you have a telephone, you say yes, even though you don't have a landline at all anymore. And just as a matter of interest, does anyone have a landline telephone in their home anymore?

In any case, after the initial shock, the companies dealing in new technology eventually realized that it was often necessary to build everything here from scratch and almost always completely differently. If they release anything, it must first be optimized for smartphones, above all, and computers only coming in for later consideration. This has led to the Nigerian counterpart of eBay completely giving up on its desktop version. This happened soon after I first appeared in Africa and was a huge shock to me. And this was my first important lesson. Although I hadn't done my homework in advance, I more than made up for it later.

Another difference which causes the big boys to stay away from Africa, and allow local entrepreneurs to take their place, is the painful birth of infrastructure.

Let's look at Amazon, for example. An internet bookstore which later transformed itself into a publisher, then produced e-readers, and still later became a supermarket for electronics, furniture, holidays, food delivery, a company building artificial intelligence, a web hosting company, and a load of other things. Meaning they started from something small as a superstructure for another business, so as to later to gobble up all their partners one by one. But when they started, they didn't own a warehouse or even a book. There was no need. They made a deal with the publishers: we get you the orders and you pay us a commission and you send the book to the customer. In Washington state, an Amazon worker sends an order to a publisher in New York state, and he calls up FedEx saying: "Hey guys, call in cos I gotta book to send," and they say "Relax, man, we'll be there in two hours," and in two days a customer review would appear from someone in Minnesota or New Mexico: "Well it's pretty good, pretty good, the book is great, got super pictures and all, but, Jesus, I had to wait a really long time, I mean up to 48 hours."

And what would this look like in Nigeria? Well, like this: after a month, waiting for the book, the furious customer would ring up Amazon and say that they can shove the book right up their ass. And it's all the fault of the infrastructure. Or actually the lack of it. Firstly, the book would somehow have to wind its way to Africa from a publisher, because there aren't too many publishers in Nigeria. By air or sea. Then someone must land it. You never know how long a container ship will be standing at the coast. If no-one has paid off the port official in advance, it could be standing there up to a month. And then the road network in Nigeria is, one could say, pretty rough. Both literally and figuratively. In order to cover a thousand kilometers here, you need two days. In comparison, in order to cover the same distance in the USA, nine hours is enough. Nobody does that because the same distance can be covered in two hours by plane. But this isn't possible in Nigeria. Although the number of airports seems to be large, nothing flies there. Suffice to say that Abuja, the capital of Nigeria, whose metropolitan area has 6,000,000,000 inhabitants, deals with the same number of passengers as pass through the airport in Gdansk, Poland, a city of less than half a million. And the main airport in Lagos, a city of 20,000,0000 people, has half the number of passengers as Warsaw, which has a population

10 times smaller.

To be frank, in order to start up any e-commerce in Nigeria, first you'd have to build warehouses, then pack them to the roof with goods, and after that create your own private delivery network. When I arrived in Nigeria, Rocket was already running one project – Jumia – which was a kind of Nigerian Amazon.com. At the time, we had a bigger delivery fleet than the entire Nigerian branch of FedEx. What is more, Shoprite, a kind of Nigerian Tesco, possesses warehouse space 10 times greater than all of its stores.

Imagine that I wanted to follow in Amazon's footsteps in the hotel reservation business. Meaning that, at a certain point, it wasn't enough that I was middle-man in booking hotels, but now wanted to open my own hotel. And let's say that I didn't even have to build one, but that I bought one for a song somewhere near the sea. And what now? There's a problem. Because first, I'd have to build a road there. And I can bet you 100% there isn't one. Meaning that there's a bit of a dirt track, or a narrow potholed strip of asphalt, while I want establish a real hotel, after all. One with a proper road. But to build that, I'd first have to bring in the materials and equipment. But to bring in the materials and equipment, I'd first have to build my own quay in the port, because bringing in such amounts of goods in a commercial manner would take me about 10 years. But wait a minute, to get to the new quay I'd also have to build a road. And so it's all a vicious circle.

At the beginning, all of these strange circumstances surprise the hell out of you. And the success of a foreign investor depends on how quickly they can swallow their pride, roll up their sleeves and get down to real work. If, despite clear market signals, they fail to realize they're heading down the wrong road, no amount of money will save them.

Figuring all this out took me a while. Over a year and several hundred thousand dollars later, I already had a completely different attitude. Although I was aware that life is full of surprises, I would simply adapt to it. I decided to be like water according to the teachings of Bruce Lee. Now's the right time to google "Be like water" and Bruce Lee. And I have to acknowledge this is the second stage in the development of Marek Zmysłowski as an African businessman: I know that I don't know. The stage of conscious incompetence. Meaning I know nothing about this world, but at least I realize it and am careful.

At this stage, I mainly concentrated on fixing what had not worked before. And there sure were a lot of such things to fix.

Let's begin with the fact that the Nigerians are born foxy devils. Depending on the context, this may be something more or less positive. Sometimes even negatively positive. Which results in them hoodwinking both hotels and their guests. And when it turns out that the customer is dissatisfied, it's not the fault of the hotel, but Jovago. And if the hotel is dissatisfied, guess what? It's all Jovago's fault.

But we were ready for this, as I learned a hard lesson just a month after arriving in Africa. It was perhaps the first and, at the same time, most crucial thing which I learned: one of the greatest challenges in doing business in Nigeria (and not only here) is service quality.

It all started with Easy Taxi, that is the Nigerian Uber, which also belongs to Rocket. My first days in Lagos coincided with Easy Taxi's first few days on the market. Which was a total flop.

So why did Uber work and Easy Taxi eventually fail? In Nigeria, Uber had started things off a bit differently from the rest of the world. Above all, it had in mind that as only rich people have nice cars in Africa, they don't need extra jobs as taxi drivers. And those who do, only have old rust buckets at their disposal. So Uber made a deal with the biggest car fleet companies and found everything in Lagos which could be rented. And then they brought in the drivers. Each driver received a fairly decent car, thanks to which they could carry out the service. Which of course came with certain strings attached. As the car didn't belong to them, they would have to take care of it. It had to be clean and smell nice and, above all, be roadworthy. One slip up and we'll take the car back, and you'll lose your job.

In turn, Rocket's development of Easy Taxi was based on already existing taxis. And ensuring an appropriate level of service proved impossible. The average Nigerian taxi driver drives a 30 year-old car and, as in Poland, is the proverbial oldster with a mustache and a car stinking of sweat and cigarette butts. And there's nothing you can do about it. As it's his car, we can go whistle. Even if we cut him out of the app, he'll do the same as before and earn his money. Even more so, in that Easy Taxi never grew to the point where drivers could afford to be genuine business partners, as they weren't receiving enough orders daily to treat it seriously.

The quality of Uber in Nigeria was really quite satisfactory. Until the appearance of Taxify, an Estonian company which used the oldest trick in the book. Taxify's employees started using Uber *en masse* and proposing that Uber drivers join Taxify also. The sweetener was, of course, a higher commission than Uber was giving and the lack of a requirement to work exclusively for them. Very quickly, every Uber driver also became a Taxify driver. And so when an order came in from Taxify, the driver dumped any orders they had from Uber to take that which was better paid. Frustrated Uber customers whose third driver in a row had cancelled their order, having previously accepted it, also set up an account with Taxify. And so when they wanted to go from A to B, they placed their order using both apps at the same time, leading to their surprise at seeing that both orders had been accepted by the same driver.

So to sum up, while using the example of the hotel sector: if by some miracle we managed to improve the quality of service in the hotels working with us, we would have totally dominated the market.

Meanwhile, the reality presented itself as follows: the customer has ordered a hotel through our service. He's seen beautiful photos, read nice descriptions and is convinced that he'll be staying in a little corner of heaven. Then, when he arrives, he doesn't get the room he ordered, the air-conditioning has broken down, the Wi-Fi doesn't work, no-one had managed to clean the room and it's on the proverbial 10th floor with no elevator.

The result was that initially Jovago had a terrible reputation. We had made a mistake in not differentiating the range of responsibilities of Jovago and the hotels in the system. The customer assessed the entire service. So, of course, he gave us one star. Once we had changed it, you could give your assessment of the quality of the app and the hotels.

But we didn't give up. In this story, I intended to be Uber, not Easy Taxi. Yeah, right. Just easier said than done. Especially at the beginning. Years later, we could strike from a position of strength: "Your hotel doesn't fulfill our requirements concerning service quality? So we'll cut your off from the system and you'll lose a shitload of money". And this works, if a hotel has had 50 guests that month thanks to us. But in the beginning, when they were getting two customers a month, they usually didn't give a fuck about us. As the old methods had gotten 10 times more guests, why change anything? We had to do it all ourselves.

Which was initially easy, but pretty tedious. Everyone knows that this kind of business has to be done quickly. Building up supply (hotels), then immediately generating demand (customers) and deriving profits from the love match established between them on my website. But of course building up demand takes a while. We were prepared for the fact that we were going to be strongly up against it during this time, even though we were doing everything we could to make sure this would be for as short a time as possible. At that time, we were working on ways to pamper our customers. In practice, this took the form of my guy, armed with information from the customer, going to a hotel to check if everything was okay. If it had been cleaned, if the appliances worked or if the hotel description was in line with the facts. If it wasn't, we made a row about it and we usually managed, as a result, to have the faults fixed or the room changed. Of course, although it wasn't easy to convince hotel owners to do this, we had been given a stick to beat them with: paradoxically, the terrible online reviews helped us out. It was pretty easy to persuade the culprit with "Hey, so you think no-one's going find out how awful your hotel is? Some hope. Look. Everything's described here. For all the world to read. And the whole world can find out that it's best not to come to you, because it's filthy/the air-conditioning doesn't work/the rooms are too small, or something else."

Although this usually worked, there were cases where they hotel owner threatened us with the police (or sometimes the army), if we didn't take down these reviews. One of my employees was once arrested for something like this. He had gone to the hotel to talk to the manager to see what could be done to improve their reviews. And later he called me up to have them removed, as they wouldn't let him leave the hotel.

And that's not all. In Pizza Hut, if you've already ordered your pepperoni on a thick crust and are just eating it, a waitress always comes over to ask if everything tastes right. Some people like it, others find it irritating, but at least everything's clear. Although I've never actually heard anyone say "No, it's terrible", there's always a way to assess customer satisfaction. And we do it also. During the hotel visits of our customers, we conduct 'spot checks'. We knock on the door and find out if everything is in line with their expectations and, if not, what we can possibly do to improve things.

And that's what we came there to do.

Hotels don't only cater for travelers. It often happens that a normal family from Lagos with a bit more money than usual, but not so much as to stay in a luxury hotel, books a weekend break at a hotel after spending the week in the noise and dirt of the city. Then you can make use of the pretty good restaurant, relax in the spa, take a dip in the pool… and not have to worry about power cuts or the lack of running water. That is, the typical problems of the inhabitants of any large city in Nigeria, and the smaller ones even more so.

And this is a very popular practice, with weekend trysts being even more popular. Nigerians are one of the most sexually active nations on earth. Of course, I have no credible research in this field, but I've never come across such levels of promiscuity, and I've been around.

Well, when our 'quality control consultant' stumbles across such a tryst, it sure isn't easy. Once, one of them returned with the left side of his face completely swollen. I asked him what had happened:

"I went to check if the customer was satisfied…"

"And?"

"And he was satisfied. Or rather being satisfied."

"Be clearer."

"Well, I knocked on the door and heard 'Who's there?'. Well, it's me, that 'It's Jovago and I'm checking…', but I hadn't finished checking, because he told me to piss off. At that, I knocked even louder, because it's my job, for Christ's sake. Eventually, they open the door and I see the guy. He looked funny as he was covering himself up with a duvet, but was trying to hide his face more than his really fat body. So you know, he looked a bit like Santa Claus. And I look and see that there on the bed was lying some kind of hook… I'm mean girl."

"Get to the point!"

"And I say to him: 'Hey, I know you! May I have your autograph?'" and here he mentioned the name of a famous sportsman, who every day declares his affinity for the Church and family values.

Unfortunately, he met with a swift, but fairly painful response. The sportsman had given it to him with an open hand, a full force. One hell of a slap in other words. In Nigeria, people of a lower social class tend to be hit by their superiors with an open hand. So the guy was as happy with his souvenir, as if he really had gotten an autograph.

Much later on, I found out that there are those who rent out five suites at a hotel, with a different girl in each and sometimes several in one room. And they have a little 'party on tour' with their buddies. With such people, especially if they're famous, it's best not to ask whether the toilet has been disinfected or the towels are clean.

In any case, eventually this Trojan work resulted in us being able to secure a satisfactory level of service quality from our partners. But let's agree that this wouldn't have succeeded if we hadn't grown. And we were growing really quickly. During all of 2014, we observed a continuous week-to-week growth rate of 5%. I'm talking here about the number of nights booked. Once hotels started getting 20% of their reservations from us, we had them in the palm of our hand. But in order to maintain quality, we also had to brainwash them a little. This is why we organized a series of training sessions, where we explained why they needed us. We didn't mention anything at all at these sessions about how cool the internet is and a how it would save their business. Actually, it was exactly the opposite. The central message was that the internet is not an opportunity, but something they needed to survive. As by now, Africa had already learned that booking hotels through the net is nice and simple, people will stop using other ways to do it. From the dozens of reservations that people were making personally or by walking in off the street, this would dwindle to just several, then to a few, with eventually no one doing it. So whoever didn't work with Jovago would die. But in order to work with us, the highest service quality had to be guaranteed. As well as payment on time.

The latter was especially important, as due to payment problems Jovago almost ended up screwed. If it hadn't been for the support of Rocket, and the fact that I quickly cottoned on to the situation, we would have ceased to exist.

In Africa, trust in the mail order business is almost non-existent. Depending on for whom the transaction is more important, the buyer plays 100% up front before the seller sends anything whatsoever or the buyer pays nothing until they see the product. Buying online increases the level of risk for the buyer by another order of magnitude. This is apart from the fact that paying online is like hotel Wi-Fi, there but not working right now. In the mind of the typical Nigerian customer, there is no question of paying in advance or paying money to a website. Nobody orders anything they can't 'touch' with their own hands. Although it's true that e-commerce is operating more and more dynamically, payment on collection comprises well over 80% of all transactions. And this meant that we couldn't put our option of immediately taking our commission into operation. Actually, we had the idea of starting a campaign to motivate customers to pay online at the moment of booking. But market research showed that we would have had to give a discount of at least 20% to convince anyone of using an option from a system completely alien to them. Meaning we would have been giving up our entire commission, as there wasn't a hope of convincing hotels to give us an even lower room rate.

So we took another route. The normal one. At the end of every month, we simply issued an invoice. And then serious problems arose. While it was true that we served several large hotels managed by international operations networks which paid up on time, most of our partners were smaller hotels which were just about breaking even. Although when they got the money from the customer they did really want to pay, by the time our invoice had arrived the cash just wasn't there. It had gone on running costs. They could of course have paid from the money they received from later guests, but it wasn't their custom to do so: "Why should I pay from the money I got from this guest? After all, you didn't send him to me." Some regularly cheated us, saying, for example, that the customer had never arrived, so they didn't owe us anything. So we ring up the customer, who expresses their surprise by saying: "What do you mean I never arrived? I'm still here for God's sake, sitting in the bathtub." So, of course, we cut such crooks out of the network immediately. Initially, they couldn't give a fuck, but then later it started to hurt a little. At a certain point about a month after being cut off, we called the hotel and said: "We had to cut you off, because you didn't pay. This month we had 40 customers for you, but had to send them to the competition. But if you promise not to cheat us again, we'll give you another chance and re-connect you to the system."

Of course, they always assured us that they would be honest in future. And you know what? We had lots of crooks, but never the same one twice. It was important to be careful that being nice was not mistaken for being weak. Sometimes you gain respect from just treating them a little tougher.

Sometimes, however, the hotel's explanation, although absurd, turned out to be true. The guests had never arrived. Or they had arrived, just somewhere else. We only caught on to this after a few months, because they also tried to cheat the system. They were capable of booking rooms in five different hotels. For the same night. A then they stayed in the one they liked the most. Since they were paying on site, there was no way to punish them for this. All we could do was throw our hands in the air and introduce a technical solution, which made booking several rooms for the same night impossible. Obviously, this wasn't easy as, after all, many of our clients were corporations who often booked 10 rooms at the same time, without providing names. So whatever we did, the hotel was furious at us, because it had a reservation, had not sold the room to anyone else, and had been left with diddly-squat in the end. And not being aware of the situation, we then issued them with an invoice.

It also happened that the guest had indeed turned up, but hadn't trusted any of the websites or the travel agents. Although he had made a reservation, he just reserved the same room on the same night on three different websites. It looked more or less like this: the customer went onto our website and looked for a hotel for himself. Then he called several other travel agents because he wasn't sure if the hotel would honor his reservation made by that travel agent he had chosen first. So all five travel agents ended up booking a room in the same hotel. It wasn't possible to establish if this was the same person, because they often provided different details. Or the hotel, as usually happened, had failed to notice. The guest arrived and paid the room rate which was lowest. Of course, the hotel had to grit its teeth as instead of five bookings, they had only one. But the best was yet to come, as all the agents involved contacted the hotel looking for their commission. So now go ahead and establish who it belongs to.

Such things were certainly of no help to us. Eventually we understood that it wasn't enough to teach people how to take advantage of online booking. We also had to join it with marketing activities.

And this was the moment I found myself at the third stage of gaining knowledge, namely 'I know that I know'. The stage of conscious competence. I knew, more or less, what worked and what didn't, in which areas you needed to be careful, and in which it was 'anything goes'. I was a long way from calling myself an African business expert, but at least I now knew I what had to do to get things going. As well as what I couldn't do.

Gaining customers through the internet undoubtedly has one great advantage. It's quantifiable. Most tactics and ideas can therefore be checked out by testing them on a small scale. Later, these can be scaled-up to see if our assumptions are correct, or if we are dealing with a coincidental correlation, rather than a real cause-and-effect relationship between the input and the result in an experiment.

Most companies which operate outside the internet invest huge amounts of money in offline advertising. Although it produces results, it is not in a way in which you can determine which advertisement works and which doesn't. But we had the comfort of being able to easily secure information on which marketing activities produce results and which didn't, while spending relatively little money each time.

The problem is that if you run an online business in Nigeria, gaining customers just through the internet is not enough. This is why we recognized that we had to find customers just as in the good old days, namely on the streets, on the radio and on TV.

Once, I gathered the entire team into a meeting room, placed a cap on the table and said something like: "Okay, now everyone throws in their own idea for offline promotion. Every idea counts. Even those which may seem stupid."

And so it kicked off. My team showed themselves to be more creative than all of last year's winners of the Golden Lion at the Cannes (the most prestigious prize in advertising) put together. Two days later, we had a list of activities which we intended to put into practice.

We started with promotional gimmicks, which is the simplest thing for companies or institutions which employ lots of people. We produced maybe 10,000 beer mats and distributed them to all the bars and restaurants in Lagos. And on the front we placed our marketing message along with a discount code, so as to track how many customers we generated through it. We handed out Hi-Vis vests with our logo and slogan to the crazy Okada riders. Not only did we take care of their safety, but because there was a whole army of Okada, we reached enormous numbers of potential customers thanks to them. Maybe not those who used the Okada, but definitely those who were passing by in their SUVs. For restaurants, we prepared paper napkins and plastic cutlery. Branded, obviously. In shops we set up stands. We published our own *Guide to Lagos,* which we distributed to all of the Nigerian embassies around the world. The booklet was, of course, to be found in every room of every hotel which worked with us.

Even though the average inhabitant of Lagos was already afraid to open his refrigerator in case the name Jovago jumped out, we were only getting going. We made a deal with two local airlines, which facilitated access to the airline ticket sales areas of airports. We helped pass the time of those poor unfortunates who happened to be flying anywhere from Lagos by telling them about our product. We had tablets, showing how to use the service and stressing how quick and easy it was to use. This actually went pretty well. People standing in line at airports who had lots of formalities to still go through were happy to see us remove at least one burden from their mind. After all, as they are already flying to some place, they'll have to find a hotel, right? Oh, yeah? Everything's already sorted out.

Apart from airplanes, we also covered the bus stations for intercity routes, but here we went one step further. Our guy would buy a ticket and spend the entire journey with his fellow passengers. At a certain moment, he would stand up, take ten tablets from his bag and ask who wanted to have a little fun. As I'm sure you've already guessed, everyone did. But before they got it into their hands, our representative gave them some professional brainwashing. The passengers got off that bus knowing that from this day forward their lives had become just a little easier. And the driver got his palms greased, just so there was no trouble.

Then we set about getting a celebrity on board. There's guy in Nigeria known as the local Kanye West and he became our brand ambassador. And this was, both for him and for us, a big deal. For him, because in Nigeria a celebrity advertising anything is a really big PR success, as only the biggest stars do it. And for us, because only telecom companies could afford to sign contracts with celebrities. So we made Jovago a player in the big leagues. However, if anyone had looked under the hood, they would have split their sides laughing. Because under the terms of our contract, in exchange for his endorsement, all our local Kanye West got was a few free nights in a hotel every month.

The next project was thought up by – wait for it – the guy who delivers our food. When I heard the idea, I understood that I was dealing with the best PR project in history. In fact, I fell of my chair.

In Nigeria, about 60% of its inhabitants are under 30 years old. And the vast majority of them are unemployed. In fact, most of them are looking for work, with the whole family often helping in this task.

In every large Nigerian town, we announced that we were looking for people to do small jobs. Check hotels, secure new partners, debt collection, simple marketing activities, handing out leaflets and so on. And although we really did need such people, we had over 100 jobs ready to go all over the country. And there had never been such a large-scale recruitment campaign. The best part was the spontaneous response of social media. People retweeted our announcement and put it up on Facebook. Hundreds of thousands of applications. Everyone in Nigeria knows someone who's looking for work. A brother, sister, friend, acquaintance, whoever. And these people answered our announcement in good faith, while simultaneously discovering what Jovago was about, what benefits it offered and so on. Thanks to all of this, not only did our recognizability increase gigantically, but we also became a 'friendly firm', seeing as any company offering 100 jobs in Nigeria must be friendly. The only drawback was that we got over 100,000 Cvs, which soon caused our servers to explode.

But we decided to ride the wave and eventually we went with TV commercials, but this is quite complicated in Nigeria, as it still happens that TV stations frequently do not keep to the terms of their contracts with their clients. They repeatedly sign contracts for a determined number of commercials, but broadcast much fewer. This is why the more serious companies, once they have signed such a contract, employ an outside company to check the number actually broadcast. And then they hire another company to check the first. And everything is fully transparent. The market has decided this. The TV station knows it will be checked, the TV inspectors too.

Such a conglomerate of con-men.

Although I was also advised to go down such a route, then my old long-forgotten buddy appeared, 'I'll show you'. Oh no, you don't.

Anyway, I recognized that we were not only not going to pay off the con-men, but we were going to whip up a total shit storm. Well, we prepared a viral message. Okay, so it wasn't very original, as McDonald's had done it years ahead of us. But we were in Nigeria and they weren't. So we announced to all and sundry that the first 10 people to call us after the broadcast of every Jovago commercial on TV would receive 1000 naira each. Which is about three bucks. As you can guess, the next time everything that could be written about us was, at least anything in print or using the more modern incarnations of the Guttenberg press.

On this occasion, TV stations did not help us out. For obvious reasons. We had bought a 1000 commercial spots altogether. Handing out $30 in prizes each time. Apart from the main expense of $500,000 on the commercials themselves, we had spent $30,000 on prizes for viewers. That is half of what we would have had to spend on TV inspection companies. What is more, we had created such a buzz about ourselves that our reach had gone many times beyond what a normal TV commercial could have guaranteed us.

We also hadn't forgotten about radio broadcasts. Radio is still a 'romantic adventure' in Africa. As the electricity is often turned off in the evening in many African countries, a battery-operated radio is often the only way to maintain contact with the world. Drivers find themselves in a similar situation, when stuck in traffic for a third of their lives, they have to have something to listen to for Christ's sake.

We introduced three advertising formats on the radio. Firstly, normal regular commercials, by which we increased Jovago's brand awareness. We broadcast those around the clock. Secondly, through sponsorship. We paid broadcasters to devote some of their time on air to talking about how nice and easy it is to book a hotel online. And thirdly, me entirely in white. Meaning using my personal brand in the promotion of our product.

I should warn you that now I'm going to get a little full of myself. Hold on tight, dear reader.

My entire celebrity story had started quite accidentally. When I appeared in Africa, the best known 'start-up expert' was a guy called Jackson. A Nigerian brought up in the UK, he had returned home after a business failure there to establish Nigeria's Netflix, streaming mainly movies made in Nollywood, the Nigerian movie industry. Just as a side note, if you have ever seen any Bollywood productions, you must also watch something from Nollywood. Once you've seen it, you can never unsee it. As I know the more I dissuade you from this idea, the more interested you'll be, just check out *Nollywood Spider-Girl* on YouTube right away.

Anyway, when Rocket entered Nigeria, Jackson had already got his business going and must have been doing well, as the amounts of money which investors had invested in him and the income which he had generated were multiples greater than other local tech start-ups. Which were actually very few in number.

And actually this guy had a very specific approach to the origin of money. In posts on his blog, he was a very vocal opponent of 'allowing' Rocket Internet into the Nigerian market. He believed that neo-colonialists were standing at the gates of Nigeria and that we would enter with such money that no one would be able to compete with us, that it would be a technological blitzkrieg, that we'd come in, plough everything into the ground and leave scorched earth behind us before our escape.

Only in describing such a scenario, he forgot to mention that the beginnings of his local Netflix had been financed by his buddy, a German, who was the *éminence grise* behind the company. And that the greatest sums of money in this business had been invested by funds also outside Africa. And that's how Jackson defended Nigeria from the foreign capital which he himself had brought in.

My Nigerian start-up premiere and first attempts at image building began with a few polemic articles which I then sent to a friendly Nigerian technology site. The first of these articles was published on TechCabal.com. I compared my experience at the school of hard knocks in the Polish start-up scene with that in Nigeria. In order to gain the sympathy of readers, I also mentioned the similarities between Poles and Nigerians, that Poles and Nigerians are entrepreneurs, as entrepreneurs emerge from a necessity for survival. Both nations have problems in this regard, as it often takes on a form of cheating the system. Religion also plays a very important role in both countries and has an influence on political decisions.

The Polish culture and language was able to survive, despite the fact that we disappeared from the maps of Europe for over a century. And this occurred with the consent of the Polish elite of the day, which placed more importance on private than national interest, a problem which is not foreign to the Nigerians. In the same way, the Yoruba tribe, one of the largest in Nigeria, has been able to survive up to today in Cuba and Brazil despite centuries of persecution and slavery.

For decades, the Polish economy after the Second World War was stifled by communism right up to the time when the Solidarity trade union movement, with Lech Wałęsa as its leader, led us into a free Europe (free inasmuch as capitalism allowed). And just a few years later, pro-democratic changes gained momentum following the death of the last (official) dictator of Nigeria, Sani Abacha, who kicked the bucket in 1998, two days before the start of the World Cup in France. Fortunately, he didn't live to see Nigeria being knocked out of its group in the first stage, following a 1:4 defeat by Denmark.

The global financial crisis of 2008 basically helped Poland. As our financial and banking market was not yet as advanced as the rest of Europe or the United States, it wasn't as saturated with junk financial products (previously known as 'advanced') which would have upset the growth of a dynamic economy. This same crisis, just as the previous dot-com bubble of 1995-2001, resulted in many educated and foreign-based Nigerians returning home with new skills which they would soon use for the benefit of the country. So Nigeria became Africa's economic engine, just as Poland had done in Europe.

Poland's start-up scene had a difficult birth. There were stages where people complained of an insufficient number of investors or too great an aversion to risk among those already in existence. Later, there was too much money for investment, which ended in the establishment of crazy businesses or irresponsible entrepreneurs receiving financing who never should have in the first place, a situation I've already described in a chapter about my adventures in Poland.

How many times have I heard pessimists in Poland complaining that new businesses were just clones of those in the States or Western Europe? Today, Polish technology is leading the world in the production of computer games and 3D printers, and we have examples of global leaders from Poland such as LiveChat, Brand24, RTB House or InPost.

The Polish tech sector grew at such a crazy rate, mainly due to that which was being criticized in Nigeria at the time, namely the influx of foreign capital. And here in my article I came to the heart of the matter, that is the problem of Rocket Internet, a 'foreign' tech giant stifling local start-ups. Nigerian critics had stated that foreign capital would capture the leading position in key areas in a fledgling online market in Nigeria or Africa. And that this would not give small players, who didn't have sufficient resources, a chance to compete with them. At the same time, there was an unwillingness to notice the enormous work carried out in educating the marketplace at least, thereby creating space for opening more businesses. If a customer had learned to buy airline tickets online, maybe tomorrow he would buy some local app. Although such changes would have happened anyway without Rocket, it would certainly have taken about 20 years longer to occur.

It was the same regarding talent. Finding the right people to employ is the most difficult task in Africa. Because while there are masses of people out there willing to do the job, those able to do it are no longer there. Only very few companies, such as Rocket, were able to afford to employ young, ambitious, but completely untrained people and then invest time and money in order to train and instill the highest business standards into them.

It somehow turned out that Rocket's greatest critics had the good fortune of having parents who could afford to send them to study abroad and then find them their first job, also abroad. Although a whole army of fiendishly capable Nigerians did not enjoy such good fortune, it was Rocket which ended up employing them.

Now, every new company opening in Nigeria, and which secures its customers online, has it easier, as they can employ those who came through Rocket. In addition, working at any of Rocket's companies works wonders on a CV when you go to an investor looking for money. Just as having worked at McKinsey on your CV would get you into Rocket. Not in my case of course. At least half of the current start-up founders in Nigeria who have managed to secure financing from foreign investors have worked at one of our companies at one stage. That's no coincidence. It's a cause-and-effect relationship.

Jackson was always critical of the importation of foreign (white) managers to run local companies in which Rocket invested. Managers such as myself. But Rocket sought them out because they had too. And cried when they had to pay for it. Because just as in Nigeria there was a problem in quickly hiring hundreds of good senior programmers, there was also a lack of good middle level managers. At a certain moment, out of 300 employees, we had 30 foreigners. But that was 'peak foreigner'. After three years, out of 100 employees, only one was en expat. In the meantime, we simply trained up local managers. Just as good, but cheaper. Foreign capital came into the tech sector in Africa, because local capital usually didn't want to. A typical African millionaire has made his money in commodities and often not in an entirely legal way. Such a guy wants to invest in a business he understands, best of all in an apartment complex in London bought in his aunt's name, in case there's a change of regime and the new one isn't so friendly.

The first real African investors in the tech sector in Africa, I concluded in my article, will be those African entrepreneurs who have first made their own millions in technology and then invest it into other enterprises. This is why the first stock market debuts of local tech firms are necessary. And it's also necessary for some huge foreign corporation, such as Microsoft or Apple, to buy an African start-up established by African entrepreneurs for big money, meaning billions of dollars. Only then will local rich people, investors and banks willingly begin to look into this sector.

And that's how, point by point, I laid out arguments for the other side. The article got a very good response. During the first month, it was read several thousand times. It was such one-sided discussion, as Jackson never took up the challenge to respond to my counter-arguments. Of course, other media outlets did that. They needed faces which would represent foreign involvement in the tech sector in Africa. With which Africa is fascinated. And a face they got.

I became famous. And lots of people liked me. I was rather the opposite of everything Nigerians thought of white people. An expat in Nigeria was usually a sailor, an engineer or somebody else in construction. A world-weary old man who was fat and had a mustache. A man who was despised by the locals whom he certainly didn't mix with. Meanwhile Zmysłowski posted up hundreds of photos showing him eating local dishes such as egusi, a soup may from plant seeds, spiced fish and kilos of chili. In Lagos there are a huge number and variety of meetings, conferences and talks. Nigerians adore talking and giving talks. For hours. And I took advantage of this. When invitations came in to take part in events on radio or television, I always agreed.

I gave them what they wanted, meaning, for instance, performing the local shoki dance (I'm begging you, don't search for this on YouTube) and obviously spread the gospel about the internet and Jovago.

At the same time, I never tried to oversell Jovago, as this could had had the opposite effect from what I wanted. I rather spoke about Nigeria and its upcoming future. About new technology. About the advantages it brings. About how the world will soon be breaking down the door to get into Nigeria and the growing potential of this country will be impossible to deny. However, I didn't avoid difficult issues. I wasn't afraid to speak about Boko Haram, even though everyone advised me against it. Put simply, while there, I felt as if I was one of the locals.

I got loads of offers to perform in various low-budget Nigerian Nollywood movies. Although one's acting ability didn't count, I decided never to venture there. I actually backed out at the last minute from filming a leading role as a white journalist in a movie called *Idahosa*. Seeing the movie later in a movie theatre in Lagos forever convinced me that acting in Nigerian movies is not my thing. That said, I didn't turn down offers to parade down the catwalk at a fashion show. Although I nearly died of embarrassment and nervousness then, I will be bragging about my photos with male and female models until the day I actually die.

And you know why Jackson was really battling against Rocket? Because just before Jovago was put into operation, he himself had invested in a hotel booking website and, what's more, had established his own start-up incubator. Rocket had not suited his plans at all, as a bigger kid had come into his sandpit and started to play with the same toys.

And coming back to our stages, just the fourth is left: 'I don't know that I know'. The intuition stage. When you just feel that this is the best decision, even though you don't know exactly why.

But your subconscious knows perfectly well and remembers why.

Chapter 11

JAGUARS AND LEOPARDS

I recently watched a certain French feature report on TV about Nigeria. It was sad and moving. And it ended with the thesis that we Europeans, a real civilization, must do even more to help these poor unfortunate, malnourished people, who no-one invests in and are generally 'dirt poor', to take care of their future.

What a crock of shit. People driven by ideology completely fail to notice how they contradict themselves. On the one hand, "Africa is wonderful and doesn't need the white man" and a second later they say "Hey, let's collect money for Africa, they need our help". Africa has become more a subject of academic than practical solutions. Everyone wants to talk about it, but most don't have much to say.

One of the most popular media myths is that a supposed ban on receiving international aid written into the constitution of Botswana is the reason why one of the poorest countries of sub-Saharan Africa has become one of the richest.

I've read this many times and corrected it as many times. But I have to bring it up once again, as it's a real scandal that people learn history and geography from memes (in fact, I've read the constitution of Botswana from cover to cover; and there isn't a single word about any ban on taking money from anyone. If anyone doesn't believe me, go ahead and read it. Botwana's constitution is available on the net).

In actual fact, in its history Botswana has received the most international aid per capita of all African countries, perhaps the most of any country in history. The initial years of its independence were financed by Britain. Later, big money came in from the USA, Germany and Scandinavian countries.

Why then did Botswana, over the space of 60 years, go from being one of the poorest countries in the world to one of the richest in this part of the world? In my opinion, mainly because it had the good fortune to have honest presidents. In contrast to the many subsequent 'presidents' of Nigeria. Even though honesty is less often a result of happiness and more often one of culture.

There are two similarities between Botswana and Nigeria. Firstly, both were ravaged by the British. Secondly, in the middle of the last century, both were found to have enormous natural resources – oil in Nigeria, diamonds in Botswana. Insofar as Seretse Khama, the president of Botswana, who served for 14 years, used this wealth to reform the country, subsequent presidents of Nigeria, of whom there were five in the same period, mainly concentrated on reforming the contents of their own pockets and those of their supporters. And those who came after them were no better. While Botswana battled with corruption, racism and social problems until these were brought down almost to zero, Nigeria simply did the opposite.

The result of all this is that Gaborone, the capital of Botswana, is a fairly modern city, built in a near-Western style, where people live well considering African circumstances (as long as they don't catch AIDS, as almost one in three inhabitants of Botswana are infected with HIV). However, not many people rise above the average, at least in financial terms. At the same time, in Abuja and Lagos poverty reigns by day, while the 'charmed life' is seen at night. The disgusting wealth of the idle rich, those who are rich by profession and birth. It's these people I now want to tell you about.

Let's begin with the fact that very few come from 'old money' families, where wealth has been passed down through many generations. Of course, there are noble families, many compared with Europe, in fact. Just in Nigeria alone, there are at least several varieties of kings…

Most of the money, however, comes from the mid-20th century, when oil was struck and the rich Western world dropped into Nigeria shouting "Shut up and take my money!". It was then that the greatest fortunes were created, with the descendants of these home-grown businessmen appearing on today's stage, meaning the second or third generation of people with money. As they say, Daddy's boys and Daddy's girls. These are the worst. Most of them haven't worked a day in their lives, or are mainly employed to smile at photo-reporters, or visiting their family businesses. Because business based on oil is the easiest money in the world. All you need are political contacts. Every so often, they award their citizens (yeah, sure, average Joes…) a piece of land with oil on it. Whether this is part of a strange secret deal or sold at a heavy discount, in any case, the land is sold for peanuts. Then a guy in a fancy suit comes to you with a cigar clenched between his teeth, carrying a beautiful leather briefcase emblazoned with the logo of Shell, Mobil, Chevron, Agip or Texaco and tells you that this is for starters. The briefcase is crammed to the brim with dollars. You hand over the keys and say "do whatever you like on my land" and they do just that, then every month they send you not enough dough just to fill a briefcase, but a shipping container. Simple. In Nigeria they produce 2.5 million barrels of crude a day. A barrel costs about $50. Meaning that the land in Nigeria is pumping out $125,000,000 daily. Annually, this works out at $45, 500,000,000 to be shared out.

People who earn such money give a pretty waitress thousand-dollar tips, having paid a restaurant bill of $10,000.

In the West, people mainly use money to improve their standard of living, whatever this hackneyed slogan means. They buy nice cars, apartments and houses. As well as expensive electronic toys and so on.

The problem occurs when you spend money with only one aim in mind: just to show that you have it to spend. The most important thing you can achieve in Nigeria and many other African countries is social advancement. It's what everyone dreams of. And to gain social advancement, you have to earn money. So it's important that everyone sees that you have it more than whether you actually use it for anything.

I see this with my own neighbors. Although I live in one of the better districts of Lagos, it's still barely the equivalent of Brooklyn or somewhere like that. A multi-family apartment block, grey and not very impressive. A neglected stairwell, unpredictable elevators. At the same time, in the car park outside there is something you wouldn't expect. A Lamborghini, a Ferrari, several Porsches, which here is considered a poor man's car, two Bentleys, an Aston Martin and at least six G-class Mercedes. My Toyota Sequoia looks like a taxi alongside them.

The richest of the rich are different. They don't live in apartment blocks, but in colossal villas which, of course, also fulfill a representative function. So they stuff them with anything they can get their hands on. On the one hand, a 1000" flat screen TV; on the other, marble, Doric-Ionic-Corinthian columns and kitsch to the max, a gigantic chandelier in the style of Louis something-or-other. I was once at the home of a client. When he welcomed me at the door around noon that day, I passed a group of people who had come to change the light bulbs. As it turned out, having signed a contract, my host turned out to be most hospitable and we had a 'small bite to eat' to celebrate the occasion. When I left a day later, the light-bulb changers were just about half-way through the job. And the garden? What garden? Land in Lagos is insanely expensive. So if you buy some, you don't do it to sow some weeds on it. There are no gardens in Lagos. Houses begin and end three feet from the fence. And the rest is paved with Baum paving stones, usually red, so the same as in Poland. Any divergence from this rule is exceptionally rare and exceptionally unwelcome. One time, I was invited to the home of a businessman, an African mogul in the airline catering business. If you fly around Africa, you've definitely had his chicken and rice. When I was going to see him, my friends told me to be careful as he was "a bit weird".

It very quickly became apparent what the basis of this weirdness was. The guy had built a house only using up half his plot of land. The rest he had transformed into a beautiful garden, in the middle of which stood a large tree.

"Great, isn't it?" he asked, as if he was bragging about a new toy.

"Beautiful and very unusual," I said, pretending to be a tree enthusiast.

"Just so you know. We live in Africa, right? So it would seem that whatever we have, we've got trees up to here. Nothing could be more wrong. Nobody sells anything like this here. I had this one brought in from Jamaica."

"What do you mean 'had this one brought in'?"

"As normal. In a container."

I've already told you a little about cars, and mentioned earlier how anyone can buy police roof lights and ensure priority on the road. But you must realize that in Nigeria there are not only rich people, but also those richer than rich. And on the road you can differentiate between four kinds of wealthy people. The first are those who buy police lights, which flash blue, but with no siren. They have them installed on the roof, behind the windshield or, a solution which is especially popular, behind a fake radiator grill. They drive around and flash their lights, though nobody takes much notice.

The second kind are those who have lights and a siren. Such people are extraordinarily irritating, because the sirens are insanely loud. So if some motherfucker like this is tailgating you and blaring his siren, you let him go through just to get some peace and quiet: "Go on for fuck's sake, get out of my sight!".

The next group are those who, apart from police lights, throw a private cop into the deal, and who travels in the car with them. This works out cheaper per month than the cost of the lights. In a traffic jam, this cop can get out of the car and politely ask other drivers to get the fuck out of there. And as they usually wear black uniforms, these drivers politely and willingly give way, no-one wanting to end up with a bullet in their head.

And the final and richest group are those who drive with neither police lights nor with their own policeman on board. Instead, sometimes in front, sometimes behind, there's a pickup-up full of armed commandos who usually don't politely ask for anything, simply because they don't have to. Traffic jams part like the Red Sea at the sight of them. The few drivers who don't manage to get out of the way are taught a lesson they'll never forget.

The funniest thing, however, happens when such rich kids head to nightclubs. Because, after all, in Lagos you can't go very far in a Lambo with the suspension just three inches off the ground. So usually Lambos are only used to go to clubs. Once I went to a party with one such guy. Let's call him David. The journey looked like this: we drove out of the garage under his apartment, travelled 200 meters and… that was it. We had arrived. Although it was 30˚C outside, you don't buy a Lamborghini to use the air conditioning. Actually, because tinted windows are mandatory in Nigeria, we drove the whole way with the windows rolled down to the max. Let the common people see who the really rich are. But the best was to happen right outside the club itself. David pulled up in the middle of the street, after which a flunky in a suit got out of a G-class SUV, got into the Lambo and drove it back to the car park. The same one we had just left.

So we go into the club. The Lagos nightlife is a subject deserving of a separate book. Especially the nightlife of its rich kids. Anyway, the first thing you see when you enter a Polish nightclub is a huge dance floor. Somewhere along the walls are normal sofas and armchairs, while on the mezzanine, and often even in a separate room, is the VIP lounge. Because the last thing they want is to be rubbing shoulders with the hoi polloi.

In Nigeria, it's completely different. Above all, Nigerians don't dance in night clubs. The dancing is done by the chicks in your box seat. So the dance floor is only there for show, while the most important place in the club is the box seat. It's usually takes the form of specially raised dais, placed right in the middle of the club, of course. Just so that no-one there can avoid seeing it and who is sitting there that evening. The day I was there, I was seated with David and 15 chicks. I didn't know them. David had spotted them, sent out a bouncer, and a moment later there they were. Each one of them could have been a Miss Nigeria. I later found out that there are girls like this in every nightclub. If there are any guys sitting in a box seat where the women are either missing or outnumbered by men, then these pussy cats spring into action. They are usually young and inexperienced, as let's say that the ones who are a little older and sophisticated have already found their 'sugar daddies'. Soon, I was convinced that under normal circumstances we wouldn't have had a chance of inviting any other girls over to the table, because they always arrive with someone. Usually in large groups. Pop into a club, have a few drinks, talk to a nice girl? No chance of this in Lagos.

But these weren't normal circumstances. Because I was with David, who wasn't only loaded, but was also famous, a legend even. As a result of which girls, who had come in their own groups, and even with their 'sugar daddies', soon found themselves in our box seat.

David showed himself to be the perfect party host. From his position of command in the center of the box seat, he issued orders to DJs, waitresses, barmen, bouncers and whoever else was there. And, obviously, to his guests, especially to those of the opposite sex. Not even a half an hour had passed before we became the center of attention of the evening. All the spotlights were on us. And smartphones. I'm sure that Nigerian Snapchat's servers were close to overloading with all the photos and films. Thank God this kind of thing only went on for a few months following my arrival in Nigeria, when I was still fairly unknown. Otherwise, I would never be able to explain this to my mother.

David ordered 10 bottles of champagne time and time again – because as I think I've already mentioned, you ordered alcohol there by the bottle not the glass – each of which cost a 1000 dollars. When an order was placed, the DJ announced it over the microphone, the lights started flashing and the crowd went crazy. Each bottle was brought over by a different girl and there was a general atmosphere as if we were footballers who had just raised the Champions' League cup into the air. Generously and even-handedly, David filled the glasses of all the guests in the box seat. At a certain moment, after the fourth round when all the glasses were full, a problem appeared when it turned out that there was only one bottle left. What do you mean? Already? Is this the end of the fanfare? The end of the Champions' League. Oh no. No way, Jose. David just couldn't take it. So just like that, he uncorked the bottle and poured the whole lot into a champagne bucket full of ice. I've never seen anyone blow a thousand bucks in such a way before or since. Then he ordered another five bottles. He then placed them on the table, after which he said: "Marek, I'm outta here. The champagne is for you guys."

Whether David left on his own or with four girls, I'll just have to leave to your imagination.

There's no better party season in the year that the period between Christmas and New Year. Then all the rich kids who have been living abroad for years come back. They leave to study or take up internships. Then they fly home and, as they have a few bucks in their wallets which go much further in Lagos than in London, then the fun starts. There's nothing worse than a young punk who suddenly feels he is better than everyone else (now, where would I know that from?). At a certain moment, I eventually understood how it all works in the fortunes of the *nouveau riche*. As the classic line says, the first generation builds the business, the second generation develops it and the third generation pisses all the money away. This is shown brilliantly in the

Channel 4 TV show *Lagos to London: Britain's New Super-Rich,* which is about a generation of the descendants of Nigerian billionaires.

I myself used to live the life of 'an out-of-town party animal'. I once went to Johannesburg. To a conference, as normal. Meaning: a few hours chatting, then 'doing business' all night. I met a certain Indian man there, let's call him Deepankar, who was an associate of the largest South African classified advertisement website, which had started as a free newspaper decades earlier. In any case, we wanted to make a certain deal over the website.

Fortunately, we found some common ground with Deepankar and decided to go to a club afterwards to talk over the details. This was right after my adventure in Cape Town, after which I almost ended up in the #MeToo movement. Even though I knew the background of my friend fairly well, I told my assistant where I was going, who I was going with and sent her my live location (thanks, WhatsApp).

Deepankar took me to an amazing steakhouse, where the owner himself brought us into the kitchen and showed us how the meat, which we later ate, was all prepared. Of course, the steaks were the best I've ever had in my life. Then we headed off to one of the best known nightclubs at that time in Sandton, the business and entertainment district of Johannesburg. Obviously, we had a table there and Deepankar started his mating dance by ordering successive bottles of champagne.

Deepankar must have been disgustingly rich, or at least wished to seem so, based on the type and amount of alcohol he ordered and which he then shared with everyone around. Our table became both the most popular table with the opposite sex and the most hated among those of our own gender. Between negotiating points 5 and 6 of our contract, my companion went crazy for a certain lady sitting with her friend at the bar. He looked at me, and I instantly knew that the future of our working together in business depended on me being his wingman. I wasn't exactly very enthusiastic, as her friend was no oil painting. 'One for the team', I thought and started to entertain this lady, who was as ugly as sin, while a besotted Deepankar attempted to chat up his beautiful partner in conversation.

Fortunately, as the girls were very respectable or, at least wished to come across so, they left about 3am, to my delight and Deepankar's despair.

The next day, about noon, I got a call from my new friend who said that the party had been amazing and that he really liked one of the girls (what a surprise) and would like to invite her out to dinner. But the girl herself didn't want to go (also really weird that she didn't want to go to dinner alone at the home of a guy she had just met), because she's respectable, yadda, yadda, yadda. Anyway, there would be three of them there. Including the ugly friend who I had gotten to know the previous evening. Meaning I had to be his wingman once again. Another one for the team. Dinner was supposed to be, as Deepankar stressed, at his humble abode.

He gave me the location of the rendezvous point and I managed to get there. Luckily, Uber works great in South Africa, although not without conflict with taxi drivers, who have several times locked Uber drivers in the trunk, before setting fire to their car. The competition in Africa doesn't mess around. Anyway, it was a wealthy neighborhood which didn't surprise me at all. However, I was surprised that the rendezvous point was just the start of our journey as… a helicopter was waiting for us. We took off from one of the heliports and after a few minutes had arrived at our proper destination. Once we landed, my almost out-of-range smartphone told me that we were several dozen kilometers from South Africa's capital, Pretoria, basically in one of the private nature reserves. Don't confuse them with our nature reserves in Poland. Here a private nature reserve can be the size of one of our provinces.

And 'dinner' really wasn't an appropriate word for the occasion. Just as with a 'humble abode'. Here, I saw an enormous residence, while 'the garden' had a mobile restaurant with several chefs and waiters bustling around. And all of this for five people. I won't go into just how wonderful the food was and how much amazing alcohol was served. Suffice to say that we drank 40 year-old wine as if it was Blue Nun. I then understood that the classified advertisement newspaper was only one of hundreds of businesses owned by Deepankar and generations of his family.

Evening fell and we moved from the garden to the villa. Around midnight, desiring to be alone for a while, I took my glass, slid back the huge glass doors and walked onto the patio on the other side of the building. I was listening to the song of the crickets and the birds. For that short moment, I felt that I would never live to see anything more beautiful, and as the garden was truly magnificent I decided to go for a walk around it. After a short stroll, I reached a fence where the most beautiful garden gate in the world had been installed. It had been hewn into a high wall and was overflowing with flowers and wild vines. Magic. I pushed the gate and had almost crossed the threshold, when I heard: "I'm sorry, Marek," with Deepankar adding, "but we rather don't go in here."

"Oh, I'm sorry," I mumbled, "I didn't know that it would bother you. Let's go back."

He just laughed. "It doesn't bother me at all," he said, "but it would bother her."

That is to say, he pointed to an 80kg spotted leopardess lying on a branch of a nearby tree and gazing straight at me. I never heard him say that it was a leopard which had lived in captivity among people from birth and had never had to hunt for food. I wasn't listening, because I was busy breaking the African sprint record.

Sometime around 2am, we were all completely drunk. And then my nicely 'toasted' Indian friend slapped me on the back and said, or rather slurred: "Marek, come on, I'll show you something."

And he led me down some steps. It took a while for us to get there, but eventually we found ourselves in a huge garage. And there stood the following: a Ferrari 250 GTO from right at the beginning of the 1960s; a Lamborghini Countach; an Isdera Imperator, which I had never seen in real life and which should be no surprise, as only 17 were ever produced; the bluest Plymouth Road Runner Superbird, said to have been brought straight from a NASCAR track; a few silly toys, such as a Porsche Carrera GT or a Mercedes SLS AM, and a load of other magnificent things. And right at the end of the hall, a special enclosure in which I saw the most beautiful herd in my life.

"My pride and joy," Deepankar said. "Here is every model of Jaguar produced in the world. At least until the 1990s. When Jaguar was Jaguar and didn't produce shitboxes for the middle classes, such as the X-type."

And he was right. Among the terribly boring and bland rides of the XF or S-type, stood genuine treasures, including the SS1 model – the first ever Jaguar production car in history – even though the company was under a different name then. According to Deepankar, it cost 1.5

million pounds sterling... in Polish zlotys that would be... I don't even want to know.

"Choose one of them for yourself," Deepankar slurred.

"Uh?," I replied matter-of-factly, my love of books giving me away.

"You're my friend," he said. "I want to give you a gift. Take something. Anything."

Well, I chose something. As I didn't want to hurt the guy by taking the Superbird or one of the Jaguars, I chose something a little more modest. I thought that the 2001 Lamborghini Diablo VT would be enough. A black cabriolet. Deepankar smiled and then walked, slightly swaying, to an armored safe, punched in the code and took out the keys and documents of the car. Then he handed them over to me, as if it was the most normal thing in the world.

"Happy birthday," he said.

"But it isn't my birthday."

"The pleasure is all mine," he grinned, closing his eyes the way drunk folks tend to do.

We went back upstairs. I left the keys and the documents on the table near the exit, as it was clear to me that his generosity had been due to the influence of alcohol and would evaporate along with its effects. Maybe I'm no saint, but I always put honesty above everything. And that's why I don't have a Lambo today.

And so that's how the rich have fun in Africa. But that's nothing. I haven't told you about the weddings yet. That's where everything just gets started. Our attitude of "There may be no money to live on, but there will always be enough money to dazzle your guests" must have been brought to Poland by Poles working in Nigeria during second half of the 20th century. Because it suits nowhere else in the word more than here. Poor families often drive themselves into lifelong debt due to a wedding. And the rich? Well, I was being constantly invited to such weddings. In no way because I am sought after in Africa. Simply because such weddings are usually so huge that I always know someone who will be at one and they invite me on the host's behalf.

Let's begin with the fact that I was one of 2000 guests. In terms of wealth, most of them were at were at my own level, meaning significantly richer than average, but much poorer than the host. This is the way it goes more or less. In coming to such a wedding, you must realize that the stars of the evening are the host and the happy couple. That's why they don't usually invite anyone who could outshine them.

Everyone who comes gets a gift. A surprising gift. It may be, for example, several rolls of toilet paper, a sack of rice, toothpaste or a toothbrush. The happy couple 'brand' these with their image. Just as in Poland bottles of vodka are personalized with labels showing the bride and groom.

And the decorations? Worth $200,000. How do I know that? Because the host did not shy away from mentioning the fact over the microphone. And I don't think he was lying. All around there were flowers, sculptures, hostesses (I'm willing to bet they were double-jobbing), paintings, artificial fountains and a vast, immense hall the size of several basketball courts divided into sectors. But not as in the West, with one section for the family and one for the rest. At the center point sits the bride and groom, the host and the most distinguished guests. Then the 'poor', me for example. And further away the plebs. Meaning those earning less than $10,000 a month. The tables in my sector had their own names. I sat at 'Omega' while those next to me sat at 'Rolex' and 'Patek Philippe'.

Tiwa Savage, the Nigerian Beyoncé, sang for the bride and groom. She got $20,000 for a 10-minute concert. At least that's what I heard. I know it wasn't much, but it was probably because she referred to the host as 'uncle'. Dozens of security guards constantly and very actively kept watch to see that no gatecrashers got into the reception. But you must realize that a crowd of tens of thousands had gathered outside the reception hall. Huge flat screen TVs continually showed slides from the life of the bride and groom, in which the dominant theme wasn't love, but expensive cars, foreign holidays, jewelry and other luxuries. Everything had fanciful captions, such as 'Janine's new G-class SUV'.

I stuck it out for three hours. Mainly because I was starving to death. Only two or three dishes appeared on the table, along with drinks and a drop of not very refined alcohol. It was obvious that what would soon be absorbed by my stomach was not fit for the approaching display of wealth. So I soon got myself out of there, grabbed my toilet paper and went for a *suya*, meaning a spicy kind of Nigerian shish kebab coated in ground peanuts which is wrapped in today's newspaper, together with slices of onion and tomatoes. One of the best kinds of street food ever.

One time, I met a guy who was trying to get into an exclusive yacht club in Lagos. In order to fulfill all the membership conditions, he bought himself the second biggest yacht in Lagos. The second biggest so as not to piss off the club president, who had the biggest one. But this guy came from the Igbo tribe and, as most of the club members were Yoruba, they told him to take a hike, as the boys didn't like the look of him. So the guy got mad, bought a bit of coastline for himself, built a colossal marina and established his own yacht club.

When you see such things going on, it begs the question as to why Africa is still so poor, when such rich people live there. Well, actually they don't live there. In building up Jovago, I had many meetings with rich people. Because the rich usually have some kind of hotel. And frequently I had to wait months, because 'the master lives abroad'. This is the way things often work here. They make big money, build houses and pay their taxes abroad. And we all know what this means for the economy.

People say that every wealthy African person, apart from having a Nigerian, Kenyan or South African citizenship, is also the citizen of another country. Even if it's St. Kitts and Nevis, Dominica or Vanuatu, thanks to which you can visit almost any country in the world without a visa. Because with a Nigerian or Polish passport this isn't necessarily so. I had always thought that getting second citizenship by paying money can only be obtained in some shady ways and that it must be extremely expensive. And by extremely, I mean millions of dollars. What I found out was something totally different. A lot has changed in the last couple decades. Many governments started treating their citizenship as a commodity. The first country that offered its passport for sale was Saint Kitts and Nevis in 1984. Today, already over a dozen nations offer citizenship—including five Caribbean island-states, Vanuatu, Jordan and, within the EU, Austria, Cyprus, and Malta. Even the Dalai Lama got himself a passport from Dominica. Programs have by far become more affordable. Citizenship of Vanuatu, a beautiful, peaceful republic on a South Pacific Island, starts from $70k and you can even pay in Bitcoin. I wanted to have such a passport for myself too, so I did some more digging around.

Let's be honest, which country wouldn't want to invite more lawyers, doctors, engineers, entrepreneurs and other successful experts in their fields to their land, so they invest and pay their taxes there? There is however a vetting process that keeps the crooked types out, your finances need to be legit and you even have to go through a health check. No place for sick people in paradise. There are many advisory companies licensed by those governments that manage the whole application and investment process. I went with the one that had the coolest looking website (obviously) and that seemed the most professional out of the few I spoke to. Migronis Citizenship had also been on the market for more than eight years already. In the startup world, that's almost like an eternity.

The hardest part of the whole process was choosing the country to get the passport of. You need to take into account their geography, as you will want to visit it from time to time and who knows, maybe make it your base. What's crucial is their tax system, quality of education, if you're planning kids in the near future, and the strength of the passport. My Polish one allows me to travel freely in Europe, but I wouldn't mind having to apply for fewer visas when traveling to Asia, Africa, Latin America and the great 'Merica', of course. I chose one of the Caribbean countries. I fell in love with their zero income and inheritance tax. I was allowed to keep my Polish passport and have dual citizenship. And most importantly, this country's significant part of revenue comes from foreign investors, offshore banking and payment processing companies. The government has a great opinion among international entrepreneurs and the likelihood of becoming a victim of criminals, as happened to me in Nigeria, was significantly lower. Instead of buying a property (minimum of $260k investment), I went for a cash donation to the government fund, which was less than half that price. It was much cheaper, but I will never see that money again. With the Real Estate option, I could sell it after 5 years and hope for a nice ROI.

After choosing the country, it was time for the paperwork. A visit to the doctor, the bank, a notary, a sworn translator, a couple of signatures on the application prepared by an advisory firm and I was good to go. The whole process was pretty straightforward, and if you ever opened an offshore company then you know what I'm talking about. It took me two weeks to collect all the necessary documents and another three months to get a shiny new, blue passport that allows flying to more than 120 countries (including EU) without a visa. I got myself a beautiful and peaceful place to pay taxes and move to, if the need comes. A plan B for safety, peace of mind, and a cool thing to show off, of course. Did it end there? Of course not. I wouldn't be myself if I didn't start thinking how to build a business around what seems to be a booming industry. The Citizenship by Investment (CIP) market is estimated at $ 20bln annually, which is twice as big as the global private yachts market. It's growing by two digits in percentage every year and it's just the beginning. But it's an industry that hasn't figured out yet how to leverage on the digital revolution and online marketing. The biggest players operate more like lawyers, less like growth-oriented, technology-driven companies. That was my aha! moment. I decided to invest in the very company that helped me, and can now proudly call myself a Partner at Migronis Citizenship. It's a pretty cool way to democratize the world. Because it's not your fault where you were born.

But let's go back to Africa and other issues. One very serious problem is access to money for those who don't have any at all. And this is not a problem peculiar to Africa. Because it wasn't the Africans who came up with the idea that a bank is like someone who gives you an umbrella when it's sunny, only to take it away when it rains. In fact, in Africa this proverb is meaningless, as an umbrella is far more necessary when it's sunny. Once I went for a drink with a western European who had opened up a start-up incubator several months earlier. As he was in need of some advice, he invited some people along who had been dealing with technology in Africa. I agreed to go, because it seemed that the guy had jumped in at the deep end just as I had done. And we had a really interesting conversation. It turned out that he had also noticed the paradox concerning access to capital.

"And so I thought to myself," my new friend went on, "that I'd become a business angel for the little guy. I established a foundation, paid peanuts for PR and what? Nothing! Not even one application. I would have understood if there hadn't been many. An unready market, lack of faith in oneself, whatever. But a big fat zilch. For six months."

An investigation into the causes required the consumption of two bottles of wine, during which the guy laid out his total business model, rules, regulations, requirements and so on. He was aware that it would be difficult for him to judge the quality of the projects because, firstly, they were at a very early stage and, secondly, he didn't know Africa at all. So he decided to check out his partners from every aspect, which gave the greatest chance statistically. But, statistically, this will not be a genius twenty-something who is too cool for school. Just a forty-something with corporate experience, preferably international. And this was one of the key criteria which my friend wanted fulfilled: "Because when I give someone money, I want to be sure that he'll know what to do with it."

The problem here was that it's the children of the rich who meet these criteria. And rich kids don't need 25 grand to start a business, because they already have it or will get it from Daddy. So you want to help? You have to go in deeper and earlier. Give them money without having graduated and this will motivate them to work. But be aware that before you start earning, you'll lose many times over.

I don't know what happened to this fired-up investor, as we never met again, but I didn't think anything would come of his business, so I'm sure he just left and went elsewhere with his money. He would have done good business in Poland. People from prestigious schools there often end up working at KFC. In fact, time and time again have I heard that eastern Europe, including Poland, is the Africa of Europe.

And if we are talking statistics, this is based on my own subjective and private scientific research called 'life', which shows that the more money a person has (which he didn't make himself), the bigger an asshole he is. And Africa has also confirmed this thesis for me. Of course, there are exceptions. You have already seen that here. The rich think that the rules don't apply to them. Insofar as in Nigeria they really don't apply to them, often this leads to absurd situations.

My girlfriend in Lagos at that time was the owner of a beauty salon and hairdressing school. And because it was a nice and fashionable salon with high prices, it was usually frequented by ladies from the upper echelons. One day, a customer came for a wig which had been ordered. Don't ask what a black woman in her sixties wanted with a blonde wig. I can only add that the fake hair industry is one of the most profitable ever. I recommend the documentary movie *Good Hair* narrated by Chris Rock if you need a business idea. Anyway, the wig had arrived 'in a tired state' from the producer and the girls at the salon were trying to freshen it up a little which, unfortunately, took some time. But this really pissed off the old dame, who caused a hissy fit in which she used arguments such as "my time is too valuable to be waiting around here", "I should be your most important customer", or "I'll tell everyone in high society not to invite you to their weddings" (I didn't really get the last one).

Anyway, the receptionist (because let's just say that in a real hairdressing salon there must be a reception desk and a VIP lounge) informed the customer that the wig would be ready in 'three minutes', after which she went into the back room to check by how much she was out. When she returned the old dame wasn't there. And along with her had gone the two cell phones used for contacting customers.

And don't even think she simply stole them. She just wanted to punish us. The girls start ringing her from their own private telephones. It wasn't until the 10th time calling that she answered and said that when the wig was eventually ready, the salon owner was to deliver it in person, apologize nicely and, of course, refund the entire cost of the wig, and then maybe the phones would be handed back. Maybe the old dame would have to think about whether they would be considered compensation for the time she had lost in working with a "completely irresponsible and unprofessional company". Of course, we called the police. Of course, she also called the police. And, of course, her police defeated our police.

In the end, the salon apologized. The phones were one thing, but after all we didn't want the old dame to tell her friends in the upper echelons not to invite us to their weddings.

Chapter 12

BLOOD RIVER

When he came in, the whole restaurant went quiet. All you could hear was the hum of the air conditioning and the clinking of cutlery being slowly placed on the tables, as if everyone was trying to do this as quietly as they could. 'I'm not here' was the message to be understood from their gazing straight at the floor.

He, however, pretended not to notice. He walked right through the middle of the room, straight to a free table. He had a tired face and a dirty creased shirt, with huge sweat stains under the armpits. He sat at the table and froze without the slightest movement.

The impasse lasted several minutes, until eventually a particularly brave, perhaps particularly cowardly, restaurant guest got up and sat two tables away.

None of the waitresses came over to him. I sighed deeply and got up from my chair. I walked over to him and asked: "What are you drinking, Abioye?"

"Whiskey on the rocks," he immediately replied. This confirmed my suspicions that he knew exactly what was going on around him. He must have known. I went to the counter and shouted to the waitresses hiding in the kitchen to immediately serve two double whiskeys on the rocks. They did as I asked, although it was difficult to find any trace of good humor on their usually smiling sunny faces. I waited until they handed me the glasses. I didn't kid myself that they would want to come out of their foxhole.

When the whiskeys were ready, I brought them over to Abioye's table. I placed them on the table, pulled back a chair and sat down. As Abioye looked at me, perhaps I noticed some kind of gratitude in his eyes.

"So it's already happened?"

"Yes," he replied.

"My sympathies."

Have you ever wondered which river in the world engenders the greatest fear? Sometimes I ask my friends this question. Without really thinking about it, they usually throw out the Amazon, as everyone knows about the piranhas and anacondas which live there, as well as the enormous numbers of natives all around, who are just waiting to hunt down white men. Or the Nile, because of crocodiles, floods, rhinos and whatever else is there. Once, someone suggested the Ganges, as they throw dead bodies into it, as well as it being the filthiest river in the world. Which is bullshit, to be honest, as the Mississippi, the river beloved of all Americans, is actually more polluted than the Ganges. Some clever guy will say the Jian, a famous Chinese river whose water is the color of blood. True, this may indeed arouse unpleasant associations, despite the fact that the Jian gets its unusual color purely from the pollution which dye-producing companies have thoughtlessly poured into it.

However, the truth is entirely different is my view. The scariest river in the world is a short one, just 250 km long, which flows through the Democratic Republic of Congo. About the same as the Western Neisse in Poland. It's barely a tributary of the major artery which the Congo undoubtedly is. Not too wide and not too deep. Neither especially inaccessible nor unprotected by spears and arrows.

The name of this river is the Ebola.

When I was a spotty teenager, just like half the teens in Poland, I collected a magazine which you had to put into special binders. My choice was *The X Factor*, a series of magazines about how aliens had built the pyramids, that a world government of lizards was poisoning us with chemicals in airplane contrails. I lapped it all up like a hungry kitten. Among all these kinds of subjects, I also recall Ebola. It was supposed to have been a virus created in special top secret laboratories, intended for controlling the world's population.

I already told you that, before my departure for Africa, I got a super-combo dose of vaccinations, but apart from that I also got a super-combo dose of knowledge on the subject of all the kinds of microbes which love killing people on the 'Land of the Sahara'. The most important advice was given to me by my mom and went something like this: "Use a condom. There's HIV there." Well, going deeper into the matter, I also found out a lot about a certain microscopic son-of-a-bitch which causes a horrible bleeding fever. It was first discovered near the Ebola river, now in the Democratic Republic of Congo, then Zaire. As Ebola is spread through fluids and not by drops traveling through the air, good personal hygiene virtually eliminates the threat. In addition, it has an inclination towards suicide, because it kills so quickly that it doesn't manage get to another host. To be frank, it's no biological weapon. Theoretically, it could be used to kill off some of the poorest countries in the world, but is basically useless on a global scale. Maybe someone's working on a mutation which will delay the symptoms of Ebola for several days. Then we're finished.

It had all started on Monday.

"Jesus Christ!" one of my employees exclaimed, looking at his laptop.

"What's going on?" I asked.

"It's nothing," he replied calmly, after which he clicked off *The Guardian* webpage and feverishly got down to work. They always feverishly got down to work when I caught them slacking.

I brought up the same article and read the headline. And went hot and cold at the same time. My eyes lit up, my heart started thumping and then, completely unexpectedly, I felt I needed to take a dump:

EBOLA PATIENT DIES IN GUÉCKÉDOU HOSPITAL

Where the hell was Guéckédou? Uncle Google soon told me that it was a town in Guinea. Just 1,500 km from Lagos. So just a stone's throw away. I just went crazy then. I had no idea how to react. After all, I knew that as long as there was no Ebola there was no problem, but once it appeared in the neighborhood it was better to get the fuck out of there. And so I got the fuck out of there. Meaning, I felt like shit, I had stomach ache and went home, where I spent two hours on the john. A few people still make fun of me today for being the only case in the world of someone contracting Ebola merely by reading about it. They can laugh all they like, because they hadn't visited Mali just two weeks previously, while I had. I was in Bamako, which was not 1,500 km from Guéckédou, but 500 km. In fact, I should have told them about it. Firstly, due to safety reasons and, secondly, because it would wipe those stupid smirks off their faces.

Although I was sick for two days, I really was sick. While some of my friends joked that I had an anti-placebo, the fact that I used five rolls of toilet paper during those two days should count for something. When I eventually returned to work from what had been just normal food poisoning, the media had already published several cases of death in Guinea and Sierra Leone. So things started to get serious. Despite this, life in Lagos seemed completely normal.

"Because you know," one of my associates explained, "it's a poor man's disease. Those from the bottom of society who usually don't even have running water. They live somewhere in the jungle or elsewhere. They eat monkeys which they hunt and when someone is close to death, they keep them at home for several days. Their level of education is zero, but because they are poor above all, they don't travel by plane. Thanks to Ebola's virulence, they generally die before they get to hospital. So you can't get it that easily. Ebola is not infectious during the incubation period. Only those with its symptoms are infectious. You can't catch it by accident. Maybe you could be bitten by a some monkey or bat or other piece of shit. So you were in Bamako two weeks ago. If you had caught Ebola, you would have certainly known about it by now. There's nothing to worry about."

Well, that calmed me down a little. Just to be sure, I reminded the Samwer brothers during our monthly call that we had Ebola on the horizon, but they politely ignored me. One was made to understand that Ebola doesn't make us money.

I knew that in the case of other epidemics, 20,000 people in the whole country had usually died. 20 million people lived in Lagos alone. Indeed, it was the perfect place for Ebola. An enormous city, masses of people on the streets, the lack of normal public transportation, very mediocre levels of hygiene. But despite everything, I recognized that I, a white guy living in circumstances luxurious for Nigeria, and being careful, aware and well-informed, would be able to ride it out.

Life went on. Ebola was with us, but as they say more in spirit than in body. People spoke about it a little, while blogs and social media wrote about it a little. And people joked about it too. And they joked more and more often and more and more intensely. Because you know yourselves how this works: when someone is afraid of something, they try to fend it off with humor. And there was something to be afraid of. Already it wasn't individual cases, with 8,000 victims in Guinea, 6,000 in Liberia and another 6,000 in Sierra Leone. The whole world was yelling not just of an epidemic, but a pandemic. The World Health Organization (WHO) established a crisis team, while airlines from Europe, Asia and North and South America cut back their flights to Africa. And even in Nigeria, people started getting nervous.

Eventually, July saw news arrive that the first patient with Ebola had been admitted to a hospital for contagious diseases in Lagos.

And then it all took off. A 24-hour hotline to Rocket HQ. Everyone wanted to know about the developing situation, the threats, their impact on the business and so on. All of the white guys on my team suddenly felt like shit and went on sick leave. Only officially, of course, as no-one even attempted to hide the fact that they wanted to high-tail it out of Africa for some time. Headquarters was upset. Motivational emails, assuring all possible aid and any other whistles and bells. Eventually, however, they understood that they couldn't conquer human fear and announced that anyone who wanted to return could. People started booking flights, which wasn't all that easy, because let's just say that it wasn't only Rocket that had European or American employees in Nigeria. Since the number of flights had been cut back, finding a free seat proved to be a miracle.

At a certain moment, I also thought about bugging out, but I quickly calmed myself down. I just acknowledged that my thinking things through had been right up to that point, and that I had a greater chance of avoiding infection in a wealthier part of Lagos than spending five hours in an airport bursting at the seams with people. Even more so, since it was already officially known just how Ebola had found its way here. It had come from Liberia. Obviously by plane. So I finally informed everyone that I was staying on in Lagos.

We had to spring into action. We bought hand sanitizers, thermometers, soap dispensers and other utensils. The guards at the entrance to the office measured the temperature of everyone entering the company. They received as their weapon modern infrared thermometers, and their task was to send everyone whose temperature was higher than 37°C home. Which was a mistake, because in the summer the temperature in Lagos can hit 40°C. If you walk to work in such heat for half an hour, your body simply heats up. So basically we should have sent everyone home. Therefore, we raised the temperature to 38°C, which was sort of pointless. If Ebola had been ravaging the neighborhood, the guards with their thermometers would have protected us from nothing.

One day, I came and saw a line of people at the entrance. The guards were measuring temperatures. I awaited my turn, came up to a huge goon and he said to me: "Well, what's this, boss. You don't have to, with you being the boss and all."

And of course he didn't want to be convinced that everyone had to be checked. He thought it was very nice of me that I wanted to be like the ordinary employees, that I was giving a good example and so on. He just didn't get it that a white guy could get Ebola as easily as a black guy. And besides, he clearly thought he was doing me some kind of favor: "Boss, you just go through to one side and remember that I'm an accommodating fellow."

Meanwhile, the city was gripped by paranoia. I think I have already mentioned that it is common to see someone injured on the streets here. And that seldom does anyone offer any help. But now things went beyond the absurd. One day, a man was found on the streets of one of the city's better districts. The man, although seriously injured, was still alive. Not only did he not receive any help, but the police additionally evacuated the entire neighborhood and would not allow the emergency services to treat the injured man. In the end, the man died and his body was left there for many hours. Eventually, a team of specialists took his body to the morgue, where an autopsy discovered that he had many internal impact injuries. To be frank, he had probably been hit by a car. In turn, at Lagos airport, just after leaving the aircraft, a man fell unconscious while still in the air bridge. The airport was closed and evacuated. Specialists were brought in who, while dressed in their ridiculous hazmat suits, came to the site of the incident and confirmed he was dead. Tests confirmed that it had been a not-very-serious heart attack. Meaning something that could have been treated, had the man received medical attention immediately.

The big money-makers from all this pandemonium were the pharmaceutical sector, to be understood in a broad sense. A very broad sense. Within three days since the first news of Ebola had broken in Nigeria, a human tsunami had washed everything there was to be had from the drugstores. And the most money was made, in my opinion, by the cell phone operators. At my company, phone ringtones were playing their melody practically non-stop. Wives called their husbands and lovers while husbands called their wives and lovers, parents called their children and their own parents, and children called their own parents and grandparents. Constantly. Every quarter of an hour there was a report: "Is everything okay?"; "How do you feel?"; "What's your temperature?"; "Oyewole's temperature is a quarter of a degree higher than normal"; "If I took a dump already twice today, does that mean I'm sick?". Non-stop. Apart from that, one of my first crisis directives was not to visit any hotels until it had all blown over, because it wasn't known whether they had any guests from Liberia, Guinea or Sierra Leone. I ordered all matters to be sorted out over the phone, which only brought about chaos.

But the thing which really got to me during this time was the complete lack of health awareness. Fine, there were guards at the entrances to shops ordering people to wash their hands in a bowl and spraying their hands with sanitizer, but the number of idiotic myths about Ebola would bring you to your knees. And here I'm overlooking those with a religious basis, such as if you prayed three times a day you would be fine, or you had to hire a witchdoctor who would protect your company from evil spirits. One of my employees suggested doing the latter. But, for instance, at a certain moment someone said that the best way was to wash your hands in the Nigerian equivalent of Domestos, as it was the most effective killer of infection. Or that it was enough to drink two liters of salt water a day in order to avoid infection. And then my people landed in hospital with stomach problems. The level of misinformation was enormous. Although almost everyone in Nigeria has a smartphone, not everyone uses it to follow up current information. And often those who even come across information about Ebola had no idea either what it is or why it's dangerous. Apart from that, there are those who are really poor, with hordes of them to be seen in Lagos. Such people lived as before, wandering the streets barefoot, eating what they could find in bins or hunting it. And it's not true that they didn't realize the danger. Actually, they risked their lives merely to survive. Whether there's Ebola around or not, you still have to eat.

I thought then that of all people I had the opportunity to change something. I was working with dozens of hotels and thousands of other companies, not only as part of Jovago, but within the whole Jumia group. I estimated off the top of my head that we had access to over a million people, which really was something. So together with my people, we decided to run an education campaign using our own resources. My graphic artist prepared a guideline, which we almost lifted entirely from the WHO website. As we were aiming for a mass message, it had to be legible, both for geniuses and those who thought cars were a form of witchcraft. We included information on what Ebola was, why it was dangerous, how to avoid and counteract it, how to act when confronted with someone ill, while taking the opportunity to debunk some of the more popular myths.

We printed off tens of thousands of them and started to have them distributed. We sent newsletters to our client and contractor databases. Apart from that, we rapidly wrote up a training program for the managers of the hotels working with us and conducted it by teleconferencing. We recognized that they were the ones most at risk and that a duty rested with them to inform the health services should they spot anything suspicious. In line with our assumptions, the knowledge gained during these training sessions was meant to be passed on to the hotel staff by these managers.

We weren't alone in our endeavors, as the Nigerian technology sector was also very active. An educational app was quickly released, which the most popular bloggers in Nigeria wrote about, then celebrities got hold of it and within a week, according to cautious estimates, all of us working together had reached over 50 million people. And that really was something.

This had proved my view that Nigerians were a little like Poles. Although they fought with each other like cats and dogs on a daily basis, in a situation of real danger they united and were capable of achieving great things. So if there was a common enemy, it was 'let's charge forward together'. Even if the enemy was a motherfucker no bigger than a micrometer.

The authorities were also quick to react. One of the first directives was an absolute ban on the hunting of wild animals. Here, there are always hunts conducted for all kinds of big cats, apes and snakes. The result of the ban was tens of thousands of protests, because Ebola is one thing, but a guy's got to eat. I heard a funny, but actually sensible, explanation that you can't get Ebola from the bite of a Black Mamba as you are long dead before this even happens. True story. The Black Mamba can grow up to four meters in length, can travel at a speed of 20km per hour and is so supple that it can bite you even on the forehead. And it kills with the same efficiency as Ebola, only much quicker. Insofar as the government wasn't concerned at all about getting Ebola from a snakebite, it was when it came to eating infected animals. Have I told you that snakes are eaten here? Although there wasn't any evidence whatsoever that snakes could be a reservoir of Ebola, the president and those around him decided it was better to be safe than sorry.

And in the end, one must say that Nigeria did perform very well in this regard. The whole world was impressed. 20 people fell ill, of whom eight died. All of them had been infected from the same sources. The disease never hit the streets.

And the actions of the Jumia and Jovago groups later found their way into an academic paper authored by a certain American doctor, who was writing about infectious diseases in large urban centers.

However, before all this had happened, I had my own moment of collapse. Even though we had the situation virtually under control, I was seized by doubt. At the time, I was overloaded with work and even more stress than usual. Not everything in the company was as I had imagined it would be, while my vision of Jovago's development diverged more and more from Rocket Internet's own vision for the company. Thanks to this, I was working more, sleeping less, eating worse, and in the end my body just said that I could do what I liked, but it was going on vacation, so all it was leaving me with were those functions necessary for survival. See you in two weeks, sucker! I got weaker, my temperature rose, I lost my appetite and was generally feeling like shit. When I started coughing, I looked just to see if I was bringing up blood. I must have said the line 'I think I've got Ebola' a million times during this period and, at certain moment, really believed it. Actually, the days passed and although there was nothing much wrong with me, science has described in great detail the cognitive error known as confirmation bias, a condition which I was also suffering from. Although I ignored lots of arguments concerning the fact that I didn't have any fucking Ebola, when the slightest symptoms appeared suggesting that I had, I treated it as a sure thing. Fortunately, instead of a hospital for infectious diseases, I went to a doctor friend of mine. When I told him that I thought I had Ebola, he could only laugh. Then he checked my heart, slapped me on the back, ordered me to stick my tongue out and confirmed that I was as healthy as a bull, but overtired, stressed out and suffering from a lack of sleep. And it would be a good thing if I took a short holiday.

Well, I couldn't disobey doctor's orders, now could I? I checked the calendar and it turned out that I had several meetings in Abuja which had been planned well in advance. And it actually even turned out alright. If I went for a week, had one meeting a day and planned the rest of my time on doing absolutely nothing, I would surely get back to my old self. And Abuja was, after all, over 500km from the danger zone. So I would get a break not only from work, but Ebola.

I booked a room for a week in the Abuja Sheraton, based on the assumption that a prestigious hotel would certainly have been made secure. I packed my things and headed for the airport. Remember Freddie? As usual, he turned out to be very useful and thanks to him I got through the crowds in record time, even though my temperature was checked five times along the way. When, at a certain moment, it was slightly raised, it seemed that I wouldn't be flying anywhere. But in the end, I flew off. And by the way, after all this hysteria, his trick of saying "Make way, I have a passenger here who's sick with Ebola" wouldn't work again.

I landed in Abuja that afternoon, checked in to my hotel, hit the sack and did jack-shit. But I soon got tired of it, as I'm just not used to this kind of thing. So in seeking out some entertainment, I came up with a great idea.

Basketball. It was just what I needed. The Sheraton had its own court. The only problem was that the only change of shoes I had were canvas sneakers with rubber soles. I had bought them when I was in Croatia for walking on stony beaches. The court was totally empty.

I warmed up with a few epic one-on-one battles with an imaginary opponent. But after about 20 minutes, my feet were so sweaty that they were sliding around inside the sneakers. I lost my sense of stability and was afraid that if I kept on playing I would twist an ankle. And then I remembered what I had seen on a basketball court in front of my apartment block in Lagos. A bunch of youngsters were playing barefoot on the asphalt and it was going great for them. So I threw off my sneakers, wiped my feet and sprung into action. I won yet another match against myself, but then lost the next one, which put me in a bad mood, though I was generally having a ball. Of course, it wasn't easy, my feet hurt, but I was able to manage. Unfortunately, I had forgotten that the Nigerians who were playing in this way had done so since they were kids and thus the skin on the soles of their feet was at least a centimeter thicker than mine. While I… at a certain moment, I felt an unpleasant burning sensation. I raised my foot and saw that one large piece of skin from my sole was just coming off. Relax. It's probably normal in such a situation. But not for me. I looked at it all and screamed: "Fuck, it's Ebola!"

It's good that no-one heard me, as I would have ended up in the local hospital. Meanwhile, however, I hid my injury away in my sneakers and ran back to my room. I feverishly thought about what to do next and recalled all the instructions that we had put in our brochures. What was in them? Oh yeah, hand sanitizer. And I happened to have one with me, after all. I reached into my bag and without the slightest consideration poured a whole bottle of alcohol-based hand sanitizer over an open wound on my foot.

"Fuuuuuuuuuuuuuuuuudge!" I shouted in excitement from exploring new levels of pain.

"Hello, sir, is everything okay?" someone from the hotel staff asked me through the door about three minutes after I emitted a ferocious roar.

"Yes, yes," I replied, swallowing my tears. "It's the TV. Sorry, I'll turn it down right away."

Since I couldn't walk, I had to cancel four of the meetings. In the meantime, my old friend Rafał, who was working in the Polish embassy, came to see me. He showed no understanding of my suffering, but cruelly mocked it. Three days passed before it healed up and since I knew that once again I had evaded a deadly threat, my mood improved.

"Tell me," I eventually inquired of him, "If it did turn out that I had Ebola, what would you do as an embassy? Would you charter me a plane? I heard that the Italians did this with one guy recently."

"Forget it. We would have sent you to a hospital for infectious diseases, the same as anyone else. From where you would certainly never have returned. And by the way, that Italian didn't survive either."

"Great. You've cheered me up no end. Your good mood surely results from the fact that you don't live in Lagos."

"No, more to do with the fact that I have my own plan. If I came down with Ebola, I would take an entire packet of paracetamol to kill the fever and get on the very first plane to Europe. It's enough to just to look okay at the airport and not have a temperature. Then, it's easy peasy from there. The plane will land, they'll take me to a civilian hospital and, if I'm lucky, someone will save my life. I recommend that you do the same."

This was the advice I got from an employee of the Polish embassy. If anyone from WHO is reading this, they're probably turning grey.

I returned to Lagos on the 19th of August. It was on that day that Dr Ameyo Adadevoh died.

'Patient zero', the person who brought Ebola to Nigeria, was Patrick Sawyer. He was a Liberian lawyer who had become infected in Monrovia, before performing the maneuver which Rafał had described. In backward, impoverished Liberia he had no chance of survival. And Nigeria, in comparison with Liberia, is like Germany in comparison with Moldova.

Anyway, that's what they say 'in town'. Officially, Sawyer was flying in for a meeting of the Economic Community of West African States (ECOWAS). In fact, a member of this organization was waiting for him on his arrival in Lagos. He immediately noticed that something was not right with Sawyer and brought him straight to a private hospital, the First Consultant Medical Center (FCMC), where diagnosis of malaria was confirmed and treatment commenced. The senior registrar of the endocrinology department there was Dr Ameyo Adadevoh, a woman universally respected due to her significant input in limiting the spread of the swine flu epidemic. A woman who hailed from the upper echelons, she was the grand-daughter of the first president of Nigeria. It was she who during her evening rounds discovered the unsettling case of Sawyer and, following a short interview, confirmed a suspected case of Ebola hemorrhagic fever. She placed the patient in quarantine. Things got very nervous, everyone in Sawyer's immediate surroundings was evacuated, although no Nigerian hospital was prepared to fight Ebola. There was a lack of equipment and qualified personnel. Dr Adadevoh dealt with the patient personally, along with a small team. In the meantime, although the Liberian government put pressure on her to discharge Sawyer from hospital due to him possessing a diplomatic passport, Dr. Adadevoh did not agree to this.

Shortly before his death, Sawyer, now probably unaware of his actions, tore off his hospital tubes and connectors and demanded to be discharged immediately. This having been rejected, he decided to break free using force. He urinated on terrified personnel and spat saliva and blood at them. He was almost at the point of succeeding, when Dr. Adadevoh dragged him back into isolation herself, which was no easy task since Sawyer weighed a good 150 kg. But he was already very weak and died four days later. And Dr. Adadevoh herself died just less than a month later. It is said that it was only due to her devotion, due to putting her own life at stake that Nigeria managed to avoid the most deadly attack of Ebola in world history. If Sawyer had got out of hospital, he could have infected thousands before being apprehended. The FCMC is surrounded by slums. Nigeria could have shared the fate of other west African countries, where 30,000 were infected, of whom over 11,000 died.

Today, Dr Adadevoh is regarded as a hero. She was posthumously awarded the highest state honors. CNN named her Woman of the Year in 2014. Recently, a movie was made based on these events, and even though it was produced by Nollywood, Danny Glover was a member of the cast. If you ever get a chance to see it, do. It's called *93 Days* and it will have you on the edge of your seat.

Abioye drank his whiskey in no particular hurry. The waitresses had closed the restaurant. The fucking idiots. They more than anyone should have known that Abioye was the person most tested for Ebola in the country. A few minutes moments earlier, I had felt a bit odd. Now, however, I wanted to show this boy some friendship. During recent times, no-one in Lagos had offered to shake anyone's hand. Indeed, that had been one of the recommendations included in our brochure. As Ebola maybe transferred by shaking hands, it was better to give up this form of social contact for the time being.

But we had known each other a fairly long time. We had started off working together at Rocket in the same office in Lagos.

He was an old buddy.

"Your mother was a wonderful woman," I said, shaking his hand.

"I know," he quietly replied, but with pride in his voice, Abioye, the well-known Nigerian entrepreneur and son of the heroic doctor, Ameyo Adadevoh.

Chapter 13

KIDNAPPED

The girl was called Paulina and she was Polish. A blonde with a pretty face. She had friended me on Facebook, even though we didn't know each other or have any friends in common. To me, this was weird to say the least… so of course I accepted her. I was just about to enter a meeting, so I turned the volume off in my phone and forgot all about it. When, however, I looked at my phone two hours later, I saw there were 11 missed calls. Along with a very accusatory text: "Why don't you answer? I have very important news!"

That was a little too much for me. I have rules. Firstly, don't call me if you haven't first asked if you can. It's the Millennial in me. Secondly, if it's that important to you, write it down and I will decide for myself if it's important to me too. It's the asshole in me. Thirdly, if you don't want to write because you're afraid that someone else will see it, that means you have something to hide and I have no intention of getting involved in such things. Fourthly… I have only myself to blame, as why did I accept the invitation? Oh, that weakness for blondes.

So I preferred to nip it in the bud. I unfriended the blonde and blocked her on Facebook.

But she didn't give up. She eventually found my business address. Let's just say it wasn't very difficult – firstname@company.com. And two days later, I get an email asking "What do I have to do in the end to get you to respond?"

I didn't write back, so she found my Twitter account. Her messages started to be more and more insistent. And they never contained any details of the matter which 'she had for me', which caused me to believe even less that this person was normal.

My patience eventually ran out (and they say that guys have a problem with 'no means no'). This was a period of enormous stress at work, which resulted in frequent irritation and not letting people off with the slightest thing.

I decided that I would find out who this crazy woman was and teach her a lesson. I'd write to her family, her boss, or at least describe the whole thing on social media.

However, the crazy woman didn't provide any identifying information on either Twitter or Facebook.

I decided to try and find her profile photo from Facebook on other webpages by using Google's picture search engine. I found the same picture of Paulina on LinkedIn, where her job was listed as 'owner of a beauty salon'. The salon was located in Warsaw's Mokotów district. And it just so happened that I would be traveling to Warsaw in a few days.

I decided to pay her a visit.

That's what I decided and that's what I did. Just before 4pm, I came to the reception desk. Guess who just happened to be engaged in a conversation on the phone.

"I think we need to have a serious talk," I said bluntly.

She looked at me, for a moment not understanding what I wanted from her. And then her eyes lit up.

"Oh my God, it's you," she whispered, not paying attention to the person talking to her on the other end of the line.

I was waiting for just such a reaction, as it confirmed that Paulina from the beauty salon was not an innocent victim of identity theft. Paulina was in fact that crazy bitch, who wouldn't leave a peaceful businessman in peace. I told her what I thought of her behavior. Concisely and swearing like a trooper. And then I turned to leave.

"Marek, wait," she shouted after me. "It's about my sister, she's in Nigeria, being held by her husband, she has no way to get out. We have almost no contact with her. The embassy can't or won't help. We don't know what to do. You are the only Pole from Nigeria who we know," she said, blurting out everything in one go.

"For God's sake woman, couldn't you have said that at the beginning?!" I shouted almost in anger.

However, my attitude changed immediately. I had often heard about the problems of Polish women who had fallen in love with guys from Nigeria. Although many of them had a wonderful life at the side of wealthy, caring and relatively faithful husbands, others enjoyed less. My friend, the consul, once visited a Polish woman lying in a Nigerian hospital with six bullet wounds. She was returning from church with her husband when they fell into an ambush. Not terrorists, just ordinary criminals, but armed with Kalashnikovs. Another Polish woman became the widow of a certain wealthy Nigerian from a province in the interior. The husband had modern views. You couldn't say the same about the family or village elders, however. And the future of the widow depended on them. Her best option was being passed on to the deceased's younger brother. She would have been wife No.5. Her worst option would have been being buried alongside her husband. It ended with her being rescued by her neighbors, who spirited her out of the village under cover of darkness.

"It's all a huge misunderstanding," Paulina explained. "You thought I was some kind of psycho-fan? Can we go and talk somewhere? There's a café next door."

Well, what could I do but agree. I had no idea if I could help, or how to help Paulina and her sister, but I wanted to try.

Aneta was Paulina's older sister. Paulina was an economics graduate, while Aneta was a confectioner by trade. Aneta had been drawn to go abroad and forge out a career in the UK, as firstly there wasn't any work around in Poland, and secondly 'Polish guys are assholes.' First she wandered around London a little, before heading north. Eventually, she ended up in Glasgow, where she found a job and her little corner of the world. Along with the love of her life. Chigozie hailed from Nigeria. Although he was three years younger than her, he had class, worked as a postman and, what's more, looked great. Aneta loved the fact that he treated her like a princess. Which should have been no surprise, as in line with what he had told her, Chigozie was the son of the king of his own tribe. And heir to the throne. He came from a small village surrounded by forests, where everyone was happy and well-off. He was only working as a postman, because he liked being of service to people.

Aneta bought all of this hook, line and sinker, to the point where she took his side, even when he was accused of stealing money from postal orders. As the heat was on, Chigozie saw that it was time to return to Nigeria. He asked Aneta if she would like to be his wife and she agreed. It had to be a church wedding, as Chigozie was a devout Christian. He wasn't actually Catholic, but that didn't pose any problem, in fact. Because they didn't have the appropriate documents to hand, the young couple decided to get married when already in Nigeria. And that's how Aneta found herself in Africa, only she 'forgot' to tell her parents about it.

Almost a year then passed, in which they'd had no contact. Her family desperately searched all over Britain for her, a search which involved the police, as well as the Polish community there.

After a year Paulina, received a telephone call.

Chigozie really did turn out to be the son of a king, or actually a chieftain. The problem here is that each one of the billions of villages in Nigeria has their own chieftain, more or less officially. And this village turned out to be an especially nasty example. There was no running water, electricity only came from a generator, while the house itself reminded one of a broom cupboard. One room, plus something which looked somewhat like a kitchen. The toilet was an outhouse, or more precisely a cubicle made of sheet metal, which was difficult to enter, since it stank so much that you could even smell it in the house.

Now Chigozie treated Aneta not as a princess, but as a wife. She wasn't allowed to leave the house on her own. If she had to go shopping, one of Chigozie's brothers always accompanied her. Apart from that, she was assigned a range of household chores, such as cooking, cleaning and washing clothes. Any insubordination meant being punished. And the punishment was always the same – being beaten – and whose intensity depended on the degree of culpability. To top it all off, Aneta also had sexual obligations towards her husband.

Although Aneta thought about escaping, she had no money to do so. She had no way to get to the airport, and even if she did, she had no documents. She was afraid and helpless.

After a couple of months, she eventually convinced her husband that if he didn't allow her to call home, her family would look for her and pick up their trail in the end. He bought it. From then on, he allowed her a five-minute phone call every month. Aneta called Paulina. Although Chigozie listened in, fortunately he understood shit. The girl quickly found a way to pull the wool over his eyes. She chattered away cheerfully, laughing on the line pretending to tell some joke while describing the awfulness of the situation to her sister.

"Up to now, we've had six conversations," Paulina told me. "Meanwhile, I was looking for someone who could help us. I contacted the embassy, but they told me that they couldn't do anything for me in this region."

The Polish embassy does not have the right to conduct 'field operations' on the territory of another country. At least officially. As it hadn't provided aid during the Ebola crisis, it wasn't going to help out some girl who had chosen the wrong husband. The embassy told Paulina that although they could inform the police, this could be risky, as it was very probable that the cops knew Chigozie and would tip him off about the situation, rather than help Aneta.

"Then I tried to find someone in Nigeria," Paulina continued, "without result. I even thought about hiring a famous reality TV detective, but there's no way I could afford that. Eventually, I started reading about a Pole who lives in Nigeria. I'm desperate, Marek."

"I've noticed."

"Will you help me?"

"Just a second," I said, wanting to gather my thoughts. "What's this village called?"

She gave me the name, and I looked it up on Google. I confess that the search results shook me a little.

"Well, fuck me!" I said, more to myself than to her.

"What is it?"

Village X was to be found 100km from city Y. A city which was becoming a more and more active region for Boko Haram attacks. Nothing major, just a few kidnappings, dozens of Christian homes burnt down, along with their occupants.

"First of all, we have to find some way of sending a telephone to her," I suggested to Paulina. "I'm returning to Nigeria tomorrow. I'll buy something with a prepaid card and we'll think about how to get it to her. I'll also talk to the embassy in my own way."

"There's no chance with the telephone. Don't you think I've already thought of that? She won't agree. She's afraid that if Chigozie finds it, he'll beat her to death. Besides, she wouldn't even have any way to charge it. He turns off the generator when he leaves home. And he's always with her when he comes back. I have no idea when she'll call again. Maybe tomorrow, maybe in a month. But when she calls, I'm going to tell her that you'll come and rescue her. Right?"

"Don't be so dramatic. It's not Hollywood. Someone will come for her, I just have to think it through first and plan things out. I'll try to get my contacts in the embassy going."

I went back to the hotel and started trying to sort things out. Firstly, I rang my friend Rafał, who worked in the embassy.

"Marek, the embassy can only help when Aneta crosses our threshold," Rafał told me. "Even if I really wanted to help her, I have no way to. Do you want me to send in Polish Special Forces? I'm clearly disposed to contacting the Nigerian police in such cases. Unfortunately, no-one is going to stick their neck out for someone of such low status. Besides, we don't have any evidence that anything bad is happening to her. You only have the complaints of what may be an over-sensitive sister. And I'm begging you not to go there on your own. There's no reason to place yourself at risk. That would be a really stupid idea," Rafał concluded.

I attempted to find someone trustworthy (meaning someone who not only wouldn't change their mind at the last minute but, above all, someone level-headed enough to be able to manage unforeseen circumstances), who would go to that village and simply get the girl out of there, but I couldn't find anyone at short notice. Although you could hire a car at the airport, since the driver wouldn't be able to deal with it, someone would have to accompany him. In any other case, I would have put up a message on Twitter, which in Nigeria has frequently turned out to be the most effective message board, but the matter was too discrete for that. I couldn't go there myself either, regardless of how brave I was or not, but because my presence there could jeopardize the entire operation, simply because I would draw too much attention to myself.

A few days later, Paulina called and things started to race forward at an extraordinary speed.

"Tomorrow, Chigozie is going off somewhere with a friend. Aneta doesn't know where. He's leaving at 8pm and returning around 5am."

"Are you kidding me? I don't have anything ready yet."

"Tomorrow is the only shot at this we've got…" Paulina wailed.

"I'll call you back."

Fuck this, I thought, I'll go. If you fall off a horse, it better be a big one. If I die, it would be for saving a damsel in distress. I checked how many hotels in city Y we were working with – we had three, although apparently there were 10 there. You'd think that if Boko Haram was operating there, the city wouldn't have hotels. But there they were. So although tourism was meager there, business was being done and people needed somewhere to take their lovers to. As long as the army was guarding the hotel. Such deals are a valuable source of maintaining military units in these areas. And the wallets of the generals.

The travel agent booking my flight and car with a driver asked me three times if I really wanted to go there and whether I had mixed up the names. Then he joked that I should have been granted a Nigerian passport long ago for bravery, as I surely wasn't Polish. He clearly didn't know much about Poles…

I had a window of eight hours, more or less, during which Aneta was to be on her own. For a 100 kilometer drive from the airport to the village, I had to set aside at least three hours, considering that the state of the roads would probably be terrible. The plane landed at about 6pm, and as the first flight the next day took off at 6am, I would have to be at the airport an hour earlier. This would give me four hours to find Aneta's home and be a possible buffer for any unforeseen circumstances. Aneta had never given away the address, as saying it aloud would have tipped off her eavesdropping husband. I only knew that I was "looking for a square yellow apartment block standing opposite a red apartment block on which there was a huge billboard for Indomie noodles, which was next to an upturned burnt out truck that has been lying there for a couple of days now." By the way, Indomie is the Indonesian equivalent of the Chinese noodle company, Vifon. Meaning totally body-destroying chemical junk food. And a basic part of the diet of the poorer sections of society, but those who can still afford to actually buy food.

The goal seemed achievable. How big could this village be? I didn't want to risk staying in any of the local hotels. These would be the first place her beloved husband would look. If I had no other way out, Plan B was to get to one of the hotels which was working with Jovago and use my influence to get them to hide us until the next flight out. But since the route to the airport would also be under surveillance, Plan A had to work.

As there were no seats left on the direct flight from Lagos, I had to fly through Abuja. And the flight from Abuja – wait for it – turned out to be delayed by an hour. "A beautiful start to the everything," I thought to myself. The last flights are always the most delayed, as they are the sum of all the other delays that day. Anyway, I was happy that it was only an hour. After landing, waiting until a bus took us from the plane to the terminal and the required temperature check for everyone arriving (a legacy of Ebola; the rules were in force for many months after WHO had declared Nigeria free of the disease), I walked out the airport door shortly after 8pm.

Fortunately, the driver, another potential weak link in the whole plan, was there and waiting patiently for me. I treated this as a good omen.

When he found out that we weren't going to a hotel, but on a journey of several hours, he almost gave up on the job at hand. I was ready for this. A bonus of 10,000 naira and another 10,000 if we returned the next morning brought back his desire to travel.

We set off. The road was terrible. It was already sunset and, of course, not only were there no street lamps but the driver didn't know the road very well. Having learned from my experience of Lagos, I ordered him to drive very slowly so as not to fall into some six-foot-deep pothole in the middle of the road. Because then we would be in the shit. Meaning deep shit. The phone signal was coming and going every minute. I would have written my last will and testament on the way, if the road wasn't so bumpy. Apart from that, the driver was always calling or taking calls on his phone. His jabbering on started giving me a headache, until I lost patience and ordered him to keep his eyes on the road.

We passed two police checkpoints and were pulled over twice, which was no surprise as few cars were moving around at this time of the evening. Because time was of the essence, these two stops cost me 10,000 naira a time. I had a damsel in distress to rescue, for Christ's sake! I was furious with myself for not thinking to hire another driver to drive ahead of us. There would be a greater probability of him being pulled over at the checkpoints by the police (or thieves, not that there's any difference), and we would drive on as they were engaged in negotiating their price.

Eventually, we arrived in village X before 11pm. And then the real problems started. In Nigeria, villages can be strung out over a distance of 10km in terms of length and breadth. A village may have five thousand people living in larger and smaller buildings and huts. By our standards, this would be termed a small town.

But above all, it was completely dark. Only the patrol station was lit. We made wrong turn after wrong turn searching for this fucking house with the Indomie billboard or the upturned truck, as absolutely all the houses were yellow. Initially, I didn't want to ask anyone on the street, fearing unwanted interest. After driving around for an hour, I had no other option. As luck would have it, no-one knew about any upturned truck or an Indomie billboard. Not a living soul to be seen and no-one to help. Eventually, we managed to chance upon a group of Okadas camping out in front of the gate of some large house and eating their supper under a battery-operated LED lamp. One of them had seen an upturned truck on the road. He said it was more or less five minutes drive away and that he would lead us there for a thousand naira. "Deal," I thought and, of course, agreed. It was long after midnight and time was running out. On WhatsApp, I had about a hundred messages from Paulina asking if I had managed to reach Aneta.

"Not yet! Finding the building is almost impossible. Aneta gave us imprecise information. I'll let you know when I know something. Don't stress me out right now," I replied.

Unfortunately, the five minutes the Okada rider said it would take turned out to be a Nigerian 'five minutes', and so we drove for a good half an hour. Until we came to an enormous upturned truck on the road... a road in the middle of nowhere. And absolutely no buildings around. It wasn't that truck... By the time we had returned to our previous spot, only 15 minutes were left to look for Aneta and take her away so as to make the morning flight. Our adventure had come to an end, our chance had gone and I had to come to terms with it.

"It didn't work out," I wrote to Paulina, then adding a moment later.

"But it's not the end. I simply wasn't able to find the house. You must get more information out of her as to how to find it. At least the name of the street, if they have names."

I returned to Lagos with a strong basis for preparing a better plan in which I had now gotten completely into. Maybe I was channeling Liam Neeson in *Taken* just a little too much. This time, I had no intention of making such stupid mistakes.

The most important thing was to assemble a team. I didn't intend to put myself at risk by being alone anymore. Insofar as this kind of recruitment really isn't easy. I wrote to friends whom I thought could help me. Each one of them turned down taking part in such a crazy venture. They also made light of the situation, suggesting that chicks exaggerate as chicks do. They just didn't buy the story or made excuses:

"How's it going?"

"Yeah, how's it going?"

"You wanna come with me to find a girl?"

"Whereabouts?"

"Oh, quite far, where Boko Haram are blowing people away."

"Hey man, sorry, but I've just remembered that I've left the milk on the cooker and anyway, I've bought an all-inclusive holiday in Botswana. You understand."

"But relax, I've already been there and nothing happened to me."

"Oh, but you see, the next time the statistics will catch up with you."

The days passed and I was doing nothing in particular. I was getting more and more irritated with my helplessness. Until I had a certain conversation, which was to change everything.

Apart from Rocket, I was also a partner or investor in several other smaller enterprises in Nigeria. One of them was a company dealing in hotel management. A so-called hotel operator. The company was run by two guys from South Africa, who had cut their teeth in the hotel business. In this game it often happens that the owner of the building and land buys a brand license for one of the international chains and then hires an operator to run it in line with the standards of that chain. In short, the chain usually earns most of the money, while the operator does most of the work. With my help, they were looking for hotels with potential, but which were not doing that well and then negotiating taking over their management.

During one such meeting, I was discussing the takeover of one of the hotels in Abuja with my partners, a hotel which had just opened, but one which the owner was completely unable to manage. Wayne, one of my partners, had just returned from an audit at the hotel lasting several days.

"If we are supposed to take over this hotel, the first thing we need to do is either change the hotel manager or immediately fire the heads of the restaurant, housekeeping, reception and sales," Wayne began.

"Why so?" I asked, "The manager's experience is impressive."

"The owner employed him and then gave him a completely free hand in taking on people who were to report directly to him," Wayne replied.

"That's seems like the standard procedure. You hire a good player and give him a free hand and responsibility," I still didn't get it.

"In Europe maybe yes, but not here, my dear Marek. You're clever, but you're still lacking experience." Wayne always liked picking on me, even if it was from the heart. "I've managed to ascertain that every single one of those he's employed come from the same tribe as himself. He's created his own gang, who'll be loyal to him above all, not to the owner. Maybe I'm over-sensitive, but my intuition, based on twenty years of experience in hotel management, tells me that this is a straight road to bribery, embezzling money from the company and abuse of power… You understand what I have in mind. We must break up this mutual admiration society and bring in someone from outside, not entangled in local networks," Wayne continued.

I had already stopped listening to Wayne as I was just dazzled. I had been looking in the wrong place all along! The best hiding place is in plain sight. Firstly, I didn't want to contact the local police, because it was obvious they knew Chigozie and would certainly tip him off, but nothing stood in the way of making contact with the police from a different state since, after all, the distance involved would only be a question of money. Plus, the probability of information leaks would be much lower. Secondly, #illshowyou came to my aid or, as a classical scholar once said, 'getting fucking angry in a positive sense'.

Don't I, Marek Zmysłowski, a man who wants to be held in high regard by everyone, have sufficient connections in order to deal with an ex-postman, the son of a lesser-chieftain? Shame on you, Zmysłowski!

I had completely limited my search for help to a small group of friends who, although I knew them well, couldn't give a fuck about such things. But such things could only be sorted out by someone high up in the police, army, government or the governor's offices in some of the provincial states. I knew lots of such people. Every respectable politician or general should own at least one hotel and two nightclubs. By the way, the lewdest strip-club in Lagos, in which naked women dance with each other and, so to speak, touch each other with certain gadgets, belongs to a high-ranking politician, a staunch Muslim. Of course, so I've been told, as I've never been to this club, and that's the version I'm sticking to, your Honor. I knew such people and had frequently received offers to do business together which, however, I had usually turned down. I just felt that we weren't on the same wavelength and, apart from that, was afraid that if the business didn't go well, I would end up covered in shit and not just in the business sphere either. So there was one man who I decided to talk to.

The Honorable Mamed, because that's how he had to be addressed, was a powerful man. Powerful because, firstly, in Nigeria a 'big man' is defined as someone with money and power. Secondly, the Honorable Mamed was nearly seven feet tall and weighed at least 150kg. We had gotten to know each other when negotiating a hotel contract in Lagos in which he turned out to be a co-owner. He then later turned out to be the co-owner of two other hotels in Lagos, and one in both Abuja and Kano. Of course, his name never formally appeared anywhere, although his sister's did instead. Before signing the contract, he invited me to dinner, an invitation I didn't turn down. As with such negotiations, after dinner we moved on to a nightclub which was owned by his sister. One must admit that this sister of his was some businesswoman. Honorable, as I'll call him from now on, absolutely loved glitz and glamour, as well as being the center of attention and compliments. He loved appearing at parties where no money was spared in impressing those present. Once, when paying a bill by credit card, he told me that although it was a government card, he had a so-called entertainment budget. A text then came to his phone confirming the transaction and displaying the available funds in the account. He showed me the screen. Although the account was in naira, I counted at least 12 zeros. 1,000,000,000,000 naira is almost $3,000,000. Not the worst government entertainment budget you could have.

So what was 'The Honorable' all about? Nigerian society is divided along class lines and although it doesn't take on such a radical form as in India, it may be shocking for Europeans used to egalitarianism. It's from this that the need arises for social advancement or displaying one's social status through money or in ways which draw your attention. Nigerians have gone much further than the typical forms of address, such as doctor, professor or engineer. 'Chief' is commonly used in the south of the country among politicians and simply important people. For even more important people, the term 'High Chief' is used. During the period of military dictatorship, 'His Excellency' was used both for state governors (usually generals) and foreign ambassadors to Nigeria, the same term of address for governors during the colonial period. In northern Nigeria, there are 'Emirs'. One Nigerian, namely Sultan Sokoto, has the term 'His Eminence' reserved for him. In the south, you say 'oba', or 'king'. During colonial times, one of the highest titles was 'Sir', as it still is today in the United Kingdom.

As architects and pharmacists were a little envious of titles such as 'Dr.' or 'Eng.' (for engineer), they demanded their own, namely 'arch.' and 'pharm.' There were also developers (in construction) whom you have to address as 'builder X' and 'builder Y'.

So in the end we come to 'The Honorable.' The was a term first-ly reserved for the members of the first parliament of the Republic of Nigeria (meaning the 1960s), while party leaders were called 'Right Honorable' (as is the case in the British parliament). Later came a military dictatorship and, after 1999, democracy was welcomed once again. And with it a bumper crop of honorables. Every chairman, councilor in state government, every member of the national assembly or parliament, every commissioner, presidential advisor and assistant was to use 'The Honorable' before their name.

So did it all end there? Of course not. Every politician who ran for public office started to demand the title from the get-go. Just for running. Meanwhile, in order to differentiate themselves from the losers, those who had managed to win used the term 'Distinguished'. I could go on, but this isn't a book about Nigerian titles. Let's go back to The Honorable Mamed. He had gained his title for working close to the president as one of his advisors on security affairs. This concerns the new president, seventy-five-year-old Muhammadu Buhari, elected in 2015 in a general election, a lover of democracy (with the small detail that he had actually ruled once before, as he had been a general during the 1980s. At that time, he had taken power as a dictator as the result of a military coup). As you can see, democracy is like old wine – the older it is, the more you like it, or something like that.

The Honorable Mamed was surprisingly young for the position he held. This had to suggest a close relationship between his father, also an army man, and Buhari. I didn't ask about such things, as I didn't want to know. At the same time, the Honorable did not fail to recall during dinner one time that he intended to direct his own career in such an effective way that he himself would become president. Since every taxi driver in Nigeria has the ambition to be the head of a huge company, it's actually no surprise that every senior official wants to be the head of the country. Although Mamed had many hotels, he proposed doing business unconnected with the hotel sector. And I agreed mainly because you don't turn down such people. This wasn't long after one the Nigerian army's clashes with Boko Haram on the border with Chad.

"Marek, my friend, how's everything with you?" the Honorable started his call.

Followed by 15 minutes of small talk about absolutely nothing, during which he asked me four times how everything was with me and I asked him three times how his family was. For a high-level Nigerian business conversation, we cut to the chase very quickly.

"Marek, I need you to do a presentation, I'll tell you more when we meet, I'm here at my hotel, come at midnight, alone."

To cut a long story short, the army was getting ready to strengthen its protection of Nigeria's land borders. The total length of the Nigerian border, not counting its coastline, is over 4,000km, most of which is not guarded in any shape or form. The generals and politicians had heard of new technology being used by the American military and wanted to have the same toys also. Someone such as myself would say that Nigeria was lucky to have people in government who were looking for new technological solutions. A cynic would say that, above all, they were looking for an opportunity in new technology to earn money from the tendering process. Anyway, the Honorable wanted to use it because, as decidedly the youngest person in his circle, he wanted to go with the technology he understood the best. In order for the task of finding clients to be awarded to him, and what went with it – responsibility for its budget. And because he didn't understand it at all, he needed me. Because I'm young, with no baggage in Nigeria, trustworthy (because I knew about his sister's business success) and, above all, white.

"Marek, next week, on Tuesday, I have a meeting with two important people to whom I've got to present our border protection systems. You know, drones, cameras and such like. I need to show them how to do it well, above all, better than the previous government. I need your help in preparing such a presentation, multimedia would be better. And even better, do this presentation together with me in front of my bosses."

"Honorable, that's only five days away. I don't know anything about it, I'm not sure whether I would be more of a hindrance than a help," I said trying to wiggle out of it, because I sensed something was up.

"Marek, don't worry about anything. You know all about these technologies and the internet like no-one else, you started up Jovago from scratch, for God's sake. Since your father was also in the army, you surely know something about such things. And, above all, I know you're able to bullshit. I've seen you in action. Besides, they'll listen to you because you're a foreigner. I need someone to prepare a presentation about what this new technology allows you to do, better with examples of companies that do this kind of thing. Surely you'll find some company in Poland, ask your father. You'll come with me, do your thing and leave the rest to me. Well, you can go now. You may have a couple of phone calls to make. And a friend is coming to see me in a moment, if you know what I mean."

"But wouldn't you like me to simply bring in the representatives of these firms to the meeting and for them to do the presentation?" I said, refusing to give up and looking for a way out of this situation.

"It doesn't work like that. At such an early stage, I don't want anyone talking directly with our people. First, we have confirm things internally. Then, the tendering process will start in which local firms will also feature. Everything must run in accordance with the letter of the law and in an honest manner. You understand, after all…"

The next day, I did indeed call my dad and got the names of a few companies.

I then contacted them and cheekily asked for a catalogue, suggesting that I had been sent on a preliminary reconnaissance mission by a west African government, however incredible that may have sounded. Strangely enough, they had no problem with that, as they are probably used to such situations. Do you know that you can buy an advanced military drone for $14,000,000? I even thought about taking one for myself.

As I already had the product, I now had to find a problem which this product solved. Or invent one. Basically, I started building a standard presentation for an investor, as it was all about making money, after all.

As it happened, with Boko Haram, ISIS etc. being around, there was no problem with finding a problem.

The meeting with The Honorable Mamed's bosses, as occurs in such cases, took place at the Abuja Hilton, in a suite hired especially for this purpose. I found out about the location of the meeting just beforehand. The driver which The Honorable had sent to the airport for me didn't breathe a word. The penny only dropped when we entered the hotel grounds. Located right behind the president's villa, the Abuja Hilton is said to be the safest place in the country. That's no surprise as apparently most of the rooms are permanently rented out by the government. In exchange, the authorities ensure its protection, starting with armored cars along the fence and an army of undercover agents masquerading as guests and passers-by around the hotel. It may also boast of having one of the highest occupancy rates of any Hilton hotel worldwide.

The Honorable was waiting for me in one of the cafés.

"Ready?" he said, welcoming me with a broad smile.

"I was born ready, Mamed," I replied calmly, even though I was really shaking like a leaf. I had never made a presentation to such a strange and mysterious group before.

"Wonderful. Listen, I'm going upstairs now for the meeting as we'll be discussing a lot of other things. We'll call you in. Just don't go anywhere. And remember, introduce yourself as a Polish expert in new technology, mention Jovago, Jumia, and then military issues and your dad. Present it so that it all holds water. When we're ready, my assistant will come for you."

"Sure, how long will it take you?"

"A few minutes, we're already finishing up," The Honorable replied, but I already knew that I would be waiting there for hours.

Two hours, three cappuccinos, a club sandwich and a piece of cheesecake later, his assistant tracked me down and brought me upstairs to the suite. I expected to see a round conference table at which men would be sitting with grave expressions and dressed in uniforms festooned with medals. Something like the war room in Stanley Kubrick's *Dr Strangelove*.

And here were four guys lying back on huge sofas. Literally lying back, meaning not sitting on their asses – excuse my French – but lying on their backs, which we were almost in a completely horizontal position, with only their heads raised with the aid of some cushions. I looked for uniforms in vain, as three of them were wearing the traditional Nigerian agbada, a long dress-like garment worn by men.

As I entered, they went quiet and looked at me with indifference. The Honorable seized the initiative and introduced me to everyone and started to list off the position of each of 'the lying men' in turn. I may only say that 'His Excellency' was the lowest rank there. The Honorable spent a long time introducing each one of them, listing off their achievements and current ruling position, and when I had begun to feel mediocre enough in the presence of such greatness, he nodded his head suggestively indicating that now was the time to approach and greet them. Not changing their supine position, the officials offered me their hand which I then held with both of my hands, simultaneously bowing low so as to display my low status and mediocrity.

As I sensed that small talk would count for nothing, I quickly got my laptop going, set up the projector and started the presentation. I began with the statistical data concerning Nigeria and the ways people crossed the border, showing the paradox based on the fact that the places on the border with the least focus are simultaneously those most often crossed. I started to present the numbers of victims and the scale of economic losses which Nigeria had sustained through unrest in the northeast of the county, and porous borders through which most of the contraband was being smuggled through. This stage of the presentation was meant to annoy them. I then smoothly moved on to showing them how not only Western countries such as the USA and Germany, but also Rwanda, were managing border control.

For the moment, I was using just slides. While speaking, I tried to pick up any kind of feedback, the slightest trace of interest. Although, of course, the Honorable was so fascinated that he nearly got an erection from watching the presentation, the lying men just lay there motionless. I got nothing back that I could consider a sign that I was getting through to them. Not good, I thought, but went on. Fortunately, I had saved the best for last. My graphic artist had put together a visualization of some military drones and had given a compilation of YouTube videos the energetic soundtrack of that fucking *Rocky* movie. Generally, the scene showed a few bad guys running through a forest and hiding among the trees while our brave drones spying on them, informing their unit, sending live feed video back and identifying the weapons held by the intruders at the same time. Then there were a few explosions, freed hostages with our noble knight marrying the king's daughter in the end.

The film did the job. The lying excellencies were visibly satisfied, with the music and visual effects having worked. There were no questions. Such important people do not ask questions just like that, as first they have to confer with each other. With my role of being a white mascot now fulfilled, I packed up my toys, bowed low before everyone once again and headed off as quick as I could so as to catch the last flight back to Lagos.

The story ended with Nigeria opening a tendering process which was won by a local company whose CEO was The Honorable's cousin. My God, it's a family of talented entrepreneurs! In turn, this company started cooperating with the companies which I had mentioned in my presentation. And me? Let's just say that Mamed and a certain Polish company are very grateful for my efforts.

And so it was then during my conversation with Wayne that I remembered the Honorable Mamed.

I called him up that evening. He rang back a few hours later.

"Marek, my friend, forgive me but I couldn't talk earlier. I can't tell you what I was busy doing, because if I did…"

"Please stop there."

"I'm joking, I'm joking. What's up with you, my favorite white Nigerian?"

I explained the whole situation to him and told him about my initial unsuccessful attempt at taking Aneta away. I got down to what we knew up to now as far as the location was concerned.

"Marek, you should have called me straight away. We'll sort it out. I'll call you back."

He called back three days later.

"Aneta is already in city Y in hotel Z. Alive and well. I have paid for her first night there. My boys are guarding her. I understand that you'll take care of the rest?" he said calmly.

"What??? How??"

"Ha, ha, I'll tell you all when we meet up. But it wasn't a difficult task."

I was off like a bat out of hell. Although this time a direct flight was available and there was a flight in three hours, I still had to get to the airport and then get through check in. Only a miracle could help me manage this.

And that miracle was called Freddie, but I've already told you about him.

I got to the location with only a slight delay. There was a guy waiting for me at the airport whom I didn't know, but he knew me, as he came right up once I had come through arrivals. Of course, the fact that I was the only white man in the airport made this a fairly easy task. He took me to the hotel. We went to the seventh floor by the elevator where Aneta was waiting for me in a room on the corner.

Emaciated and neglected-looking, but happy. She cried when she saw me and heard me speak Polish. And threw her arms around my neck.

And how had The Honorable solved this problem? Nothing could have been simpler for him. He just sent eight of his guys dressed in military uniforms and carrying Kalashnikovs in two pick-up trucks. Although the journey took them 12 hours one way, no police check-point dared to pull them over. They arrived there during the day and found the right house no problem, because they knew how to talk to the locals who knew exactly where the white woman lived.

A shocked Chigozie didn't even attempt to argue with armed soldiers. End of story.

We put Aneta on a flight to Abuja, where a driver had been hired to collect her. I gave her some cash for small expenses and paid for a hotel literally 300 meters from the Polish embassy. I only breathed a sigh of relief when I received the news that she had crossed its threshold. The girl was safe. The embassy would not be handing her over. The case was, of course, pretty complicated. Aneta didn't have any documents or personal belongings. Although issuing a new passport wasn't a problem, as Aneta's Nigerian visa had run out, there was risk of her being held at the airport during her departure. Fortunately, this time the embassy used its contacts and I then received a photo through Messenger from Aneta showing her at Warsaw Airport with Paulina.

"Marek, you'll be our honored guest as long as you live," Paulina wrote.

These events made me feel so good about myself that those girls owe me nothing.

Chapter 14

HOUSTON, WE HAVE A PROBLEM

During the first two years at Rocket Internet, I felt like Charlie in the chocolate factory. It was as if I had found myself in an enormous theme park, where there were the most wonderful carousels, Ferris wheels, rollercoasters and so on spread over a 1000 hectares. I was grateful to Rocket for betting on a lunatic from Poland, rather than employing some egghead from McKinsey or PricewaterhouseCoopers, as they usually did. I was completely happy doing what I love, in a region I had fallen in love with. I had got a taste of international business and built it up a rate you would see in Silicon Valley but, above all, had been given a huge amount of freedom to make decisions. And, above all, I had produced results.

We had opened branches in 17 countries, had hired about 400 people, 20,000 hotels all over Africa had signed contracts with us, and we were making a thousand reservations a day. Nigeria, the apple of my eye, generated about 70% of Jovago's entire income, had the lowest customer acquisition cost and the highest average booking value. Actually, this was helped by the fact that hotels in Lagos are some of the most expensive in the world. We gradually prepared to start selling airline and bus tickets. In the internal audit of partners running Rocket companies, twice in a row I received the highest possible grade. For its own internal need for a case study, Rocket used the growth of Jovago as an example for other partners in other regions. Everything had gone wonderfully, damn difficult, but wonderfully all the same.

The development of a company once it has reached a stage of maturity isn't easy. And it was especially difficult at Rocket. They really are wonderful at securing funds from investors: business angels; venture capital funds; private equity; corporations and institutions such as the International Finance Corporation (IFC), the investment wing of the World Bank. They do great work in rapidly firing up new businesses in many markets at once and generating their first income. Because if Rocket is good at gathering money off investors, it's absolutely brilliant at optimizing processes and driving up results.

But there are some things in business which need to be built from scratch and from outside. Vision, leadership, corporate culture, those things which allow you to hire great local employees and motivate them to come up with innovative solutions to solve local problems. Such things can't be bought easily, not even for a lot of money.

What I valued most in my working with Paris and Berlin was the freedom I was given. Along with my team, we produced the results which we had agreed to and which satisfied the investors. But how we actually did it was our business. Taking into account cultural differences, both those between nations and within them (such as tribal, language or religious differences), the freedom to make decisions was deeply promoted throughout the hierarchical management structure. At the same time, we tried to keep it as shallow as possible. And I won't be taking the credit for thinking up such an approach to expanding business in emerging markets. The absolute leader in this area is Coca-Cola. There are regions of the world with no running water, electricity or phone coverage. But you can still buy a Coke there. For me, Coca-Cola was always the global brand with the most amazingly effective marketing. I started to study the available material regarding its strategy, until eventually the penny dropped. Coca-Cola is not a global firm, but a 'multi-local' player. In every country there's a different board, a different production line, a different bottling plant, different logistics, different sales. Everything is made to suit local circumstances.

Initially, Rocket gave us a free hand and allowed us to make mistakes, above all. As everyone knows, learning from one's mistakes is the best teacher. When I arrived in Africa, I wasn't an expert in anything. I just had lots of luck, but I also did a huge amount of work. I very quickly understood that Africa is different. A plethora of companies who have achieved success in other regions of the world have failed in Africa. Even Rocket had problems. And that's why it acknowledged that it needed a guy who not only built companies, but would redefine know-how so that new procedures could later be implemented in other businesses on this continent. And that suited me. I wasn't only deeply convinced that this titanic work aimed at educating the market would be used by other tech companies, but also, as is the nature of things, by the competition.

And, for a while, everything worked very well. During my time there, Oliver Samwer took the trouble to visit us once. It was an inspection visit, a year after Jovago went into operation. The fact that he flew in only once and just for Jovago's first anniversary was a good sign as it turned out. Samwer only went traveling when something had been fucked up. And there was a by-now infamous rule that he would fire someone on every visit 'so as to help management team get rid of their weakest links', as he said. The monthly video-conferences which we conducted with him always followed the same course, more or less. On his laptop he opened up the Excel file which we worked on daily. It basically contained information on every aspect of the operations of the company, several dozen financial and operational indicators, namely KPIs (key performance indicators), which were updated on a weekly basis. He picked out one of the indicators for himself, went so deeply into the nuances of the given KPI and hauled the culprit over the coals for so long that the manager responsible could no longer recall sufficiently detailed information so as to defend himself from the hail of questions. And that's exactly what Samwer was waiting for, to fuck the poor unfortunate out of it right and proper. I really, really enjoyed it, as it reminded me of the late-lamented Felix from my old company Efect. I knew that fucking someone out of it up is part of the motivational process. While the other boys were shitting themselves in fear before the video-conferences, I was as excited as a kid waiting for a ride at a funfair.

However, his first visit to our office did not pass off without some nerves, when it turned out that he didn't like the shape of our company.

That he would be checking out the qualifications of the people I had hired, people who, at least in the initial phase after all, wouldn't have swept you off your feet. We had just trained them up. A story about the founder of Apple swirled around my head. Sometimes Steve Jobs could turn up in the open space section, occupied by the lower ranking employees, walk up to some programmer or someone else and ask him what he actually did. If the cat had got the guy's tongue or he replied in an incoherent or rambling manner, he was fired. Samwer had a similar reputation. So I decided to conduct a pre-emptive strike. Before Oliver's visit, I held a major briefing for the entire hundred-strong team at our Lagos office. I told them the story about Jobs. I taught them that they had to look as if they were completely engaged, that they had to put aside joshing around, as for someone used to the German coldness in Samwer's style of communication, this may be interpreted as laziness and a lack of focus.

As Samwer was flying into Lagos at 4am, I assumed that he'd go to the hotel, sleep for a few hours before appearing at the office at 9am on the dot. Just in case, I went there myself at 7am to make sure that everything was as it should be. So I walk in and there he already is, sitting and working at a laptop. He had taken over a free desk in the corner. He impressed me. Also for the fact that even though a billionaire, he still flew everywhere in economy class.

"What's going on here, Zmysłowski? Seven a.m. in the morning and no-one in the office! Apart from that, it's as dark as hell. The lights don't work, how do you manage with this building?"

Although he thought he had found a reason to fuck me out of it, unfortunately this time he was wrong. I explained the principles of how the generators worked and saving investors' money during night-time standby systems.

As I had taken him by surprise, he didn't reply. He agreed and I now knew that he would spend all day looking for something to pick us up on. Just as a mother-in-law on her first visit to the newly-weds home.

"Challenge accepted. Mr. Samwer," I thought to myself and smiled at the comic nature of the situation.

Explaining such things to someone who had just arrived in Nigeria was something I was already well used to. After a year in Nigeria, apart from my duties at Jovago, Rocket had also placed supervision of administrative issues regarding expats in Nigeria on my shoulders. This mainly concerned accommodation, drivers, travel and everything which was to make living in Nigeria easier. At one time, the Nigerian branch of Rocket had over 30 foreigners. These demeaning additional duties had come to me as, after a year in Nigeria, I was the cofounder with the longest tenure at Rocket there. This tells you something of the scale of difficulty in working both at Rocket and in Nigeria. But on the other hand, there were princesses, and here I'm not linking this only to the female sex, among the middle management level of Rocket, who complained that the water in the pool wasn't being changed often enough, or that the film they were watching on Netflix was lagging too much.

But coming back to Samwer, we were almost finished with our round of meetings in each department. Nobody got fired. The people working in the open space section were also on their best behavior. They sat quiet as mice, their headsets on, no pointless breaks, no leaving for a quick cigarette break, no chit-chat, total focus. They must have only been stressed out when 'that Samwer' came next to them.

At the end of the day, Oliver took me aside for a face-to-face meeting.

"You know," he said, "it seems everything here is fine. Work is going efficiently, the people are disciplined. But there's no energy here. You know, such a company has to live, people have to talk with each other, walk around the office, always be running for coffee. I don't feel the excitement that this team is building something big together," he said.

Oh great, I had dropped myself in it by telling all the staff to be quiet. But it wasn't over yet. In the conference room I had a poster. Four drops of various liquids on a white background. They were labeled blood, sweat, tears and champagne. It perfectly outlined my beliefs. In order to drink champagne, you have to open up your blood vessels, work up a real sweat and cry an ocean of tears due to pain, exhaustion and sacrifice. I had made a motto for myself from this poster and told new employees the meaning of this image at every induction training session. And here Samwer sitting opposite me, looks at this poster and says with a smile, "Maybe you've only been concentrating on the last one, right Marek?"

"Well, fuck me right!" I, Marek Zmysłowski, company founder and manager with a myriad faults thought to myself. With a slight allergy to Excel and not possessing the greatest focus on details, if there's one thing I do well it's that I can build up a team, motivate them, sell them a vision and introduce energy to their work.

And this Zmysłowski got praise for his numbers, but hammered for his lack of energy. Well done me.

And when did my marriage to Rocket start to fall apart? Around two years after the wedding. The honeymoon had lasted a very long time. But what went wrong? Differences over the way our child, Jovago, should be raised.

Let's go back to Rocket's global strategy. You enter an emerging market, you bet on long term economic growth, which is based on demand from the local inhabitants of that country, globalization, which is based on consumer behaviors becoming similar, and the spread of new technology, which moves most of these behaviors onto the internet. Therefore, you build a business from scratch in a market that's still small. You become the market leader. Now, your business can grow because the whole sector is growing, not only due to what you snatch from the competition. If you command an army which is struggling through the jungle, cutting down trees so as to clear a path to get to the enemy, once in a while you have to stop and send a scout to the top of the highest tree. So that you don't accidentally find out that you're hacking a path where you shouldn't, as the enemy has changed position. The scout has a thankless job, as no-one wants to know that he's wasted his efforts.

The online travel sector was new for Rocket. And here we're talking about one of the biggest online business sectors in the world. We entered this sector at a time when there were already over several hundred such businesses on five continents. So it was inevitable that the Samwers had less time to comprehend it and notice the global changes emerging within it, which could have an impact on the entire point of the strategy in this particular field.

Changes which I was closer to and were more visible to me.

And what is more important, I had begun to notice gaps in our strategy.

As Jeff Bezos, the head of Amazon.com, once said, his company's strategy was based not on trends, but things which didn't change. For

Amazon this meant offering the greatest choice at the lowest prices, because they believed and still believe that these are values to which the customer will always pay attention.

But everything in turn. An online store or an eBay-like platform are characterized by the fact that both the sellers and the customers are overwhelmingly based in the same country. A synergy of marketing strategies aimed at both groups appears. What is more, it is difficult for something like Amazon to fight for a Nigerian customer, who wants to buy something from another Nigerian, for example, as with Jumia, which is based in Nigeria. On top of that, Amazon doesn't have either any logistics or organizational structures which are essential in order to run a business directed both at those who want to buy and sell in the same country. This is why in Nigeria, Jumia only competed with other much smaller online stores. But what it was actually competing with was the Nigerian habit of not buying online.

The situation with online travel was completely different. Firstly, we weren't dealing with goods which had to be delivered from the seller to the customer. Secondly, even if Jovago dominated the hotel reservation market in Nigeria, even if you could book a room at any hotel in Nigerian on our website and every Nigerian knew that "if you need to book a hotel, book only with Jovago", we would still lose 30% of the market of so-called 'inbound travelers', meaning those flying into Nigeria from abroad for the purposes of business or pleasure.

In Nigeria, this factor was indeed rare, as it's not a country known for tourism. However, in countries such as Kenya or Tanzania, foreign visitors accounted for two-thirds of the entire market. And in order to compete for this market, we'd have to compete for customers traveling to Africa from the States, Europe, India and China. And who would we be competing with? Booking.com and Expedia, of course, meaning the two behemoths controlling over 80% of the global online travel market, and what we wanted to be in Africa, as currently these two giants are concentrating on south-east Asia and Latin America.

I knew that, sooner or later, Expedia and Booking.com would open an office in Lagos and start meeting with hotels. And then they would always have more to offer than us, such as customers from their markets. The hotels weren't going to say 'I don't need you as Jovago fills all my rooms for me'. Although we had grown rapidly, we still needed a little humility. Jovago was making a thousand bookings a day while, globally, Booking.com was making almost two million.

Therefore, while the strategy of 'the internal market' worked for online trade, it may not work for online travel. It was irrelevant that we were building up a local position, as this would not stop the giants from entering the market. The question remained: instead of pretending that this would never happen and just clearing a path in the wrong part of the jungle, wouldn't it be better to get ready for the entrance of the big boys and, paradoxically, maybe become stronger due to their competition?

In working with hotels in Africa over several years, I had observed them change their attitude to technology. I knew that they were getting better and better at using it. Right at the beginning, let's call it Stage 1, you had to explain what the internet was and why they needed to be there. The hotels in Stage 1 had no idea about marketing online and were unaware of the changes emerging in customer behavior. Essentially, this was no surprise, since the hotels were busy with customers who hadn't paid, while the officials were dreaming up newer and newer reasons to conduct inspections in order to get their palms greased. Hotels had also had to contend with dishonest taxi drivers taking their customers to their competitors. But if you went to a hotel and said "You don't have to understand how I send customers to you, but when he comes and pays, you hand over my commission", then of course they agreed. Europe had gone through Stage 1 during the 1990s, thanks to which the current big boys appeared – Expedia and Booking.com – who today dictate terms and conditions to the hotels, as the hotel sector itself was too fragmented to be ready in time.

Hotels had not built their own channels for selling rooms and were dependent on platforms, agents, services and so on. Airlines learned from the mistakes of the hotels and started building their own channels for ticket distribution in advance and freed themselves from the travel agencies before it was too late.

But let's return to hotels. Such a hotel from Stage 1 signed a contract with Jovago or Hotels.ng and during the following months, much to their surprise, received more and more customers from these weird 'online agencies'.

The hotel owner thought to himself: "There's something to this internet after all. Let's check what else we can do there". And in this way the hotel moves into Stage 2 on the way to adapting technology. In Stage 2, the hotel invests in its own website, offering the possibility of booking rooms, while also looking for the highest number of online travel agents which would send them customers.

And you can find such hotels on Expedia and Booking.com and, if they search well, there are also hundreds of other smaller ones which send customers to Africa from time to time. And the greater the number of agencies the hotel works with, the less they will want to pay Jovago for each customer, because now they have other options and can go somewhere else, if they can't make a deal with us.

The common denominator for the first two stages is sales. Sales, sales, sales and a little bit more sales. No-one thinks about a program which would gradually allow you to better control the amount of soap in the hotel storeroom, if they are only fighting for total occupancy. No-one's going to also think about an automatic email sending system for booking confirmations, for example, in a country where human labor is so cheap that it pays to employ a 24-hour porter to open and close the gate than install a remote-controlled automatic gate which will only work when the power is on.

Technology which allows one to cut costs and increase effectiveness constitutes Stage 3. When it seems that you have maximized your income thanks to the internet, you look at your costs in order to continue increasing profits. And then, in fact, hotels are more open to talking about the general property management systems (PMS) offered by IT companies. At this stage, hotels also use software such as Channel Manager, which allows you to manage, in one place, hotel prices and availability in all of the online travel agencies immediately.

Hotels entering Stage 4 are so convinced by new technology, that they are inclined to take the risk of employing their own IT and online marketing people.

A side-effect of Jovago's operations was moving hotels from Stage 1 to Stage 2. We sent them more and more bookings, which resulted in them becoming more and more interested in the internet, while simultaneously becoming more easily available to our competitors, because they could find them on our website. Expedia wasn't going to have to hire an Okada driver to bullshit that his uncle was getting married. Expedia would just have to send an email. Jovago had cut off the branch on which it was sitting.

So what would Booking.com and Expedia do now? Here, once again, for help I used the letters which the boards of these companies had sent to investors on the occasion of the publication of their quarterly figures, as well as press interviews with their CEOs and directors. Booking.com and Expedia are giants which are buying up companies developing software for hotels all over the world. Why? For reasons of loyalty. Hotels aren't loyal towards travel agencies, as they treat them as a necessary evil. But what's the deal regarding software? How many times have you been in a service company and seen that you are being served by someone using a computer monitor with a black and white interface from the 1980s and early 1990s? Companies don't like change. And software changes above all. That's why once software is sold to a company, it'll stay there for years and years. Because even if after some time it'll be totally out of date, as long as it still works no-one will want to go through the pain of change.

So it was becoming more and more obvious to me that the enemy was securing his position in a new field. The field of B2B, or business-to-business.

Booking.com allowed millions of customers to book hotels around the world, and 'deliver' them to the hotels. And now they wanted to deliver a host of other things to these hotels, including software. I knew that within time hotels would be looking for their own solutions and Jovago would have serious problems. It wasn't going to happen right now. Not in a year, but in five or 10 years, for sure. And such a possibility needed to be considered in Jovago's 10-year strategic plan.

I had another problem in Jovago which was Jumia, Jovago's sister company. Jumia was the first business Rocket had established in Africa, while being the most capital intensive. It was actually Jumia which, apart from conducting online sales, had to first import these goods and keep them in huge warehouses, as well as building its own fleet of delivery vehicles. In 2015, Rocket had seven different businesses in Africa, namely: Easy Taxi (a competitor of Uber); HelloFood (food delivery); Carmudi (advertisements for buying and selling cars); Lamudi (advertisements for buying and selling property); Kaymu (a clone of eBay); Jovago and Jumia (a clone of Amazon.com).

The last of these generated 85% of the costs of the entire group. All of our companies belonged to a specially created entity, Africa Internet Group. And this entity (entirely managed by Rocket Internet) collected more money from investors for all the businesses at once. What was obvious during conversations with investors was that Jumia was always the decisive element, as it was the largest in terms of income and costs. The other companies got money as 'by the way'. The downside of this was that the investors did not place very much weight on the other businesses and couldn't have helped any other way except with money.

So, in short, the situation was like this: the further they went into to a forest, the less they could see for the trees. The bigger Jovago got, the more complex its model of operation would become, while an investor who doesn't understand your business is a ready-made recipe for disaster.

So it's *quid pro quo*. The model of delivering investment 'leftovers' under the aegis of Jumia had worked a treat, as long as it was generating growth and the investors were throwing their money into the furnace and didn't ask questions. Such a model suited us, the partners and managers of the other companies, as we weren't concerned with looking for investors. And each of the start-up CEOs agreed with me that this was one of the most time-consuming and stressful parts of running a company.

The problems began when Jumia stopped growing. One of the main reasons for this was the economic crisis that hit Nigeria in 2015 and whose indirect causes were, more or less, elections, falling oil prices, economic problems in China and a thousand other things. A feverish search began to find ways to save Jumia's growth. And what do you think was the easiest way? Cut the budgets of the other companies, including Jovago.

At one moment, we had to pull a TV advertising campaign because the entire budget had 'moved' to Jumia. I had no choice, but to go along with it for the sake of the group – one for the team.

I sensed that such situations were going to happen more and more often. I recognized that it was high-time that Jovago left the Jumia nest and operated more independently on the investment market. We were, at the end of the day, the rising star of Rocket Internet. Jovago had the healthiest indicators of the entire group regarding the cost of securing customers, customer value over time, or the outgoings-income relationship.

I wanted to secure a big financial investor for Jovago, one from the big VC funds which frequently invested in companies from the online travel and travel tech fields and often launched them on the stock exchange or sold them to other giants.

It was summer 2015. A big meeting in Paris of all the boards of Rocket's African companies was drawing closer. I had prepared to make a presentation of these new threats and recommend additional changes to our operations. I didn't expect too much resistance from Paris regarding the B2B direction and, as they had always given me freedom in the end, why would it be any different this time? At the same time, I wasn't sure what their reaction would be to the proposal of Jovago finding investors directly. I presented the concept at the next meeting in Rocket's Paris office, the same one in which I had been recruited.

"Marek," began Ezra, one of Rocket's investment bosses in Africa. "It seems as if you want to direct attention from our focus of building the largest online booking website in Africa. Software for hotels looks interesting and you could certainly make money out of it. But it's distracting you. Remember what Steve Jobs said? Focus like a laser."

"I understand you perfectly, Ezra, but this is not about what I want to do beyond building the Expedia of Africa. This is about what Jovago must do to become this Expedia."

"Let's return to this subject in six months or so, please."

I already knew that 'six months or so' meant 'never'.

"Right, okay, and what about the issue of finding outside direct investors just for Jovago? I don't want to be dependent on Jumia any longer. It seems that when Jumia sneezes, Jovago catches a cold. This isn't healthy for our development."

"Don't worry about that, Jumia's problems were temporary. Please concentrate on managing and growth as you are able to do. Leave the investors to us."

And that's how the French hung me out to dry. It was on that very day, or while drinking wine alone in a Paris hotel that evening to be more precise, that I understood that my adventure with Rocket was gradually coming to an end. I had no idea then what the real reason what for their turning me down was, and that they already had very concrete plans regarding Jovago, which they didn't want to share yet. However, I took it as not heeding my words, which was even more demotivating. I knew that the love had died in our marriage and couldn't even remember the last time we had got it together. We were only together for the money, the fame and so that my aunt wouldn't barrage me with questions at Christmas about when I was finally going to get hitched.

I returned to Lagos and got down to doing what they asked, just somehow without the verve that I once had. But soon I got an email which raised my spirits. The Rocket's Middle East Internet Group, knowing the case study of Jovago in Africa, was very keen to have such a business model in their own portfolio and start with Pakistan. They wanted to enter into a joint venture: we would help them develop this business and manage it, while they would pay for everything from their own budget. I was psyched up, as it was as if we were having another baby with Rocket. Maybe this would save our marriage?

We got down to work. Of course, I offered all the help I could and our Pakistani colleagues were happy to use it. Talks took place virtually every day. We trained up a new team. It was clear to me that although Pakistan was demographically really similar to Nigeria, they were coming across very different problems from us. However, we prepared them for what could happen, how to find solutions, which areas to analyze, who to talk to, who to watch and this kind of thing. It took us several months, but all of us had done a great job. Jovago Pakistan was launched and the first results regarding how quickly it had secured hotels and generated bookings were better than in Nigeria or Kenya. It began to look really great. Jovago had become an intercontinental enterprise. Up to the moment I began to be seized with doubt. I recalled how much hard work we had put into developing Jovago in Africa. Did I really want to go through that experience all over again? Pakistan could end up being a shot on target. But what then? What would that mean for the way the whole organization was managed? I had come to love Africa and wanted to concentrate on her. I had a good life here, had friends and a girlfriend. Flying around the continent of Africa was tiring and time-consuming enough. Flying from west to east takes six hours, north to south takes 10. Now there was going to be the Middle

East and Asia thrown into the deal? Jesus, are there even any bars in Pakistan?

I had not yet managed to start thinking over this problem properly, when it turned out that Rocket had already come up with a solution for me.

One day I got a call from Ezra.

Ezra doesn't call, he just wants to see your reaction to the information he's passing on. Because it's your reaction that's the more important thing in such a conversation.

"Marek, as you yourself have noticed, Jovago is getting bigger and bigger. Our operations in Africa will be complemented by Pakistan, with other countries soon joining it," Ezra began.

"Yes, I know. I planned that myself," I joked, not yet suspecting where the conversation was heading.

"Uhhmm, well, yes, yes. As I said, we are dealing with several branches on two continents with over five hundred people working in the organization. It's high time to unify the processes between the countries so that the company can better manage things centrally. For this job someone strong in finance is needed, a kind of engineering leader and less a visionary leader."

"I totally agree with you, Ezra. For some time now we have begun to implement some of the most tried and tested processes in Nigeria in other countries. At the same time, the most important thing in this whole transformation is not to kill off our local approach, not to destroy the morale of our local teams and not to stop trusting their experience and intuition. It's also a question of priorities – just three months ago, you told me 'Marek, maintain growth. I trust your judgment over other priorities', while on the other hand recently blocking my recommendation at the general meeting of investors. If the most important thing is the unification of processes, I'll employ good financial and operational directors and they'll support me in this."

"Uhhmm, well, yes, yes. You know, the situation has changed a little..."

"Alright, just come out with it, as you haven't been too talkative lately."

"We've decided, for the good of the company, that it's necessary to create the main department of Jovago Global with its headquarters here in Paris. This will oversee Jovago Africa, Jovago Asia, and soon perhaps, Jovago South America," Ezra said in one go.

"Okaaayyy? Does that mean you want me to move to Paris?"

"No, it's best if you stay where you are and keep doing what you do best, building up Jovago Africa. We... have already hired the CEO of Jovago Global with whom you'll be working on a daily basis. He's building a small team in Paris which is supposed to support, not limit your operations. Yadda, yadda, yadda..." I didn't listen to the rest.

In working for as rapidly developing a company as a tech start-up, you must invent and discover yourself anew all the time. The company which hires you today is a completely different one from six months ago. The same concerns the founders above all, perhaps. A company goes through the following stages: embryonic, launch, growth, development and maturity – the range of names is as numerous as the people describing them. The most important thing is that the subsequent stages demand different strengths from a leader. Although a visionary is more necessary at the beginning, he won't pull the company through the first stage if he's not a good builder. The bigger the organization, the more necessary it is pay attention to detail, as it's in the details the potential for improvement lies. The problem is that there are very few founders who are capable of having all these skills or able to learn them so quick as to keep up with the development of the company. Aware of their own limitations, leaders hire suitably strong deputies. If you're a good motivator, get yourself a good financial director. If your strong side is finance, you're going to need suitably good sales chief, and so on.

Rocket did not want to give me such an opportunity. I was to stay on in Lagos and manage an organization called Jovago Africa. Meaning being a puppet boss. All the key decisions would now be taken in Paris. Rocket, a company for which I had busted my balls, for which I had built a business from scratch in one of the most difficult markets in the world, had carried out a hostile takeover on me.

One day, I felt like the most important guy in the company and the father of all kinds of processes, while the next day they made me just another employee. They didn't even give me a chance. They didn't invite me for a meeting, they didn't propose that I present my the vision which I had had in my head, for Christ's sake. Meaning I had presented it at the last board meeting. Maybe they just didn't like it. They didn't consult me over their thoughts and fears, nor did they suggest finding a solution together. The crazy Pole was getting more and more difficult to work with because he was getting more and more ideas of his own and wanted to do things his own way. I wasn't one of them anymore. It was only now that I realized that, right up to the end, I hadn't established any kind of friendship with anyone at Rocket. My friends were Nigerian, not expats. We were cast from different moulds. And, above all, I wanted to make Jovago independent of Jumia. This was now too much. Because they couldn't get rid of me, as it would look bad from the outside, they decided to check my ambitions by placing me under an umbrella. At the head of Jovago's main department, they had put in one of their own. Some guy called Pierre, a Frenchman – who else? Although he had been in Africa only once, he had worked for 10 years at McKinsey, of course. With whom? With Ezra, of course.

"They've treated you like a black," my sales chief joked, adding when I didn't laugh straight away, "You know, like one of us, not one of them."

The comparison then hit me, although of course I understood it a little differently: or as Schiller wrote: "The Moor has done his duty, the Moor can go". A disgustingly racist saying that actually described how I felt like no other, namely once you've served your purpose, you're no longer needed. No, sir. It's not going to be like that. And although I maintained my composure, while knowing that I had found myself flat on my ass, and realized that I couldn't act rashly, nervously and emotionally, I knew that very day, as soon as I had put down the phone on which I had heard the fateful news, that there was going to be war.

Straight after this conversation, an email was sent to all of the country managers.

"What do you think of it?" Elizabeth, the manager for Kenya wrote immediately.

"It might be a good solution for the company. We'll wait for the details," I replied, even though my entire body and soul wanted to write something else.

And war broke out straight away with Pierre, the new president of Jovago Global. I remember our first meeting. I had gone to pick him up at the airport. The guy was much much smaller than me, which immediately started to worry me that he might try to overcompensate in dealings with me. Smiling broadly, I bent down so that my face was at the same height as his, a sight which must had looked comical from outside, and looking into his eyes said:

"Hi Pierre, how nice to see you."

"Hi Marek, the pleasure is all mine!" and we both knew straight away that this wasn't going to end well.

When we arrived at the company, I gathered the whole team together so as to present Jovago's new acquisition and attempt to explain to everyone what was going on. Over a hundred people met in our open space office; this was a new office, one we had just moved to from our beloved attic space. I started with a short motivational talk in which I explained how wonderful it was that Pierre had joined our family and that Paris would be supporting Jovago Africa. Those who had been working with me the longest sensed that something just wasn't right. Then I introduced Pierre, who stood before them and started selling them his version of why things were so beautiful, since things were so hopeless.

"Alright then, as you can see, we have bright prospects before us," he concluded. "Do you have any questions?"

Michael raised his hand. But there's something you must know about Michael: he's the laziest employee I've ever had in my life. But a sly fox at the same time, who, like no-one else, could lie to you while looking into your eyes with a smile on his face. This was his last month working with us, as I had taken the decision not to extend his contract a long time before.

And so Michael says: "Hello, I have a question. Why is Marek not doing your job? Then someone from our local team could have been promoted to take Marek's place."

The room started humming with approval of these words. Pierre went goggled-eyed and started to stutter. Believe it or not, he loosened his tie with a shaking hand.

"Immediately withdraw Michael's dismissal," I quickly wrote to the HR department. "After all, everyone deserves a second chance."

And it was in such an atmosphere that my conflict with Pierre was born. He knew that his appearance had totally upset my world. And I knew that my presence in the company would hinder his career. A conflict in which I had all of Jovago on my side and he had Rocket on his. It hurt me, because I love Rocket, but seemed like Rocket didn't love me back anymore.

Pierre also helped us with our costs. Namely, that the costs of running his Paris office, along with salaries and travel costs to Africa, were thrown onto all of our local companies, which now had to chip in to build the company's structures in Paris.

I've previously mentioned how, right from the get-go, we had image problems. When they called us neo-colonials. When I patiently explained that we weren't neo-colonials, we just wanted to play a part in developing the economies of Africa, provide it with knowledge and train up staff. All of my team were locals. In the Nigerian office, apart from me, there was one Dutch woman, one Indian and 120 Nigerians. I taught them what they needed to know. I promoted the best of them to management jobs. I tried to create an environment for them to implement their own ideas. The result of this was that I had trainees who were better educated than many managers. And I had managers with more experience than many directors of finance, marketing or even operations.

Pierre had joined us so as to support us in optimizing costs and standardizing processes. The first thing he started to do was to build a main team, his own team. For every position we had in every country at middle management level (marketing, PR, customer services, control, finance, sales), he created a central position to which its local equivalents had to report. Although he had 10 positions to fill, he never once asked if this could be someone from our local teams who would be perfectly suitable for promotion and who, by the way, knew the company and Africa from the bottom up. Their main function was to take in young guns straight out of consulting companies. You know the type – guys in New Balance sneakers, jeans and button shirts. Rocket was constantly repeating the mantra that these were internal consultants who were there to support and help us, not rule over us and complicate things. Of course, the reality showed that they were deliberately taking more and more power for themselves. This is the organizational dynamic and I knew it would end like this. Anyway, the most stupid thing was these guys weren't capable of doing anything. Meaning they certainly were capable. They were black belts in Excel. Okay, in certain respects they were far more capable than me. But they 'couldn't do Africa'. Their training alone, when counting their continual traveling between Paris, Lagos, Nairobi and the other offices, was to last six months and soak up a good half a million dollars. And this was to meant to be the optimization of costs? Straight away Pierre had tripled my personnel costs, just like that. I mean, I hope you don't think that a former McKinsey consultant was going to work the salary of a Nigerian manager? Systematically, one after another, they took away the possibility of making autonomous decisions from my people. The first to crack was my marketing manager, who had been with me from the beginning.

"Marek, I can't do this. A month ago, I was responsible for a huge TV and radio campaign from which we generated an additional 10,000 bookings. And now I can't put a fucking photo on our company Facebook page without the permission of Paris. This is an insult. They're treating us like school-kids, despite us having more competence than them. Recently, some idiot added a post promoting Lagos and put up a photo of Lagos in Portugal!" she complained.

And despite my assurances that all of this was temporary and that we would sort out the issue – which I didn't believe myself – she left the company. I myself also started to think about leaving. I had completely lost my energy and motivation. My options for shares in Jovago had already been cashed in, so I could leave and not lose them. Maybe this was an opportunity to start a new chapter in Africa? I was in a comfortable situation, as every possible option was open to me. Focus on investment in start-ups as a business angel, establish my own fund, or maybe start something again from scratch? I was subconsciously waiting for Pierre to do something that would send me over the edge completely. I didn't have to wait long.

It was no secret that Jumia had incurred enormous losses. The situation wasn't helped by the situation in the Nigerian market, which I described earlier. As if there wasn't enough bad luck around, one of our major investors pulled out, namely MTN, one of the biggest cell phone operators in the world. A year earlier MTN had bought 30% of Africa Internet Group (our umbrella company). As it turned out, MTN was supposed to pay for its shares in installments, if it was happy with growth. Well, however, apparently they didn't pay the second installment. Up to today, no-one entirely knows if this resulted from actual dissatisfaction or maybe due to the fact that the newly elected government of Nigeria had slapped MTN with a $5 BILLION fine for violating rules and not switching off unregistered SIM cards in time (actually, it was punishment for the fact that MTN had maintained close ties with the previous government).

I well remember my last meeting with Pierre. So there we were, sitting opposite each other, and he says "Marek, we're meeting so that I can inform you that, together with the board of Rocket, we have decided to unify all of our African companies under one brand – Jumia. From now on, Jovago will be known as Jumia Travel and Jovago's entire budget will come to the group."

"What?" I screamed and then… the cat had got my tongue. I thought for a moment of what this actually meant. And it meant that Rocket had done exactly the opposite of what I had assumed. That instead of taking Jovago out from under the supervision of Jumia, they had buried it even deeper.

"It's for the sake of us all," Pierre went on. "One strong brand in the online sphere. There won't be Kaymu, there'll be Jumia Market. There won't be HelloFood, there'll be Jumia Food. There won't be Jovago, there'll be…"

"I know what there will be, I'm not stupid. Stop fucking around, Pierre. This for Jumia's sake. But it's the death of Jovago. A company that was meant to be the Expedia of Africa will now become a category of an online store!"

"We have to balance costs. Jumia has been feeding us. If we allow it to collapse now, soon it…"

"I couldn't give a fuck."

"Uhh, excuse me?"

"I couldn't give a fuck, Pierre. I couldn't give a fuck about Jumia. I won't save Jumia to the detriment of Jovago, my project which I spent three years working on. And tell that to the Samwers. Let them take Jumia and shove it up their ass. And you with it."

"Marek, maybe you don't understand…"

"Maybe it's you who doesn't understand, you idiot. Actually, it was with that stupid smirk on your face that you signed your name to a document which resulted in you becoming a nobody. Everything will go to Jumia and Jumia will manage the project. And who are you? The head of a department. Without any power, any real influence on the development of the business and without anything at all. You've destroyed everything we've built. You've transferred the processes to Paris, where there are people working over us that know Africa from my YouTube videos, if at all. You've moved finance to another continent, depriving me of the chance of reacting quickly, you have financing for two months ahead. What are you able to plan in such a period? Congratulations. You're a stupid ignoramus."

That was last ever face-to-face meeting with Pierre. We never saw each other again. That same day I sent an email to Paris handing in my notice. Ezra tried to convince me to change my mind, but it was too late. He also proposed that I take on different projects in other countries, because the management of various Rocket companies was leaving *en masse* at the time and there were lots of high-ranking positions to fill. I didn't want to become permanently employed by Rocket and didn't do it. I had come to build a business and had done it.

It was important to Paris that my departure be as smooth as possible, without any media drama or the *en masse* departure of my subordinates. We agreed the terms of my bonus and the issue of securing my shares. We agreed that my official reason for leaving would be something that I had wanted to do for ages, meaning investing in and helping other companies to develop in Africa, which had been difficult to do, as Jovago was taking up all of my attention. That this had been agreed a long time before and that we had been gradually preparing for a new person to take over my duties. A necessary condition, one which I insisted on, was that my position not be taken by another European sent from Paris to Lagos, but someone from our local team, a person nominated by me. Since we were allegedly copying Booking.com, we could also copy their approach to recruiting managers from within the company. And that's the way it also happened.

The next stage was informing my team of the new situation. Breaking up has never come easily to me. For many years, I couldn't look people in the face and give them the bad news. I never broke up with any of my ex-girlfriends, instead I deliberately became a worse and worse boyfriend until they were so frustrated that they dumped me themselves, at which point I breathed a sigh of relief.

Initially, I invited all of my 10 managers to a meeting. Each one of them had gotten to know me in our small office in the attic. We were almost like family. When I explained things to them, I broke down and started to well up. Everyone was crying because they felt my pain and also knew why I was leaving. It was one of the saddest, but most beautiful moments of my life. There, in that small room with a view of the mosque across the street, I felt that we had really built something.

Later came the whole Jovago team in Lagos and conference calls with the other countries. That was a little bit easier.

After all that, as was our habit, we organized an informal leaving get-together with my managers. Without Pierre, obviously. People started asking about what was next. I told them that I would leave everything unchanged where they were concerned. They were to continue with the vision of building the leading online travel company in Africa. And when they said that they didn't want to work with another manager, well, that set me off crying again. Jesus, crying again within such a short time. The last time I had cried was during *The Lion King*. Because Dad had drunk all my coke.

"Listen," I told them in the end, "The measure of the true success of a manager is that the company continues to function well after he leaves. That's why you can't be silly. Stay on, develop Jovago and fight like lions. Or like leopards, because the leopard is the real King of the Jungle. Fight for everything that we put into it. Don't leave the company just because I'm leaving. Of course, it's very nice and all, but completely pointless. Work for the company, not the boss. If you leave, it means that I haven't built a great place to work."

Well, I turned out to be a hopeless manager. During the first week after my departure, over a dozen people left. Later, we held a press conference and an official farewell party for our partners, hotels and airlines, at which I said that everything was going great and that although I would now be getting involved in other ventures, I couldn't say what because it wasn't the right time, and that this move had been planned for ages. I smiled for the cameras and it was a sincere smile. I was relieved that I had gotten out of it in the end. Then there were meetings with our most important partners, the transferring of duties and so on. I had kept my side of the bargain regarding a smooth departure.

The most curious thing was that this whole optimization of costs didn't help very much. In 2016, a report was published from which it came out that Jumia's income had fallen by 40%. But attention needs to be paid to the fact that in the meantime it had already managed to absorb Jovago and five other smaller brands. Therefore, Jumia's losses were so great that swallowing up the other companies hadn't helped. The potential of these brands was wasted. A whole army of capable people in which we had placed years of investment was lost. Jovago had become a division of Jumia, without any understanding of the specific nature of the business. Without the understanding of headquarters and the investors.

The result? Jovago Pakistan came back to me with a proposal to take the helm of investment in their Asian sector. Even though I could have had a grand return like Steve Jobs, as my mind was already elsewhere, I turned them down.

And Pierre? Having good relations with the top brass isn't going to help you forever if you haven't produced results. Eventually, he was moved somewhere else and left Rocket quickly after that. Right at the end, my contacts in Expedia informed me that they had been offered Jovago Africa for sale.

Everything happened that I was afraid of occurring if we don't change our attitude. It was a sad victory for me.

Today, several years after describing the events above, Jumia's headquarters is no longer in Paris, but in Dubai. I read an interview with the current board of directors, in which they bragged that moving everything to Dubai was an issue of optimizing costs and the logistical benefits of managing an African business. I wouldn't be surprised, if in the near future I read that the next step would be moving the office to guess where: "From the beginning, I believed that the office should be in Africa since, after all, we are running an African business. This why together with the board we've come up with the brilliant idea of moving everything lock, stock and barrel to Lagos."

Chapter 15

DAVID AND GOLIATH

"It must have been a real traumatic experience for you," said Joanna down the phone, a girl I had gotten to know during my time at Efect, and someone I talked with from time to time. Now she was enjoying success as a psychologist and sometimes I got the impression that I had become for an object of clinical interest for her. "You know, with that Jovago, you must have been through a lot."

"Yes," I replied. "A lot. And I'm sorry I can't talk right now. Actually, I'm in therapy."

At that, I hung up, put my phone away into a waterproof pocket in my life-jacket and twisted the throttle of the jet-ski I had rented two days earlier in Zanzibar, my favorite place on the east coast.

I had powered it up a little too much, so the girl sitting behind me fell into the water. She couldn't drown as it was too shallow and I almost busted my ass laughing.

I was actually having the best holiday of my life. I had set aside a couple of weeks for chilling out on the beach. Zanzibar is the most beautiful place in the world, right after Cape Town, of course. The best weather, the most wonderful company; what fucking trauma was that girl going on about? I will never understand shrinks.

But as everyone knows, vacations come to an end sometime and you've got to start doing something once again. As I was heading off to Zanzibar from Lagos, I made a bet with myself I would spend my entire time there thinking up a new business idea. But it had ended up with me thinking up everything during the flight. So during breaks between jet-skiing and exotic massages (I'm talking about normal massages!), I dreamt up the concept and contacted investors who might be interested in such an idea. Although it was meant to be a business that would grow to the value of about $100,000,000 within a few years, I didn't have the resources to finance and lead it to profitability exclusively from my own money. And even if I could have, I wouldn't have done it, as I had already been through that. Never invest all of your money in one business, no matter how much of a sure thing it seems.

I went back to Nigeria, flew into Abuja and visited a hotel which was being managed by my partners from South Africa. We were negotiating the taking over of another building and it was a long night. While traveling to the airport the next day to catch a flight to Lagos, I could still feel effect of these 'negotiations' in my blood. As the flight was late, I settled down in the VIP lounge, drinking a cold beer for medicinal reasons (that's the version I'm sticking to). And then suddenly I get a phone call from my Nigerian lawyer, Rafiu, who asks when we can meet. Things like that are never a good sign. As I told him I was out of town, he gave me the following account: he had received a letter from Jumia's lawyer, immediately ordering me to cease any kind of activities coming under the clause of banning me from conducting direct competition, yadda, yadda, yadda. And that if I didn't put things in order, I would have to pay them $100,000,000 in compensation, would lose the right to work in Nigeria, and that their witch doctor would cast a spell causing me to get malaria and Ebola.

I had just gotten over the frustration connected with my departure from Jovago, and now this. To say I was fucking mad is an understatement. They say that alcohol brings out aggression. Even though I'm like Winnie the Pooh after a few drinks, when it comes to a hangover, you'd better keep your distance. The company to which I had devoted several years of my life, which had rewarded me by replacing me with that stinky-breathed short-ass (I know being short wasn't his fault, but I sense that universal forces had a hand in it having sensed something about him), now wanted to sue me due to some rumors which only made me realize that I had fewer loyal friends than I thought. And those guys from Jumia hadn't even called me to ask if this was truth or rumor, but just sent the lawyers in straight away. I knew that Pierre (who was still with Jovago then) was behind it all. Right from the beginning, all of his actions towards me had a personal character. He just couldn't get over the fact that nobody in the company ever accepted him and had to get himself through some insecurity concerning me. So I picked up my phone and tweeted something like: "Jovago, the company I founded, wants to sue me. How could you be so stupid, you little French men." Oh, that Twitter always gets me into trouble. Once, I allowed myself the luxury of commenting that riding a jet-ski around the lagoon in Lagos is for those who don't have the balls to ride a motorbike. Well, when I then wanted to join the Jet Ski Riders Lagos private club, which would give me access to their private restaurant and marina right in the city center, they recalled that post.

But coming back to the subject. To be clear: I have nothing against the French. I had Ezra and Pierre only on my mind. Of course, I quickly understood that my actions had been a little impulsive and deleted the tweet. But you know how things work. Journalists had made screenshots and nothing ever disappears from the internet. Website after website started calling me, and all the tech elite was talking about whether Zmysłowski is sound, or not necessarily so, after all.

The accusations against me were entirely baseless. Firstly, even I didn't know at the time what exact form my new company would take and what precisely it would be doing. I only knew that I wanted to build something at the interface of the internet, software and hotel sectors. Jovago, sorry Jumia Travel, simply assumed that I would go into direct competition with them and wanted to scare me off. Not on your life, I was still going to do my own thing. Of course, there was never any court case with Jumia as, at the end of the day, they were afraid of showing themselves up and never actually sued me.

And what was going through my mind at the time? The longer I worked at Rocket, the more I understood that the model which we had chosen was flawed. From working with us, hotels in Africa had often begun a romance with the internet. You give them an inch, they take a mile. Once we had taught them how to use online booking, their managers understood that they didn't have to work exclusively with us. That there were more and more online travel agents, and, as using their services cost nothing apart from a commission, you could link up with several or a dozen such websites and glean customers from all sides. Loyalty? How can we discuss loyalty since the market is like an enormous competitor who calls you every minute shouting "Hey, take my customers."

Well, Zmysłowski thought to himself that instead of fighting it, he should go along with this trend, even speed it up. Good companies react to change. Bad ones don't notice it. Great companies are ahead of it. I recognized that it was completely irrelevant where the hotels got their customers from. Managers place no importance on that. The important thing is that the rooms are occupied, that they don't pay too much for customers and that the customer comes back. Instead of saying "Hey, sign a contract with me and I'll get you new customers", I was saying "Hey, sign a contract with me and everyone else will get you new customers too". To be frank, I decided to be a middleman to the middlemen. If travel agencies are middlemen between the hotel and the customer, then I wanted to be a middleman between the hotel and the travel agent. So as to get my hands on every online transaction in all of Africa, no matter through which travel agent the booking had been made.

Of course, in order to achieve this, you have to give 'something' to both sides, hotels and travel agents. What could I offer the latter? Above all, know-how and contacts with the former. After the success of Jovago, a large number of competing travel agencies had appeared on the market which, however, did not have as much clout as Rocket's money. And, right away, I could equalize these opportunities in a very simple way. And what value did I place on the big players, such as my baby, Jumia Travel? I knew perfectly well what a headache it is to take on a thousand hotels at once, take care of payments, confirm bookings in person, and so on. Jumia was like a bookstore that had to negotiate the sale of books directly with the author. But my new business was to be a distributor which would solve this problem. And also save Jumia a ton of money. I was aware that initially Pierre would not want to give me the time of day, but recognized that the market would rapidly force him to do so. If it started to lose customers to local competitors, he would come running. And to be honest, I kind of miscalculated on that. Initially, anyway. And I'm not only talking about Jumia, but the other travel agencies. But more about that in a moment.

The next major challenge was keeping the hotels sweet. I would have to think up something really special for them. Leaving aside the fact that thanks to HotelOga, as my Nigerian baby was called, they didn't have to sign a contract with a succession of travel agencies, because they get them all as part of a package along with the software, we also provided them with a system facilitating much more effective business management. While working at Jovago, I had noticed that most hotels still used paper and pen. They would go onto the internet, receive a message from a travel agency and then write it into a proverbial notebook. Meanwhile, we were guaranteeing them software which would not only automatically fill in the information from the travel agency, but also manage the reservation, allow one to calculate the hotel's occupancy rate for a given period (thanks to which the manager would know whether they should lower prices, because rooms were unoccupied or raise them due to high demand), as well as manage the following: divide out the work of housekeeping services; calculate all costs, thanks to which the manager would know if the chamber maids were siphoning off cleaning products or not; monitor the technical state of the rooms, the room temperature, media usage… the only thing the software didn't do was make the coffee. And this would all be on your tablet or smartphone! Although not every hotel had a computer, every, absolutely every manager had a smartphone.

I went in with the assumption that this would tie the hotels in to a long term relationship. Because I wanted to guarantee them the absolutely most up-to-date, most intuitive and most practical system imaginable. Created especially for them, tailored to their needs, actually going beyond their needs. I was convinced that if the hotels took on our software, they would never change it.

I was only afraid of one thing. Namely, that I was possibly proposing too much regarding the current degree of technological advancement in Africa. I've already outlined four stages as regards to the implementation of new solutions. Just to recap: the first is when a computer is used for putting a potted plant on the monitor, maybe to play a game of Patience; the second is when the user gets used to the internet, is able to operate it fairly independently and, in any case, notices the benefits that flow from using this tool in business; the third occurs when the user looks for solutions themselves, notices that their co-educator has been trying to hide them from this, meaning a lack of a connection to a single source of information or income and the possibility of independently influencing processes in the company; and the fourth, when the user is not so much looking for new solutions but wants to create them. Where hotels are concerned, this is usually the moment when they start hiring their own specialists in IT, marketing and sales and whoever else, so as to run their business with the least amount of involvement from middlemen.

When I started the Jovago company, we were at the first stage. When I left, we were at the second. But HotelOga had crossed the space-time continuum in that it was entering a system in the second, or even the first stage and immediately changing it to the fourth stage. Our software was nothing different than a digital equivalent to that in sales and marketing departments, while we ourselves took on the role of IT manager as, after all, we had guaranteed full maintenance for the software, thus complete after-sales service.

Keeping this in mind and being afraid of repeating the problems with Mementis, that is not wanting to enter the market too early, I had to develop an attractive funding model. One which would result in the production of the software not being linked to excessive risk. We knew that if they had to pay for the software up front, they would never go for it. At least not in droves, as we wanted. They didn't yet understand how HotelOga could improve how their business functioned. In order to convince them, they would have to get it for free.

We constructed the contract in such a way that although the whole system and its subsequent use was free, we would be taking a small percentage of each transaction. Secondly, we created the following sales spiel: "Thanks to our system you precisely know how many rooms are free, which ones they are and for how long. We connect them to all the travel agencies and so no matter what, when a customer searches for a room, your offer will always appear there. In addition, you'll know if your chambermaids are fiddling you out of cleaning products."

We wanted to use a model which they already knew well – a commission on transactions. And this, of course, posed a certain problem. After all, hotels had been trying to get rid of middlemen, not add yet another layer of them. And here they had to pay not only the travel agents, but us as well. The added value we were giving them was huge, but delivering this value is one thing, seeing it is another. I found a way to do it. After my adventures at Jovago, I knew exactly how difficult and expensive the process of securing hotels to work with in Africa was. And then you had to get your money out of them. But thanks to our existence, most travel agencies would be able to impose lower margins – they knew that they didn't have to sign contracts, maintain personnel, conduct negotiations, as we would do it all for them.

Travel agencies would agree to work with 'our hotels' for a lower commission than if the hotel had to work with them directly. We would be able to keep the difference for ourselves. I assumed that if I managed to sign contracts with the biggest travel agencies in the world, then the hotels working with us as their agents would pay them less. Meaning that by negotiating a discount, I was to create the space for my own commission.

It worked.

To be honest, I didn't expect everything to take off so quickly. And I'm convinced that the good relations which I had managed to build up with partners over several years made a huge difference. I received many formal and informal declarations of cooperation.

So I got down to work on a pitch deck, or an investment presentation in other words. Apart from myself, the team comprised Maciek, my old buddy from my Efect days, from whom I had learned the internet sector. When the time came for the favor to be returned, I invited him to join my own project. We met up in Warsaw, I told him about it and he got fired up. He said he was willing to join as a partner, had a few bucks and was in. Which really suited me, as I knew that Maciek had a whole set of the best programmers in Poland, which was a huge asset when it came to a business based on selling software. For my part, I had some money and a lot of African know-how to bring to our common venture. And my immaculate haircut. That was enough for Maciek.

The finished pitch deck was one of the best I had ever put together. Although the business I was planning had many moving parts and was difficult to comprehend for someone outside the sector, on the slides it looked nice and simple. After two months, and before we had broken digital turf, we had half a million bucks at our disposal. Let's just say that it's best to gather up money before income starts coming in, or after gaining profitability. Everything in between is just an ordeal.

Anyway, I put in $200,000, the rest came from two other entities, an Indian investor, Ramesh, and a Polish investment fund, SpeedUp. However, it wasn't the pitch deck which guaranteed us the money, but reputation and contacts. I only offered the investment to those people with whom I had done business before, or those who knew me well.

I had known the boys from SpeedUp basically since they started. I presented Mementis to them, they turned me down. I presented MotoRaporter to them, they turned me down. But we had always remained in contact and they knew all about my subsequent business ventures. This time, despite the very exotic location, they didn't turn me down.

I had gotten to know Ramesh a year earlier at a conference for investors in Lagos. He comes from a very wealthy Indian family. Currently, together with his brothers, cousins, aunts and uncles, he controls a conglomerate dealing with logistics, the chemical industry, the food sector, property, medical care and God knows what else. As Ramesh told me, his father had made his fortune doing business with the Nigerian government when it was still ruled by military dictators.

I have to confess to something. I was afraid to take money from and get into a business bed with a truly local, Nigerian partner. I fell for a stereotype. I heard too many stories of expat founders being kicked out of the country after being considered "not needed anymore". I preferred to deal with another foreigner, one who was already successful locally, who might understand my African challenges better, and support me when the bad guys come after me. Ramesh was born and raised in Africa, but had graduated from one of the best universities in the world and gained international business experience. For me, he combined the best of two Worlds, the Nigerian and the Western one. Time will show whether Nigeria can be more civilized than the West.

To be blunt, Ramesh was well set up, but despite this, he seemed as someone very hard working and organized while being an extraordinarily nice guy. Although I felt that someone like that must have another face that they only show while doing business. And this wouldn't be a nice face. In spite of all that, his attitude impressed me and gained my admiration. And it seemed that I impressed him too. Mainly with freshness and passion. And creating start-ups.

Me and Ramesh just got on, a lot you could say. He was in Lagos every two weeks. And every two weeks I got an email from his secretary with an invitation to dinner. We ate at his penthouse, where he had an Indian chef permanently employed to cook Ramesh his favorite cuisine. Or we went out on the town, to his friend's restaurant.

These dinners often ended up with us at a nightclub. Ramesh loved to talk, especially after a couple of drinks. And, well, I just listened. About his problems with his wife, kids, mistresses and businesses.

"You know what I'm lacking in business, Marek? That note of excitement, that sense of being cool. This year, I've already made a clear $10,000,000 and it's only May. And it doesn't get me going at all. I would love to pack it all in and join a team that's changing the world and building a unicorn," he told me after a few drinks.

"I think you've been reading TechCrunch too much, Ramesh," I said, "But I think I know what you have in mind. You don't have to pack everything in at once, for God's sake. You can begin with investing as a business angel. Or as a partner in an investment fund."

"Don't you think I've already done that? I've put in a couple of million into one of the biggest private equity funds on the continent. This problem is that I'm far away from their businesses, my role is now basically receiving annual reports from portfolio companies. Which I also don't like, just like the people from the whole of this fund."

"Alright then, but have you maybe tried investing directly in some tech company in Nigeria or somewhere else?"

"Sure. I've invested in Nigeria Payments (here Ramesh gave me the name of a start-up which I have to keep secret, both for the sake of the company and its founders). Do you know them?" Ramesh asked.

"Of course I know them! It's one of the few huge successes of companies in Africa involved in fintech," I said excitedly, referring to companies dealing with technological innovation in the financial sector. "Funds from Silicon Valley have invested in it."

The founder of Nigeria Payments is an experienced and very well respected person in the sector, whom I know personally. We'll call him Ademola, as I'll be talking about him later.

"Well, yes, yes. So they say… but you know, I'm not happy. Ademola was my good friend. I was at his wedding. I invested in Nigeria Payments very early. And then everything went wrong."

"But what?" I asked, surprised.

"They've stopped treating me with respect, as an investor. I don't feel important, they don't want to listen to my advice. Generally, it seems to me that they want to kick me out of the business. Now I'm suing them, and the courts are just the beginning. You'll see, they'll come and apologize. They had no idea what I'm capable of. This is Nigeria, you can have anyone put in prison here, it's just a question of money. Well, no matter. Let's order some drinks! Waiter!"

Ramesh's attitude to Nigeria Payments and Ademola surprised me. I had the chance to talk about Nigeria Payments with a friend who manages a smaller fund investing in this company. Thanks to him, I got a fairly good handle both on its financial situation and how investors are treated by the company. Everyone talked about it in glowing terms. This paranoia regarding respect and control, as well as the irrational fear of being cheated, did not match the picture of Ramesh I knew. But I just put it down Ramesh's ramblings down to his weak Indian head for whiskey. I decided to ignore the situation and not dwell on the subject in any way.

This would turn out to be the biggest mistake of my life.

Getting back to business, me and Maciek were ready to go. We divided out the responsibilities. Maciek took on all tasks connected with building the technology and operations, running it from Poland where he was based, where we had the developers and a local polish entity to hire them, while I dealt with sales, negotiations with travel agents and contracting hotels via our Nigerian entity. From day one, we were an international business and that was exciting. It was also convenient for our investors. SpeedUp, due to European Union constraints, could only invest in an EU entity, while Ramesh wanted to invest his local currency - Naira. So we set up both entities at once, Ramesh got the shares in the Nigerian one, SpeedUp - the polish one. Both entities couldn't exist without each other, the Polish one controlled the technology, the Nigerian one - the business contracts. It was like in this joke, where a patient at the dentist's grabs the doctor's balls during the time of the treatment. The four of us also agreed that once the startup proved itself, we would invest in corporate governance, setting up a mother entity in Dubai, Mauritius or Delaware. For tax reasons of course. The mother company would then own 100% shares of the local entities, while we get shares in the mother company. Such a structure is very costly and we wanted to see traction first, to rationalize such a high overhead cost. Fun fact: Rocket had opened a software development center in Portugal, where all its websites were built. Jovago had to be its internal customer. That was an order. And it was totally absurd, a view I repeatedly raised at many meetings. Since they wanted to cut costs, that was where they needed to start. It seemed to the Samwers that anyone who had the opportunity to work at Rocket felt that they had grabbed Steve Jobs by the hind legs. But this didn't concern the developers to the slightest degree, cut off from all the 'adventures' related with building up a business. They hadn't been given the title of 'Honorable', but the not-entirely-true title of partners or cofounders. They were just normal kids working 9 to 5 in a normal office and, as with everyone working this way, were looking at the clock every half an hour to check how much more time they had to sit on their asses. All that connected them with Africa was a map on the wall. And an out of date one at that, missing South Sudan, and so a good symbol of their involvement. Neither the money, nor the challenge involved were particularly worthy. There was nothing they hadn't already done many times in the past. The cost of their work was decidedly unrelated to its quality. They did shoddy work, weren't open to change and, in addition, changed jobs regularly, which necessitated the constant organization of 'onboarding', or staff training sessions.

Although Rocket didn't give a fuck what I thought, from the beginning myself and Maciek assumed that all the IT work would be done in Poland, since Maciej was based there. Not to repeat the Porto mistake, we gave our two key developers Szymon and David shares options and made them our partners. We got an absolutely perfect product into our hands. In addition, we could design it in such a way as to be the best functioning product on the market for which it was meant. Software for Nigeria must be simple because, firstly the costs of data transfer are incredibly high and, secondly, Nigerians are just learning to work with new technology. And so we had got everything we wanted from our programmers. A wonderful, simple, easy-to-read product. We had worked on the basis of the most popular hotel software in the world and had asked our potential African clients which options were 'must have' and which they wouldn't be using. We focused on 20% of the functionality which fulfilled 80% of the requirements. You have billions of functions on Facebook but you mainly write posts and comments, click likes and share content. Its remaining functions may as well not even exist. I mean when was the last time you published 360° photos, transmitted something live or used promoted posts? Business is one thing, but in your private life? Almost certainly never. That's why our software had no whistles and bells. But it worked intuitively.

Even the name was no accident. For Nigerian operations, we have secured a fantastic local name "HotelOga". For our future international growth, we chose "HotelOnline" and registered it in Poland, where our technology was being built. 'Oga' is a very popular word in Nigeria. If you met a Cockney while walking through the east end of London, maybe not now but half a century ago, he might have said "Spare a shillin', guv'nah?". So 'oga' is actually boss or governor. Or 'guv' even better. With the exception that 'oga' only has positive connotations in Nigeria, in that it expresses respect, not taking someone lightly. So why did we call our project HotelOga? Most companies involved in B2B sales focus directly on the decision makers at the highest level of the organization possible, yet forget about those who'll end up using the product. But we knew that the success would depend on whether the lowest-ranking employees would like it or not. It was obvious to us that the managers or CEOs would like it. But it was 'ordinary people' who would be using it on a daily basis and for whom we needed to design something nice and easy. Something they would tell each other about with an ear-to-ear grin: "You know, we've got this new program called 'Guv', of all things. Can you imagine that?".

Within three months, we had secured 500 hotels ready to work with us. But a quite unexpected problem appeared with the travel agents. I met the bosses of all the big ones: Wakanow, Hotels.ng, HotelNowNow. And even though I knew each of the founders pretty well, because it's a small world, each of them drew out their decision, afraid to tell me that they were not in. And I thought that they would be the easiest to convince. At that time, I had the first demo version of the application.

I showed them how it worked and how they would benefit from it. I told them that the hotels were queuing up to work with me and if they didn't buy their ticket soon, the train would leave without them. But to no effect. They weren't buying it and that was that. Eventually at a meeting with one of the CEOs, and with me having pushed him up against a wall (not literally), he told me told me straight: "Marek, we've spoken among ourselves and none of us are going in. It's a dangerous project for us. Although you are not a competitor, your development will speed up the entrance of foreign competitors. Sorry."

I was angry with him, because he had said something completely different between the second and third lap dance at the Lagos strip club where we had gone a week earlier to "conduct negotiations."

The local websites knew that the big boys would come in sooner or later. And had decided to do everything to ensure this would be later. What did this mean for me and the hotels? A hotel which had started to use the HotelOga app had to constantly receive emails and make calls regarding bookings to the local agencies manually, because they didn't want to update information directly on our system. The agencies were stubborn and deliberately increased the workload of both the hotels and themselves, just to hinder our development. A case of cutting off your own nose to spite your face. Pierre, still fueled by personal emotions towards me, went even further. Jovago threatened hotels it will take them off the platform if they start using HotelOga.

Jovago and other local OTAs also counted on soon building their own competitive solution to HotelOga. But I knew that this was doomed to failure from the start. Firstly, no competitor travel agency would integrate with the software of another. Secondly, the hotels wouldn't take software from a travel agency, as it would allow them access to all the hotel's data, including average occupancy rates, income and customers sent by other travel agents. Such information could later be used during negotiations for rates of commission for each customer. The closer the hotel was to bankruptcy, the more it would pay.

I knew that I had to hold out and just do my own thing. The only chance to overcome this impasse would be reaching a situation where the hotels were receiving a sufficient number of bookings through agencies automatically connected to HotelOga for them to no longer want to work with a few rebels on a manual basis. And for them to say: "Either connect up to HotelOga or get lost". I had come across exactly the same situation at Jovago, when signing contracts with the biggest hotel chains like Radisson or Accor. They sent me off to integrate ourselves with their software deliverers, because they themselves weren't going to respond to emails and be bothered with some little agency in Nigeria.

This is why I focused precisely on that which the local agencies wanted to delay. Namely, on inviting the greatest number possible of foreign booking websites to broaden what they had to offer with Nigerian hotels. Why had they not been in Africa before? Of course, they could have could swallowed up the fledgling market no problem, but at an enormous cost. They would have had to open an office, send out teams of people or find people here, spend a long time getting hotels to sign contracts. Meanwhile, I could offer them everything on a plate. They wouldn't even have to lift a finger. They would need neither people nor know-how, as I had both. They wouldn't need to sign contracts with hotels as I had already done it. Every contract between a hotel and HotelOga would also regulate the rates for travel agencies. A bit as if you came to these agencies and said: "Hey, I'll give you billions, in exchange for a small commission". Who wouldn't go for that?

Insofar as I wanted to be the good guy here, I acknowledged that firstly I would sort things out locally. That I would be developing local travel agencies, even Jovago (Jumia Travel) with my old buddy Pierre at the helm. The mints would be free. I believed that the market would first be satisfied and take off and that sites such as Booking.com and Expedia wouldn't devour everything that hadn't headed for the hills at once.

And if they don't, they don't.

And so I sent emails to my contacts in these tech leviathans.

Booking.com responded the same day. Expedia the next day, and TripAdvisor, Hotelbeds, HRS and a couple of others after a week. And all of them invited me to meet them at their headquarters. The first of these emails was interesting, as they offered me a job.

Although the first meeting with Booking.com took place at their office in Amsterdam, it turned out to be not as easy as I had expected. They told me that they agreed with all the theses of my presentation. What's more, for a long time they believed that the market had become so saturated that the only option for them would be B2B solutions. They had been working on their own software for some time and asked if I would like to be the head of the department introducing this software to the market. I turned them down, however.

"Do you think our project is not good?" they asked me.

"On the contrary. I think it's very good. So good, it's bad. In putting software into hotels, you become even more dependent on each other. You are part of a duopoly with Expedia and you want to be even stronger. I want to be on the light side of the Force. I believe that the companies building software for hotels should not be related by shares with travel agencies."

"You're an idealist. Like Icarus."

"Maybe I am."

"But you know how Icarus ended up, right?"

"He became a legend," I laughed in reply and went on saying, "Leave B2B in Africa to me. I already have a really good handle on things. You'll enter a channel which won't be servicing you exclusively, but will open a route to a market worth billions of dollars. And it'll cost you as much as you spend on corporate catering."

"An awful lot," the head of finance blurted out.

"Oh yes, could you pass the croissants?" asked the head of the programmers.

Everything I had told them was in a freestyle manner. I wasn't prepared for such a course of the meeting. I talked about how difficult, but essential the right strategic decisions were. Sometimes, it's better to take a smaller piece of a bigger pie. That although everyone would like to have a monopoly, the market doesn't like monopolies and that in Africa, similar to the so-called civilized world, very soon the market would be dictating the conditions to entrepreneurs, and not the other way round. I even managed to work-in a Steve Jobs story. By introducing the iPhone, Apple killed off the iPod. Journalists and armchair experts accused Jobs of cannibalizing his own products. And he just replied: "If you don't cannibalize yourself, someone else will". And he was right. Sometimes, it's better to kill the goose that lays the golden eggs, if you can replace it with one that shits platinum.

As I saw how they were in fact nodding their heads reluctantly, I went a step further. I told them that for several years, I had been running an extensive educational campaign in Nigeria. That everything I had presented in my pitch deck, I was also telling hotel bosses. That they already knew what they can demand and what they don't have to agree to at all. So, to be blunt, Booking.com may be a giant, but it was going to have to play by my rules. This was quite audacious, especially since I had not prepared myself for such an exchange of blows.

In the end, Booking.com came on board and, in the same way, Expedia, TripAdvisor, HRS and a few more. Although this was a good sign, half of our anticipated income which was meant to have come from local agencies that had, however, turned us down, had evaporated. And this was crucial income right at the beginning. The company was not capable of surviving from just working with foreign websites – we needed local players.

I faced a difficult decision. I could have either cut all my costs, delay and postpone the solicitation of hotels and gradually increase earnings through small costs, waiting patiently for better days. And pray that some competitor with millions of investors would not open up. Or I could race forward, in spite of everyone, in spite of the market. Instead of slowing down at the wall and going around it, just put the pedal to the metal and smash right through it, counting on the toughness of my head and character. Meaning take even more money from investors right now, so as to cover the hole in the budget. Of course, I choose Door No. 2. I hadn't come to Africa and built something from scratch in some start-up to abandon it all now: "Either you do it 100%, Marek, or you go back to Poland and find yourself a cushy little job", I persuaded myself. Although the cash we had gathered together at the beginning was meant to last us for two years of operations, it would only last nine months due to the fuck-up by the local agencies.

So as to keep ourselves afloat, we starting preparing for more rounds to secure finance from the market. Series A. Have I told you what the particular stages of getting money are? First, there's the so-called angel round, meaning looking for a wealthy 'sugar daddy' who invests money at the start-up phase of the project. Then there are further rounds, namely seed capital, series A, B, C and so on. Until the end, when the company is going great, the IPO (initial public offering) or stock market debut takes place. So we began to gather money from the financial market for Round A. I was very confident and intended collect money in the style of Rocket. Since they had collected $500,000,000 in previous years, I wouldn't have any problem with getting a measly two big ones for 20% of the company. Meaning I had valued it at $10,000,0000 . Why? Because in less than a year, we had built the largest tech company in the hotel sector in western Africa. Because we had our own technology tailored for Africa, because we had the best possible team. Because we had signed a contract with GLO, a Nigerian telecom company, that every hotel using HotelOga would have free internet. This caused a sensation all over Africa. Because even the high and mighty Google discussed our technology at its annual conference in San Francisco, as an example of one perfectly suiting the market. We knew the market like the back of our hand and had the largest agencies in the world working with us, as the only company from Nigeria. Just because.

I put together a new and even better presentation than the one before. I knew exactly which kind investors we would require. I stayed far away from local business angels and investment funds. I didn't trust their sources of money. Nor did I trust their knowledge and patience.

As I had confessed earlier, I had heard one too many stories about situations where conflicts within management boards ended badly, very badly.

Example 1: The largest supermarket chain in Nigeria. A man from outside Nigeria, the company's CEO and shareholder was a neighbor of mine. When Nigeria went through a crisis which hit Jumia badly, especially its sales figures, the supermarket boss started looking to save money. He started cutting the salaries and 'entertainment budgets' of the board of management and the supervisory board. You must remember that two-thirds of the posts are occupied by those who are the Godfathers of the company. These guys call up the state governor or chief of police when the company needs help. So that a health inspector doesn't hold out for such a large bribe or so that the harbormaster doesn't keep containers of French cheese in a refrigeration unit with the electricity deliberately turned off for too long. And so on. Such temporary cutting of salaries seems entirely understandable. Lead by example and we'll take care of the company's future, right? Well, not necessarily. The CEO encountered categorical opposition at the top. But he didn't go soft and enforced his decision. Within a week, he had stopped being my neighbor. The next morning, instead of his driver, two border guards came knocking on his door. He was informed that his permit to live and work in Nigeria had been revoked. Forever. He had 15 minutes to pack his bags and was escorted to the airport.

Example 2: A German-Nigerian construction firm. During the glory days, meaning before the Chinese arrived and started to make everything four times cheaper and ten times faster, it had employed over a thousand foreign engineers, built an airport, roads and bridges. Despite protests from their Nigerian partners, the Germans send a new financial director to Nigeria who was supposed to analyze the company's situation which was much worse than one could expect. It was as if money was... just disappearing. The financial director started introducing changes and started an internal investigation. Although this was not an easy job, he liked Nigeria. Mainly because he could realize his passion of off-road motorcycling as much as he liked. He had his favorite route outside Lagos, where he went with a friend every weekend. During one of these trips he fell victim to extraordinarily bad luck. Someone had strung thin wire among the trees in a place where the road was straight and even, and where you could go hell for leather. I would have like to write that the wire cleanly beheaded him and he didn't suffer. Unfortunately, it only cut half way through his neck and threw him off the bike. It sliced through his windpipe and blood vessels. He was suffering for well over 10 minutes.

Therefore, I wanted to secure money from a foreign investment fund, even better if it was one that specialized in the complex sector of online travel and travel technology. The kind which would strongly support me in global partnerships. Because I also had dreams of entering the Asian and South American markets. After all, even if we weren't there first, we could always enter by buying up a local competitor. This was a round in which failure was not an option.

And what kind of businesses fail to take off most often? Those destined for success. To say I had suffered a defeat was an understatement. I had made contact with 150 companies, pitched my idea to them face to face over 30 times. All of them wanted to talk to me. None of them wanted to immediately invest.

I could write a separate book about the mistakes I made during my first approach to Round A. To cut a long story short, I didn't manage to get to those with balls big enough to take the risk of running a tech business in Africa. Or in other words – I wasn't able to set their minds at rest regarding this risk, to mitigate them. I spent a total of a couple of weeks in the States talking to investment funds in Silicon Valley, the ones that are always bragging about seeking out the greatest innovation and taking risky decisions, on the condition that the start-up concerned is no more than a 15-minute Tesla ride away. I wasn't able to convince them either of the business model or the huge market we're talking about.

The travel tech funds which understood my business were just not interested in Africa yet. There was still too much going on in the travel sector on other continents. Instead of positioning ourselves as a business from Nigeria which would conquer Africa, right from the beginning I should have sold it as a Polish-Nigerian company which specializes in emerging markets all over the world. But that which seems obvious in hindsight, wasn't so obvious then.

Things started heating up and time was running out. It was one of the most stressful and worst periods of my life health-wise. I was working all the time, sleeping very little, was on edge and pissed off by the slightest thing. Although I didn't pay myself anything and covered most of the incidental costs of the company with my own money, I didn't have the right to demand the same of my team. Who were so understanding anyway.

As if that wasn't enough, Ramesh started to play up. We were not getting along as we used to. He couldn't understand why we needed to raise money again, why we weren't already profitable yet and why I was flying around looking for investors, instead of focusing on the business locally, as if inviting people with more money was all I wanted to do. While our second investor, SpeedUp was supportive in my situation and satisfied with the reporting, Ramesh wanted more and more reporting, spreadsheets, files, as if we were already a multimillion dollar enterprise. SpeedUp understood startups, Ramesh wanted us to run like he run his old family business.

But he was right about one thing – I had ceased to get it. There's this saying: 'If everything is under control, you're working too slow.' Well, we were working real fucking fast, and there was very fucking little under control. Our priority was to maintain growth in securing hotels because there's nothing worse than things slowing up half way during negotiations with investors. That's like a girl's make-up coming off half-way through a date. I knew that if we didn't keep up the pace of sales, we wouldn't secure the money. And then none of it would have counted. This is why all of the other operational challenges were put off for the future.

At the end of the day, we were a small start-up company, with a total of 15 people in a team divided into four shareholders. We trusted people and didn't need contracts. Formalities are for people, not the other way round. You can always sort out the formalities later, right? Wrong, actually.

And then he appeared. Biruk. An Ethiopian with an American passport. Another perfect combination of the best of the two Worlds, I thought. By his own description, he was a specialist in operations, finance and securing investors. He had been introduced by a mutual friend, which cut a lot of ice with me. Indeed, Biruk's CV was so amazing that I immediately wanted to frame it and hang it in my office. He came to the interview in an expensive suit and shoes, with a gold watch on his wrist, while the vision that he conjured up before me made me want to shine those shoes for him. After 15 minutes of conversation, I knew I had my man. To me he was the vice-president of financial affairs/operational affairs/Jesus Christ, Our Lord and Savior. A perfect American accent and a CV with Lehman Brothers, the World Bank and several months of working with Jumia on his CV, among other things. When asked why such a short time, he replied that he had been employed on a particular project as a director of operations and so, once he had set up the processes, he left. I believed him, because I wanted to believe him.

When he left, I breathed a sigh of relief. Some time earlier, I had understood that we needed someone to focus on securing investors. As Maciek and I had to watch over the business, we didn't have time for it. Talking with investors was like pulling teeth. And someone had to test and introduce the software, someone had to establish cooperation with new hotels and new travel agencies, and someone had to promote it all. "There's something I just don't like," said Ifechi, blurted out unthinkingly. Ifechi was a guy who had worked for me for some time at Jovago, until he was fired by Pierre because he had allegedly turned up for work drunk. Just one thing: Ifechi is a Muslim and doesn't drink. From his own account, it concerned something else. Namely, for mentioning my name during talks with Pierre one too many times. Okay, maybe the guy doesn't have an instinct for self-preservation, but because he knows marketing, I took him for ourselves.

"What don't you like?" I asked.

"Such a successful guy – he says – and he wants to work for a failing start-up?"

"You're a failure yourself!"

"Alright, alright. But it's weird right? Maybe you should call..."

"I'm not calling anywhere. And certainly not Rocket. I'm telling you, he's our man. I know what I'm talking about."

Now, whenever I talk with Ifechi on Skype, he always greets me with the same words: "Hi Marek, didn't I tell you so?" There's no-one on earth who annoys me as much as he does.

But we're getting ahead of ourselves. Biruk made me a proposal. He would join the company as vice-president. He would sort out our finances, deal with the reports for the investors (including for the more and more unbearable Ramesh), take over all my talks with new investors and help in ending up with success. He was also supposed to invest $20,000 of his own money, and then work with us for a minimum of six months. After this time, he was to receive a 5% stake in HotelOga. Additionally, if he managed to secure finance to the value of at least $2,000,000, his stake was to be increased by a further 10%. Of course, meaning he would end up with a total of 15% of something valued at 10 big ones. So he was to earn almost $1,500,000 in the clear for six months work. Not bad. Biruk cheerfully accepted such terms. At the time, every dollar counted for us. Because being short of one dollar was almost like being short of two dollars. And two dollars was almost a 1000 naira. And a 1000 naira was...

We had dropped our pants for Biruk, the company dropped its pants. He got HotelOga on a silver plate. And a good look at our financials, bank statements, and every one of our databases. I introduced him to all of our investors who we were talking with, he was supposed to close the deal with them. Biruk was given the right to issue orders to my people without my involvement, just so as not to slow things down. Full transparency and trust. Only for some reason my partner Maciek did not take to our new Messiah and put up resistance to showing him our system. He considered him a Slick Willie, with a decidedly oversized ego. Although Maciek's ego isn't the smallest either, his intuition is better than mine. Insofar as I didn't listen to him then. We had a company to save for Christ's sake! I myself had introduced Biruk to SpeedUp and Ramesh with the promise that from that day

Biruk would fulfill all of the investors' demands. SpeedUp had never had major concerns and actually supported us. Of course, this really concerned my little Indian friend. If only Ramesh was happy.

The following months passed. And what was the only result of Biruk's work?

A shiny, new, sweet-smelling... 50-page business plan full of corporate jargon bullshit and even more complicated Excel files with the budget. Apart from the self-praise and promises which he flooded us with at every monthly meeting, we had made no progress. But it was a fact that Ramesh had stopped calling me at 6am daily. As it happened, I was really happy with that, as my relationship with Ramesh had deteriorated incredibly due to the situation at HotelOga. Before Biruk had appeared, we had had one hell of a row to the point where I threw the phone down. At that time, I was a real bundle of nerves and wasn't always able to control myself. Sometime, I forgot that I was talking to my investor and screamed as if talking to a buddy. I just exploded and shouted: "Ramesh, stop fucking around in my business and let me do the job. I know what I'm doing. I have the most skin in the game here, I'm risking the most. You don't understand tech businesses. You're old and made your money in old businesses. Wait a second! You didn't even earn that money, your father did. You're not happy with any of your other investments. Maybe it's time to look for issues within yourself? Maybe fix your marriage instead of throwing your frustrations on me?"

Words can hurt. And I'm good at verbal martial arts. And I know how to make someone suffer with wounding words. Especially a friend you know much about. But Ramesh was a guy with an enormous ego and a ton of money which fed this ego. He took insults badly and never forgave them. Something which I was about to learn.

The three potential investors, people which I had still invited for talks, kept delaying after several rounds of negotiations talks run by Biruk. At the eleventh hour, I myself found Rohit, an investor from India, unrelated to Ramesh in any way, who quickly threw in another $100,000 and which gave us another few months of life. Biruk hadn't organized a single meeting with the investors from his own network of contacts. Instead, weird games started. Biruk singled out two issues which he really pressured me over. One day he declared that our office was too expensive, but no problem, he had a solution – a good buddy of his had just opened a co-working space and would definitely give us a great discount.

At the time, I didn't realize just how dangerous this proposal was, but I turned him down anyway. I didn't want to change the office. My people felt fine there. And these people were my greatest capital. Many of them had come from Jovago. They had handed in their notices, because they wanted to work with me. And I tried to take care of this team as best I could. I won't hide the fact that things weren't pretty. But no-one turned their nose up at it. None of my old teammates anyway. By the way, remember Michael? The guy I wanted to fire from Rocket, until he showed me how he wonderfully he fucked up Pierre at the organizational meeting? Well, he was the first to leave Rocket and now he was working for me. And the sly bastard had made it.

One way or the other, my team liked that office and I didn't see any reason to change it. And also because the owner of the building was a friend of mine and I knew that if I wasn't able to pay the rent he wouldn't just kick me out after a week. Besides, we were paying the market rate, not overpaying. And above all, we had other priorities than arranging a big move of all the furniture, docs, hardware and people.

But then Biruk came up with something else. One of our biggest pains in the ass was the long time our partners took to pay over the money. Both hotels and travel agencies. In theory, it was the perfect solution. In the case of a booking, when a customer pays up front directly to a travel agency, Expedia for example, Expedia transfers the money for all its bookings to us, then we, having taken our commission, transfer it to the hotel. Expedia paid late, but regularly. In exchange, I didn't have any problem with chasing down hundreds of small hotels for small sums of money. I could have also taken charges owed to us and the agencies (such as Booking.com) by the hotels from the transfers to the hotels, in cases in which the customer had paid the hotel for their stay just on arrival. Everything would have worked fine if we had a float of money as a 'buffer'. But we didn't have any cash in the piggy-bank, as everything that was coming in was being used the same day to cover payments for the previous month.

My old buddies who I had gotten to know at Rocket gave me a helping hand. Some time before, they had left Jumia and founded a company dealing with factoring, meaning fast, small loans for companies guaranteed by the invoices which the borrower was issuing their customers. I had been using their help almost from the very beginning of HotelOga's operations. In fact, they had offered me preferential terms. An honest rate of interest for our situation. Needless to say, as a company we had no chance of getting a loan from a bank. It worked in this way: right after registering a booking, the factoring company sent us its value and we would return the money once we had received a transfer from our partners. It was a very convenient solution, but above all one which was crucial for our survival. Well, when asked at one of our meetings about potential investors, Biruk replied that although there were none, he knew instead how to save every penny. And factoring, in his view, was an unnecessary expense, as he had a friend who would lend us the money at a cheaper rate.

This was just too much.

"For fuck's sake, Biruk. First of all, I didn't employ you here to have you wheedle your friends in. And second of all, since the time you appeared, our factoring partners are the only thing, apart from me and Rohit, who are directing any capital into this company. Do you understand what I mean?"

"No."

"Somehow that doesn't surprise me at all. Let me explain this to you: either you get down to serious work and bring us an investor, instead of dealing with bullshit, or we are done."

"How dare you speak to me like that!" Biruk, just like Ramesh, couldn't stand my 'hard' feedback. "And secondly, this was an act detrimental to the company!"

"You're right, Biruk, employing you was an act detrimental to the company."

"Fine. We'll see what Ramesh has to say about this."

And this was news to me. I didn't know that they were so tight with each other. Ramesh had been my good friend and it was me who introduced them. And now he was aiming to use him against me. This feeling really started to get me. I felt that Biruk was hiding something. I didn't think much longer. I had a hunch and decided to act on it.

"You know, Biruk," I said calmly, "You're right. I'm sorry. I'll take back what I said about firing you if you don't get down to work."

"Well, Marek, I think the next time you'll think twice before speaking to me like that," Biruk said, feeling even more sure of himself.

"I'm firing you right now."

"What?!"

"You're fired. I'm terminating the contract due to the failure to fulfill duties on your part. I've had enough. This collaboration isn't working. Meetings with you are long, exhausting and make me feel more stupid than I was beforehand. But above all, you haven't fulfilled your basic task of finding an investor. You haven't advanced this company one millimeter. The new budget which you ordered to be prepared, as I know that you certainly didn't write it, was a smokescreen. There is no indication that this is going to change. I'll give you back your money. However, you don't deserve to get shares for obvious reasons, as you haven't worked for them. Excuse the form, but in a moment you'll receive the relevant document in this matter."

"You have no right to do this!"

"Go cry somewhere else, Biruk."

I had already stopped listening to him. I left to make a phone call, because I realized that I shouldn't sack Biruk without Maciek's agreement.

"Listen," I said meekly into the phone, "I've just fired Biruk."

"Jeeesus, why took it so long!" my partner replied.

Biruk didn't come to work the following day. Neither did two other employees. Wale, whom I had recently employed, and Towulani, who Biruk had employed himself. Both of them were helping him with 'finances'. Neither of them responded to emails, texts or answered their phones. Something here clearly stank. I started to examine and delve deeper into the facts. Trawl through emails, ask around, check out contacts.

And what did I find out? Only that for a long time Biruk had been having regular meetings with Wale and Towulani, the same two guys who had disappeared that day. Out-of-office meetings. None of them had announced these meetings either in the daily or weekly reports or in conversations with me. I found an email sent by Wale straight to Biruk and Ramesh. Both Biruk and Wale were either so careless or confident that they had used the company email box to which I had the right to look at. When I read the subject of the email, I started fuming. It was called "Stuff we can use against Marek to remove him from the board".

What I had found proved that Wale was indeed a fantastic analyst, patiently analyzing and gathering evidence, because that's what I had employed him to do. I never suspected, however, that he was corruptible, deprived of a moral backbone, a weasel who would find facts to suit any thesis. And so, for example, in his report he exposed such crimes as payment for a booking from one of our partners, Expedia, had not been transferred right at the beginning of the company's operations to the company account in Nigeria, but to the company account in Poland. What he had forgotten to add was that HotelOga comprised two companies: one Polish, one Nigerian. Expedia transferred the money to the account in Poland, which would in turn send the money further on to Nigeria. Taking into account that it's a listed company in the USA, as well as its internal rules, Expedia couldn't send dollars directly to Nigeria. Of course, Wale forgot to remember that all the right amounts to the dollar later arrived in the company account in Nigeria. And that throughout the whole time, HotelOga had an external financial auditor, recommended by Ramesh, who was analyzing the cash flow on a monthly basis and never flagged anything even slightly suspicious. The whole report was full of half-truths, clearly written with the aim of having me thrown out of the company. Both Wale and Towulani obviously knew that their secret machinations with Biruk were about to come out. They now work with Biruk in the same company. Since they are rather unemployable after what they did, he must have brought them in. His promise of HotelOga shares in return for playing a part in the hostile takeover scam didn't quite materialize.

The first thing I did was something I should have done a long time beforehand. I called an old friend who had worked as a financial director at Jumia. In fact, I had become very good friends with Natalie and we're still in contact today.

"Marek, that guy was the greatest bullshitter of my entire career. We fired him after a couple of months when we figured out that all the guy could do was talk. Don't tell me that you were taken in by him too?" Natalie asked.

"Uuhh, you know, it's breaking up, I'll call you back!" I was embarrassed to admit it. How could I have been so blind!

The next person was Richard, the owner of a large Nigerian media company, and the man who had introduced us.

"Marek, forgive me for introducing you to him. At the time, everything between us was okay. But this guy promotes himself as an African Gordon Gekko, as a great rebuilder of companies. His father made his money in the first private businesses in Ethiopia, and it's thanks to him that Biruk has any money and an American passport. He milked money out of me for consulting services, as I was falling into even worse difficulties. And then he proposed that I appoint him vice-president, because only then would he be able to get anything done! Nice try."

I wouldn't be surprised if the $20,000 which Biruk gave me was the same money wrung out of Richard. In contrast to Richard, I hadn't lost any money paying Biruk. But I had lost something more valuable – the time which was supposed to have been spent on saving the company. From these conversations and slowly analyzing the last few months, a true picture of Biruk developed. Yet another rich kid who had watched *Wall Street*. One with a Daddy's boy complex. He just had to be important, had to be the boss. And he believed he was so smart that he would be fast-tracked to the head of the company. Through a hostile takeover.

"Business is like chess. And I'm like Kasparov. Now you're thinking about moving a pawn. But I'm already analyzing all the possible combinations five moves ahead." His little saying had then struck me as slightly cheesy, but still a bit cool. Now, I took it up differently.

And when I put the pieces of the puzzle of past events together, Biruk had done something which had dispelled all my illusions. He called up Maciek and tried to convince him to join him and have me kicked off the board. He promised Maciek additional shares. In fact it was no surprise that someone like him had no sense of honor, loyalty or honesty. Of course, Maciek stood right by me. It was now clear that Biruk was trying to force a company takeover. And this report was the basis on which the supervisory board (which Ramesh headed) could get rid of me and put Biruk in my place. He had planned it all out. He had deliberately delayed finding an investor, so as to drive the company into a situation with no way out, up against a wall and then blame it all on me. And then he would ride in like the cavalry to save the day. And his attempt to move our office? If it had worked, of course his buddy would not have let me in to my own office. But it was obvious that Biruk couldn't have done it all on his own. He must have had at least two shareholders on his side in order to have the power to vote me out. Maciek could be counted out. So there was SpeedUp, Ramesh or Rohit, who had just joined the board. And just who he had wrapped around his little finger became apparent only the next day, when Ramesh sent me a letter containing the information that he had made Biruk his representative and that all issues had to be sorted out through him.

I was shocked. But I should have expected this and I had only myself to blame, especially after the course of my last conversation with Ramesh, during which I brought up my knowledge about his personal issues just to piss him off.

Initially, I had no idea by what miracle Biruk had persuaded Ramesh to work together. Then I found out that he had worked on his sense of paranoia. Ramesh saw people who wanted to cheat him everywhere he looked. First, Ademola from the start-up finance company who wanted to destroy him, and now me. First, Ademola had been a friend who had betrayed him, and now me. And now Biruk was his new friend. Biruk had spread rumors that we wanted to sell the business secretly and take the money and run from Nigeria. You know, a kind of Nigerian anti-scam. Instead of bringing dough into Nigeria, we were going to take it out, thus exacting revenge for all those letters starting 'Dear Sir, I am John Smith, a lawyer, your relative Nhlanla Zyslovsky has just died and left you an inheritance of [in words] 10 million dollars. In order for me to transfer it over to you, you will have to pay a fee of yadda, yadda, yadda.'

And it was amazing that Ramesh bought this story hook, line and sinker. He now believed that Zmysłowski had wanted to cheat him right from the very beginning. Which is why Zmysłowski had employed Biruk and given him access to all the documentation so that Biruk could figure out that something was wrong. And apart from that, when Biruk started to think things over, it was right then Zmysłowski introduced him to Ramesh so that Biruk could protect Ramesh. Of course, Ramesh bought this story, as he wanted to believe it and because he needed Biruk. Just as I had believed in Biruk the Messiah, because I wanted and needed to believe it.

But something in Biruk's plan hadn't worked out. He had put too much pressure on me to change the office and the factoring company and did not foresee that my intuition would sober up. I had interrupted his winning streak too early. He had not yet managed to lure in SpeedUp or Rohit, although I know he wouldn't have had a chance with them. They were my team and there had never been any friction between us. And, above all, both the boys at SpeedUp and Rohit were able to take feedback on the chin, while being well capable of busting my balls when I needed it. And I respect that.

Shortly before firing Biruk, I had established contact (and here I must stress it was me who did it, not Biruk) with a certain start-up from East Africa. It was called Safari Sunset, and although their headquarters were in Kenya, they were involved in more or less the same thing as us. Everything was run by two Norwegians. They had been on the market for much longer, for over three years. But they didn't have their own technology. They had licensed it from a company in India. Ahh, India again! They had the same number of partner hotels as we had. Why had they grown so slowly? Because they had gone along the route where I hadn't wanted to go: slow organic growth, resulting from its own profits, not being swamped in high overhead costs or building own tech. They traded having a long term advantage with the comfort of lower costs short term and risks of being cut out any time by software license provider. They didn't want to or couldn't grow from cash injections from investors apparently. The interesting thing was that now they were thinking about moving into west Africa, while our plan was to move into east Africa, once we had secured financing. So we would have ended up as competitors and losing money fighting among ourselves instead of building up a market together. I proposed joining forces: we would merge the companies on a 50-50 basis and together take money from investors. We would become one company. Although we didn't have much time for checking each other out, it seemed we were on the same wavelength. I wanted to believe in this. For Norwegians, they were totally laid back. However, everything had changed for me after my experience with Biruk. A real war had broken out between Ramesh and us and I was afraid that this would scare Safari Sunset off. After all, no-one wants to invest in an enterprise that's riven with internal conflict.

I tried to straighten everything out. I had to convince Ramesh that

Biruk had pulled the wool over his eyes. I tried calling him, but he didn't answer the phone. I called mutual friends to try and talk him round. I wrote to all of them. I was so stressed, that I didn't sleep the whole night. All of them apologized to him on my behalf and asked him to talk to me. Eventually, he agreed to talk to Maciek. Only to Maciek. That was even better, as he would hear confirmation of my story from someone else. My partner was up to the job alright. He told him all about the situation with Biruk, how that he had done absolutely nothing for four months – on the contrary, he had put off the investors which we ourselves had found. He explained how Marek was busting his ass, trying to save and develop the company, and how he regretted saying what he said about Ramesh. Eventually, Maciek managed to talk Ramesh round. He rescinded Biruk's position as his representative, something which was especially important and satisfying for me, given what Biruk had wanted to do.

We entered into a preliminary agreement in which we confirmed, within a few months, that Ramesh would receive shares in a newly established company merged with Safari Sunset. I also promised that I wouldn't take revenge on Biruk. Karma would deal with that. I was relieved, as I was at last ready to sign a contract with the Kenyan Norwegians and put the company back on its feet. And the company really needed it. Neither myself nor Maciek had paid ourselves a salary in a year. Meaning at all. Although I hadn't even counted how much money in total I had put in to cover running costs, it would easily work out as double what I had initially invested. What was worse, I also hadn't paid my staff for two months and knew that either we had to find shelter or we were finished.

The only problem was that Daniel, Safari Sunset's CEO, also knew it. He smelled our blood and then unexpectedly changed the rules of the game: "We're still going in on the deal, but we want a 80/20 split. 80% for us, of course :-)" is was more or less the message they graced me with. To be blunt, it was no longer a proposal for cooperation. It was just a common or garden takeover. But I wasn't in much of a position to refuse. At the same time, however, I knew I wouldn't be working with Safari Sunset after something like that. They had used me once, and only once. But the worst thing was that the change as to the split wouldn't allow us to get out of the terms agreed with Ramesh. And renegotiating the agreement with Ramesh would be taken as betrayal and playing for time right from the beginning. We were in a black hole twice as deep as before.

With HotelOga, I had put everything on one card when I decided to race forward. The plan didn't work. Tough. Business is not all about success, you learn from your mistakes and I had learned a lot. That was the day I understood that I wouldn't be introducing HotelOga to high society. Because either we would collapse or be taken over by people I had no intention of working with. So I then conducted a review of my goals. One way or another my adventure with the 'Guv' had come to an end. Above all, I wanted to secure the future of those who had believed in me and invested their careers (my wonderful team) and money (the investors). I also wanted the company to survive and continue to conquer the world, even without me. And so I got down to working twice as hard.

As Maciek attempted to gain a little more time for me, he started negotiating the details of the deal with the Norwegians. Although they were, of course, inflexible, given that they weren't in a hurry, they were also quite patient. Meanwhile, I managed to conduct a 'Tour de Despair', meaning I reactivated all the contacts which I still had. I visited old partners, clients and competitors. I crossed the thresholds of Wakanow and Hotels.ng, meaning those who had blocked me out. I even wrote emails to Ezra and Pierre with offers to bury the hatchet. I swallowed my pride for the greater good. I flew to South Africa to meet with the board of SouthAfricaSoftware, a large IT firm with 20 years experience, and enjoying great esteem both in the field and among its clients. HotelOga wouldn't have had a chance of existing, if SouthAfricaSoftware had wanted to enter Nigeria earlier. In fact, I had modeled myself on their solutions when developing the initial concept of HotelOga.

And here an opportunity appeared. As it turned out, for some time SouthAfricaSoftware had been watching our activities. Actually, the thing here was that this didn't concern our software at all, but our client database, contracts with hotels and my Nigerian team. They were curious about how quickly we had grown. As the late-lamented Felix once said: "There's no secret at all, it's just that no-one busted their asses as hard as we did." In turn, SouthAfricaSoftware had its own technology, although ours was newer, and preferred to improve its own rather than patch it up with ours. To be frank, they recognized there was a chance for them to get themselves into Nigeria through an acquisition. By the way, a few funny things came out. Among which was the fact that my old friend Pierre had met with SouthAfricaSoftware many times, as he wanted to integrate Jovago with them, instead of me. He was concerned to have an alternative for hotels, in case they started asking too much about integrating with HotelOga. During these talks he had really run me down. Saying that I had run the company badly, that I had really been fired by him, that in breach of my contract I had introduced direct competitors to the market, and had poached their best employees. And another time he had said that Jumia Travel would be the perfect partner for them because from the beginning of its operations it had high earnings and is the fastest growing enterprise in the online travel sector in all of Africa, that it has virtually no competitors in Nigeria, and that the employees which Zmysłowski had poached were poor performers anyway, whom he would have fired himself long before, had they not had contracts.

Helen, the founder of SouthAfricaSoftware, noticed Pierre's looseness and ferocity, which naturally influenced how his words were perceived. Later, when she mentioned to him that she was close to making a deal with HotelOga, he was meant to have given her the friendly advice to change the name of my company after acquiring it. Because it was very ill-judged and had bad associations for everyone.

Just as a side note, Helen had founded this company with her husband many years before and currently comprise almost a monopoly in South Africa. She told me that when she first sent hotels software on CD, they put it in to their car radios hoping to hear music. Helen's calm, composure and experience was the thing I needed. I saw how she treated her company employees and knew that my team would be in good hands if this deal went through. But, above all, their office was in Cape Town! Ten points just for the choice of location.

After meeting Helen, I returned to the hotel and wrote emails to everyone that I was indefinitely indisposed, called room service for a burger and a glass of wine (alright, a bottle) and started scheming. I knew I couldn't leave the hotel without a solution. Time had run out. Safari Sunset was starting to lose patience and Maciek couldn't lead them on for much longer before they changed their minds. It was the same with Ramesh – if I didn't have a sensible alternative, once he found out that the previous agreement would have to be renegotiated, there would be war. His lawyers had already sent two reminders. I knew that if I didn't write back within a few days, things would get bad, very bad. Ramesh had totally and utterly lost it and wouldn't be listening to any rational arguments. But in the end, and above all, if the staff didn't get paid and the hotels, payment for bookings, there wouldn't be anything left.

I turned the mirror in the room into a temporary blackboard and started writing out the situation on it with a marker.

Above all, Safari Sunset needed our technology. If it was to develop any further, it had to move away from using the software it had been using, which was not in fact tailored for the African client. The merger with Safari Sunset would continue along the start-up route. Every employee would feel like a partner and have share options. Merging with SouthAfricaSoftware, although a safer option offering better pay and stable employment, did not offer share options. SouthAfricaSoftware already had other ambitions and was a company at a different stage of development. Even though perhaps its appetite wasn't smaller, it certainly ate more slowly. My Nigerian team needed more stability than adventure, as living in Nigeria is an adventure in itself. The staff at HotelOga had gotten to know Helen during her visit at our office in Lagos and expressed an interest in merging with SouthAfricaSoftware. Our team in Poland – Maciek, Szymon and Damian – definitely had ambitions to continue the development of the company and build something bigger and so preferred joining the Norwegians. Safari Sunset, which had changed the terms of the proposal, mainly referring to HotelOga's financial situation, was afraid that it would have too much impact on opportunities for fast development and securing money after the merger. In turn, SouthAfricaSoftware was inclined to pay cash for the company and not ask too many questions.

I thought up the following: SouthAfrica Software would buy the Nigerian team from HotelOga and take over its hotel contracts. It would pay off all the company's debts and, thanks to its reputation, it would straighten out and calm the situation with the travel agents. No-one would turn down SouthAfricaSoftware.

The cash surplus left over from this transaction would allow us to buy Ramesh out. If he wanted to leave the company already and not create more bad blood, he could go right ahead. If not, a cash surplus in the account would sure help HotelOga.

Although Safari Sunset would be merging with an admittedly slimmed down HotelOga, it would be merging with what it most wanted, namely the technology and our brilliant team of programmers headed by Maciek. I would gradually and painlessly withdraw from this set-up, and wouldn't be involved in the decisions of the board in which there were already too many egos. I would be satisfied more or less with the position of a passive investor who once in a while would have something to say at meetings of the supervisory board. Having a portfolio of guaranteed share in Jumia and HotelOga, I could calmly plan out my next steps. After merging with Safari Sunset, HotelOga was to take on more international name – HotelOnline, the official name of our Polish company, and one which I had also thought up.

Technically, the mergers were to take place in a way that we would establish a completely new company in Dubai in which all the parties involved would receive shares, namely: our Safari Sunset partners; me; Maciek; Ramesh (as long as he wanted shares instead of cash); SpeedUp; and Rohit. Then all the shares of the local companies (those from HotelOga and those from Safari Sunset) would be transferred in their entirety to the mother company, HotelOnline in Dubai. The only crucial condition HotelOga had to fulfill was not to enter the Nigerian market for a year so, as to give SouthAfricaSoftware time to integrate with the team. After this period, may the best man win.

I knew that even if all sides agreed to this angelic/diabolical plan without hesitation, it would still take a few months to implement. But we didn't have a few months.

An additional requirement for SouthAfricaSoftware would also be a deposit of 10% of the agreed amount. Payable immediately, as a sign of good will and a lack of an impulse to mess around, as had happened with the Norwegians. Of course, the deposit would be returned if the transaction did not go through, which I ensured through an additional personal guarantee. If the company collapsed, I would return the deposit out of my own pocket.

The concept was ready. I knew that an entire day on the telephone awaited me. Anything could happen. From that day on, we still had to make a multi-million dollar business out of HotelOga, while I would be sending everyone their notice that evening. "Marek, get a couple of hours of sleep. We won't think up anything else. Tomorrow you have to be, both of us have to be, ready to rumble. Tomorrow is most important." Maciek wrote.

I just managed to write to our lawyer to set aside the whole day, as it would be necessary to write and edit the contract as it was being put together. I set my alarm clock for 8am, so as to recharge my batteries, and fell into bed. I fell asleep before my head hit the pillow. This plan had a one in a million chance of succeeding. Such plans succeed sometimes.

SpeedUp and Rohit were in first. "Gentlemen, we trust you know what you're doing, we're in favor," we heard.

Then came SouthAfricaSoftware's turn. Following six hours of constantly being on the phone, calling each other back, discussions and negotiating details, SouthAfricaSoftware said 'Yes'!

We started to put the contract together. I was euphoric, but curbed my enthusiasm so as to get ready for Safari Sunset. The biggest problem was the year-long ban on entering Nigeria. This was the largest market in Africa, which of course they knew and had been sharpening their teeth to get at. They didn't want to give in. We agreed to a two-hour break for discussions in our groups. It was the same with the next conference call.

"We consider the blockade on Nigeria to be unfair. We want the possibility of starting operations in that country straight away."

"Gentlemen, firstly, you are not in a position to tell me what is fair or unfair. Need I remind you who changed the conditions of this merger at the last moment? SouthAfricaSoftware is actually cleaning up the mess you made. If you want this deal to go through, this condition is non-negotiable. Take it or leave it. It's 6pm, if you don't call back before 8pm, consider our proposal withdrawn. Goodbye".

And with that I hung up. I was playing for the highest stakes, bluffing, pretending to be confident in the comfort of my negotiating position. The reality couldn't have been further from the truth.

"Are you sure that you did the right thing in ending the conversation like that?" Maciek asked.

"Of course, I am!" I wrote back to him on WhatsApp. Of course, I wasn't.

The next two hours were the longest of my life. I had to sit at the computer and be ready for anything. But as long as I didn't know where we stood, I couldn't do a thing. I went on YouTube to watch films such as *People are awesome 2015*, but was so nervous that I couldn't focus on any of them for longer than 15 seconds.

The phone rang at 8.01pm. "We have a deal. Send on a copy of the contract. As today is Friday, we'll send back any changes on Monday. Our lawyer doesn't work weekends."

Although the sly bastards had made the decision in a minute, they deliberately waited right to the end just to torment us. That one minute after eight was a symbol they were on top. I didn't care for those ego trips anymore.

That was the first weekend in months that I slept properly. I woke up and got out of bed with a smile on my face. My bad luck must have reached its limit. Things had begun to settle down. I even began to think that maybe those Norwegians aren't so bad after all. Don't blame the player, blame the game. Helen sent on confirmation of the transfer of the deposit and I was really grateful for her trust and quick decision. I know she must have had to go far beyond her comfort zone to agree to everything and then push this through in Cape Town.

That Sunday evening I was already visualizing Monday. I knew that it was only when the money came into the account that I would be able to pay people their salaries and pass on the good news at the same time. That evening, I would have Safari's contract. This would allow me to join it together with the project in the SouthAfricaSoftware contract, as well as the letters of intention from SpeedUp and Rohit approving the decisions Maciek and I had made. This was meant to divest Ramesh of any doubts whatsoever, regardless of how paranoid he was and much his mind had been affected by Biruk. I imagined an evening conversation with Ramesh at which I would finally have an opportunity to apologize to him for my hurtful words, by which I had deliberately wounded his pride. In turn, he would apologize for attempting to exact revenge through business. And I imagined that we all lived happily ever after...

Monday morning, 7am. An email arrives which definitely wasn't what I had imagined. An email from Ramesh's lawyers, with a document attached:

"Information concerning the legal conflict between Marek Zmysłowski and Ramesh regarding control of the company and a call to abandon any business talks with HotelOga." What was in the document? Part of it contained the accusations from the report prepared by Wale. The document had been sent to everyone that Biruk knew about, because I had given him this information myself. All of our investors, all the travel agents with whom we had been working, Booking.com, Expedia, Travelstart, SpeedUp and a couple of others. And the aim of the report? Totally an attempt to destroy my image and discredit me as a person. "That'll cheer Pierre up", I thought. But there was something else in the document. And it went like this: "Mr Ramesh is convinced that this concerns attempted fraud. We will hold to account both legally and publicly anyone who makes a deal with Zmysłowski or HotelOga without my knowledge or agreement. Ramesh." And this sentence was the problem.

That evening, Helen called me with the news that SouthAfricaSoftware was pulling out of the deal:

"Marek, we're a big company, we have a lot of money and a reputation to protect. And Biruk knows this, and knows that if he sues us we'll be happy to settle for a sum of money greater than his entire investment in HotelOga," she said.

And so now everything was fucked up. I had only needed a few hours or so to be able to send Ramesh the good news. He had interpreted the silence on my part as me scheming against him, and not working on his behalf. He had killed the woman he loved, because he thought she was cheating on him. I was forced to let people go and terminate our contracts with hotels, as we were in no state to continue operations.

The Nigerian team let go by HotelOga could walk into any job they wanted. The best were recruited by SouthAfricaSoftware, which didn't have to pay anything to get them anymore. And gradually it started to sign its own new contracts with the hotels.

As a business, HotelOga almost became worthless. All that was left was the technology which would also lose its value if it wasn't developed. Fortunately, Safari Sunset was not scared off by Ramesh and Biruk's illegal threats and completed the deal and merged with us. However, the amount of shares which was granted to Szymon, Damian and Maciek from the company in Dubai was pathetically small – we're talking a fraction of a percent. The more the boys realized this, the more they felt like hirelings. The board was to be almost completely controlled by the Norwegians. Only I had still enough shares to be able to decide anything. But I was emotionally exhausted by this rollercoaster ride. I just wanted to finish this chapter of my life.

It was then that I decided to make a decision which was fatal to my wallet, but wonderful for my sense of well-being. I divided my shares into three and sold them to the boys for a token fee. I was just lucky I was out this drama. More important to me than money was that HotelOga, now already HotelOnline, would be a great company which I could be proud of establishing. Thanks to the shares from me, the boys would have more of a say in the company and regained their motivation. I only wanted one thing in return – that they would take care that there were also shares in the company in Dubai waiting for Ramesh. The fact that he had worked to the detriment of the company was one thing, but the fact that he was also a shareholder was another. I had no right to take his shares from him. Anyway, the courts would decide how the damage Ramesh and Biruk had wreaked was to be repaired.

And regarding one's reputation, it was Daniel from Safari Sunset – the guy whose greed had triggered it all off, the guy who had pulled out at the last minute from a contract with equal terms for both sides – who was himself fired by all the other partners and the board, when it came out that there were fairly serious irregularities in the way the company was run by him. Any decision-making power and control of the company was taken away from him by new investors and he was given a puppet "chairman" position. I recalled how he had argued for a last-minute change in the terms of the merger. He then said with a smirk on his face:

"Well, Marek, you should have managed your company better."

Karma works. I paid all of HotelOga's debts from my own pocket and returned SouthAfricaSoftware's deposit. For everyone, HotelOga was Zmysłowski and Zmysłowski was HotelOga. And my reputation was very important to me. And I'm in Africa for the long haul.

Chapter 16

MISS WORLD
AND THE TERRORIST

Leaving HotelOga and moving to Cape Town on my 31st birthday set a year of change in my life. Change which had entered my head on turning 30 (for all you readers in your twenties, if you think that this psychological barrier between a two and a three at the front of a number changes anything, then you thought right. Something just popped in my head then. Like an oil can whose leaking contents had greased my wheels).

I had spent a large part of my time during recent years in airports and airplanes. I had to learn how to live out of a suitcase, not large ones, but hand luggage, as airlines had often lost or stolen my bags. This forced me to take a very practical approach to the material things needed on a daily basis. This forced minimalism began to come to me more and more easily, until I realized that it had become second nature. Recently, I went on a two-week motoring holiday where, despite having unlimited baggage allowance, I fit everything into a rucksack, as I simply didn't know what else to take.

Minimalism has brought me freedom. Not necessarily savings, as it wasn't about that. I always spend a lot on traveling, food and life. Five years in Nigeria has gotten rid of my desire to drive. I don't want to drive anymore. I have a driver and always use Uber when I'm out of town, thanks to which I'm more efficient while on the move. I work on my laptop or snatch forty winks between meetings and get some energy for a longer, more productive day. I've limited my wardrobe regarding the number of colors and types of garment, which has given me freedom and saves energy, as I don't need to decide what to wear in the morning.

I've also realized that, during the last 10 years, I've been in business for the wrong reasons. I simply wanted to be the center of attention and wanted to win. I wanted to prove to everyone that I can, that I deserved respect, that I'm not an object of ridicule. Put simply, I was fulfilling the needs of the 15-year-old me. Those things which I had always lacked – to be picked for the volleyball A-team, to be able to regale classmates with jokes that were funny enough, to catch the attention of girls in the classroom. So that I wouldn't be misunderstood: this was one hell of a motivating factor, and an effective one too. But one which had always left me longing for more. You'll always find someone who has a bigger company than you, is more handsome, has more money and nicer pictures on Instagram. It started to get to me that really the greatest internal joy came from the building process. From stages 0 to 1. When everything was still in chaos. When you had to drive everything on yourself, as no-one else would do it for you. Everything higher than this – from 1 to 10 and from 10 to 100 – was someone else's job. I find this difficult, as it demands things from me which are not my strong points. I prefer to focus on my strong points and make them stronger.

I had stopped having fun at Jovago because we had gone from stage 1 to 1o. Pierre was only an excuse: if he hadn't been there, I would have found another reason. I left HotelOga because instead of building up a business, I had to mess around first in office politics, and then save the company. It was obvious that my sharp tongue hadn't helped me with certain investors and employees and everything could have gone better had I been more mature about things.

Coming to such conclusions liberated me. I decided to give myself a break from founding more companies for the moment. Investment was also not for me yet. I had already invested in five companies in Nigeria and lost a packet. And how I did I invest in companies? Did I pay attention to the market and analyze their business models? Hhhmm, maybe. Did I pay any attention to the quality of the team?

Not so much. I invested in businesses about which I had once thought "maybe it would be cool to develop that". There was no wonderful investment theory behind it. If not for a couple of bull's-eyes in hotel sales transactions in which I had taken part, and a couple of deals like the one with military drones, I would have left Nigeria only with the bags I came with.

Five years in Lagos had also left its mark. This city is a drug. More like cocaine than weed, though. An addiction where you experience everything with double the intensity. There are no normal parties, just epic ones. There's no such thing as working calmly, but only working your ass off. Let's just say that no one comes to Lagos for the lifestyle. At Rocket Internet, despite everything, I had a billion-dollar company behind me, which could get me out of any trouble. With HotelOga, I was on my own. Due to problems at the company, life in Lagos in overdrive, indigestible food and the ubiquitous alcohol which flows through business, I became neurotic and had problem with my liver and weight gain. But that wasn't the worst of it.

The worst thing was that my whole adventure with HotelOga had also sustained collateral damage. As I've mentioned, Keyshia was a beautiful Nigerian girl, born and raised in the States. As if being gorgeous and educated wasn't enough, she was also independent. She ran her own business selling women's products. We had gotten to know each other in Lagos where she had flown in for a cousin's wedding. We fell in love with each other straight away, at least, that's how it seemed to me. I persuaded her to move to my place in Lagos, thanks to which we could be together and she could expand her business in Nigeria. She agreed, despite the fact that the traditional Nigerian part of the family weren't too impressed with us living together unmarried. Keyshia was also with me when my dad died. Whom I hadn't seen once since moving to Nigeria, something I couldn't forgive myself for long afterwards.

Unfortunately, the love on my side only lasted a few months. We were arguing more and more, while our personalities were not conducive to civilized arguments. The situation started reminding me of my experience with Klaudia. Do I always attract women with 'character' or are they all like that? Or even worse, is it my behavior that drives them crazy?

I had no strength to work on our relationship, as HotelOga was all that counted. But on the other hand, I didn't have the courage to look her in the eye and tell her I no longer loved her and then go through the emotionally exhausting process of breaking up and moving out. I just put it off. I convinced myself that the relationship would last, or maybe would right itself – it would just have to wait for the moment. Because first I had to deal with HotelOga and couldn't fix two things at once, for Christ's sake. But that was the worst thing I could have done. Because the frustration which I was experiencing in business drove me to nightclubs, which worsened my relationship with Keyshia, who had already been forced to forgive a lot. By the end of the relationship, I was the worst kind of guy you could imagine: unfaithful, uncaring and disrespectful. And it's not important what shortcomings were on the other side. What is important is that I didn't end it in time. And the more I put off this difficult conversation, the more I hurt us both. Thanks to this relationship, although I don't know what kind is perfect, I do know which kind is unacceptable. But Keyshia became stronger because of it and probably now knows what kind of guy to avoid and at what stage of life to avoid them. And that was the last lesson for a newly-minted thirty-year-old.

A change of scene brought me back to life. I changed my diet, life-style and got back into working out. Within weeks of moving to Cape Town, I felt ten years younger. But I didn't move to my beloved city straight away. The process of renewal had started earlier. First I flew to Bhutan, a less commercial version of Nepal, with tens of Buddhist temples. It's very difficult to get a visa there, unless you have Indian citizenship, for which you don't need one at all. Bhutan maintains very good relations with India as a counterbalance to its non-existent relations with neighboring China. The border between China and Bhutan is basically closed. Bhutan just doesn't want to go the way of Tibet.

Rohit, HotelOga's last investor, came to my aid. He knew what I had been going through in recent months and offered me this trip as a form of gratitude. He was the co-owner of several companies in Bhutan and organized everything for me. I spent two weeks there wandering around the mountains and meditating in Tiger's Nest temple, one of the most picturesque human-made buildings on this planet. You have to see it, or at least Google it. Meditation might be the single most useful tool for an entrepreneur to regain his mind clarity during stress. You can apply it anywhere, anytime, you don't need any equipment or sign up for classes. You can apply it instantly to calm yourself down when something unexpected happens. You can also "train" it regularly to improve your overall mind wellbeing. The same thing applies to Yoga, which I can practice in a hotel room, when there's no gym around. I always thought it was a thing for tiny little women with fancy mats in a park, but a 30min Yoga session can leave me more tired than free weights. I then took another trip, both metaphorically and literally, to and in Peru. My curiosity about ancient plant medicine started with Tim Ferris podcasts and then grew with books from Graham Hancock and Michael Pollan. I took part in a shamanic ceremony with Kambo and Ayahuasca.

All these travels were the best thing that had happened to me and helped me understand myself, define a clear plan for the future and simply become a stronger, healthier man. I want this book to be everything, but 'life coaching' or another "meditating raw vegan woke yogin hippie" bullshit, but I do believe that CEOs, Entrepreneurs and people in general pay way too little attention to how our body and brain biology affects our performance and its effect on the people around us.

I also decided to spend the next two months in the States and check out if the American Dream was all it was cracked up to be. For the first month, I rented an apartment in the center of San Francisco, 10 minutes walk from the famous Pier 7, a legendary place for skateboarders which I had seen in American movies copied from friends on VHS tapes. I was in the Mecca of business tech and a temple of skateboarding. And then I got thinking that if I hadn't given up my skateboard in high school and packed in my coding studies at university, I could have ended up living here as a developer by day and skateboarder by night. How much different my life could have been.

I visited Silicon Valley. Polish friends working at Facebook, LinkedIn and Google showed me around their company headquarters. Google definitely had best lunch on offer. For those few weeks, I lived like all of those making a career and doing business in the tech sector. I worked remotely from cult cafés such as Peet's and Philz in Palo Alto. Once, I sat at a table next to Peter Thiel, a partner at PayPal, and Travis Kalanick, who created Uber. Every day, I met friends and friends of friends living there for coffee, lunch or drinks. At the weekends we went visiting the vineyards all around Napa and Saratoga.

In one respect, San Francisco beats the hell out of every other corner of the earth I've been to. The average IQ per square meter. I've never felt as dumb as I did in San Fran. In every street side café sat someone more ambitious and smarter than me. But I knew that they certainly weren't working harder than me. And they didn't have as much passion as me. And they couldn't drink as much vodka as me.

For the next weeks, I chose as my base a gorgeous loft right by Venice Beach in Los Angeles. Not only a Mecca for skaters, but also bodybuilders, hippies and other interesting people. On a rented motorbike, I travelled around Hollywood and Santa Monica and wanted to live for a while just as I had dreamed in high school. And I'm glad I did, because now I know that it isn't all as wonderful as it seems. The American Dream is over-hyped. San Francisco is overcrowded, expensive and full of homeless people, while Los Angeles is enormous, jammed with traffic and dirty. Cape Town, apart from the slums on the coast, was for me a combination of the best of San Francisco and LA. A flowering tech sector, but also a center of showbiz, beautiful people, even more beautiful natural surroundings and magnificent food. During my last few days, I couldn't wait to get back to Cape Town at last, this time for longer. Julius Caesar once said that he would rather be first in an Alpine village than second in Rome. If Rome was Silicon Valley, highly developed, full of talented people jostling each other for fame, glory and money, while of course 'making a better world in the process', then Africa was my Alpine village. Where I could build something from 0 to 1. In which every newly opened business has a real influence on its environment, as it solves real problems and isn't just another way to kill time on your smartphone. It's for this reason alone that in a few decades my Alpine village will be bigger than Silicon Valley ever was.

Meanwhile, information about my African business adventures had reached Poland. There wasn't a day when talking to a friend, a friend of a friend, or a friend of a friend of a friend, that they didn't ask about the possibilities of expanding their own business in Africa. More and more important companies started looking for advice. As one of the classical scholars once said: "Every problem has a solution. And if it doesn't, somebody makes lots of money from consulting".

The time had come to exploit the gallons of sweat and tears, the millions of air miles, the thousands of meetings and the hundreds of key relationships. Not to build my own company, but to work for someone else. And it turned out that my ego, now rigorously dematerialized from my time with the Buddhist monks from Bhutan, had absolutely no problem with it.

During the next few months, I enjoyed life and work as never before. I divided each month into a week in Cape Town, Johannesburg, Lagos and Nairobi, helping to open offices and securing initial partners for companies in the adtech, fintech, e-commerce and on-demand logistics sectors (and a few more cutting-edge abbreviations). Generally, I stuck with the internet, which had basically permeated through everything already. As luck would have it, everything I touched went right. I remember putting a post on Twitter: "That feeling when everything is going so well that you wonder what you'll fuck up and when". Karma had to sweep through and decided that I deserved something for having to cross paths with Karol, Pierre, Biruk and Ramesh. Having found my niche in business, gotten my health back and achieved emotional balance, I once again felt ready for a more stable relationship. "Your wish is our command", the cosmic forces declared.

As it happened, I was in Johannesburg. I had finished a fairly okay-ish date on Tinder. At the same time, the place my assistant had booked was charming. The roof of the Southern Sun Hotel with a magnificent view of the sunset. I had just led my would-be girlfriend to a taxi and decided to go back up alone, finish my wine and enjoy the views from the bar outside.

At the bar sat one other guy, one with Asian features. He was chatting loudly and happily with the barman and I guessed from his accent that he was definitely American. We got talking and Johny turned out to be a straight-up guy. His family had come from Vietnam, but he was born in the States. His father, a billionaire (I always have the luck to end up meeting rich kids), had made his fortune from importing everything he could get his hands on from the old country. And Johny? Well, Johny is the CEO (i.e. the Chief Entertainment Officer) of the family vineyard, golf course and restaurant in California. Although I didn't ask him straight out, I guessed that Johny had come to South Africa to check out investing in one of the hundreds of vineyards here. As it happens when chatting over a few drinks, we talked about life, relationships, as well as fast women and beautiful cars. Johny listened to my stories about my going through woman after woman until, somewhere between the third and fourth bottle of wine, he piped up:

"Marek! I haven't known you long, but I have a feeling we're going to be friends. And I help out my friends. And it seems to me that you don't have great friends. You've got to get to know my crew!"

"That's really nice of you Johny, but I think you've had too much to drink. You Asians can't hold your drink, right?" I joked.

"Watch it, 'cos in a second I'll sort you out with one of our martial arts! Bottoms up!"

About two in the morning, the barmen very firmly chased us away to our hotel rooms. I exchanged cards with Johny and we went to sleep.

The next day, about 8am, I get a text from Johny:

"Hey buddy, I keep my promises. Drop into the bar tomorrow. I'll introduce you to Team Miss World."

"Johny, are you still drunk? :-)" I asked with an emoji.

Johny didn't reply. A few hours later he sent a photo. In it was Johny in front of a statue of Nelson Mandela. And with Johny? Seven extraordinarily gorgeous women. In ball gowns. I don't have to add that Johny only reached up to their t... eeth.

"I'll be there in 5 mins", I replied straight away.

What was going on? Well, Johny's father – apart from being a billionaire – was also a co-organizer of Miss World. I'm not talking about the Trump-sponsored Miss Universe, but the older and more dignified competition in which there are no bathing costume displays and where the only required criteria for entry is, for example, documented but above all effective work on behalf of the local community. As it happened, the Miss World team, both the runners-up, as well as the continental queens, were in South Africa, having been invited by the Nelson Mandela Foundation and helped it with fundraising. And everywhere Team Miss World goes there is a manager, a press officer and staff of hairdressers, stylists and whatever else, as well as Johny. He deals with security and talks with sponsors. Johny also makes sure that members of the public don't have access to the team. But that's not how you treat an 'old' friend from Poland.

And since we're talking about Poles, each one of us has at least two superpowers. Firstly, we have mastered the Polish language. Secondly, we know how to get a party going. From the moment I entered the elevator to the roof, for the next three hours I was the best version of myself ever. I was aided in this by the amazing local wine, of which I ordered plenty so they could try this magnificent South African ambrosia of the gods. Julia, the president of the entire Miss World organization, an older and more serious lady in the prime of her life, was taken aback that Johny had let a member of the public in to their private party. She asked me in front of everyone:

"So what do you actually do, Marek?"

"It's interesting you ask. I've been asking myself that question during the last few months. The best answer I can give you is that I'm an entrepreneur and focus on the internet and this sector gives me freedom. And I try to build companies in markets where everyone says that it's much too early for the internet. So perhaps thanks to me it may be a little less early. I started with a hotel booking site called Jovago which…"

"Oh my God! Jovago! I know that for God's sake!" shouted Miss Africa, "I use your site in Kenya!"

Paraphrasing Leonardo DiCaprio in *Django Unchained*, if I had Team Miss World's attention, now, following that scream from Miss Africa, I had everyone's attention. Thank you, Mr. Samwer.

I started chatting up Miss USA, Miss Australia, Miss Belgium, Miss Kenya and Miss Puerto Rico. All of them were extraordinary women, fulfilled, educated, ambitious, devoid of insecurities and, by the way, amazingly open, friendly and down-to-earth. Simply great girls. Then I decided to chill on the sofa for a moment and gaze once again at the Johannesburg sky. It turned out that I wasn't the only one with that idea.

"May I sit down?" I asked the woman occupying one of the sofas. She turned around, and from that moment my life was never the same again.

"It wouldn't be polite to say no, now would it?" she teased.

Yaritza was phenomenally beautiful, tall with coffee & milk colored skin, curly hair, delicate elongated facial features and a smile which was out of this world. She was from the Dominican Republic, had started her career as a nurse in order to additionally graduate from journalism school. She was only 23, but was already presenting her own talk-show on the biggest national TV station there and had acted in eight full-length feature films. And she had returned to college, this time to study acting. In her free time, she taught English and singing for free to children from the deprived areas where she herself had been raised. She emanated extraordinary warmth and natural charm. Oh, and by the way, she was the first runner-up Miss World in 2016. The next hour we spent talking about the history of the Caribbean islands, artificial intelligence, personal development, anthropology, longevity, stoicism, minimalism and… the Second World War.

Before I knew it, the clock had struck 11pm and Team Miss World had to return to their rooms, as the next day at 10am they had to depart by coach for Soweto, where the beauty queens had to distribute meals and big smiles to the local community. So as to be ready for 9am, they had to rise at 6am.

"It was nice to talk to you, Marek," Yaritza said, and left.

I sat there like a jackass with a broad grin on my face for another half an hour. And I didn't even get her email address. I could have found her on Instagram, but my message would have drowned among the thousands of requests sent daily from an army of stalkers, perverts and more or less disgusting creeps.

Suddenly, I remembered Johny – since he had brought me here, he would help me get her number! Despite everything, I knew that I would have to do something else to dot the i's and cross the t's. I came up with a brilliant idea. Yaritza had told me that she had joined the team in South Africa two days late, because one of her connecting flights from the Dominican Republic had been cancelled. Due to this she didn't get a beautiful handmade bracelet as a welcoming gift, just like everyone else. She regretted not having had the time to do any shopping and didn't know if she would have any time to see South Africa again. I decided that by some miracle I would find this bracelet and give it to her tomorrow before her departure. And then we would live happily ever after.

This was a serious problem. The whole team was to leave at 10am. Most of the jewelry shops only opened at 9am. And we're talking about Africa, where the concept of punctuality is fairly complicated. If that wasn't enough, my flight to Nairobi was at midday. This meant that I had a 30 minute window between 9.15 and 9.45am in order to find, by some miracle, a shop that would happen to have these unusual bracelets, return to the hotel, count on a stroke of luck that Yaritza would actually be in the lobby, hand her the present, romantically depart, struggle through the traffic to get to the airport, and make my flight with no time to lose. What could possibly go wrong?

Anyway, I was proud of myself. Such a plan wouldn't have put Ocean's Eleven to shame. And there my pride ended, because as I was going to sleep I was so preoccupied with the evening's events that I forgot to plug in my phone to recharge it. I also forgot to charge my Powerbank. I was woken by the knocking of an overzealous chambermaid. It was 9.35am.

"Fuuuuuuuuck!!!" I shouted and leapt out of bed.

"I'm sorry, I don't understand, sir," the chambermaid said through the door. I had to make a decision right away. The rational option: I go straight to the airport for my flight to Nairobi, I still had a chance to get there no problem, Johny would send me Yartiza's number and I would try my one-in-a-million chance of contacting her. It would end with an exchange of pleasantries, and then she would ditch me. Over my dead body! I bet everything on the turn of a card and called reception, requesting they order me a taxi now. I couldn't order an Uber as my phone was dead. I packed my stuff like a soldier ordered to move out, saving myself my morning ablutions.

9.40am: I check out at reception. The taxi is already waiting for me as the driver has just brought someone else to the hotel.

9.50am. We arrive at the first local bazaar which the driver remembered. By some miracle, one stall was open. The woman running the stall had those bracelets! Fortunately, they weren't as unique as I had thought. I gave the only banknote I had on me.

"But that's three times less than the price I'm asking!"

"Where is the nearest ATM?" I asked nervously.

"Not far, about five minutes drive."

I already knew what their five minutes meant! I now recalled the twists and turns of Nigerian timekeeping.

"I don't have that much time! It's a matter of life and death. Either you take what I have or we don't have a deal," I started to negotiate the Nigerian way.

"Ohhh, alright then, go on then. I'm starting the day at a loss."

"Thank you, you don't even know how important this is!" I shouted, already jumping into the taxi. With the wind at our backs, we would be back at the hotel a few minutes after 10am. I managed to let the driver in on the game during our crazy drive through the city. He showed concern about my story. And also showed concern about the bonus which I had promised him if we succeeded.

I fell through the revolving door back at the hotel with the little box in my hand. Out of breath, I started to look around the lobby. Literally at that moment, the doors of the elevator just a few meters in front of me opened. Yaritza was clambering out of it with her suitcases, accompanied by two friends. Laughing and engaged in conversation, in the light of day, and lightly made up, dressed in a comfortable shirt and jeans, she looked even more beautiful than the day before. Emerging from the elevator, she looked around and saw me, out of breath, sweating and in a crumpled shirt. For a second, she was dumbstruck.

I took advantage of that second to run over to her. With the agility of a street seller of perfume, I pressed the gift into her hand, and before she could protest, stole a kiss from her on the cheek. Then, maintaining a safe distance (protecting her from my all-night breath without having brushed my teeth), I blurted out: "I've solved the problem connected with your delay in coming to South Africa. And now I must run so as not to have a problem being delayed in Kenya!" and dashed to the taxi.

Now, I just needed yet another miracle. Kenya Airways, despite the financial problems it was having at the time, was known for being relatively punctual. However, I couldn't check in online, as I still hadn't managed to charge my phone. I prayed to the cosmic forces for it to be at least half an hour late. The road to the airport was fairly passable. I rushed into the departures hall a few minutes before 11am. Although the check-in desks were closed, a few members of ground staff were still standing around at one of them.

"It's weird that the system still allows me to check you in. Normally, this would be impossible at this time. But there were technical problems and the plane will be about half an hour late. You are really lucky today."

"You don't even know how lucky," I chuckled to myself. That day nothing would have amazed me.

The wheels of the Kenya Airways Boeing 787 Dreamliner hit the tarmac in Naroibi a few minutes before 6pm local time. I had managed to charge my phone during the flight, and now switched off flight mode and waited a few seconds for it to connect to my local SIM card belonging to the Kenyan division of the Indian telecoms giant, Airtel. I had over a dozen local SIM cards, one for each country visited. Straight away, I was inundated with an avalanche of messages, including one from a particularly important person.

"Dear Marek, your gesture was completely unnecessary. But I can't deny that it was extremely nice. Thank you. If you're ever in Santo Domingo, you have a friend there."

Attached to the message was a selfie showing her with the bracelet on her wrist. I decided to go in for the kill.

"Dear Yaritza, I'm delighted that the bracelet has found it proper place. It just so happens that in two weeks I'll be in your neck of the woods on business and will surely manage to get away for the weekend to your home town."

Yaritza was surprised. No less surprised than my assistant, whom I asked to check how big the Dominican Republic was and whether there was any money to be made on the internet there. After all, I was flying there on business!

Two weeks later, at the beginning of August 2017, I landed at the airport in Santo Domingo where she was waiting for me. More beautiful than ever.

These were the happiest two weeks of my life, during which Yaritza taught me about the history and culture of her country, allowing me to get to know her better in the process. And she also discovered more about me. It was an interesting experience, after my years as a pseudo-celebrity in Lagos, to see how at almost every step she was being asked for photos and autographs. It was almost impossible to spend time together in public places in peace, which is why, on the second day, we escaped to picturesque Las Terrenas, an even more beautiful part of the island than the more well known Punta Cana, but unsullied by commerce and tourists.

This part of the Dominican Republic is unbelievably safe, while the country itself is generally safe compared with Nigeria and South Africa. Enormous, stunning houses, whose value was certainly in tens of millions of dollars, stood completely unfenced, barely a few meters from a public beach. Experience has taught me that the height of the fences around the most expensive homes is a general indicator of the level of safety in a given country. In the Dominican Republic, I felt the same as I had done in Bhutan, only this time I had my better-half with me. The more we talked, the more we discovered how similar we were to each other. The circumstances and series of events through which we had come to know each other, starting with a failed Tinder date, then me accosting Johny at the bar, ending with the huge stroke of luck when searching for the bracelet and catching the plane, only made everything seem magical.

Of course, during my entire stay I slept in a separate room, but by the time I flew out of the Dominican Republic after two weeks, we were officially a couple and have been inseparable until today.

We saw each other every two or three weeks and spent at least another two weeks together. This was a period when we racked up an awful lot of air miles.

As the end of 2017 was drawing near, one of my goals was to do everything I could to close the chapter of my life entitled 'HotelOga/HotelOnline' and make sure that Maciek and the other boys would still develop a company whose future was not without significance for my image. As it happened, Maciek wrote me a message that we had to call each other, as some new problem had appeared on the horizon. I was then in Santo Domingo, Yaritza had gone to do another episode of her evening talk show, while I had the opportunity to go up on to the roof of our apartment block and gaze at the fabulous but diabolically short sunset, call up Maciek and ask what was going on.

"It's not good, Marek," Maciek began. "Ramesh has gone rogue. He's as stubborn as a mule. Insofar as they have mules in India. No rational argument will get through to him. He absolutely denies that any of his or Biruk's actions have damaged the HotelOga merger. He's rejected accepting shares in the mother company in Dubai. He's sticking to the story that the value of the shares has been artificially lowered and that we have deliberately engineered this situation. He doesn't even want to hear of agreement. But what's the point of explaining. Look at this screenshot," he said and sent on a screenshot of a conversation with Ramesh on WhatsApp.

"Maciek, I can wipe my ass with your money. Last year I made 25 big ones in the clear. I'll hire the best lawyers in Poland". After threatening to hire those who worked for Polish business mogul, Jan Kulczyk, he added "Your head and Marek's belong to me. You're a con-man and Marek is an idiot. I'll destroy your reputations. Have a nice weekend, it may be your last," Ramesh wrote to Maciek.

I called Rohit, our other Indian investor, whose head office was in Calcutta and where it was just the crack of dawn.

"Jesus, Marek, do you know what time it is?" he asked, still half asleep.

"Sorry, my friend, but you have to see this. I've just sent you something on WhatsApp. It's from Ramesh. Please advise me how I should deal with someone like this".

Rohit went quiet for a moment, then he sighed, cleared his throat and began saying: "Oh. Marek… Perhaps we should have had this conversation earlier. As you know, Indian society in strongly class-based and is divided into different castes. And this is no accident. Ramesh comes from the caste of businessmen. They achieve enormous success. And at the same time, they are assholes of the highest order. If you even once get under the skin of one of them, they will never, I mean never, let it go. In his mind, you have offended his pride. He has become the laughing stock of his family and even if you sort it out, it will, as they say, still leave a bad taste in his mouth. He will now do everything to avenge this insult. There is a joke in India about his caste, that if you see one of them in a forest walking with a viper, make friends with the viper. I think you understand what I mean…"

After so many months had passed, this guy had not gotten over it one iota. Insofar as I could understand Ramesh's motives, just why because of my insult he still wished to believe the bullshit Biruk was telling him was absolutely incomprehensible to me and I wasn't able to imagine in what way he wanted to harm us. Apart from the barrage of insults, of course, which he was only aiming at Maciek for the moment. Even if he sued me, Maciek or the company itself, he would be immediately be crushed by the weight of evidence we had, namely the emails, the bank transactions and the testimonies of our other partners which showed that the accusations were divorced from reality.

And then I remembered a joke told to me by one of my friends in Nigeria, a very highly placed director of a bank: "You know, Marek, why Nigeria always occupies second place in the rankings of the most corrupt countries in the world? Because it can pay off all the rankings so as not to be placed first."

Ramesh's lawyer in Nigeria was a woman named Florence, whom I had had the opportunity to meet during my many meetings with him. She had been educated in Britain, and had a perfect British accent, something more valuable than many diplomas. She seemed to be very loyal to him and Ramesh admitted that once she had borrowed a large sum of money from him, which had rescued her from difficulties and was now paying it off by working for him for half-nothing. However, I remembered her as a reasonable, down-to-earth professional lawyer. I contacted her and proposed a meeting on neutral ground. I wanted to present our version of events. I counted on managing to persuade her to present this to Ramesh, if he didn't want to hear it coming from my lips.

Surprisingly, Florence agreed to the meeting, which was to take place a few weeks later in London. As our meeting place, she chose a restaurant in the Law Society building, which I took as a positive sign and a hint of good will from the other side. I mean, she could have proposed meeting at Novikov, the infamous Russian restaurant and haunt of gangsters, or even a graveyard.

On the day of the meeting, Florence was waiting for me in meeting room hired for the purpose. I smiled broadly at her and greeted her with a hug. I was honestly happy that meeting was taking place and hoped that thanks to her common sense we would soon sort out this difficulty. The first surprise was waiting for me at the reserved table.

"Marek, please meet Anna from a law firm from Poland."

"Oh, hello. They say you have good intentions when you come to a meeting alone. Bad ones, if you are with bodyguard. Very bad ones if you're with a lawyer!"

Neither Florence nor Anna laughed.

During the following 20 minutes, I explained the whole story of HotelOga step by step, starting with the investments by Ramesh and SpeedUp, through the employment and then firing of Biruk, and concluding with Ramesh's blocking of the transaction which was meant to save the company, and the irony that Ramesh was the one with a grudge against us. The women made frantic notes and asked additional questions and I had nothing to hide. Because if you're telling the truth and haven't done anything wrong, you don't have to watch your words, right? That's at least the way it seemed to me.

Florence allowed me to finish the story, before saying:

"Marek, I sympathize with you. Maybe I shouldn't say it, but I've worked with Ramesh for years and I don't think you realize what Ramesh is capable of. He was able to be provoked by something much smaller than your insults directed at him during your phone call. And now he is under strong influence of power-hungry Biruk, who hates you to the core. Do you realize that we know the story about all your travels? And our knowledge doesn't come from your social media, but from the Nigerian police. They have access to the Interpol database and we have access to them. We know what you're doing, who you're with and where you travel to. Lately, you've been frequently traveling between Santo Domingo and Cape Town, right?"

I was dumbstruck.

"Ramesh has made the matter clear," Florence continued. "Either you hand over twice what he invested, or Ramesh and Biruk will destroy you."

It took all my strength to keep control of myself, while saying: "I understand that the aim of this meeting was to set out the matter clearly from your side. You will not hear anything from me now. First, I need to contact my partners, and then I will present our join position to you."

Anna took advantage of my silence to say:

"You've had a very good run in the media for the last couple years. Journalists tend to like you. This may end. It would be better for you to hurry with your reply."

She had made a threat hidden behind the veil of concern.

This was now too much for me. I stood up and walked out. The adrenaline now hit me while I was on the street. I went for a long walk in order to cool off. As the Law Society building was right in the center of the old part of London, there was something to see. I had a lot of things to think over. No, I wasn't going to allow myself to lose it. That night I changed all my passwords and installed additional anti-virus programs. And I ordered a couple of spy gadgets allowing me to record conversations I was having. I was kicking myself that I hadn't recorded this last one. That's how those who prematurely assume goodwill on both sides end up. I hadn't appreciated Florence's loyalty and bluntness – she must have really owed Ramesh an awful amount of dough. I contacted my own lawyers in Poland and Nigeria, both of whom were very familiar with the situation, as I had worked with them for years. Both said with one voice: "For Christ's sake, it's obvious the guy is trying to scare you. You haven't done anything wrong. But no one can stop Ramesh suing you as much as he likes and depending on how much money he has. Remember that his lawyers are paid by the hour, including Anna, Florence and all of Kulczyk's lawyers whom they are scaring you with. But he'll get over it sooner or later, the bills will start mounting up and the results won't be there. Don't pour petrol on the fire, don't insult either him or his lawyers! This must blow over. Eventually, he'll get tired of it, stop causing problems and take those shares."

Talking with the lawyers calmed me down. Maybe they really did want to scare me and make a quick buck. Ramesh had already changed his mind about investing, as all the tech start-ups had irritated him the way a wife irritates a husband and "had not shown respect". So now he wanted to take his money and, thanks to Biruk, find a very convenient excuse: "For God's sake, all of them wanted to swindle me right from the beginning! But now I'll show them!"

Christmas was approaching and I wanted to make a quick trip to Lagos for some business meetings, just before people go on holidays. Yaritza's birthday was on the 17th of December, so I went do the Dominican Republic to celebrate with her, then quickly catch a flight to Lagos and leave Nigeria on a flight to Poland on the 23rd.

But the Universe sent Yaritza to my life for a reason. Not only had she organized her Birthday party, but also a surprise early Christmas dinner for me and her family, so she could introduce me before I left. They absolutely amazed me with the sheer amount of positive energy and love. I was the freaking happiest guy on the planet. I asked Yaritza if she wanted me to cancel my Lagos trip to stay a couple days longer, before leaving for Christmas to Poland. And If she agrees to come with me, so I could also introduce her to my family. She happily agreed. What we didn't know at that moment is that she saved my life that day.

I wrote an email to Florence that I would contact her during the last two weeks of January, when all the investors would come together. The following day, we took a plane from Santo Domingo to meet my family in the Polish mountains on St. Stephen's Day. We spent two days on the piste, where I tried to teach Yaritza to snowboard and which was no easy task, given that she had never seen snow in her life before. We flew to Barcelona for New Year's Eve where, on the stroke of midnight, we declared our love for each other yet again by eating twelve grapes in accordance with Spanish tradition. We agreed that if we ever decided to move to Europe, Barcelona would be first on the list. After Barcelona, we returned to Poland for a few more days.

14 January 2018, Frederic Chopin Airport, Warsaw.

Yartiza had flown off to Brussels, from where she had a direct flight to the capital of the Dominican Republic, while my plane to London, where I had a few business meetings, was to take off an hour later. We went through security together and were able to say goodbye right at the gate to her plane. Although boarding had already started, we dragged out the moment we separated right until the end. Yaritza started to well up.

"I love you, Marek," she said.

"I love you too," I replied. "Go now, or they won't let you board!"

The truth was that something must have also gotten into my eye.

Yaritza entered the airbridge, turned around for the last time, blew a kiss and began to disappear among the other passengers. I let out a deep sigh. Meeting that woman, then falling in love with her MUST have exhausted the limits of my happiness for the next 10 years. "I wonder what will be fucked up now", I thought before managing to get to passport control, which was necessary before flying to London. I gave the nice lady from the Polish border guard my passport, along with an additional temporary one. Space had run out in my main passport, as some countries seem to be so insecure that they compensate with the size of their stick-on visas and stamps (I'm talking about you, Ethiopia). As I was thinking about Yaritza all the time, I initially failed to notice that the lady was staring at the screen for longer than usual.

"Is everything okay?" I asked, pretending to be concerned, but really wanting to get out of there fast. I was used to border guards taking their time to look at my visas, as they were surprised at someone having two passports and, above all, the fact the Polish one was issued by the Polish Embassy in Abuja, Nigeria.

"A problem with the system. You'll need to wait a moment," she returned to staring at the monitor and made a phone call to someone.

During the moments I spent waiting, I looked around and saw that the neighboring lines were moving without delay. I was slightly irritated by this and wanted to tell her that maybe only her computer was having a problem. However, I didn't manage to say a word before hearing a voice from behind.

"Mr. Zmysłowski? Please come with me." It was a uniformed border guard accompanied by another colleague.

"Does this have something to do with my passports? They are completely genuine, you can check with the embassy," I said, trying to understand whatever was going on in this situation.

"Please follow us, you'll find out everything in a moment," the guy clearly didn't have the desire to talk to me here. We started to attract the attention of the other passengers. I could feel people looking at me. I'm sure they thought I was a terrorist, as I had a long beard and a dark tan.

I was taken to a small room with two chairs, a table and no windows at all. I was, however, allow to keep my things, which I took as a good sign. It must be a passport problem. I've been through well over a hundred airports in my life, and none are as overzealous as the Polish border guard. At the same time, I started to get worried I might miss my flight. Boarding would finish in 20 minutes. After a few moments, two other border guards entered the room. The first – older, fatter and with a tired and irritated expression on his face – and his partner, younger, dressed in a uniform T-shirt, seemed more pleasant and less jaded.

"Marek Zmysłowski?" the older one asked, just as a formality.

"That's right. Are you my savior who is going to help me explain this misunderstanding?" I asked, pleadingly looking for a smile on his face. I was waiting in vain.

"Mr. Zmysłowski, Interpol have placed you on Red Alert. It was issued on the basis of a warrant for your arrest and extradition from the Nigerian government. You are under arrest and will be handed over to the Polish prosecutor's office. You will hand over your possessions to my colleague. If you wish to contact anyone, it would best if you did it now." He got up, walked out, slammed the door behind him, slamming down my whole world at the same time. My mind and body went cold.

"Well, buddy, I've heard lots of stories come through here, but if the Nigerian government is looking for a white guy, you must have really been up to something. I'm guessing it's not alimony, right?" the younger guard started chatting to me, visibly impressed and intrigued by my presence. "What could a normal-looking, respectable guy have done to end up in such a place?"

"Do you know, maybe, what's going to happen to me?" I said, trying to control my increasing jitters, having decided to get any helpful information out of him that I could.

"Well, my friend, I don't know what things are like with Nigeria, but I know from experience that you'll be in custody until they sort out the formalities regarding the extradition, and that could last even a few months. Well, then it'll be a plane and straight into custody in Nigeria... I don't envy you. Alright, listen, you'll have to hand over your things to me. If you want to inform anybody, do so now. I'm going for a smoke, I'll be back in three minutes and will be taking everything. You're on camera, so don't try anything stupid."

With my hands shaking, I took out my phone. I first called my assistant: "I've been arrested at Warsaw Airport. Nigeria wants my extradition. I don't know anything else. I don't even know where I'll be tomorrow. Inform my lawyer in Poland immediately. Get him to send on the information to our office in Lagos and then come straight to Warsaw to explain what's going on. Cancel all my meetings for tomorrow in London. Jesus, what am I saying? Cancel all my meetings this week! Just in case. Oh, and call LOT Polish Airlines to tell them not to wait for me with boarding! I don't want them shouting my name over the public address system."

The second phone call was to Maciek: "Ramesh and Biruk are up to something. I've been arrested at the airport. I'm being threatened with extradition to Nigeria and imprisonment. But please don't tell anyone until I find out more."

Now it was Yaritza's turn. I decided to send her a text instead of recording a message on voicemail. I was afraid my voice would start to crack: "Honey, I may be out of range until tomorrow because I don't have a local SIM card for London. I'll call you tomorrow. Love you."

"What a hopeless cover story," I thought, but I didn't have either the time or the ability of thinking up anything else. I didn't want to worry her. I was hoping that by some miracle everything would sort itself out by tomorrow. And if not, I should at least already be in a condition to talk with the lawyer, and then he would pass on further information.

The young border guard returned just as I had pressed 'send' on my phone.

I then had to hand over all the items in my possession. Fortunately, I hadn't checked in any baggage and had everything in my hand luggage. I signed a custody report and an inventory of personal property.

"Now, we're going to the car, you'll be transported to the pre-trial detention center at Mokotów Prison," he said.

"Is this really necessary?" I said, gesturing towards the handcuffs hanging off his belt.

"It's regulations," he replied.

On the evening news, when the police are leading away some handcuffed criminal under the glare of flashing cameras, they at least put some kind of jacket over his head. But I had to be paraded along a line of passengers waiting to board a coach. And the way they looked at me... well, I'll never forget it.

The journey lasted about 25 minutes. Never in my life have I looked at cars, passers-by and buildings with such a heavy heart as I did when looking out through the small window of the prison van. Once in custody, I had to strip off completely and be searched by a guard, in case I was hiding anything which could hurt myself or my fellow prisoners. Fortunately, as my Chelsea boots didn't have any laces, I didn't have to walk around having gone through the humiliating procedure of taking them from my shoes. I was assigned some bedding and something small, hard and rank which the guard called a pillow for some reason.

They guard began leading me to my cell. And Jesus, if watching all of those Hollywood action movies was to be of any use, it was to know how to act when making a first impression on entering a cell full of other inmates. I stood up straight, put on my best Steven Segal expression, and had already put together a story in my head how during a fistfight in Lagos, while rescuing a beautiful girl from unwanted attention, I beat the crap out of three assholes and their dog, who later turned out to be extremely rich (not the dog) and who were now seeking me out the world over in order to exact their revenge. Especially, on behalf of the dog.

The door opened, I took a deep breath and entered ready for a fight over the top bunk and to beat the shit out of the biggest guy in the cell. As in prison, as in business. You'll never get a second chance to make a first impression. I walked in. I looked around. I was alone. I had gotten an individual cell.

"Goodnight, Mr. Zmysłowski. Rise and shine at 6am. For breakfast, it's tea with sugar and bread with pate." The guard closed the door and bolted it.

Initially, I was happy with this turn of events. I had avoided confrontation with any cellmates – after all, you never know who you're going to get. I had no idea as yet what loneliness could mean. It wasn't until after a few minutes that I realized that the deafening silence and being left all alone with my thoughts was the worst thing that had happened me that day. The initial pressure and adrenaline rush went away to be replaced with despair, helplessness and, for the first time in my life, simple, straight up, deathly fear. I was in constant shock. Disbelief started to be mixed in with feverish thoughts. What's this all about? What's going on? Is this part of some kind of candid camera TV show? Has someone put me in a parody of Kafka's *The Trial*? I'm considered a fugitive by the GOVERNMENT OF NIGERIA? I didn't do anything for Christ's sake! Ramesh and Biruk! They're all behind this. But would they be able to pull off such a trick? Do Ramesh's contacts really go so high?

Then came the time for fire and fury. I swore that no matter how long it took and how much it would cost, I would get those who had set me up. And they would bitterly regret doing so. Then came the jitters: "Oh my fucking God, I'm going to fucking prison in fucking Nigeria!"

I recalled a book by Michał Pauli, a Pole who had spent six years in one of Thailand's toughest prisons. Sentenced for smuggling a small amount of drugs, he received twelve death sentences. His life was miraculously saved and he returned to Poland due to the intercession of several Polish presidents. In his book, he describes the terrible prison conditions and how he eluded death on many occasions. If the difference between the standard of living of Thailand and Nigeria rests on the difference in the standard of their prisons, all due respect Michał, but I'm on a sure-fire route to writing something even more terrible. Regarding the descriptions of the conditions, of course, not the quality of the book. The book was amazing.

I was afraid how my mother would react, a woman who had recently been widowed and was bringing up my teenage brother alone, taking care of my grandparents nearly in their nineties, as well as working all the time. It wasn't enough that I wouldn't be able to support her, but would myself become her greatest burden. I completely came undone when it entered my head that I would never see my beloved Yaritza again, just as we had just started a wonderful life together. I cried for a good few minutes, sitting curled up on my bunk. Crying allowed me to discharge some emotions and I began to regain my composure: "Pull yourself together Zmysłowski. It's exactly such situations which build character! Everything that hits you now and during the following days, weeks and maybe even months, is part of building up your resistance. Everything you go through will be a lesson you'll use in the future", I said in an effort to motivate myself. I remembered Cyprian Kosiński, whose biography I had read while traveling to Africa and whose story had inspired me. Although he was a professional volleyball player and captain of the Polish national team, he chose a career in business and moved to the Congo (formerly Zaire), where for many years he managed factories and built housing developments, befriending, in the process, local people and, naturally, politicians. He also ended up in custody, for over a month, due to accusations which were later withdrawn. And Kosiński himself was awarded compensation.

I got up from my bunk. I thought that sitting there motionless would neither allow me to focus nor my mind gain control of the stress, allowing confusion to set in. I started walking back and forth around my cell. Five steps forward, turn around, five steps forward. Physical movement allowed me to regain the feeling of being in control of the situation. I repeated to myself that it would all end well sooner or later. After all, I had done nothing wrong. I could defend myself in any independent court. But what chance of finding an independent court did I have in Nigeria? I began preparing a list in my mind of all my close and not-so-close friends who could help me. I bet on a more or less positive scenario resulting from being possibly released from custody the following day, following a meeting with the prosecutor, right up to landing in custody in Nigeria and preparing myself for various kinds of accusations. From fraud to murder. After all, I could be set up for anything. About three hours and 15,000 steps later, I was already convinced that I would not think up anything else, while remembering every detail of my plan, having repeated it to myself several times. This gave me a minimum of a feeling of calm and having influence over the situation. Actually, those three hours could have been two hours or five hours – I didn't have a watch, after all, and in January in Poland it's dark from 4pm to 8am.

Then came the turn of things which were beyond my control. It had been 16 years since I left the confines of a Catholic school, which had given me both a wonderful education and a fear of institutional forms of any kind of religion. Over the years, my beliefs had flirted with atheism, deism and mysticism. But at such moments, a man desires to believe. As they say, there are no atheists in foxholes. I started praying to my version of God and speaking with my dead father, wherever he was. After praying, came time for meditation which I had discovered while in Bhutan. That night, although I didn't sleep for many hours, meditation helped me survive fairly calmly until morning.

My dear reader, do you know that feeling when you wake up in terror from a nightmare, only to realize a moment later that it was all a bad dream? You're enveloped by a sense of relief, you smile... well, actually... I wasn't the lucky guy to wake up and realize such thing. It hadn't been a bad dream after all. I was woken by the door being opened and it took a few seconds before I remembered where I was.

Despite this rude awakening, tea and pate sandwiches never tasted so good. Nothing had passed my lips for almost 24 hours. Along with my breakfast, the guard threw in a crumpled, weeks-old copy of Car World magazine. I read it from cover to cover several times at least. If anyone wants to know the most common faults in a used Skoda Octavia II 1.9 TDI, I'm your man.

The rays of sunlight falling through the barred windows partly covered with tape brought with them rays of hope, in that something was happening. And for something good to happen, anything needs to happen.

And it happened. I was taken to the district prosecutor's office on Chocimska Street in Warsaw. There, in the prosecutor's private office, Krzysiek, my lawyer, was waiting for me. I had never been so happy to see a lawyer in my life. Also greeting me was the prosecutor, a guy of about 40 in a very nicely cut suit.

"How do you feel, Mr. Zmysłowski?" he asked.

"Apart from the fact that my assistant booked me into a fairly average hotel, pretty well. I'm going to have to place a negative review on TripAdvisor. And change my assistant."

"You don't need to change her, it wasn't her fault at all," the prosecutor said, getting the joke, which meant either he had good news or he wanted to sweeten the bad news. "We've already been talking to your lawyer, Mr. Zmysłowski, who has presented his power of attorney from you. Today's meeting is only for the purposes of information and concerns the substantive facts. A proper interrogation will occur at a later date. In short, you are accused by the Nigerian government of fraud on a grand scale. If convicted, you are facing anything from seven to twenty one years' jail time. That's according to Nigerian law. The Nigerian state prosecutor issued a warrant for your arrest, which was confirmed by the district court in Lagos, Nigeria. In the Interpol system there is also information that a decision has been issued to block your bank accounts in Nigeria. Now the good news. You will not be extradited to Nigeria and will be released from custody today. Poland does not hand over its citizens to other countries just like that. The Nigerian side must first send over all documentation concerning the matter for me to examine it. It will not be until you are called for interrogation here that it will be decided what will happen next and whether action will be taken against you here in Poland. Therefore, I strongly suggest staying in this country until the matter is resolved. As long as a red alert is in the system, you risk being arrested crossing any international border. In Poland, you'll risk at least a repeat of the situation which occurred yesterday. In every other country, you'll risk arrest and extradition. Would you like to make any additional statement?"

I didn't want to make additional statements, just give the guy a hug, but since it wasn't the done thing, I hugged Krzysiek the lawyer instead. I wondered if would bill me for that too, citing 'working under difficult conditions'. I did, however, make a statement in accordance with Krzysiek's suggestion and under his direction, as the lawyer knew which breaches of the law to draw attention to. The statement ran more or less thus: "I am a respectable businessman with a clean record. I have fallen victim to corrupt officials working on behalf of a dishonest, vengeful former business partner. Poland, I love you."

"Mr. Prosecutor, one more question," I said, stopping at the door. "On which day did the red alert appear on the system?"

"December 22nd."

They day before my initial flight out of Nigeria. The day after landing in Poland from the Dominican Republic, after a last minute change of plans thanks to Yaritza. The day after landing in Poland for the first time in several months. If the alert had appeared on any other day before December 22nd, I would be rotting in custody in either South Africa, Kenya, Bhutan, Thailand, the Dominican Republic or the USA, waiting for extradition. My visit to Barcelona hadn't been picked up by the system, thanks to the fact that Poland and Spain lie within the Schengen Zone and so no-one had checked my passport at the airport.

Three weeks after being released from custody, my grandmother died. I was able to say goodbye and be at the funeral. If I had been in custody abroad, no-one would have cared about the fate of some Polish guy and they would have gladly gotten rid of the problem by sending me on somewhere else. Not to mention the difficulties in contacting lawyers, family and the costs involved in that. The worst day of my life turned out to be the greatest stroke of luck in my life. Thanks, Dad, wherever you are.

I got my possessions back and we went outside.

"What do you want to do now?" asked my lawyer.

"First, I need to brush my teeth."

Never, and I mean never was I so happy to see anything at all. The feeling of leaving custody, after it had seemed that you would never see the world again, is equal to absolutely nothing else. The tears streamed down my face once again. During the previous 24 hours, I bawled my eyes out more than in the previous 10 years. I called Yartiza and told her everything. As I predicted, my voice was cracking when I was telling her about what I had felt thinking about her in the cell. She was furious with me that I hadn't told her the truth right from the beginning.

"Don't ever do this again. We're together for better or for worse. Oh yeah, and I definitely resent the comment that if they had arrested you in the Dominican Republic you would be sitting there until the time of your extradition. Don't you remember the traits Jeff Bezos looked for in his partner?"

"You sure have a good memory, honey," I laughed, because I knew exactly what she was referring to. "Yes. Bezos wanted his woman to be able to get her man out of prison in some exotic country."

"Exactly! It's just a pity that they didn't arrest you someplace else. I would have proved it to you. You don't know yet what I'm capable of."

How could you not love a woman like that?

Fortune had allowed me to win the battle, but there was still a long road to winning the whole war. As everything indicated that I would sitting in Warsaw a little while longer, I rented an Airbnb in the center. I started by checking out what the prosecutor knew about my bank accounts. I hadn't used my account in Nigeria for several months, as Nigerian cards using local currency are blocked abroad by most payment terminals. These were the days when the Federal Bank of Nigeria was fighting devaluation of the naira to the dollar, due to which it set ridiculous monthly limits of $200 or $500. I tried making several online payments on Nigerian websites, with the configuration of my server so that the site would think I'm in Nigeria, but they didn't go through. I tried several local ATMs, and nothing. I called up my own banker, Dotun, who had been serving me for a good few years.

"Marek, your current account and savings accounts have been blocked, I can't say anything more. It would be best if you came to see me in the branch personally, we'll talk it over. Are you in Lagos?"

"Dotun, first of all, why can't you tell me?! You're talking about money which I own. And secondly, doesn't the bank have a legal duty to inform me about something like this?"

"Marek, come to the branch, we'll talk."

I didn't like Dotun's secretiveness and his pressuring me to meet in person, even more so at his branch. Never before did he have a problem sorting things out over the phone or coming over to my home.

"I'll call you back, Dotun," and I hung up.

That wasn't the end of the strange news of that day. In the afternoon, my Nigerian phone rang. It was Ruth, a journalist friend from one of Nigeria's business newspapers.

"Marek, we got a tip-off that reportedly you were arrested in Poland today. Is this true?"

"Ha, ha, ha, if I had been arrested, would I have a cell-phone on me?" I bluffed.

"It's good it's not true. But we have received some documents anonymously and I wanted to ask you a few questions before we publish them."

"Ruth, listen, you know how dirty business can get in Nigeria. I'm in conflict with my former business partner. Everything points to the fact that he's resorting to all manner of activities to discredit me."

"I understand. And is this why you don't want this publicized? You're doing wonderful things in Africa. The media like you and will help you put out your version of events."

"The media like you. That could all end..." I immediately recalled the meeting from London and the nasty smirk of that lawyer Anna when she had said those same words. I was starting to join the dots.

"Ruth, listen. If this all comes out too quickly, we'll have a damp squib on our hands. I haven't yet gathered all the necessary documents which would make this matter more interesting for you, and which strengthen my defense. Let's do it this way, please hold off from publishing anything. And in exchange for that, when I'm ready, I'll give you an exclusive interview and the scoop on publishing it in Nigeria. Do this for me please, for old times' sake."

"Okay then, Marek, good luck. And call me!"

In accordance with the law, the Polish prosecutor had informed the Nigerians immediately after my arrest and sent a request for full documentation on the matter to be sent on. Someone in Nigeria must have tipped the press off. More than likely, the same person who had arranged my arrest warrant. I needed to immediately verify the hypothesis that Ramesh and Biruk were behind it. And that their executors were Florence, Anna, plus several other people in Nigeria for sure. Straight away, I sent an email to Florence and Anna and CC-ed Ramesh and Biruk, which said more or less:

"Dear Florence, Dear Anna,

I just had a very unpleasant experience last weekend at the airport and at the Polish prosecutor's office. I'm aware of the activities of Ramesh and Biruk with the Nigerian police and Interpol. I also know about communication with the Nigerian press and the blocking of bank accounts. I'm very much surprised and frightened by the whole situation.

Let's sort out this matter as quickly as possible. Please. What sum of money is Ramesh demanding from me to make all my problems disappear?"

Anna called me back within an hour. It was as if the other side had been expecting an email from me. The answer sounded more or less like this: "Mr. Zmysłowski, we are happy that you have changed your attitude. The required amount is US$300,000. Only after the payment of this amount in its entirety will the prosecutor withdraw the accusations concerning you, will your bank accounts be unblocked and will you be able to regain your freedom without risk of extradition to Nigeria," she said over the phone.

They wanted $150,000 more than they had invested. Anna called this 'costs of legal services plus interest'. Ramesh wasn't doing this for the money, but was doing it to satisfy his ego and to teach me a lesson. If it had been any different, I would have expected at least another zero at the end. It was Biruk who had hatched the plan for money, as he had nothing to his name and has never earned any more money than whatever his father allowed him to have. Perhaps Ramesh had demanded a low enough price, so that it wouldn't seem like typical extortion, and so that a few crumbs would fall from the table for Biruk. I wonder how much of the 'costs of legal services with interest' was designated for the Nigerian officials and prosecutors who had signed documents where necessary, in order to block my accounts and issue an alert to Interpol and now, with 'the wave of a magic wand', would cause everything to be dismissed and overturned.

Where do you start if you want to win a war? With recruiting the best generals. I started by implementing one of the plans I had thought up the previous night in the cell. Although my current lawyer, Krzysiek was amazing, he specialized in commercial company law. I needed someone with experience in international cases, civil cases bordering on criminal matters. I established contact with a specialist perfect for this task. Artur ran a highly regarded law firm in Warsaw called "AK LEGAL", and had gained notoriety when he managed to have the sentence of an American court declared invalid regarding a very well publicized precedent-setting case between the family of the prime minister's family and a certain political weekly magazine. In addition, he brought in, as a consultant, Jerzy, an energetic 60-something whose superpower was that he had altogether spent several decades in diplomatic posts in Nigeria, Kenya, South Africa and Zimbabwe, and so no-one knew the complexities of business, law and diplomacy in Africa better than he. The case with Nigeria was not so easy. Although Rafiu, my Nigerian lawyer, had been working with me for years, could I trust him in the face of what had happened? Rafiu knew Ramesh. I couldn't rule out that Rafiu was working for him and that this had been the reason why I hadn't received any information on the subject of the actions being taken against me, which had ended with a warrant for my arrest. Just in case, I found a midway solution regarding my doubts around my Nigerian lawyer. Matthew, a British citizen who had been living in Nigeria for more than 20 years, recommended his own lawyer to me, one with the very serious-sounding name of Daddy. From that day on, Daddy received information concerning all the legal steps in Nigeria which Rafiu was proposing. In the meantime, I received all the documentation he had prepared for analysis.

To complete the team, we were still lacking a specialist in matters connected with Interpol and coercion regarding the issuing of red alerts. I probably read and watched everything on the subject available on the internet. It turned out that Interpol has a growing problem with corrupt countries using baseless red alerts to hunt down and persecute various individuals. Interpol, despite having been established as an independent institution and without a shadow of a doubt as to the justification and motives of its actions, also accepts grants from private institutions. For example, it took €20,000,000 from FIFA just months before the outbreak of an enormous corruption scandal in this organization. Could the heads of FIFA have wanted Interpol on their side, as they knew that they would be up against the wall? I don't know. The cherry on the cake was the arrest of the head of Interpol (yes, the head himself) by the government of China (yes, China) on accusations of corruption (yes, corruption).

International pressure for the reform of Interpol deepened, once information came out about the hunting down of political opponents in Turkey, Azerbaijan, Saddam Hussein's Iraq and Putin's Russia.

It was in this way I discovered *Red Alert*, written by Bill Browder, and published in 2015. Browder, through his managing of the Hermitage Capital investment fund, was the largest Western capital investor in the Russian stock exchange at the beginning of the 20th century. At one moment, he was managing a portfolio worth in excess of $4,000,0000,0000. He concentrated shares in undervalued companies in the commodities market, purged them of unprofitable old boys' networks in it for the bribes, before restructuring them and watching his property grow. However, at a certain moment, he pissed off one oligarch too many. His visa was revoked and he was deported to the UK, while part of his company was taken over. He continued the fight for justice from his London office and tried to run businesses in other parts of the world. One of his Russian lawyers was arrested and beaten to death while in Russian custody. But for Browder, the Russian prosecutor's office issued a red alert through Interpol in order to hunt him down and have him tried for alleged financial fraud. Thanks to wonderful lawyers and media pressure, he managed to get Interpol to withdraw its red alert order. In Russia, however, he's still a wanted criminal.

For several years now, the United States has been blocking the property of Russian oligarchs and criminals, obstructing them from enjoying the spoils gained as a result of their operations in Russia. In fact, these blockades and freezing of shares occurs due the so-called Magnitsky Act, passed by Congress.

Magnitsky was Browder's lawyer, the one who ended up murdered, and Browder has sworn to continue his fight against dishonest oligarchs, including Vladimir Putin. Today, Browder is considered Putin's No.1 enemy.

Reading this book gave me goose bumps. Nigeria was often called 'Russia without the snow' by my Moscow friends. Some many things in it were similar here. Although my experience was similar to Browder's, the scale of my businesses and the magnitude of my enemies was much smaller. Well, Rafiu, my Nigerian lawyer, had a good life. Maybe that's why he was working for Ramesh?

Without a second thought, I found Browder's website and email address. I wrote to him hoping that someone in his office would forward on my message. The next day, I received a reply.

"Dear Mr. Zmysłowski,

My name is Theodor Bromund and I work with Mr. Browder on issues concerning the abuse of Interpol. I would be willing to hear more about your case."

Theodor turned out to be an analyst working for an American

think-tank and had helped Browder have Magnitsky's Law passed by the United States government. He contacted me from a law firm in Miami, which specialized in cases with Interpol.

My team was now complete. I was ready for action, even if it would cost me more that the amount my enemy wished to extort from me.

Chapter 17

WAR AND
(THE LACK OF) PEACE

We started by buying time. Ramesh and Biruk had received information that first I must secure the money as, after all, he had blocked my account himself. And this would take me several weeks at least. I still planned to draw this out as long as was necessary for our operations, and as long as it was possible without arousing Ramesh's suspicions. The good news was that we were basically over the worst. The only thing which Ramesh could do to cause me further damage was to ruin my image through attacks in the media.

I didn't believe that Ramesh was inclined to resort to using violence against me in Europe, although nothing would have surprised me at that stage.

We divided our strategy into four acts. As Agatha Christie once wrote a story called Three Act Tragedy, I had to be better and add one more.

Act One: Local operations in Nigeria, with attempts to defend ourselves, as well as prove our innocence and the illegality of the activities of the prosecutor to the Nigerian courts. This would gradually allow us to bring about the withdrawal of the red alert notice by the Nigerian branch of Interpol. For obvious reasons (as everything had begun with corruption in Nigeria), this act seemed the least possible to win, unless

Rafiu was a genius lawyer and unless we would be lucky and come across an independent judge, not belonging to people paid by Ramesh and Biruk's people.

Act Two: Operations directly with Interpol headquarters in Lyon, France. It was here that we had the greatest chance of an honest examination of the case. In other matters similar to the withdrawal of my red alert notice, this would be drawn out over several months or even a decade or more. There was no such option, no chance I would wait that long – I had gotten too used to the warmth of Africa. Meanwhile, I would have to freeze through this Polish winter.

Act Three: Get the international media and justice organizations interested, in order to put pressure on Interpol and hurry up its operations regarding Act Two. This would be connected with the fact that Ramesh's activities would be publicized and that he would no longer want to reach agreement with me. But I was hoping that if we managed to score big in Nigeria, Ramesh would lose his main bargaining chip.

Act Four: A counter-attack. If we managed to gather together a sufficient amount of evidence regarding the activities of Ramesh and Biruk, we'd be able to file a case against them in European Union or USA, for instance, and get them with their own weapon – a red alert notice. Only this time, it would be justified. Although I hoped that both Biruk and Ramesh would at some point rethink their behavior and back down, so I wouldn't be forced to launch Act Four and waste my energy, time and money.

The curious thing about the whole situation was that, although I was a fugitive from the law, we had no formal knowledge regarding by whom or for what. In order to have the case thrown out and to show the falseness of the accusations, they first had to be examined in detail. We didn't even know at which police department or prosecutor's office we had to file a request for the presentation of information and the indictment to be able to build our defense.

Such disinformation was planned and deliberate. Up to today, Nigeria has never sent any documentation related to the case to the Polish prosecutor's office. The Nigerian Department of Foreign Affairs did not respond to the diplomatic note sent by the Polish ambassador in Abuja, immediately after my request for help. The lack of response to such an official note is a scandal in itself. They did send a fax of the application for my extradition to Nigeria. Once again with the very laconic justification: 'for large-scale fraud'. And the basis for this? The testimony of Ramesh and Biruk that I had defrauded them while running HotelOga. Namely, that I had promised mountains of gold and had taken the money. Then, I had driven the company to bankruptcy, while transferring all the profits to Poland. Meaning the typically common 'Polish prince' scam. Without any evidence, but just a completely illogical testimony was enough for the Nigerian police.

On the one hand, the lack of detail worked in our favor because it showed the prosecutor the real motives of the other side. We already knew that no accusations would be filed against me either in Poland or Nigeria. However, the lack of information was slowing down our defensive operations in Nigeria.

My bank was our starting point. It was, after all, a private organization, listed on the stock exchange. One which took care of its image in the eyes of its customers and shareholders. Rafiu, my Nigerian lawyer, rapidly sent a letter of my behalf with a demand to unblock my accounts immediately, as well as for a statement of the legal basis of the bank's actions. A few days later its legal department, covering its ass, sent a scan of a letter which had been sent to it by the Nigerian police department in Alagbon, located in the Ikoyi district of Lagos. Thanks to this we now knew who had dealt with the case, also finding their signatures at the district court in Lagos where the decision had been made to freeze my accounts. It was this court which had signed the warrant for my arrest.

One sentence in the scanned document struck me, namely an order from the police to the employees of the bank: "Allow payments in, stop withdrawals, card transactions and transfers. Inform the police in case of a visit to the bank. Aid in arrest."

And that was it, if we're talking the loyalty of bankers. I don't know if Dotun, the employee of this bank who had been serving me, was working for Ramesh, but it was Ramesh who had recommended him to me when I was opening my company and private bank accounts.

Because of my doubts concerning Dotun's honesty, I became more and more distrustful of Rafiu.

The first surprise. The police department in Alagbon apparently rejected accepting correspondence from my lawyer three times in a row. No-one wanted to talk to him once he told them whom he represented. The second surprise. The documentation concerning my case in the district court concerning the warrant for my arrest and the freezing of my assets just disappeared... Of course, the court has the duty to place all of its files in its archive. Rafiu received unofficial information from an employee at the archive that the 'documents have been mislaid'. So Rafiu filed an official letter with a demand for the documents to be handed over. Surprise, surprise, although the letter was allegedly accepted, the employees taking in the document did not agree to any formal confirmation of them doing so.

To be sure that Rafiu wasn't bullshitting me, I send Daddy, my other Nigerian lawyer, to check the situation at the police station and the court. He was treated in the same manner. So I regained my trust in Rafiu a little, even more so when he made the following proposal:

"Marek, the district court and playing around with the police is a waste of time. We have to go to the federal court and sue all of them."

"All of them? Meaning who, Rafiu?"

"The bank, for illegally freezing your assets, because the documents which they received were issued by an authority with no right to do so. And the Nigerian police for violating your basic human rights, such as your right to a defense, a right to information on the accusations against you. After all, no-one informed you their actions, no-one summoned you for interrogation, and the documents in the district court have 'disappeared'. In the worst case scenario, if they decide to defend the case, as part of it they will have to show us the documents on the basis of which they wished to have you arrested. Although we'll lose on that issue, we'll be able to defend ourselves on the real issues. And if they don't decide to defend themselves, this will inform the court that it was all a big scam. And we can win on that issue. And if the court rules that the bank and the police acted illegally, this will aid us greatly in our talks with Interpol. If we are very fortunate, we'll get a good judge, and in case the police and the bank put up no defense, we'll win two hearings, three at the most!"

Even though this was a crazy plan, we had nothing to lose and the rest of the team supported the idea. A case was filed as 'Marek Zmysłowski vs. the Nigeria Police Force and Zenith Bank Nigeria'.

I demanded $100,000 compensation for moral and material damages. When you're in the game, you've got to be ready to go for broke. They say that fortune favors the bold.

And boy, did it favor us. The time for the first case was already set for March, which in Nigerian, even Polish circumstances was fast track. It seemed that the Nigerian federal court worked much more efficiently than anyone had supposed.

The judge assigned to our case was Judge Hassan, a Muslim from the Hausa tribe. According to Jerzy, our team diplomat, Hassan was one of the most inflexible and incorruptible judges in Nigeria. The fact that Jerzy knew of him filled me with optimism. When the time for the trial came, lawyers for the bank filed a statement saying that: "We have nothing against Marek, we were only acting on the orders of the police, so Your Honor, please leave us alone." The defense lawyers for the police never showed up, despite having received trial letters and a summons.

This was our first success. Judge Hassan decided to give the police a second chance, and set a date for the next hearing for April 23rd. And they police failed to show up again. They were so afraid of showing the documents of the case, that they decided to lose now just to keep what they had been up to a secret.

About 1 pm, Rafiu sent me a message: "The federal court has acknowledged that the freezing of your assets was illegal and that the process of your arrest was unconstitutional and has ordered the withdrawal of the warrant for your arrest. Oh, and you've been awarded 2,000,000 naira in compensation. Now, we only have to wait five working days to receive the decision in writing and then 90 days for the ruling to come into effect. In the meantime, the police have the right to appeal the sentence and then we start everything from the beginning."

These were the longest five working days of my life. I was afraid that the documents would magically disappear, as they had done at the district court. On the fateful day, I wrote to Rafiu probably every five minutes, asking if they had been released yet. Eventually, five minutes before the court closed, he sent me a photo taken with his phone. He was holding the original copy in his hand.

Now something even worse awaited me – the longest 90 days of my life, waiting for the ruling to come into force. I didn't just sit around twiddling my thumbs. I got down to work. I wanted to get the most information I could from my accusers, information which I could then use against them.

Gathering evidence about the police, the bank and God knows who else, all working corruptly together, was still very difficult. These people must have known each other for years and it was certainly not their first 'joint venture'. We couldn't find anyone 'inside' who wanted to cross over to our camp. Very few people had the courage to talk with me about such things, from a distance, over the phone. I was afraid of giving this task to a third party. I took the risk of the other side giving me away or being so careless that Ramesh and Biruk would find out about my activities. Things went better with Anna, the over-zealous lawyer, who became easier to draw things out of. Ramesh must have promised her a good percentage of the money squeezed out of me. We had several conversations over the phone, which, of course, I recorded.

Here, I played the role of a lost and frightened businessman. So lost that I didn't even have my own lawyer and just wanted to put this horror show behind me once and for all. At all costs - $300,000, for example.

And our lawyer lady friend bought it and put pressure on my weak points. During one conversation, she passed on the message that Ramesh was getting more and more impatient.

I arranged a meeting with Anna – the first since our memorable time at the Law Society restaurant in London – during which we were to establish the details of the transaction and the agreement connected with it. I was wired up with two separate hidden microphones. One in my pen, the other in my glasses case.

"Anna, let's turn off our phones, okay? We'll be talking frankly and I don't want to be accidentally recorded, as later my goodwill may be used against me," I began, turning things around.

"That's no problem, I'm already turning it off, see for yourself," our lawyer friend said, turning her phone off in front of me. "Marek, Ramesh will not present his proposal for the terms of the details of the transaction and agreement, if you don't confirm that you are ready and able to transfer the money."

That didn't surprise me. Ramesh didn't want to take a risk and open himself up, if he didn't know that I was living in fear and had the money, and that he was the one on top who was calling the shots. Showing my ability to pay would be a risky move. The Polish lawyer suggested that if Ramesh believed I was broke and that he wouldn't get anything out of me, he might just give up on his own. But it didn't seem to me that he was sufficiently sorry for me to sort out everything with Interpol and the courts. After all, he wasn't going to pay for that out of his own pocket.

I pulled out my laptop, logged in to my bank account, turned the monitor towards her and showed a bank balance which would satisfy Ramesh's demands.

"Is that enough?" I asked. "Please tell Ramesh that I won't be transferring this money to anybody until I see the agreement. Even if his people put a gun to my head."

"A little dramatization won't hurt", I thought to myself.

That was enough. We moved on to the details. I received a copy to look over. In it, Ramesh and Biruk had committed themselves, once I had transferred the money to an indicated account in Dubai, to sending me the following documents. Firstly, a confirmation from Interpol that the Red Alert notice had been withdrawn, Secondly, a letter from Interpol to the Polish justice system concerning the withdrawal of accusations in Nigeria. And thirdly, confirmation from the Nigerian Ministry of Justice of the discontinuation of all investigations against me.

Ramesh declared he would sort out all of these matters as if he was lord and master of all of these offices. And I had everything in writing. I can only add that if an investigation had been initiated by an official institution, he wouldn't be able just to sort it out by saying "Oh, I was only joking". Unless it wasn't a real investigation. The same with the sentences of the courts! Even though someone had already checked to see if things could be 'wiped from the memory' of Themis, the mythical carrier of the sword and scales of justice.

Although we had recordings, emails and Ramesh's threats, we needed to dot the i's and cross the t's. I wanted to have Ramesh on tape, admitting straight to my face what he had done and why he had done it.

The last time we had spoken was a good year earlier when the memorable conversation took place, during which I told him to fuck off. I took a chance and sent him an email.

"Dear Ramesh,

I hope, like me, that you think it's important that we finish this matter as soon as possible. If you wanted to teach me a lesson, then it worked. I hope that my actions with Anna have convinced you that I am treating the matter seriously and am ready to transfer the money, if I gain certainty that this will set me free. In order to gain this certainty, I need to talk to you. Please call me."

Stroking Ramesh's ego worked. He called me that very evening. I had just come back from training, and managed to get my recording software fired up before calling him back.

"Marek!" Ramesh said in a self-satisfied manner on answering the phone. "I'd ask how you were, but it's probably not appropriate, ha, ha, ha," he continued.

"Maybe a little bit, Ramesh, I'm in a terrible situation. You've taught me a lesson. I've been through nightmare and can only dream about waking up from it as soon as possible. You've won, Ramesh. I'll pay you what you want. Just tell me by what miracle you were able to turn the courts and the police? That's unheard of. And above all, how can I be sure that once I send you the money, you'll be able to sort this out?"

"Marek, everything is a question of money. You are not a criminal, of course. All the officials, prosecutors, judges... all they care about is money. I paid them to start hunting you down and issue the arrest warrant. They'll take it down, if I pay them off."

The call lasted a good 20 minutes. Basically, I didn't have to draw anything out of him. Ramesh was so confident. Even though Ramesh was speaking to me, it was his ego talking. He also said one more important thing that confirmed my suspicions about Biruk. "Marek, Biruk is a crazy guy, I can't tell you much, but he is crazy and wanted to go after you more than I did."

In hindsight, it all seems so clear. Biruk, Pierre, Ramesh and Daniel shared the same traits. A mixture of huge, but fragile ego, inferiority complex and jealousy towards me. I know that type so well, I was one of them for most of my life, but throughout all these months of our interaction I had even more personality issues than them, and the way they were treated by me, drove them crazy. All they wanted was respect and admiration... what they got instead was me looking down on them, giving harsh feedback and orders. Their motivation to hurt me was similar to what drives a younger sibling not loved enough by the parents.

I should have given them more love.

There's no way to place a value on the recordings of my conversations with Anna and Ramesh. This additional evidence would not only strengthen my arguments in front of Interpol, but would also allow the Polish prosecutor's office to commence an investigation. Although bribing a Nigerian official in Nigeria is not a crime in Poland, even if a Pole is the victim, the threats and blackmail I had faced certainly fitted the definition of illegal activity to be prosecuted for.

We also hoped that when we informed the press of the matter, people from Nigeria who had valuable information would begin to contact us. I had a feeling that this wasn't the first time that Ramesh and Biruk had used such tactics. I didn't have to search very long. Eventually, I had to call Ademola, the founder of Nigeria Payments, who Ramesh had been complaining about. I opened up to him so as to gain his trust. He repaid me with a similar level of honesty: "Marek, you're not the only one. There is an undergoing court case between us and Ramesh. As we're currently at the stage of gathering the next round of investment, I can't put up with the publicity and the scaring off of investors. And he knows it. Someone's got to stop him from such actions. I wish you luck and let me know if you need any help."

Ademola gave me the details of another businessman. The owner of one of the first supermarkets in Lagos. It was yet another story about the forced sale of shares through being scared off by the involvement of corrupt officials. Apparently, Ramesh had quarreled with them over dividends from an investment and decided to make a point in his own peculiar way.

Well, here we are talking and in the meantime 90 days had passed since the court judgment. We had won. In the Nigerian highest court. Against the Nigerian police! But it wasn't just my victory. It was a victory for the Nigerian justice system. That maybe it sometimes has its challenges, but this time the justice in Nigeria won, and I'm so grateful for that.

As the Gloria Gaynor classic says 'I will survive'. I'm going to hang that court judgment up in my office, right next to my extradition warrant and the print-out from Interpol about me being a 'Wanted Fugitive'. Pity it didn't say 'Dead or Alive', that would have been something.

Then came the time for the second stage. Dealings with Interpol HQ. The Polish legal firm, which was my main legal representative, as part of its cooperation with the lawyers from Miami and thanks to documentation supplied by Rafiu, prepared a document explaining the entire case, outlining the establishment of HotelOga, HotelOnline and all its subsequent twists and turns, stressing the pointlessness and illegality of the actions of the Nigerian authorities, Ramesh's and Biruk's links with these authorities, as well as the mass of other court judgments and cases which strengthened out argument. All the documentation, together with transcripts of the conversations, came to almost a thousand pages. The document was sent off and all we could do was wait.

Well actually, there was one other thing we could do. We moved on to the third stage: The media pressure.

It takes the Super Global Police only a couple of hours to put you on the wanted list. It can take years to take you down. With an estimated of 20,000 Red Notices being active at any given time, the complicated legal structure of the organization (that makes it almost impossible to sue Interpol for its wrongdoings) and only a handful of in-house lawyers to analyze thousands of complaints about baseless Red Notices, the problems in dealing with this international organization can be bigger than the issue itself that brought you there. Interpol simply allows the local offices (as in my case – corrupt Nigerian Police) to put data directly into the global system, but applies a time-consuming and financially destructive procedure to undo it. People who ever dealt with fighting with some illegal content on social media platforms know what I'm talking about. The platforms usually distance themselves from taking responsibility for the content, allowing by default for everything to be put out there and only react when enough users report it.

I needed to do something to speed my case up. Otherwise, I will wait years for any decision. Interpol doesn't like media attention, nor any human rights attention. Frankly, Interpol doesn't like any attention at all. I needed to use that angle. It was tricky though. If I overdo it and attack Interpol too hard, I might antagonize people working there. I needed their attention, but also sympathy... I have antagonized enough people.

I was able attract with my case the interest of Amnesty International and Open Dialogue foundation. I was able to get meetings with their local heads, who sympathized with my issue. I was extremely grateful for that, especially after I learned what type of other abuses they are dealing with on a daily basis. Rapes, war crimes, police tortures, unfair jail time, to name a few. For a moment, I even felt bad for even asking for help. I was healthy, had access to lawyers, I was able to still move around within a region. I was great timing for me to talk to Open Dialogue Foundation, they were in the process of preparing a report on Interpol for the European Union Commission. Their focus was the misuse of Red Notices and the impacts this had on human rights, as well as lack of international accountability for Interpols actions, or lack there of. Not only did Open Dialogue send a formal letter to Interpol, expressing concern about my treatment in Nigeria, but they have also included my case in a report that European Union Parliament members will read. That was huge.

Now, it was time for the shit to hit the fan. I was aware that me going public with my ordeal would antagonize a lot of Nigerians. It was impossible to make my case loud without attacking corrupt Nigerian institutions. I couldn't just omit that corruption was at the core of this problem. Ramesh and Biruk didn't want to take me to court (if I had done anything wrong), because they knew they would simply loose, but it was so easy for them to use the police to force me to do what they wanted.

According to Allianz Global Corporate & Specialty Report, in 2017 Nigeria was the 4th most corrupt country in the World. In 2018—THE MOST corrupt state on Planet Earth. And what is the most corrupt institution in Nigeria? According to the Global Corruption Barometer, the Nigerian National Bureau of Statistics, the NOI Polls Organization, and The Independent Corrupt Practices Commission… it's the Nigerian Police.

One thing I learned about Nigerians is that they love to complain about their government, but if an outsider tries to do the same, they will go after you with passion. My D-Day was February 14th, 2019. I published on Medium.com "How building the Amazon of Africa put me on Interpol's Most Wanted List" and all the hell broke loose. In my post,

I went hard on corruption, provided plenty of sources about the state of corruption in Nigeria to back up my personal experience. I drew attention to problems within Interpol. I made a statement that the vision behind Interpol is noble. We need Interpol. But we don't need an organization that is abused and spreads corruption and the abuse of power between countries. I explained my situation, without referring to Ramesh and Biruk by their real names. I stated that I respect non-disclosure agreements, personal rights and personal data of all the people involved. So-called 'calling out' maybe a morally good thing for many, but it's not allowed according to the law. I may have known what Ramesh and Biruk did to me, but until I get a court verdict that defines them as criminals, I had no right to name and shame them. I stated that I will happily disclose all the evidence as soon as possible, in the light of the law, and in the courtroom, if I ever get a chance to. I also wanted to send a signal that in all of my fight, I still remain reasonable and I'm willing to settle. Because every fight costs a lot of energy and other resources.

What was the reaction to my post? Thousands of people made their support of my cause very clear. But then thousands, just like I expected, went after me. They didn't care whether someone broke the law or not. What mattered for them is that their country is under attack. I become the "Polish fraudster", "the white savior", "the Rachel Dolezal of Nigerian Tech", "the attention whore", and my personal favorite, "the unappreciative white small dick with no lips who was welcomed by mother Nigeria with open arms and now shits in his own birdsnest". They forgot that since 2013, I've been featured in hundreds of articles, interviews and videos, done not less keynotes. All with a combined audience of a couple of million readers and viewers. My narrative was always clear: Africa doesn't need bad charity, Africa wants to do business with you. Africa still suffers from bad past PR, but it doesn't show the full picture, so I focused on the good one. My TEDx Africa, Stupid talk was one of the examples. I was a white person talking about Africa, not because I'm 'whitesplaining' Africa, but because people from my part of the world wanted to hear story from someone like them. My Nigerian haters didn't care about that and they didn't care that in the same article I made it crystal clear that I'm not attacking the country, but the corrupt people in its institutions. They didn't care that I acknowledged that the people that abused the law had non-African passports. If it wasn't for the Nigerian Federal Court, and for the Nigerians who helped me, I wouldn't have been able to win many of the battles ahead of me.

The first wave of Nigeria's defenders was just the beginning. A week after my post, Ramesh and Biruk sent their dogs. Up until my Medium post, Ramesh and Biruk were convinced that I'm still about to pay them the money, still buying some time by negotiating whether I should send them money to Nigeria, or they would send someone to collect cash, which would give the Polish police the opportunity to arrest that person. But when my post got published, they knew they were in hot water and desperately needed a plan B, a new narrative to save their face. They were not happy, that's for sure.

A blog post emerged accusing me of "defrauding" my investors. The Post was written by a person not known personally to me, whose connection to the case remains unknown. The author refused to date to answer questions from numerous journalists about his involvement in the case, which wasn't a surprise for me. I had to give it to them though. The libelous post was written in an eloquent manner, contained many screenshots of some docs which seemed like evidence.

And that post was a first win for me. Why? As I explained earlier, our biggest problem during the legal fight in Nigeria was the planned disinformation. You can't defend yourself if you're not given access to relevant legal documents. What my Nigerian lawyer Rafiu learned, is that after we won the case in the Federal Court against the Police, the Police commissioner didn't appeal, but instead, they apparently filed a separate arrest warrant, with the same content. They played cat and mouse not only with us, but also with the highest court! We knew it happened but we didn't know the details and case number. And that number emerged in the libel post. The author used it as an argument against me. We were able to trace the docs in the court this time. And guess what? The court asked Police for the evidence supporting my arrest warrant, and they, of course, didn't present anything. They didn't show up to the court hearing again. The second arrest warrant was dismissed just like the first one. We didn't even have to move a finger.

My second win was that the author of the libel post had also shown a screenshot of an email correspondence with Ramesh and Biruk's Polish proxy, Anna the attorney. They screenshotted one paragraph too many, probably due to haste. In the screenshotted paragraph, Anna expresses her fear that if it became public knowledge that she took part in this blackmail, she would be in deep trouble in Poland. It looked like the greedy Polish lawyer finally realized what she had gotten herself into.

Those were my two wins, thanks to these defamation attempts. What were my losses? Well, they came from a direction I was expecting the least. I have considered myself a person that was liked by many, with exceptions like Jackson, a Nigerian Netflix dude I have mentioned before. What I didn't know is that there was an army of people like Jackson in the Nigerian tech sector, many quietly hoping for me to slip up.

People I knew personally, that never asked me a single question about the case, went on Twitter and posted "I always knew he's a fraud!", "get out of my country, colonizer!". People I would meet regularly at conferences, that would always smile and chat with me, sometimes ask for favors. Now they showed their real face.

It was an eye opener. Many people in Nigeria didn't like my activity in their country. Many local tech entrepreneurs didn't like the fact that a white person is promoting their own black country. I was their competition for business, spotlight and money from foreign investors. Their negative experiences (often very valid) with racially-biased white people got channeled against me. The libel post was the manna from heaven they were praying for. They did not wait for my rebuttal or my statement and my evidence regarding the accusations. That would only confuse them. What they got in the libel post matched perfectly their emotionally predefined opinions about me.

I have also gotten hundreds of messages from people in my circles showing support and offering help, but going through my own "You too, Brutus" phase was painful. But it was a social detox I needed to undergo, in order to make my body healthier and free of human toxins. So I waited three long weeks, until the dogs got tired of barking.

That's when I broke my silence. I published a rebuttal, a 25 minute-read behemoth article that one by one ripped to shreds every single lie, half truth and contradiction from the libelous post. Those who wanted the truth, and an overwhelming mass of evidence, got it. Those who felt comfortable with their position wouldn't have changed it and read the article, even if I got a naked Margot Robbie to read its 30 second summary. Many people reflected on their premature accusations and apologized to me. Most of them didn't have the guts to do so, and I'm totally fine with that.

Santa Claus came early in 2019. First, in April, Jumia (together with Jovago a.k.a. Jumia Travel) did an IPO on the New York Stock Exchange. On May 31ˢᵗ, Interpol sent me an email. It started with: "After careful examination of the documentation provided by both sides; Marek Zmysłowski and the Nigerian Police (…)" – That was already amazing, the Police finally replied to someone! Then the email continued: "The Interpol commission has concluded that the dispute between Marek Zmysłowski, Ramesh and Biruk has purely civil character, Nigerian police actions were against the Interpol International code of conduct. The commission has decided to immediately remove the Red Notice regarding Mr Zmysłowski from the International Interpol database. The commission has also instructed all Interpol member countries to do the same with their respective local databases."

That verdict goes on my wall as well, obviously. By the way, it took a Nigerian court a couple months to clear my name. It took an international justice organization almost two years to do the same. Who's more civilized now, huh?

It was over. I could travel the world, work, love and enjoy life once again. In the very beginning of my problems, since that night in jail, I was driven by revenge. And oh boy, revenge can be a strong driving force. I have made many bad decisions as a CEO, was arrogant with people I worked with, I was filled with ego. But never ever have I deliberately done anything with bad intentions to hurt my business partners. And accusations of that drove me mad. I needed that drive. I had an unimaginably hard task ahead of me. I had to fight on so many, expensive fronts. At the same time, I was cut out from my assets and sources of funding. I had to reinvent myself, find new ways to make money. I had to have laser focus on the goal. I worked harder than ever. It still amazes me, but I made more money dealing with Africa remotely, than when I was based there. During many sleepless nights,

I was filing court documents with my left hand and writing this very book with my right. Yaritza was there with my all the time, changed her life and moved to Europe to be with me. The first thing I did after we rented a flat, was to order a huge poster with a view of Camps Bay and the Twelve Apostles Mountain. So every time I went to sleep and woke up, I had my eyes on the prize.

I am happier with my life now than ever before. I am stronger and healthier than even before. I don't seek revenge anymore. The next time I see Pierre, Daniel, Ramesh and Biruk, I will shake their hands and say "Thank you for making me a better person".

I know myself a lot better too. I know what I want. Above all, I know what I don't want. Working in new, emerging African, Asian or South American markets is a risky business. I know that more than anyone. But nowhere else has given me such satisfaction in building something from scratch as here. So you want to help a poor kid with a swollen belly? Don't send money to those who broadcast tear-jerking ads on TV. From every dollar you send, that kid will maybe get ten cents. If he's still alive to get it. So you want to share the happiness you were lucky to enjoy because you were born into a home with running water, electricity, and parents who sent you to school so you wouldn't have to beg on the streets? So get a flight to Africa and spend your tourist dollars supporting some local business. Or come here, not to work for some charity, but to start up a small business, employ an African and invest in them. Above all, don't believe the stereotypes. In my case, the trick fate played on me was that I was so afraid of taking on Nigerian business partners, that I fell victim to an Indian and an American, while friendly Nigerians were the ones who helped me get out of trouble the most. Capitalism is by no means perfect, as it creates dangerous corporations and destroys the environment. But there is nothing better for improving your standard of living over the long term than free enterprise.

I've always wanted to write a book – I just wanted have it ticked off my list, along with all my other life ambitions. When I starting writing, I was motivated, above all, by a desire to share my story. Following my adventures in Nigeria, I also wanted to write about what had really happened in case I suddenly 'disappeared'.

Maybe someone will learn from my mistakes. And now, writing the conclusion, I now know what a great lesson this book has given me. It's only describing things in hindsight, in a cool manner, when you already know the additional circumstances of every situation, that allows you to notice the mistakes you made. And I made lots of them. I only have myself to blame for most of the sorry situations in which I found myself. I would have avoided them had I had more good sense, maturity and wisdom.

But if I could turn back time, would I have made different decisions? I don't know. After all, they've made me what I am today. "Good decisions come from experience. And experience? That mainly comes from bad decisions."

If you enjoyed this book, don't be a stranger. Maybe write a review on GoodReads or Amazon, buy it as a gift for someone close to you? Or maybe just post what you think of it on Social Media. All of the income from its sales goes to the MaYa Foundation. A small charity organization I founded together with Yaritza. A charity which aims to fix the broken charity model. A foundation with ambitions to become, thanks to technology, one of the most efficient, transparent, and sustainable charity organizations out there. Read more at www.marekzmyslowski. com

THE END